THE GOLDEN PATH

This exhibition and publication are made possible through the generosity of Robert and Debra F. Hartman.
The Leon Levy Foundation and a private family foundation have both provided generous grants to support this project.
Additional support was also provided by the David Berg Foundation.

THE GOLDEN PATH

Maimonides Across Eight Centuries

FEATURING HIGHLIGHTS FROM THE
HARTMAN FAMILY COLLECTION OF
MANUSCRIPTS AND RARE BOOKS

EDITED BY
DAVID SCLAR

YESHIVA UNIVERSITY MUSEUM

First published 2023 by
Liverpool University Press
4 Cambridge Street
Liverpool
L69 7ZU

Yeshiva University Museum
15 West 16th Street
New York, NY 10011
USA

David Sclar has asserted the right to be identified as the editor of this book in accordance with the Copyright, Designs and Patents Act 1988.

British Library Cataloguing-in-Publication data
A British Library CIP record is available

ISBN 978-1-80207-788-9

Published in conjunction with the exhibition *The Golden Path: Maimonides Across Eight Centuries – Featuring Highlights from the Hartman Family Collection of Manuscripts and Rare Books*, organized by and presented at Yeshiva University Museum (YUM) at the Center for Jewish History, New York, from 4 May to 31 December, 2023. Exhibition team: David Sclar, Exhibition Curator; Gabriel M. Goldstein, Interim Director and Chief Curator, YUM, and Exhibition Project Director; Ilona Moradof, Associate Director of Administration and Special Projects, YUM; Bonni-Dara Michaels, Collections Curator, YUM; Ilana Benson, Director of Museum Education, YUM; Sharon Liberman Mintz, Project Advisor; Barbara Suhr, Exhibition Designer.

Front Cover Images:
1. Maimonides autograph, JTS Library, MS 8254, fol. 7r.
2. *Sefer ha-Mitsvot*, Hartman Collection, MS 5, fol. 66v.
3. *Thesaurus Antiquitatum Sacrarum* (Venice, 1744), Yale University Library.
4. *Sefer ha-Emunot* (Ferrara, 1556), Hartman Collection, RB 18, fol. 1r.
5. *Moreh Nevukhim*, Mantua State Archive, fol. 142v.
6. Ben Shahn, *Maimonides* (1954), The Jewish Museum, New York.

Back Cover Images:
1. A. R. Oleosa, *Statue of Maimonides* (Córdoba; dedicated 1985).
2. *Mishneh Torah*, British Library, Harley MS 5698, fol. 252v.

Flap Images:
1. *Commentary on the Mishnah*, Bodleian Libraries, Oxford, MS. Pococke 295, fol. 184v.
2. *Mishneh Torah* (Amsterdam, 1702), Hartman Collection, RB 8, vol. 1, fol. 1r.

Typeset by Carnegie Book Production, Lancaster
Printed in the Czech Republic via Akcent Media Limited.

Panel from a Torah Ark door [Egypt, 11th century], The Walters Art Museum and Yeshiva University Museum. Photo by Susan Tobin.

CONTENTS

FOREWORD FROM THE PRESIDENT

New Wine in Old Bottles: Maimonides on the Legal Status of Muslims

It is particularly fitting to open this exhibition volume on the lasting impact of Maimonides by noting a central feature of the Great Eagle's thinking and worldview. For Maimonides, there were many cultures of wisdom to study and disciplines to master, but the goal of these intellectual pursuits was to uncover the truth which is embodied by the Torah and its teachings. Maimonides traveled many intellectual roads, but for him it was all one journey. It is this fundamentally religious journey that not only defined Maimonides's intellectual pursuits but also deeply impacted the course of Jewish history. One subtle and poignant example of this Maimonidean approach and impact is the way in which Maimonides addressed the legal status of Muslims. Scholars have discussed at length Maimonides's legal treatment of Muslims, especially his position that Muslims do not have the status of idolaters in Jewish law.[1] This position led to Maimonides's lenient ruling regarding Muslim wine, which, he argued, was a stance shared with 'all of the Geonim.'[2] However, despite rooting himself in the past Geonic halakhic tradition, a close reading of the text reveals a distinctly Maimonidean treatment of this matter, reflecting the way he integrated his philosophical positions in his interpretations of *halakhah*.

A passage from the Talmud tractate *'Avodah Zarah* 64b sets the stage for our discussion. In the Talmud, there are three opinions mentioned about the legal status of wine with respect to a *ger toshav*, defined by Maimonides as a non-Jew who observes the seven Noahide laws: 1) it is prohibited to receive benefit from the wine; 2) it is permitted to drink the wine; 3) it is permitted to receive benefit but prohibited to drink the wine. The accepted ruling in post-Talmudic literature is to permit benefitting from this wine but prohibit drinking from it, while the medieval sages debated whether this ruling only applies to wine touched by a *ger toshav*, wine owned by a *ger toshav*, or to both cases of wine owned or touched by a *ger toshav*.[3] Maimonides, in his *Mishneh Torah*, codified this ruling for *ger toshav* in both of these cases.[4] He also applied this ruling to the non-Jews of his day, writing that Muslims – who are not considered idolaters – are included in the exception case of *ger toshav*, whose wine it is

1 For review and analysis of material relating to Maimonides and Muslims, see Marc B. Shapiro, 'Islam and the Halakhah,' *Judaism* 42, no. 3 (1993): 332–43; David Novak, 'The Treatment of Islam and Muslims in the Legal Writings of Maimonides,' in *Studies in Islamic and Judaic Traditions*, ed. William M. Brinner and Stephen D. Ricks (Atlanta: Scholars Press, 1986), 233–50; and Daniel J. Lasker, 'Tradition and Innovation in Maimonides' Attitude toward Other Religions,' in *Maimonides after 800 Years*, ed. Jay M. Harris (Cambridge, MA: Harvard University Center for Jewish Studies, 2007), 167–82.

2 *Mishneh Torah*, *Hilkhot Ma'akhalot 'Asurot* 11:7.

3 See, for example, *Tosafot* on *'Avodah Zarah*, 64b, s.v. *la-'afuke*, and R. Aaron *ha-Levi*, *Bedek ha-Bayit* printed in *Torat ha-Bayit le-ha-Rashba*, ed. H. Zimbalist (Tel Aviv, 2002), *bayit* 5 *sha'ar* 2:11 (147); *Shitat ha-Kadmonim: 'Avodah Zarah*, ed. Moshe Y. Blau (New York: Deutsch Printing & Publishing Co., 1969), 138 (*'Avodah Zarah* 57a).

4 *Mishneh Torah*, *Hilkhot Ma'akhalot Asurot* 11:7 and 13:11. On the status of wine improperly left in the possession of a *ger toshav*, see *Hilkhot Ma'akhalot Asurot* 13:12.

prohibited to drink but from which one is permitted to derive benefit, while wine from Christians, deemed idolaters, is prohibited according to the general rules of *stam yenam*.[5]

The significance of this ruling is that Maimonides was the first rabbinic authority to contextualize the conversation about Muslim wine within the laws of *ger toshav*. The Geonim who previously ruled on the status of Muslim wine compared the case to that of wine touched by a newborn child.[6] Maimonides was well aware of the Geonic framework for this discussion, as indicated by a later responsum he penned which cited this reasoning.[7] Nevertheless, he located the law about Muslim wine in the *Mishneh Torah* within his discussion of *ger toshav*, rather than according to his earlier ruling about the newborn child.[8] Why would Maimonides consider the case of Muslim wine more comparable to *ger toshav* than the newborn child?

This subtle difference between Maimonides and the earlier Geonim could be understood as pointing toward a more fundamental distinction between them. Scholars have already noted the significance of this ruling in their analyses of the legal status of Muslims according to Maimonides,[9] but the earlier Geonic material on this issue provides a sharp relief to better appreciate the novelty of this ruling within the broader framework of Maimonides's thinking.

The backdrop of this analysis is the recognition that the founding and spread of Islam forced early medieval sages to define the halakhic identity of Muslims in order to determine whether Talmudic laws against idolaters applied to their contemporary circumstances. Some extant Geonic sources advanced a lenient ruling in respect to these laws because Islamic religious services prohibit images and idols.[10] Other Geonic sources categorized Muslims as idolaters.[11] This position is often cited in connection with the view that there are pre-Islamic pagan remnants within the practices of Islam, such as a tradition stating that an idol stood in the Kaaba.[12]

5 See Howard Kreisel, 'Maimonides on Christianity and Islam,' in *Jewish Civilization, Essays and Studies*, vol. 3, ed. Ronald A. Brauner (Philadelphia: Reconstructionist Rabbinical College, 1985), 153–62; and Lasker, 'Tradition and Innovation in Maimonides' Attitude toward Other Religions.'

6 See *Teshuvot Geonim Kadmonim*, ed. David Kassel (Berlin: Aryeh Leib Zarinzansky, 1848), *siman* 46, 9a–9b; *Ḥemdah Genuzah*, ed. Ze'ev Wolfensohn and Schneur Z. Schneursohn (Jerusalem: Yisrael Baeck, 1863), *siman* 113–14, 19b–20b; *Halakhot Pesukot min ha-Geonim*, 22. A version of this responsum is cited in the Ashkenazic halakhic literature in their discussion of wine touched by a Christian. See, for example, *Tosafot, 'Avodah Zarah* 57b s.v. *la-'afuke*; R. Barukh ben Isaac, *Sefer ha-Terumah* part 3, ed. David Abraham (Jerusalem: Mekhon Yerushalayim, 2010), *siman* 169 (217); R. Isaiah di Trani the Elder, *Tosafot ha-Rid* (Lvov, 1862), *'Avodah Zarah* 57a *Mahadura Kama*, 40a s.v. *tinok*. For detailed analysis of the development of this issue in Ashkenaz, see Haym Soloveitchik's seminal works on this issue: *Principles and Pressures: Jewish Trade in Gentile Wine in the Middle Ages* (Hebrew) (Tel Aviv: Am Oved Publishers, 2003) and *Wine in Ashkenaz in the Middle Ages: Yeyn Nesekh – A Study in the History of Halakha* (Hebrew) (Jerusalem: The Zalman Shazar Center for Jewish History, 2008).

7 Itzhak Shailat (ed.), *Letters and Essays of Moses Maimonides* (Hebrew) (Jerusalem: Shailat Publishing, 1995), 428–31; see Shailat's comments for proof that the responsum consists of two parts, though earlier printings presented them as entirely separate (425).

8 *Mishneh Torah, Hilkhot Ma'akhalot Asurot* 11:5.

9 For example, see Lasker, 'Tradition and Innovation in Maimonides' Attitude toward Other Religions,' 179. See also Novak, 'The Treatment of Islam and Muslims in the Legal Writings of Maimonides,' 237, who sees in this ruling an earlier rabbinic notion of non-Jewish monotheists, although as we will soon develop, this ruling is reflective of a distinctly medieval and Maimonidean treatment of this matter.

10 See Geonic responsa published by Meir Z. Weiss, 'Seridim me-ha-Genizah,' in *Festschrift zum 50 jährigen Bestehen der Franz-Josef-Landesrabbinerschule in Budapest*, ed. Ludwig Blau (Budapest: Alexander Kohut Memorial Foundation, 1928), 77–97 (95) (Hebrew section).

11 R. Abraham ben Isaac of Narbonne, *Sefer ha-Eshkol*, 77–78; *Teshuvat Geonim*, ed. Simha Assaf (Jerusalem, 1927), no. 50 (62); R. Zedekiah ben Abraham *ha-Rofe, Shibole ha-Leket*, part 2, ed. Menahem Hasidah (Jerusalem 1969), 12; Simcha Assaf, '*Teshuvot Geonim*,' *Kiryat Sefer* 1, no. 2 (1925): 117–41 (124).

12 See R. Abraham b. Isaac of Narbonne, *Sefer ha-Eshkol*, part 2, 78. For an example of a responsum that differentiates between the early and later generations of Muslims, see *Sefer ha-Eshkol*, part 2, 74, s.v. *ve-nish'al*. For a review and analysis of the sources related to this tradition, see Bernard Septimus, 'Petrus Alfonsi on the Cult at Mecca,' *Speculum* 56, no. 3 (1981): 517–33.

While Maimonides in the *Mishneh Torah* clearly chose one side of this debate, stating definitively that Muslims are not idol worshipers, one could detect that Maimonides differed from the Geonim in their underlying reasoning by the fact that he located this law related to Muslims within the context of *ger toshav*. A good introduction to understanding this point is found in Maimonides's letter to Obadiah the Convert.[13] In this letter Maimonides addressed the claims that Muslims are idolaters because an idol was hidden in their main sanctuary and because Islamic religious practices simulated earlier pagan practices. Maimonides countered these claims by stating that '[idolatry] has long been severed from their mouths and hearts; and they attribute to God a proper unity, a unity concerning which there is no doubt.'[14] In contrast to the Geonim who focused their halakhic argumentation on the practice of Muslim worship, Maimonides based his halakhic analysis on the intellectual mindset of Muslims. According to Maimonides, the central defining issue is not whether there is an idol in the Kaaba or if current Muslim religious practices have the same form as earlier pagan ones, but the fact that Muslims have the correct intellectual understanding of the unity of God, which defines them as non-idolaters.[15]

Highlighting the gap between the position of the Geonim and that of Maimonides is a statement in one Geonic responsum that classified Muslims as idol worshipers even if they themselves were not aware of the pagan elements in their cultic practices.[16] Such a perspective focused on action. To Maimonides, however, a monotheist could not be considered an idolater for an act that either unintentionally simulates a pagan ritual or is directed toward a building that unknowingly contains an idol.

In this light, with respect to the laws of *stam yenam*, Maimonides's distinction in the *Mishneh Torah* between a newborn child and *ger toshav* depended on a notion of two kinds of non-idolaters: one whose actions are not defined as idolatrous, and another who fundamentally maintains the correct set of intellectual beliefs. While the actions of the newborn child cannot be considered idolatrous, both because there is no intentionality and because there is no awareness of idolatry and its rituals, a *ger toshav* is fundamentally not considered an idolater because he is a monotheist. Thus, it is logical for Maimonides to place Muslims and any other non-Jew for whom there is a presumption of monotheism in the same category as *ger toshav*.[17]

While it appears that Maimonides is simply citing a previous ruling from the Geonim in codifying his position on Muslim wine, in fact one can see in his codifications an innovative perspective that defines idolatry according to intellectual belief rather than action. This ruling is aligned with Maimonides's philosophical views and reflects a broader innovative move by Maimonides to identify a new category of non-Jew in rabbinic sources, one who is a fellow monotheist due to shared beliefs. Maimonides found halakhic basis for this new legal category in his original interpretations of the rabbinic sources related to *ger toshav*. His understanding of *ger toshav* manifested itself in a number of legal rulings in the *Mishneh Torah* and significantly influenced the way in which subsequent medieval rabbinic authorities conceptualized and developed the Jew–Gentile relationship in their interpretations of *halakhah*.[18]

13 Shailat (ed.), *Letters and Essays*, 238–41.

14 Translations of this letter are based on Septimus's translation in his 'Petrus Alfonsi on the Cult at Mecca,' 522–24.

15 For more on Maimonides's view of idolatry as an intellectual error, see Moshe Halbertal and Avishai Margolit, *Idolatry*, trans. Naomi Goldblum (Cambridge, MA: Harvard University Press, 1992), 108–36.

16 *Sefer ha-Eshkol*, part 2, 78.

17 See David Freidenreich's treatment of this matter in his *Foreigners and their Food: Constructing Otherness in Jewish, Christian and Islamic Law* (Berkeley: University of California Press, 2011), 209–16, and his 'Fusion Cooking in an Islamic Milieu: Jewish and Christian Jurists on Food associated with Foreigners,' in *Beyond Religious Borders: Interaction and Intellectual Exchange in the Medieval Islamic World*, ed. David M. Freidenreich and Miriam Goldstein (Philadelphia: University of Pennsylvania Press, 2012), 144 60.

18 For more on Maimonides's influence on medieval discourse relating to *ger toshav* and the Jew–Gentile relationship, see Ari Berman, '*Ger Toshav* in the Halakhic Literature of the High Middle Ages' (PhD diss., Hebrew University of Jerusalem, 2016).

On so many topics, in so many ways, Maimonides's writings altered the course of Jewish history. This exhibit, with its broad range of manuscripts and early editions of Maimonides's varied work, tells the story of his widespread impact and influence. I am deeply thankful to our dear friends Debbie and Bob Hartman, whose Maimonidean collection and generous support form the basis for this exhibit. The lay leadership of Yeshiva University Museum has always been a source of great strength for Yeshiva University, from its founders Erica and Ludwig Jesselson, whose profound legacy is being continued through the trusteeship and leadership of Michael Jesselson, to the current devoted chair Rachel Laufer.

I am deeply thankful to the entire Yeshiva University Museum team led by Interim Director and Chief Curator Gabriel Goldstein, and to David Sclar, exhibition curator and editor of this important publication. We are truly grateful as well to the world-class scholars who have contributed to this volume and the generous partners who supported this project.

This exhibit reflects Maimonides's influence as well as his core values, which also form the worldview and aspirations of Yeshiva University. The basis for our educational enterprise is epitomized by Maimonides's intellectual quest for truth, which is rooted in his belief that seeking truth widely enhances and enriches our understanding of the truth of Torah. I am honored to introduce the journey of Maimonides and his works to our readers, who through this volume and exhibit can better develop their knowledge of Maimonides, Jewish history, and the values on which to build their lives.

Ari Berman

PREFACE FROM THE DIRECTOR

> The general principle is that one should follow the midpoint quality of each temperament until all his intentions are aligned on the middle path. This is what is implied by Solomon's statement: 'Level the pathway of your foot, and all your ways will be sound' (Proverbs 4:26).
>
> Maimonides, *Mishneh Torah*, *Hilkhot Deot* 2:7

Maimonides's Golden Path, drawing on the famed Golden Mean of Aristotle, established a path of balance and harmony that shaped history over centuries. Yeshiva University Museum (YUM) is very proud to present this exhibition and to publish this important companion volume – to journey along Maimonides's own path and then across the generations and around the globe to consider how his writings were understood and received.

We explore the teachings of the sage, his cultural milieu in medieval Spain, Morocco, and Egypt, and then consider his lasting impact over generations. We see how Maimonides was understood, how his teachings were interpreted, reshaped, or challenged, and how communities worldwide claimed and established their own identity as his rightful heirs. We examine this through a lens of materiality – through manuscripts and rare books, and also through art, visual and popular culture.

We are very grateful to the many individuals who have helped us to create this important project. This project is built on the powerful vision and commitment of Robert and Debra F. Hartman. Bob Hartman's love of and enthusiasm for Maimonides's teachings and ongoing living legacy inspired him to form a world-class collection and then to work in partnership with Yeshiva University Museum to share these treasures with the public. We are privileged to be able to work with the Hartman family to build this exhibition project and to bring these amazing manuscripts and rare books to our Museum's visitors.

The vision and planning for this exhibition began with the Hartman Family Collection, and this publication and our exhibition in YUM's Popper Gallery at the Center for Jewish History continue to be centered on these most impressive holdings. We realized that to convey the full beauty and impact of Maimonides, both in his own time and across the centuries, we needed to supplement the Hartman Collection items with select special loans from other collections.

Yeshiva University Museum is so very proud to be able to bring together this powerful gathering of materials related to Maimonides. We are humbled to be able to borrow such treasures from the most important repositories in the United States, Europe, and Israel. We express our heartfelt thanks to all of our lenders – the Hartman family, prestigious international rare book libraries and museums, and to other private collections. We are greatly indebted to the professional staffs of these important institutions worldwide for helping us to secure and coordinate these important loans and to present these prized treasures to our Museum audiences.

It has been our great pleasure to work with David Sclar as the guest curator for this exhibition. David brings a rare combination of skills and knowledge to this project – great academic expertise in Jewish history, research, and texts; connoisseurship and expertise in analyzing, understanding, and interpreting manuscripts and rare books; collection and exhibition curatorial experience; and practical know-how, coupled with a nuanced educational outlook and the sensitivities of an active teacher seeking to engage students of all ages and backgrounds.

Sharon Liberman Mintz, the Exhibition Special Advisor, has been a crucial member of our project team. Her scholarship, experience, and networks have been central to our success. David, Sharon, and I happily and effectively worked together on previous, highly successful YUM projects, and it has been a great pleasure to reunite for this effort, which we are confident will bring even greater success and attract significant audiences.

This exhibition project was launched under the leadership of Jacob Wisse, Associate Professor of Art History at Yeshiva University and the former Director of YUM. We are grateful to Jacob for his enthusiasm, scholarship, and vision that helped to first shape this exhibition initiative.

Yeshiva University Museum is proud to serve as a public face of the University, welcoming broad audiences from across the University community and beyond. The University is a crucial backbone to the Museum's efforts. We are extremely fortunate to work in close partnership with Paul Glassman, Yeshiva University's Director of Scholarly and Cultural Resources. Paul brings experience, creativity, and an ongoing willingness to help to all of the Museum's efforts.

We are also greatly appreciative of the many members of the University's staff and faculty who have and will continue to help us with the many aspects of this exhibition project. We express our thanks to Miriam Berger, Shulamith Berger, Selma Botman, Thomas Cannon, Nick Chen, Hanan Eisenman, Daniel Forman, Debbie Freeman, Stuart Halpern, Jacob Kramer, Andrew J. Lauer, Susan Meyers, Victoria Mezo, Ronnie Perelis, Daniel Rynhold, Daniel Satlow, Julie Schreier, Ludmilla Simon, Michael Schreiber, Doron Stern, and Sam A. Yospe.

We feel particularly privileged that Rabbi Dr. Ari Berman, President and Rosh Yeshiva, Yeshiva University and RIETS, has chosen to include his scholarly writing and ideas in this volume. We are very grateful for Rabbi Berman's enthusiasm for this exhibition project and for all that it represents for the University, the Museum, and all our audiences.

We express our thanks to Rachel Laufer, Chair, and to all the members of the YUM Board of Overseers. As we were preparing this exhibition project and publication, we were saddened by the passing of two longtime, stalwart YUM board members and devoted friends, Ludwig Bravmann ז"ל and Lucy Lang ז"ל – we continue to be inspired by the pathways they helped to forge for our institution.

We are fortunate to be a Partner Organization at the Center for Jewish History (CJH) and to share this wonderful facility and prime Manhattan location with our four partner organizations – specialized archival and library organizations. United on one site, we form a powerful, inspiring hub of Jewish historical research and public intellectual activity. We express our thanks to the Center Board and to Gavriel Rosenfeld, CJH President, and Rio Daniel, CJH CEO, as well as to all Center and Partner Organization staff members and to the facilities and security team. We are delighted to continue to work with Sean Naftel, CJH Exhibitions Services Manager.

Yeshiva University Museum's small staff is exceptionally talented and devoted. This major project was demanding, and in many ways an outsize reach, for a tiny team of highly experienced, skilled museum professionals. Their talent, creativity, determination, and commitment have made this a reality. I am greatly indebted to them for their support, good humor, encouragement, and intensive hard work. I express my most sincere thanks and admiration to Ilona Moradof, Associate Director for Administration and Special Projects, Bonni-Dara Michaels, Collections Curator, and Ilana Benson, Director of Museum

Education. This exhibition and publication project would not have been possible without their exceptional efforts and skills. Our thanks also to our Student Assistants, Sheindl Berger and Yitzhak Graff, and to YUM's docents and volunteers.

We are delighted to work again with Barbara Suhr as our exhibition designer. Barbara's skills, visual creativity, and visitor awareness have helped us to build an exhibition that is beautiful and engaging. Our thanks to our cartographer Anandaroop Roy for creating the elegant and accessible maps for our publication and exhibition.

I am personally and professionally grateful to many friends and colleagues for their ongoing encouragement, ideas, and enthusiasm. We have greatly benefited from their advice and actions, and they have been an ongoing resource for Yeshiva University Museum's efforts. I express our thanks to Avi Decter, Jennifer Ellis, Grace Cohen Grossman, Michael Jesselson, Sylvia A. Herskowitz, Felicia Herman, Rachel Lazin, Mary Smart, Amedeo Spagnoletto, Miriam Wallach, Shelby White, Melissa Martens Yaverbaum, Sally Yerkovich, and Carole Zawatsky.

We are very grateful to the scholars who have served as the authors of essays in this volume. Their articles are intriguing, thoroughly researched and conceived, and highly accessible. Yeshiva University Museum is delighted to co-publish this volume with Liverpool University Press. We express our gratitude to Alison Welsby, Editorial Director, and to Carnegie Book Production for all of their encouragement and hard work to ensure the beauty and quality of this publication.

This exhibition is only possible due to the generosity of our donors, who recognized the powerful potential, importance, and impact of this project. We are very grateful to Robert and Debra F. Hartman for their generous support to make this project a reality. YUM is also very proud to have been the recipient of several generous grants from prestigious foundations to support this important exhibition project. The Leon Levy Foundation and a private family foundation have both provided generous grants to support this exhibition. Generous support was also provided by the David Berg Foundation, with additional assistance from the Zoltan Erenyi Charitable Fund. The costs related to the loan and display of the Royal Danish Library's illuminated *Moreh Nevukhim* manuscript were supported, in part, by a grant from the American Scandinavian Foundation.

In his essay in this volume, Tzvi Langerman discusses how Maimonides's opinions on anecdotal evidence in medicine are relevant and parallel to recent issues addressed while confronting the unknown in the early days of the Covid pandemic. This exhibition in many ways marks Yeshiva University Museum's return to robust activity following a period when we, and almost all cultural organizations, were physically closed and then less than fully active on-site. Museum visitors stayed away from our facilities due to reasonable concerns about infection and illness.

With *The Golden Path* we mark the enduring impact and ongoing reception of Maimonides's teachings across the generations. As we invite and celebrate the return of Yeshiva University Museum's broad audiences, we hope that this exhibition also signals a renewed golden pathway for Yeshiva University Museum's enduring impact.

Gabriel M. Goldstein

PREFACE FROM THE COLLECTOR

During my late 30s and early 40s, I went through a period of analyzing my religious beliefs and devotion. Needing to bridge the past and the present, I searched for a way to synthesize my faith and logic. My introduction to the *Moreh Nevukhim* (*Guide of the Perplexed*), authored by Maimonides – known traditionally as the Rambam – changed my life. Over the next several years, I immersed myself in the work of a teacher who spoke to me clearly and directly.

Close friends knew about my internal transformation, as I would bring it up at every Shabbat dinner, much to their chagrin. My friend Gershon Bassman introduced me to Aaron Stefansky ז״ל, a rare book dealer from Lakewood, who said in short: 'I know you have a fascination with the Rambam. I have a book that has come to my attention that you should look at.' I had never thought of nor had much interest in old manuscripts and books, but when he presented a fifteenth-century Italian manuscript of the *Moreh Nevukhim*, I immediately identified with it. Seeing and holding a 500-year-old piece of Jewish history had a magnetic connection to my own life as a child of Holocaust survivors, as a refugee from Hungary. This book had traveled a long way and had somehow survived countless and unknowable events. It was a testament to the Jewish people and our continuous survival.

From that initial attraction, I started actively searching for other Rambam books, guided by specialists in Hebrew manuscripts and early printing. Early in this period, I spent a remarkable afternoon with Dr. Menahem Schmelzer ז״ל at the Library of the Jewish Theological Seminary, where he showed me some of the treasures of the Rare Book Room, opening my eyes to magnificent texts, the beauty of scripts and bindings, and the intangible but unforgettable feel and smell of old books.

The subsequent twenty-year interval, in which a hobby turned into a passion, has initiated further growth. I wanted to know the personalities behind each book's production, as well as its historical journey and its provenance. I studied these texts and gained an appreciation for the depths and beauty of the Rambam. This path helped me develop a much fuller, richer spiritual life. I spent wonderful time with my children and grandchildren exploring these rare books, and I witnessed the impact it had on them. Their faces glowed with awe and amazement in beholding something so old, so rare, and so meaningful.

It is for that reason that I have intentionally opened this collection to the community in which I have lived and thrived. I am forever fascinated with the moments when people recognize the significance of this material and the emotional, transformative power these volumes convey.

I have been fortunate to collect important manuscripts and early printed books, such as a fourteenth-century *Pirke Moshe*, with an inscription from an 'inquisitor,' and the *Mada, Ahavah, Zemanim* (Venice, 1665), with the surprising image of Sabbatai Tsevi riding on a lion. Among the most meaningful pieces in my collection is the *Mishneh Torah* published by the Bragadini press in Venice in 1550–1551. This four-volume set belonged to generations of the Katzigin family, who used it to record births, deaths, anecdotes, poems, and more. My whole life has been focused on building a strong and stable Jewish family – to keep family together (KFT) – much like the Katzigins, with a historical narrative of survival, growth, and harmony.

The deep emotion and spirit that I have been fortunate to cultivate through the Rambam now reaches a culmination with this exhibition at the Yeshiva University Museum and the printing of this catalogue. It brings together everything that I have worked to accomplish over the last forty years. It inspires in me a great feeling of pride, joy, and humility in one unusual conglomeration of emotions.

I am grateful to many people who have facilitated and joined me on this journey. Thanks to Aaron Stefansky ז״ל, Dr. Benjamin Richler, Dr. Menahem Schmelzer ז״ל, Sharon Liberman Mintz, and David Wachtel. In addition, my heartfelt thanks to Yeshiva University Museum and the full exhibition team for making this publication and exhibition a reality. Their skill, creativity, and hard work have ensured the quality and success of this project.

My journey would not have gained momentum without the mentoring and sophisticated talents of David Sclar. His depth of knowledge and insight into rare Jewish books and manuscripts always guided my growth. I am forever grateful to him and his loving family for letting me share the past fourteen years with him.

I want to thank my beloved children and grandchildren for their love and support of my passion: my sons, David and Mark; my daughters, Rena and Julie; and their spouses, Chaya Tova, Ephraim, Nathan, and Penina. Each of you, in your own special way, has enhanced this journey. My grandchildren and great grandchildren – Sarah, Yehuda, Reuben, Allie, Sonny ... Shira, Raizy, Yitzchok, Ahron, Hannah, MoMo, Talia, Rikki, Binyomin, Mikey, Sonny, Sara Leah ... Jonathan, Hershel, Jacob, Layla ... Aaron, J.J., Asher, Shaya, Nani ... Meir, Rikki, Azi, Leah – forever inspire me. They are living links in the chain of Jewish history.

Special mention to Reuben, Jonathan, and Aaron who have assisted me with the books over the years.

Finally, to my true partner in love and life, Debbie, my devoted and always supportive wife. You have paved the journey with your love, wisdom, and grace. And I know that all our true family blessings come through you. My undying love, respect, and admiration for sharing this with me.

In closing, I hope as you spend some time with these treasures, you start to feel the power of the Rambam's words and thoughts as they come alive.

In his introduction to the *Moreh Nevukhim*, the Master utilized Proverbs 25:11 – 'A word fitly spoken is like Apples of Gold in settings of silver' – to illustrate the possibilities of learning and life itself. When you see a beautiful screen of silver filigree, you are enchanted by the delicate work of the artisan. If the artisan placed an apple of gold behind the decorative silver filigree screen, you might see the shape of the apple appear behind the screen. Some stop there and look no further. With intense focus, however, you can see through and behind the screen. To your surprise and delight, its interior becomes clear and you realize it is an Apple of Gold.

My wish is for you to spend the time and effort to make discoveries of your own and be inspired by these books to love Jewish history and learning.

With a sense of gratitude and humility to Hashem,
Robert Hartman

INTRODUCTION

Dedicated to the memory of Menahem Schmelzer זצ״ל
– gentleman, scholar, librarian, teacher –
without whom this work would not have come to fruition.

[Only] *the Creator knows how I am able to write such a letter to you. I have had to flee from* [a demanding] *public, isolating myself in a hidden place. Sometimes, I have had to lean against the wall; other times I have had to write supine out of physical feebleness....*

If you want to [travel here to] *confer with me on matters of wisdom, do not hope for even a single hour, either during the day or at night....*

Every day, I head to [the Sultan's court in] *Cairo early in the morning. Even if there is no impediment, or if nothing unusual happens, I return* [to Fustat only] *in the afternoon.... Before I arrive, the porticos are full of people – prominent and common people, judges and officers, a mixed multitude, awaiting my arrival....* [Upon arrival,] *I dismount and wash my hands. I go out to placate them, to beseech them to wait a little longer while I eat quickly....*

I treat patients until nightfall. Sometimes – [I swear by] *the veracity of the Torah – I do not conclude until at least two hours of darkness have passed. I deliberate with them while lying down from sheer exhaustion. By nighttime, I am so weak that I can converse no longer....*

Moses ben Maimon (Maimonides; Rambam) to Samuel Ibn Tibbon[1]
8 Tishre 1511 *la-shetarot* (= October 7, 1199)[2]

1 For the letter in full, concerning primarily Samuel Ibn Tibbon's efforts to translate *Moreh Nevukhim* (*Guide of the Perplexed*), see Itzhak Shailat (ed.), *The Letters and Essays of Moses Maimonides* [Hebrew] (Jerusalem, 1995), 550–51. For English translations of the full passage describing his daily activities, see Jacob Rader Marcus, *The Jew in the Medieval World: A Source Book, 315–1791* (Cincinnati, OH: Hebrew Union College Press, 1990), 348–50; and Franz Kobler (ed.), *A Treasury of Jewish Letters: Letters from the Famous and Humble*, 2 vols. (Philadelphia, PA: Jewish Publication Society of America, 1953), 1:208–13. On the importance of the letter, see Doron Forte, 'Back to the Sources: Alternative Versions of Maimonides' Letter to Samuel Ibn Tibbon and Their Neglected Significance,' *Jewish Studies Quarterly* 23 (2016): 47–90.

2 '*Le-minyan shetarot*' (lit. Era of Contracts) refers to a system of yearly reckoning corresponding to the foundation of the Seleucid Empire in 312/311 BCE.

Composed toward the end of an active and productive life, these words evoke attentiveness, conviction, commitment, confidence, and maybe fatigue. The author sought to discourage his disciple from visiting him in Egypt and perhaps gain comfort for decades of dedication. Like all else he wrote, the text proved relevant beyond its original context and intent, and it emits a spirit of intensity and forthrightness that still resonates.

Maimonides lived between 1138 and 1204, the descendant of a long line of rabbis, judges, and scholars.[3] At a young age, he fled persecution in his native Córdoba with his family, eventually landing in the Moroccan city of Fez in 1160. He pursued studies in rabbinics, science, and medicine, and began earnestly to put his own ideas to paper. In 1165, he traveled to the Holy Land, residing there for five months before finally settling in Fustat (now part of modern-day Cairo). Over the next four decades, Maimonides led the Egyptian Jewish community and served as a court physician to the political elite of the Fatimid and Ayyubid dynasties, which ruled much of North Africa and the Middle East between the tenth and thirteenth centuries. All the while, he produced masterpieces in *halakhah*, philosophy, science, theology, and ethics, and guided Jewish communities all over the world with his expansive knowledge, deep wisdom, and innovative thought.

During his lifetime, Maimonides was a rabbi, jurist, Talmudist, philosopher, physician, astronomer, and communal leader, as well as a son, brother, father, and husband. We have more source material from or about him than possibly any other medieval Jewish figure, and more has been written about him than perhaps any other Jew in history. Maimonides's significance within the realm of post-Talmudic Jewish thought cannot be overstated. He earned epithets like 'Great Eagle' (הנשר הגדול) and the 'Western Light' (הנר המערבי), and once received a letter that commenced with more than 120 words and acrostics of praise.[4] His *Commentary on the Mishnah* proved indispensable for centuries and was an oft-printed addition to volumes of the Talmud. His *Mishneh Torah* (*Repetition of the Law*) transformed halakhic discourse and was so profound that even its detractors could not deny the author's immense accomplishment. His *Moreh Nevukhim* (*Guide of the Perplexed*) stirred a multigenerational controversy but came to be universally regarded as the ultimate Jewish medieval philosophical text. His treatises – on medicine (*Pirke Mosheh*), forced conversion (*Igeret ha-Shemad*), the resurrection of the dead (*Ma'amar Teḥiyat ha-Metim*), and more – had an immediate impact and then remained relevant for centuries.

Arguably, no other individual has had a more pervasive or enduring effect on Jewish religious life over the last millennium. Maimonides's written work – whether penned for the few (*Moreh Nevukhim*; medical treatises) or the many (*Commentary on the Mishnah*; *Mishneh Torah*; epistles) – almost immediately attained near-canonical status and has perpetually spawned new audiences. His voice, in all its scope, has sparked interest in assorted social and political circumstances, across diverse intellectual and cultural environments. Jews of medieval Spain and Yemen, early modern Venice and Istanbul, modern Germany and Lithuania, and contemporary Israel and the United States have regarded Maimonides as the archetype of a common heritage.

The reception of Maimonides's texts and ideas, and the personal and collective evaluations of Maimonides the man, have served as Jewish constants through incessant change. Even when developing contrary views, halakhists, philosophers, kabbalists, Christian theologians, and modern political theorists have engaged with and responded to his carefully constructed words. Scholars continually work to reinterpret and recontextualize his work, while innumerable students (in the academy and in the yeshiva) toil to

3 Recent scholarship has overturned the long-held belief that Maimonides was born in 1135; for Maimonides's words to this effect, see Yosef Kafiḥ (ed.), *Mishnah 'im Perush Rabenu Mosheh ben Maimon ... Seder Tohorot* (Jerusalem, 1963–1968), 738. For a detailed explanation of the dating of Maimonides's birth, see Herbert A. Davidson, *Moses Maimonides: The Man and His Works* (Oxford: Oxford University Press, 2005), 6–9.

4 Cambridge University Library, T-S 12.822; see Israel Friedlaender, 'Ein Gratulationsbrief an Maimonides,' in *Festschrift zu Hermann Cohens siebzigstem Geburtstage* (Berlin: Bruno Cassirer, 1912), 257–64 (261–62).

comprehend the master's words. Maimonides's name and invented likeness appear on schools, hospitals, storefronts, clothing, stamps, and more, lending gravitas and validity to any and all ventures. The well-known statement 'From Moses to Moses, none arose like Moses' (ממשה עד משה לא קם כמשה) – a celebration of the ancient Moses and his medieval namesake – speaks to more than mere legacy. It reflects a relationship between the echoes of an amorphous past and the desire for clarity in an ever-evolving present, making the story of Maimonides's 'afterlife' as much about the inheritors of his work as it is about the man himself.

The Golden Path: Maimonides Across Eight Centuries traces the impact and reception of Maimonides and his thought through a study of materiality, specifically the production and dissemination of textual objects. It focuses on manuscripts and rare printed books from the Hartman Family Collection, including: Yemenite manuscripts ranging from the late thirteenth century to the early twentieth century; early printed books from the Italian peninsula, the Ottoman Empire, and Central Europe; texts produced by and for Christian audiences; a fifteenth-century manuscript of *Moreh Nevukhim* with an illustration of the *Maʿaseh Merkavah* (Account of the Chariot of Ezekiel's Vision); and copies of rival editions of the *Mishneh Torah* issued in Venice in 1550 and 1551 that preceded and perhaps precipitated the confiscation and burning of the Talmud in 1553. The provenance of many of these volumes is extensive and distinguished, with some once held by rabbis David Oppenheim, Yiḥye Tsaleḥ, Samson Raphael Hirsch, and Samuel Salant, printer Abraham Pescarol, Karaite Isaac ben Moses Mangubi, philanthropist Moses Montefiore, bibliophile David Solomon Sassoon, and scholar Moritz Steinschneider. The assembly of this collection serves as its own active engagement with Maimonides – the use of and working with ideas and ideals, responsibilities and expectations, struggle and hope.

The Golden Path consists primarily of two sections. The first presents highlights from the Hartman Collection, exploring specific manuscripts and imprints within their historical, cultural, and Maimonidean contexts. Entries emphasize Maimonides's thought, its varied reception, and Jewish book history; each is meant to stand on its own while contributing to the overall endeavor. The catalogue unfolds chronologically, with some objects grouped together when best discussed in tandem. Each entry provides a catalogue number (cat. no.) as well as a Hartman manuscript (MS) or rare book (RB) number. Measurements of manuscripts appear in centimeters (width x height of the covers), while the sizes of printed books are given as 2°, 4°, 8°, or 16°. Transliteration follows standards set by the Library of Congress, with diacritics primarily employed for the letters *ḥet* (ח) and *ʿayin* (ע). Common English names and spellings are used, including the all-important Maimon, though most scholars agree that the name was in fact Maimun (מיימון).[5] Brackets are used when definitive publication information is unknown. Hebrew dates are converted to the Gregorian calendar for ease of reference, though the Julian calendar may have been in use at the particular time and place under discussion. Notes to each entry include relevant but not comprehensive bibliographic information; English titles are provided for Hebrew publications that originally appeared with one. The accompanying map, beautifully executed by Anandaroop Roy, records places of publication – cities and towns when known, regions when not specified – of objects from the Hartman Collection presented in the catalogue.

The second section contains eleven chapters by leading scholars on a wide range of topics, each complementing objects from the Hartman Collection introduced in the first section. The essays by Tzvi Langermann, Yosef Tobi, and Daniel J. Lasker shed light on Maimonides's immediate impact on particular subjects and communities. Ephraim Kanarfogel, Evelyn M. Cohen, Edward Fram, Joanna Weinberg, and Roni Weinstein each uncover ways in which Maimonidean ideas and texts were viewed and utilized in the medieval and early modern periods. Irene Zwiep, Marc B. Shapiro, and Maya Balakirsky Katz engage with the appropriation of Maimonides in the modern period, providing

5 Arnold E. Franklin, 'The Mystery of Maimonides' Puzzling Name,' *Mosaic*, May 5, 2020, https://mosaic-magazine.com/observation/religion-holidays/2020/05/the-mystery-of-maimonides-puzzling-name/ (accessed November 8, 2022).

perspectives on the ubiquity of Maimonides that persists in our own day. These essays indicate the depth and breadth of Maimonidean scholarship and point to the challenges in defining Maimonides and his impact. To the credit of these scholars and their respective specialties, such a task necessitates an alliance of *Maimonidean* effort. It is clear that only a path that rejects confinement – akin to Maimonides's own negative theology[6] – may illuminate the vast and variegated narrative.

An appendix lists objects included in the exhibition on loan from other institutions and private collectors, most notably a portion of an eleventh-century Torah Ark door from Egypt (presumably known to Maimonides), jointly owned by The Walters Art Museum and Yeshiva University Museum; Maimonides's autograph manuscripts from the Bodleian Library at the University of Oxford and the Library of the Jewish Theological Seminary (JTS); the fourteenth-century illuminated *Moreh Nevkhim* housed in Copenhagen's Royal Danish Library; a magnificent fourteenth-century illuminated *Moreh Nevukhim*, largely unknown and now preserved in the Mantua State Archive of the Italian Ministry of Culture; Isaac Newton's notes on calendar reform (in which he cited Maimonides), held by the National Library of Israel; and portraits of Maimonides by Jack Levine and Ben Shahn, housed in the JTS Library and the Jewish Museum, respectively.

The seeds of this project were sown nearly fifteen years ago, when I first started cataloguing volumes in the growing Hartman Collection. My deep gratitude to Bob and Debbie Hartman and their loving family for their confidence throughout this long period, and for looking after me so graciously during visits to their home. Innumerable people assisted through the initial stages of the project, as well as the more recent efforts to put on the exhibition and produce this accompanying catalogue. Thanks to Jesse Abelman, Ardon Bar-Hama, Shuli Berger, Piet van Boxel, Francesca Bregoli, Evelyn M. Cohen, Jeffrey Culang, Zvi Erenyi, Yoel Finkelman, Elli Fischer, Arnold Franklin, Rahel Fronda, Matt Goldish, Mark Hartman, Yossi Hacker, Marc Herman, Brad Sabin Hill, Martina Mampieri, Hadassah (Michelle) Margolis, César Merchan-Hamann, Sabrina Mingarelli, Rachel Misrati, Estee Morgenshtern, Judith Olszowy-Schlanger, Jordan Penkower, Angelo Piatelli, Shaul Regev, Pinchas Roth, Marina Rustow, Shalom Sabar, Menahem Schmelzer זצ״ל, Emile Schrijver, Jerry Schwarzbard, Yael Sela, Yitzchak Shailat, Amedeo Spagnoletto, Aaron Stefansky ז״ל, Daniel Tabak, Nina Taub, Magda Teter, Eli Varenberg, David Wachtel, Heide Warncke, Gabriel Wasserman, Joanna Weinberg, Tina Weiss, and Havva Zellner.

Special thanks to the contributors to this volume, each of whom graciously and judiciously responded to my request for expert yet accessible essays. Deep gratitude to my friends Ari Kinsberg, Phil Lieberman, and Shaul Seidler-Feller for answering endless questions with thoughtfulness and alacrity. I must also acknowledge that preliminary cataloguing of several items was conducted at various points over the last two decades by Benjamin Richler, Menahem Schmelzer זצ״ל, Daniel Tabak, David Wachtel, and others who remain anonymous, without which this venture would have taken much longer and been far less fruitful.

Of course, nothing would have come to fruition without the dedication and expertise of the exhibition team. Thanks to Ilana Benson, Paul Glassman, Bonni-Dara Michaels, Ilona Moradof, and Barbara Suhr for their thought, effort, and perseverance. Particular appreciation to Gabriel Goldstein, for his wisdom and guidance; Sharon Liberman Mintz, for facilitating the project at its inception and for sharing her expertise; to Jacob Wisse, for shepherding the exhibition in its first stages at the Museum; and to interns Sheindl Berger and especially Yitzhak Graff, for adeptly assisting on a host of bibliographic and research queries at a moment's notice. Thanks also to the teams at Liverpool University Press and Carnegie Book Production for their professionalism, to Alison Welsby and Alexander Marsden in particular for their patience and thoughtfulness, to Lucy Frontani

6 Shlomo Pines (trans.), *The Guide of the Perplexed* (Chicago: University of Chicago Press, 1963), vol. 1, part 1, ch. 58.

for designing such a beautiful book, and to Connie Webber of the Littman Library of Jewish Civilization for connecting us with her colleagues at LUP.

Limitless gratitude to my parents, Abe and Nancy Sclar, who instilled values of learning and humility, and who helped with this project from beginning to end. Love to my children, Noa, Avraham Hayim, and Ayala, each of whom offer worlds of those same values and so much more. And Yafit – may we continue to journey together on the middle (*golden*) path described by Maimonides in his *Mishneh Torah*, *Hilkhot De'ot*.

David Sclar
Shevat 5783 / February 2023

Paths of Maimonides and His Impact

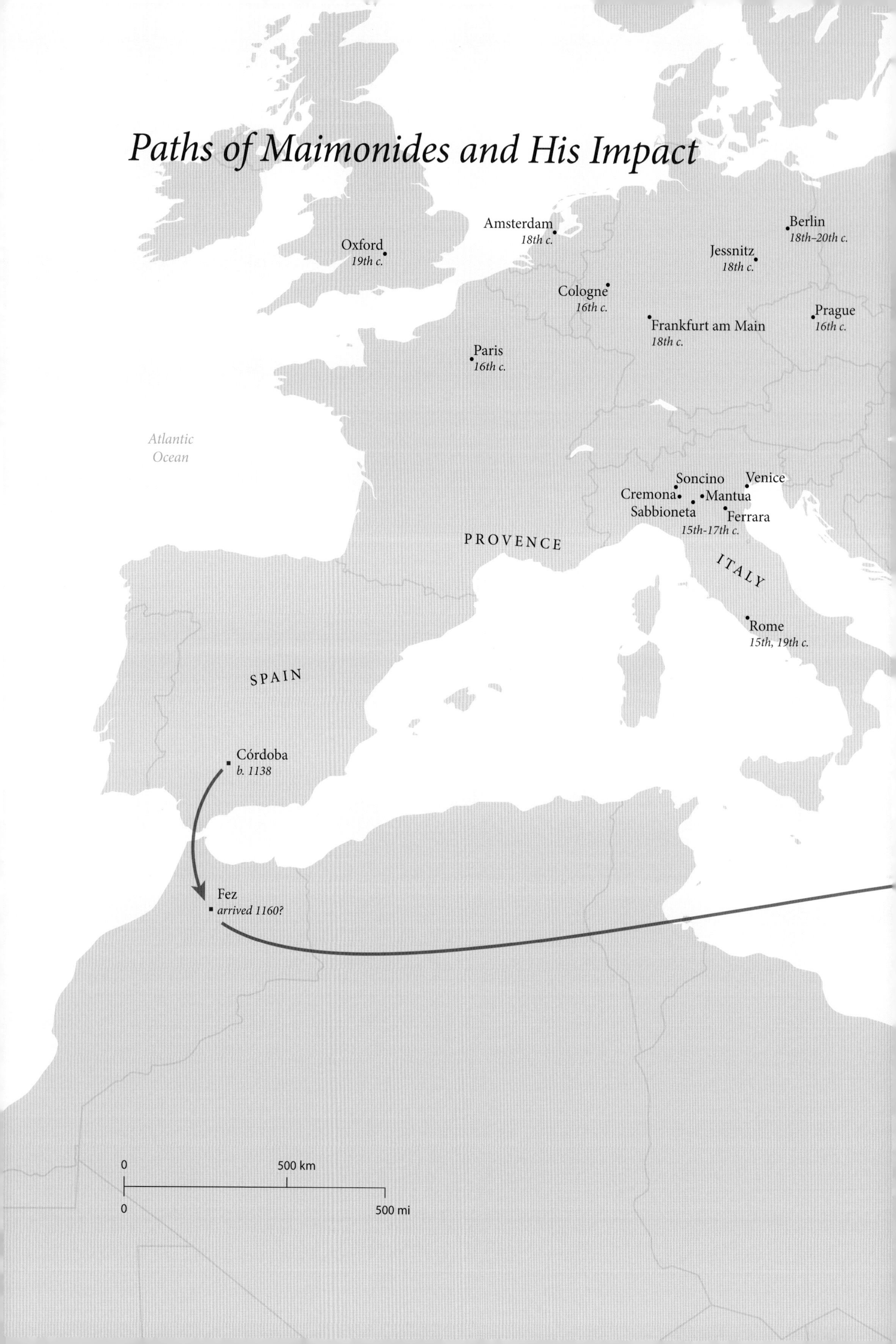

▪ Place in which Maimonides resided
• Place and century of production of manuscript/printed book in catalogue
Brest (Brisk)
20th c.
Lviv (Lemberg)
19th c.
Black Sea
Istanbul (Constantinople)
16th c.
Mediterranean Sea
Acre
arrived 1165?
Alexandria
arrived 1166?
Fustat (Cairo)
arrived 1168?; d. 1204
Red Sea
14th-20th c.
YEMEN
ʿAmran
Darb al-Ḥanashat
Sanaʿa
Guran
Salf Banei al-Qadi
Arabian Sea
Detail of Arabian Peninsula

CATALOGUE

Cat. nos. 1–9: 13th–15th centuries

Cat. nos. 10–24: 16th century

Cat. nos. 25–31: 17th–18th centuries

Cat. nos. 32–38: 19th–20th centuries

דלאלה̈ אלחאירין (מורה נבוכים)
Dalalat al-Ḥa'irin (*Moreh Nevukhim*; Guide of the Perplexed)
[Yemen, ca. 1280–1330]
MS 11. Manuscript on paper; 2ff.; 12.5 x 21.5 cm, 19 x 20 cm

כתאב אלחקאיק
Kitab al-Ḥaka'ik (*Sefer ha-Amitiyot*; Book of Truths)
[Yemen, 14th century]
MS 15. Manuscript on paper; 48ff.; 18 x 24 cm

Maimonides's *Moreh Nevukhim* (*Guide of the Perplexed*) stands as the most significant philosophical work composed by a Jew during the medieval era. Although veritably a work of Jewish philosophy, it so masterfully presented general philosophical issues of the day that it was long regarded as much more than just a work for Jewish readers. It is part of the broad transcultural genre of philosophy that Muslims, Christians, and Jews delved into between the eleventh and fifteenth centuries. Having occasionally presented philosophical ideas in several works when pertinent to the larger context, including in his *Commentary on the Mishnah* and *Mishneh Torah*, here Maimonides comprehensively presented his system of philosophical thought.

Maimonides composed *Moreh Nevukhim* in Judeo-Arabic (entitled *Dalalat al-Ḥa'irin*) between 1185 and 1191 as a three-part treatise sent to his disciple Joseph ben Judah of Ceuta, who had sought to reconcile the books of the Prophets with his metaphysical studies. As such, Maimonides devoted the bulk of the work to explaining certain words and passages found in the prophetic books of the Bible. The author's illumination of biblical homilies led to the climactic section expounding the Bible's two most enigmatic chapters – *Ma'aseh Bereshit* (Account of the Creation) and *Ma'aseh Merkavah* (Account of the Chariot of Ezekiel's Vision) – as well as a philosophical explanation of the commandments. Through it all, Maimonides presented his views on Torah, prophecy, providence, evil, and the existence, unity, and incorporeality of God.

Maimonides did not intend for his philosophical magnum opus to be widely disseminated. However, the work proved profound, serving as a guide for faithful Jews who, having delved into contemporary philosophy and science, were perplexed and even embarrassed by a literal reading of the Bible. Descriptions of God in anthropomorphic and anthropopathic terms, accounts of prophetic visions, and depictions of angels interacting with humans seemingly contradicted rational thought. Maimonides sought to reconcile two truths: the Torah, as it was revealed to Moses by God, and philosophy, as presented mainly by Aristotle and as translated and interpreted by the great Muslim scholars Al-Farabi, Avicenna, and others. Maimonides argued that no contradiction existed between the Jewish religion and contemporary science and philosophy. Any apparent inconsistency could be resolved by correct interpretation. The unique, proper perspective would in fact reveal 'the science of the Law in its true sense.' The inner meaning of the Torah was contained within the challenge presented by philosophy. Assimilating the knowledge presented in *Moreh Nevukhim* by understanding the spiritual meaning of the text would unlock the 'secrets of the Law.'[1]

1 Shlomo Pines (trans.), *The Guide of the Perplexed* (Chicago: University of Chicago Press, 1963), vol. 1, part 1, intro.

The text's impact is unparalleled among medieval works on Jewish philosophy. For centuries, almost every philosophical work produced by a Jew cited, commented upon, or criticized the *Guide*. Rationalists utilized it as a foundation text, literalists decried the dangers to which it could lead, and kabbalists lamented Maimonides's failure to reach the ultimate level of mysticism. *Moreh Nevukhim* even served as an entry point into Enlightenment philosophy and modern European society for Jewish thinkers in the eighteenth and nineteenth centuries. Baruch Spinoza (1632–1677), Moses Ḥayim Luzzatto (1707–ca. 1746), and Moses Mendelssohn (1729–1786) all engaged with Maimonides's work, even as they developed thought that ran contrary to his. Naḥman Krochmal called his own philosophical treatise *Moreh Nevukhe ha-Zeman* (A Contemporary Guide of the Perplexed). Furthermore, Maimonides's *Guide* had a strong influence on Christian scholastic thought, with several Christian scholars, among them Thomas Aquinas (1225–1274), citing Maimonides by name.

Nevertheless, *Moreh Nevukhim* engendered intense controversy, which ebbed and flowed, in several stages and under varying circumstances, for centuries. Opponents feared the potential corrupting influence of philosophical speculation and argued that Maimonides and other philosophers did not represent Jewish thought faithfully. The first decades of the thirteenth century saw bans and counter-bans levied between rationalist and traditionalist camps. Traditional sources in support of Maimonides, including a late thirteenth-century letter from Hillel ben Samuel of Verona, claimed that a campaign to ban *Moreh Nevukhim* and *Sefer Mada* of the *Mishneh Torah* resulted in a public burning of his writings in Montpellier in 1233. Although an anti-Jewish campaign in Paris included a public disputation in 1240 and, two years later, the burning of 24 wagonloads of rabbinic texts, scholars are skeptical that Jewish opposition to Maimonides directly led to Christian-propagated destruction.[2]

By the middle of the thirteenth century, the Maimonidean controversies had little to do with Maimonides himself. His thought and authority were generally, and sometimes unreservedly, accepted, but some thinkers continued to warn against the study of philosophy. In 1305, Solomon ben Abraham Adret (Rashba; 1235–1310) issued a ban against the study of philosophy before the age of 25.[3]

Just as Greek philosophy had reached medieval European societies through Arabic translations, Maimonides's philosophical treatise was disseminated through Hebrew translations.[4] Two distinct Hebrew renditions of the *Guide* were made almost immediately after its composition. The first was a literal translation made by Samuel ben Judah Ibn Tibbon, a member of the great Provençal family that produced physicians, philosophers, and translators. He corresponded with Maimonides, and generally sacrificed style for accuracy in order to provide the non-Arabic speaking Jewish world with the most precise rendering of Maimonides's philosophical thought. In contrast, Judah ben Solomon al-Ḥarizi, a poet and translator also from Provence, translated the text in a simple and clear biblical Hebrew that approached the original text quite liberally. This rendered the translation of literary value, but it also drew much criticism.[5]

Ultimately, Ibn Tibbon's version served as the authority for Jewish students of *Moreh Nevukhim*. Approximately 170 manuscripts of this translation are extant, and it became the

2 For an overview, see Jeremy Cohen, *The Friars and the Jews: The Evolution of Medieval Anti-Judaism* (Ithaca, NY: Cornell University Press, 1982), 52–60. For a recent evaluation of the validity of the event, see Yossef Schwartz, 'Persecution and the Art of Translation: Some New Evidence of the Latin Translation of the *Guide of the Perplexed*,' *Yod. Revue des études hébraiques et juives* 22 (2019): 49–77.

3 See Gregg Stern, *Philosophy and Rabbinic Culture* (Abingdon: Routledge, 2009); Marc Saperstein, 'The Conflict over the Rashba's Herem on Philosophical Study: A Political Perspective,' *Jewish History* 1, no. 2 (1986): 27–38.

4 When asked by the rabbis of Lunel to translate his *Moreh Nevukhim*, Maimonides replied that he wished he were young enough to do so; see Franz Kobler (ed.), *A Treasury of Jewish Letters: Letters from the Famous and the Humble*, 2 vols. (Philadelphia, PA: Jewish Publication Society of America, 1953), 1:216.

5 Yair Shiffman, 'The Differences Between the Translations of Maimonides' *Guide of the Perplexed* by Falaquera, Ibn Tibbon and al-Harizi, and their Textual and Philosophical Implications,' *Journal of Semitic Studies* 44 (1999): 47–61.

Fig. 1 *Dalalat al-Ḥa'irin* (Moreh Nevukhim) [Yemen, ca. 1280–1330], MS 11.

basis for all printed editions of the *Guide* in Hebrew.[6] Meanwhile, al-Ḥarizi's translation found reception among Christian scholastics, no doubt due to its easy-to-read prose. Latin translations of the *Guide* circulated as early as the 1240s and appeared in print in Paris in 1520 and in Basel in 1629.[7]

These Judeo-Arabic fragments in the Hartman Collection are among the earliest known exemplars of Maimonides's original text of *Moreh Nevukhim*. They consist of I:68 and II:24, exploring the intellect of God and the motion of the planets, respectively (Fig. 1).[8]

Maimonides's impact on Yemenite Jewry is well known.[9] His *Igeret Teman* (Epistle to Yemen), written ca. 1172, bolstered local Jewish communities then under pressure to convert to Islam or to follow a would-be messiah preaching of the imminent redemption. Written with clarity and compassion, for laypeople rather than for scholars per se, the Epistle provided a lifeline. In return, Yemenite Jews absorbed his writings wholeheartedly and added a line to the Kaddish prayer in his honor.[10]

Moreh Nevukhim had as much impact on Yemenite Jewry as Maimonides's other works. Religious thinkers adopted Maimonidean positions and methodology,[11] as well as the

6 Colette Sirat, 'La composition et l'édition des texts philosophiques Juifs au Moyen Âge: quelques exemples,' *Bulletin de Philosophie Médiévale* 30 (1988): 224–32.

7 The first was printed by the Dominican priest Agostino Giustiniani (1470–1536); the latter, of superior quality, was printed by the Protestant Christian Hebraist Johannes Buxtorf the Younger (1599–1664); see Joanna Weinberg's essay in this volume.

8 Tzvi Langermann, 'The "True Perplexity": The *Guide of the Perplexed*, Part II, Chapter 24,' in *Perspectives on Maimonides: Philosophical and Historical Studies*, ed. Joel L. Kraemer (Oxford: Littman Library of Jewish Civilization, 1991), 159–74; Herbert A. Davidson, 'Further on a Problematic Passage in "Guide for the Perplexed" 2.24,' *Maimonidean Studies* 4 (2000): 1–13.

9 See Yosef Tobi's essay in this volume.

10 On Maimonides in the Kaddish prayer, see Mordechai A. Friedman, '"In Your Lifetime and in the Lifetime of our Lord Moses Maimonides"' [Hebrew], *Zion* 62 (1997): 75–78.

11 See Tzvi Langermann, 'Yemenite Philosophical Midrash as a Source for the Intellectual History of the Jews of Yemen,' in *The Jews of Medieval Islam*, ed. Daniel Frank (Leiden: Brill, 1992), 335–47; and on the *Guide* in Islamic lands, see Langermann, 'Sharḥ al-Dalāla: A Commentary to Maimonides' *Guide* from Fourteenth-Century Yemen,' in *Cultures of Maimonideanism*, ed. James T. Robinson (Leiden: Brill, 2009), 155–76.

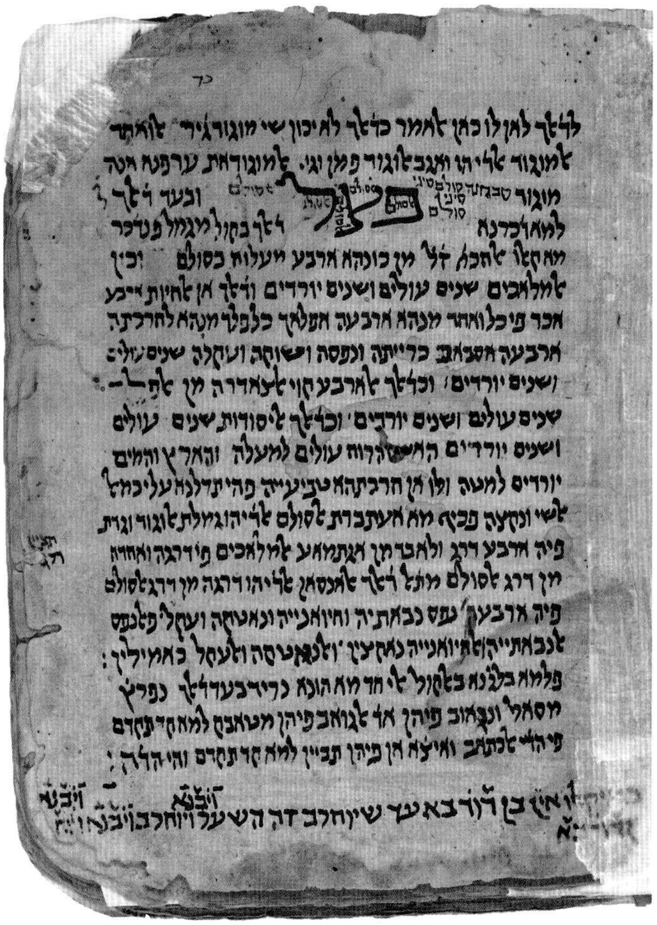

Fig. 2 *Kitab al-Ḥaka'ik* [Yemen, 14th century], MS 15, fol. 24r.

emphasis on identifying knowledge of the truths (*ḥaka'ik*) that underlie the surface of the Torah. However, as in thirteenth-century southern France, Maimonides's ideas helped inspire philosophical exegesis that generated controversy, like the present *Kitab al-Ḥaka'ik* (Fig. 2). Its central themes include 'the structure of the cosmos, the intellect as the source of all forms, the human soul, a theory of consciousness, the purpose of man, emanation, man as microcosm, and the exoteric (*zahir*) and esoteric (*batin*) meaning of the text.'[12]

The manuscript of *Kitab al-Ḥaka'ik* in the Hartman Collection was published by Yosef Kafiḥ, with an introduction by Yosef Tobi and an apparatus providing sources.[13] The work's importance lay in its penetration and adaptation of Maimonides's philosophy, and in its representation of a rich Jewish intellectual and cultural life that produced thinkers incorporating Neoplatonic, Sufi, and Isma'ili thought. In addition, it reflects the influence of non-Jewish intellectual trends on local Jewish culture at a time when Yemen was a bustling entrepôt connecting the Islamic world to India.[14]

12 Binyamin Abrahamov, '*Kitab al-Haqa'iq* and Its Sources' [Hebrew], *Daat: A Journal of Philosophy & Kabbalah* 55 (2005): 31–39 (32 n. 12). See also Meir Bar-Ilan, 'He-'arah Numerologit 'al Meḥaber "Kitab al-Haka'ik," Ḥakham she-lo Noda bi-Shemo,' in *'Ateret Yitsḥak: Kovets Meḥkarim be-Moreshet Yehude Teman: Mugashim le-Yitsḥak Kerner*, ed. Yosef Tobi (Netanya: ha-Agudah le-Tipu'aḥ Ḥevrah ve-Tarbut, 2003), 73–80.

13 Yosef Kafiḥ, *Kitab al-Ḥaka'ik: Sefer ha-Amitiyot le-Eḥad me-Ḥakhme Tsa'dah, Teman, ha-Me'ah ha-14* (Tel-Aviv: Afikim, 1997).

14 For one such twelfth-century philosopher, Nathanel al-Fayumi, see Yosef Kafiḥ (ed.), *Sefer Bustan al-'Ukul* (Jerusalem: ha-Agudah le-Hatsalat Ginzei Teman, 1953/4).

פרקי משה (עם לוחות הפועל)
Pirke Mosheh (Aphorisms of Moses), with Anonymous Medical Treatise
and *Luḥot ha-Po'el* (Astronomical Tablets)
[Provence, 14th century]
MS 6. Manuscript on paper; 79ff.; 14.5 x 21.5 cm

In addition to his expertise in philosophy and *halakhah* and his role as a communal leader, Maimonides also practiced as a physician and was widely known for his medical scholarship.[1] Although he did not specify with whom he studied, he may have learned medicine from his father.[2] He composed several medical works, some on general themes and others on specific ailments. He classified medical practice into three divisions: preventive medicine, healing of the sick, and care of recovering patients, which included the elderly. His approach, in consonance with his general worldview, was strictly rationalist. He encouraged experimentation and research, and opposed the use of charms, incantations, and amulets.

During most of his time in Egypt, Maimonides served as a physician for the Fatimid and Ayyubid courts. His brilliance and success were noted by Muslim scholars during and after his lifetime. Ibn Sana al-Mulk, a contemporary poet and judge (*qadi*), remarked: 'Galen healed the body alone; Ibn Imran (= Maimonides) the body and the spirit as well. In his knowledge, he stands at the head of the physicians of our age, and in his wisdom he also cures the illness of foolishness.'[3] Ali Ibn Yusuf al-Qifti recorded (the oft echoed story) that Richard the Lionheart, King of England on crusade in Palestine, tried to entice Maimonides to leave his post serving Saladin in favor of serving as his physician.[4] Ibn Abi Usaybi'a, a thirteenth-century physician who knew Maimonides's son Abraham, praised him in his biographical encyclopedia of notable physicians and quoted a laudatory poem from Qadi Sa'id ben Sana al-Mulk:

> I see that Galen's medicine is for the body only,
> but Maimonides' medicine is for mind and body.
> If he were to treat Time with his medical knowledge
> he would cure it of ignorance with knowledge.
> And if the full moon were to seek his medical advice,
> the fullness it claims would be fulfilled,
> And he would treat, on the day of its fullness, its spots
> and cure it, on the day of its invisibility, of its sickness.[5]

Pirke Mosheh, known in its original Arabic as *Fusul Musa*, is the most famous and widely quoted of all Maimonides's medical writings. It consists of aphorisms from the Greek physician Galen (ca. 130–201) and some Arabic authors, as well as Maimonides's commentary and his own original maxims. His most ambitious medical composition,

1 See Tzvi Langermann's essay in this volume.

2 Joel L. Kraemer, *Maimonides: The Life and World of One of Civilization's Greatest Minds* (New York: Doubleday, 2008), 88–91.

3 Moshe Halbertal, *Maimonides: Life and Thought*, trans. Joel Linsider (Princeton, NJ: Princeton University Press, 2014), 63.

4 Bernard Lewis, 'Maimonides, Lionheart, and Saladin,' *Erets-Yisrael* 7 (1964): 70–75.

5 Ibn Abi Usaybi'ah, *Anecdotes & Antidotes: A Medieval Arabic History of Physicians*, ed. Henrietta Sharp Cockrell et al. (Oxford: Oxford University Press, 2020), 222.

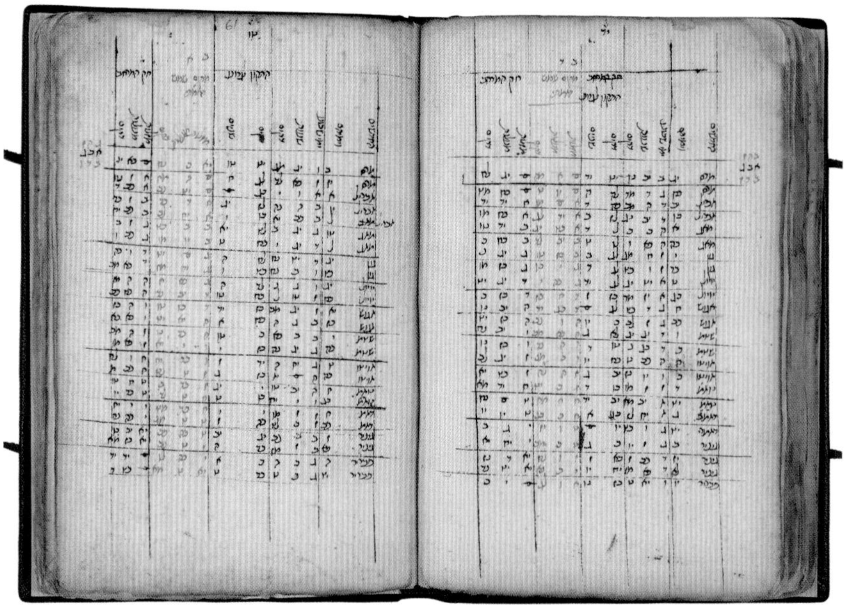

Fig. 3 *Luḥot ha-Po'el* [Provence, 14th century], MS 6, fols. 60v–61r.

Maimonides spent many years composing this work, combing through thousands of pages of Galen's works.

Pirke Mosheh was twice translated into Hebrew by scholars in Rome. The prolific author and translator Zeraḥiah ben Isaac ben She'altiel Ḥen completed his version in 1277, and Nathan ben Eliezer ha-Me'ati, called the 'Prince of Translators' and the 'Italian Tibbonide,' concluded his own a few years later. Zeraḥiah was born in Barcelona, while Nathan's place of origin was likely Cento (hence his toponymic surname, from the Hebrew *me'ah*, for one hundred), a small town between Ferrara and Modena on the Italian peninsula. Zeraḥiah's translation has survived in at least 15 manuscript copies, while Nathan's translation is extant in at least 24. Ironically, most of the manuscripts of Zeraḥiah's translation stem from Italy, whereas most of Nathan's originate from Spain.

Manuscripts consisting of only select treatises of *Pirke Mosheh* are very rare, and those copied in Provence rarer still. The present manuscript consists only of treatises 5, 6, 10, 11, 12, 13, and 14 (ordered differently), and includes many variant readings, sentences, and passages that are not found in printed editions.[6] Apart from a folio excised from the final quire the manuscript is complete, indicating that the scribe was either working off another select manuscript or produced this as such with intent. At the beginning of treatise 12, in which Maimonides discussed *hakazat dam* (bloodletting), the scribe included related text from chapter 2 of treatise 9. It follows Nathan ha-Me'ati's translation, which did not appear in print until the nineteenth century (see cat. no. 34).

This manuscript also includes an anonymous medical treatise in 13 chapters, translated into Hebrew from Arabic by Solomon of Narbonne (fols. 26r–44v). The text is incomplete, ending in the middle of chapter 10, though it also includes supplementary material from the translator. The only other known copy of this work is an incomplete manuscript produced in 1452, which includes the text from the middle of chapter 2 until the end.[7] The introduction is known only from the Hartman manuscript, from which we learn the translator's name.[8]

In addition, this manuscript contains *Luḥot ha-Po'el* (fols. 46r–79v), astronomical tables prepared in Perpignan by Jacob ben David Yom Tov Po'el, court astronomer to Pedro IV of

6 Süssman Muntner (ed.), *Pirke Mosheh bi-Refu'ah be-Targumo shel R. Natan ha-Me'ati* (Jerusalem: Mossad Harav Kook, 1959); Fred Rosner (ed.), *Maimonides' Commentary on the Aphorisms of Hippocrates* (Haifa: Maimonides Research Institute, 1987).

7 St. Petersburg, Institute of Oriental Manuscripts, MS B 133.

8 On the present manuscript, see Moritz Steinschneider, 'Salomon de Melgueil et Salomon Orgerius,' *Révue des Etudes Juives* 5 (1882): 277–81; and on this medical treatise, see Steinschneider, *Die hebräischen Übersetzungen des Mittelalters* (Berlin: Kommissionsverlag des Bibliographischen Bureaus, 1893), 752–53.

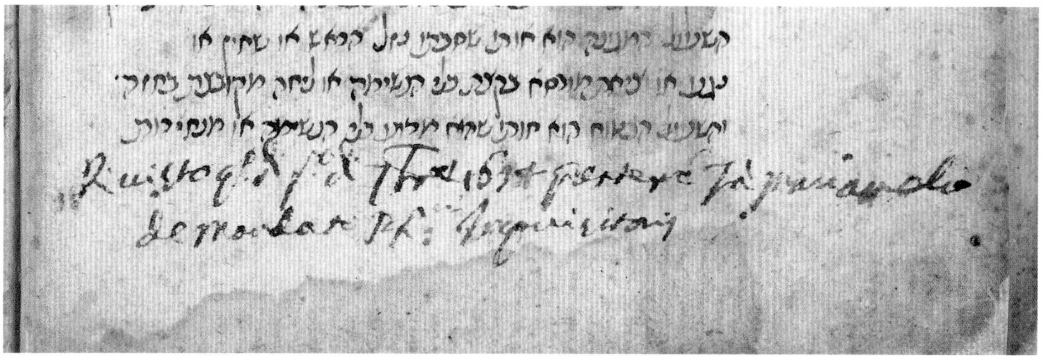

Fig. 4 *Pirke Mosheh* [Provence, 14th century], MS 6, fol. 22v. Detail of censor's signature.

Aragon (reigned 1336–1387) (Fig. 3). Jacob composed *Luḥot ha-Po'el* in Hebrew, although the names of the months appear in Spanish in Hebrew characters. The work appeared in Latin translation in the fifteenth century and served as the subject of several Hebrew commentaries. About 40 manuscript copies of *Luḥot ha-Po'el* are extant, but just one can be dated to a specific year in the fourteenth century (1395) and only three or four others can be dated approximately within that century.[9] The watermarks of the present manuscript indicate that it was written ca. 1370–1380, only a decade or two after Jacob first composed the work in Perpignan.

The manuscript consists of different hands, inks, and scripts, though it is uniformly of the same paper stock throughout. It consists of an unusual quire count: 11, 11, 4, 4, 4, 5.[10] Notes by the bibliographer and historian Moritz Steinschneider appear throughout and on the rear endpapers. The manuscript is one of about a dozen that bear the censor's signature of Marc Aurelio, whose full name and the cities in which he was active are unknown, though the inscription here indicates he examined this book on February 1, 1634 at the request of the 'Inquisitor' (fol. 22v) (Fig. 4).[11]

The manuscript probably made its way from Spain to Italy with Sephardic exiles in the fifteenth or sixteenth centuries. Its owners are unknown until the modern period, when it passed to the Italian scholar, philosopher, and Bible commentator Samuel David Luzzatto (Shadal; 1800–1865). Subsequent custodians (though not necessarily 'owners') included Steinschneider, Salomon Halberstam,[12] Judith Lady Montefiore College in Ramsgate,[13] and Jews' College in London (see cat. nos. 5 and 33).

9 See Bibliothèque Nationale, Paris, MS. No. 10,901; Adolf Neubauer, *Catalogue of the Hebrew Manuscripts in the Bodleian Library and in the College Libraries of Oxford* (Oxford, 1886–1906), no. 2072, 2.

10 A page was excised from the final quire.

11 The inscription reads 'Revisto questo die prio di Febraio 1634 quarente me Fra Marc Aurelio de mandato reverendissimi inquisitoris.' (Thanks to Piet van Boxel and Joanna Weinberg for help in reading the inscription in its entirety.) A similar inscription is found in Herbert Loewe, *Catalogue of the Manuscripts in the Hebrew Character Collected and Bequeathed to Trinity College Library By the Late William Aldis Wright* (Cambridge: at the University Press, 1926), 109 (no. 118). Abraham Berliner referred to him as 'Marcellino' in *Censur und Konfiscation hebraeischer Buecher im Kirchenstaate* (Berlin: H. Itzkowski, 1891), 10; no additional sources are found in William Popper, *The Censorship of Hebrew Books*, intro. Moshe Carmilly-Weinberger (New York: Ktav, 1969).

12 S. J. Halberstam, *Kohelet Shelomoh* (Vienna: A. Fanto, 1890), no. 148.

13 Hartwig Hirschfeld, *Descriptive Catalogue of the Hebrew Manuscripts of the Montefiore Library* (London: Macmillan, 1904), no. 439.

3

מלות ההגיון
Milot ha-Higayon (Treatise on Logic)
Translated by Moses Ibn Tibbon
[Spain, late 14th–early 15th century]
MS 7. Manuscript on paper; 12ff.; 21 x 25 cm

Maimonides composed his *Treatise on Logic*, known by the Arabic name *Makalah fi-Sina'at al-Mantik*, at a pivotal time of his young life. He and his family had left their native Córdoba in 1148 to escape the Almohad persecutions, and they wandered through Spain, North Africa, and the Land of Israel before settling in 1165 in the relative safety and security of Fustat (today part of Cairo). During this period, Maimonides's writings included the present work, a short treatise on the Jewish calendar entitled *Ma'amar ha-'Ibur*, a commentary on tractates of the Babylonian Talmud commonly studied in Iberia, and his monumental *Commentary on the Mishnah*.

Scholars have debated the authorship of this *Treatise on Logic* and its date of composition. Herbert Davidson has argued that the work contains no particularly Jewish or Maimonidean elements, and pointed out that neither Maimonides nor Samuel Ibn Tibbon, translator of *Moreh Nevukhim*, ever mentioned a *Treatise on Logic*.[1] However, the general consensus is that it indeed stemmed from Maimonides's pen and that he wrote it while still a teenager.[2] The work offers a clear and concise exposition of nearly 175 terms used in discussions of logical theory. This includes physical, metaphysical, and ethical vocabulary, making it an introduction to philosophy as well.

The work was translated into Hebrew at least three times, as well as into Latin, Italian, French, German, and English. The majority of Hebrew manuscripts of this treatise follow the translation of the author, translator, and physician Moses Ibn Tibbon, son of Samuel Ibn Tibbon. Over centuries of study, numerous commentaries on the treatise were written and published. Its popularity rose during the eighteenth and nineteenth centuries with the increased study of philosophy, and one such commentary was composed by the father of the Jewish Enlightenment (*Haskalah*), Moses Mendelssohn (1729–1786). The work has appeared in print at least 17 times, including in Latin (Basel, 1527), German (1805, 1822, 1833, 1828), French (1935), and English (1938). Yet the printed editions contain numerous textual corruptions.

The text of the present manuscript offers a more accurate rendering of the original Arabic than the standard editions (Fig. 5). A comparison to those found in Israel Efros's edition shows some variants.[3] In addition, the manuscript contains marginal notations in several hands, including a contemporary Sephardic script and another in a sixteenth- or seventeenth-century Sephardic script.

1 For a historiographical overview and his own argument, see Herbert A. Davidson, *Moses Maimonides: The Man and His Works* (Oxford: Oxford University Press, 2005), 313–22. Davidson criticized scholars for going so far as to specify Maimonides's age at the time of its composition without 'a shred of evidence' (318 n. 53).

2 Israel Efros, 'Maimonides' Treatise of Logic (*Makalah Fi-Sina'at al-Mantik*): The Original Arabic and Three Hebrew Translations,' *American Academy for Jewish Research* 8 (New York, 1938): 3. Efros's work here encompasses this entire volume of the journal.

3 For instance, Efros's chapter 8 reads: והמפורסמות כידיעתנו שגילוי הערוה מגונה וכי חסדי המטיב ביותר נכבד נאה ומקובל (Efros, 39–40 [Hebrew text]). Hartman MS 7 contains a reading not recorded as a variant: והמפורסמים כידיעתנו שגלוי הערוה דבר מגונה וכי חסדי הגומל ביותר נאה ומקובל (fol. 5v).

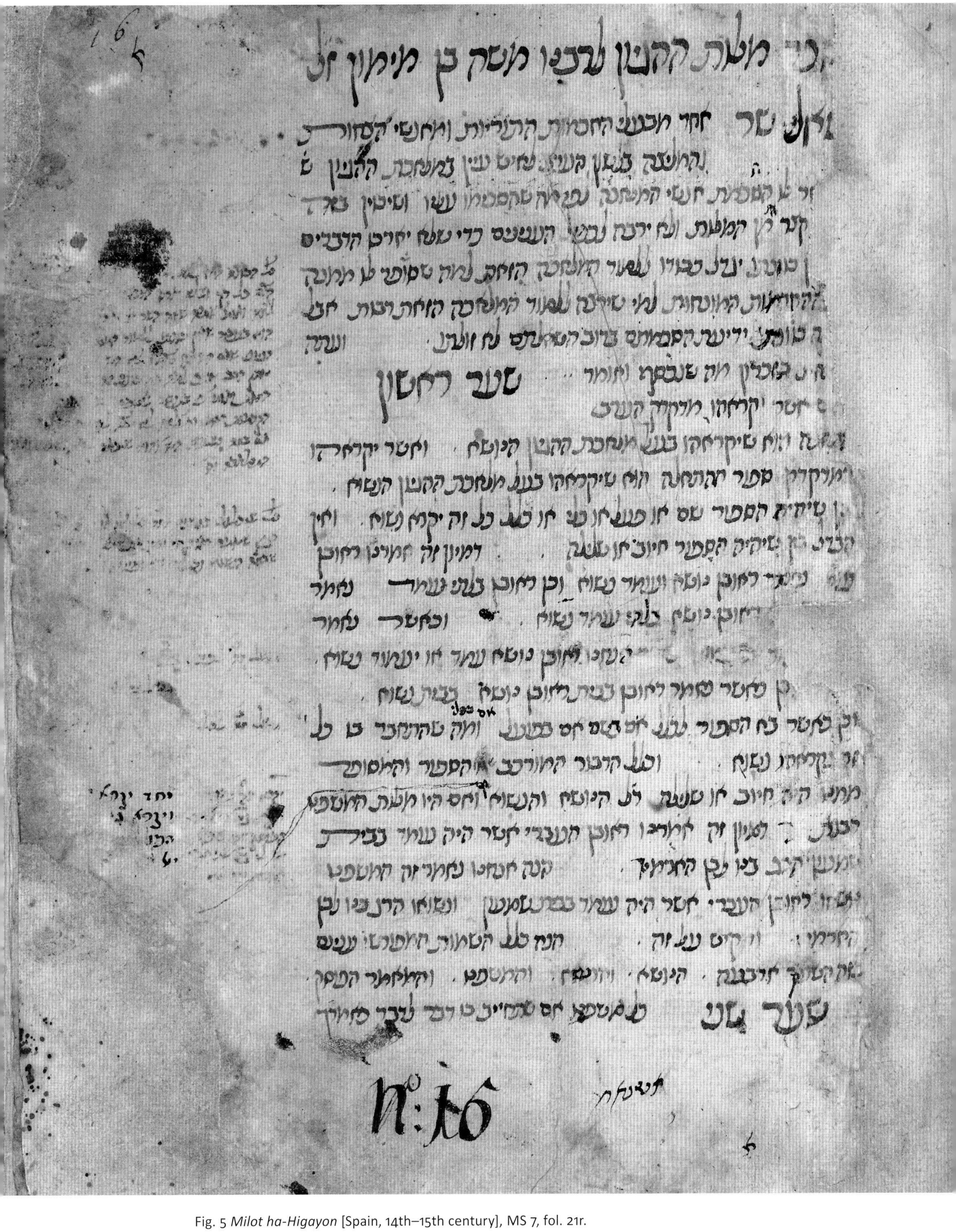

Fig. 5 *Milot ha-Higayon* [Spain, 14th–15th century], MS 7, fol. 21r.

4

משנה תורה: ספר מדע, ספר אהבה, ספר זמנים
Mishneh Torah: Sefer Mada, Sefer Ahavah, Sefer Zemanim (Repetition of the Law: Book of Knowledge, Book of Love, Book of Times)
[Yemen, 14th century]
MS 14. Manuscript on paper; 175ff.; 19.7 x 26.7 cm

משנה תורה: ספר טהרה
Mishneh Torah: Sefer Tohorah (Repetition of the Law: Book of Purity)
[Yemen, 14th century]
MS 2. Manuscript on paper; 275ff.; 19.5 x 25.5 cm

משנה תורה: ספר נשים
Mishneh Torah: Sefer Nashim (Repetition of the Law: Book of Women)
[Yemen, 15th century]
MS 22. Manuscript on paper; 278pp.; 18.5 x 24.1 cm

משנה תורה: ספר קדושה
Mishneh Torah: Sefer Kedushah (Repetition of the Law: Book of Holiness)
[Yemen, 15th century]
MS 3. Manuscript on paper; 88ff.; 19.3 x 25.9 cm

Maimonides composed the *Mishneh Torah*, also known as *Yad ha-Ḥazakah* (The Strong Hand), between 1170 and 1180 while living in Fustat (near Cairo), adjacent to the Fatimid dynasty's seat of power. Consisting of 14 'books' – thus, the Hebrew designation *yad*, the numerical value of 14 – it encompassed all details of Jewish law. With his unique clarity and eloquence, Maimonides intended to provide a systematization of the Oral Law, whereby no person who mastered the Written Torah and embraced his *Mishneh Torah* would ever need to study or consult any other reference work of *halakhah* to live a fully Jewish life. Composed in Hebrew, rather than Talmudic Aramaic or the vernacular Judeo-Arabic, Maimonides's purpose was to provide all Jews with a clear guide for practicing and deciding law.

His sources included the Tanakh, the Babylonian and Jerusalem Talmuds, the *Tosefta*, the halakhic *midrashim* of the *Sifra* and *Sifre*, the responsa of the Geonim, and the rulings of Isaac Alfasi (Rif; 1013–1103) and Joseph Ibn Migash (Ri Migash; 1077–1141). There is no discussion of Talmudic interpretation or methodology and there are very few citations for sources or arguments, an indication of Maimonides's confidence in his authority but also cause for significant concern, controversy, and study. In contrast to other medieval Jewish law codes, the *Mishneh Torah* sought to address Jewish law in its entirety, including topics pertinent to the Temple service and not merely those relevant to a Jewish exilic existence. The sequence of chapters is arranged according to subject matter, rather than the order of the Talmud or delineated intellectual principles.

These four manuscripts of the *Mishneh Torah* in the Hartman Collection were all produced in Yemen in the fourteenth and fifteenth centuries. Yemenite Jews adopted Maimonides's halakhic rulings in toto, making manuscripts like these especially reliable representations of the original text. Three of the four were owned by the great Yemenite scholar R. Yosef Kafiḥ (1917–2000), who edited a critical edition of the *Mishneh Torah* based largely on early manuscripts and translated and authored commentaries on the works of Maimonides and other rabbinic figures. Kafiḥ inherited the volumes from his grandfather,

Fig. 6 *Mishneh Torah* [Yemen 14th century], MS 14, fols. 59v–60r.

R. Yiḥye ben Solomon Kafiḥ (1850–1931), a noted scholar of Sana'a who collected manuscripts of classic texts and founded the *Dor De'ah* (enlightened generation) movement (see cat. no. 37).

Hartman MS 14 is comprised of fragments from seven undated manuscripts copied in Yemen during the fourteenth century, though there are pages that may have been written earlier (Fig. 6).[1] The value of this assemblage of manuscripts rests mainly in the opportunity to compare medieval Yemenite scripts and to document textual variants. The texts stem from the first three books of the *Mishneh Torah*: *Sefer Mada* serves as an introduction to theology, indicating the author's intention to provide a work representing the totality of *halakhah*; the book engendered controversy for centuries, particularly for laying out a system of belief. *Sefer Ahavah* contains laws regarding prayers, blessings, and ritual objects used in everyday life, including *tefilin* (phylacteries) and *tsitsit* (fringes on square-cornered garments). *Sefer Zemanim* centers upon Jewish festivals and provides a particular contribution to the laws regarding the sanctification of the new moon.

Hartman MS 2 consists of the tenth book of the *Mishneh Torah*, *Sefer Tohorah*.[2] It largely deals with the state of purity required for entry into the Temple, addressing specific topics like the impurity of a corpse, the Red Heifer, *tsara'at* (often misrepresented as leprosy), food, utensils, and ritual baths. This is one of very few fourteenth-century Yemenite manuscripts of *Sefer Tohorah* known to exist, though the first section of it appears in a fifteenth-century hand (fols. 1–76).[3] Notations appear throughout in several hands, and many chapter headings consist of colored ink. Before entering the Hartman Collection, the manuscript

1 Kafiḥ used them to edit *Sefer Mada*, *Sefer Ahavah*, and *Sefer Zemanim* in his edition of the *Mishneh Torah*, referring to them in the apparatus with the designation of MS פ.

2 Formerly Kafiḥ MS 71.

3 Fols. 64r–66v, 123r–123v, 213r–213v, 233r–234v, 238r–239v, 275r appear in a still later hand.

Fig. 7 *Mishneh Torah* [Yemen, 15th century], MS 22, fol. p. 130.

was owned by Aaron ben Zeḥariah ha-Levi (fol. 146v),[4] David Ibn Ali (fol. 152v), Moses ben Nissim al-Arussi (front flyleaf), and the Kafiḥs mentioned above. There is also a note recording the birth of Joseph ibn Joseph ibn Mauda (מעוצ'ה) (fol. 145r).[5]

Hartman MS 22 is a copy of *Sefer Nashim*, the fourth book of the *Mishneh Torah* (Fig. 7). It largely consists of laws related to family, with Maimonides addressing marriage, divorce, *yibum* and *ḥalitsah* (laws relating to a levirate marriage), sexual violence and abuse, and a *sotah* (a wife accused of infidelity). Once part of the world-renowned Sassoon Collection, the nearly complete manuscript is one of only a half-dozen or so similar codices produced in Yemen prior to the sixteenth century.[6] The Sassoon family, in the West labeled the 'Rothschilds of the East,' originated in Baghdad and built a trading empire that spread to Bombay, Shanghai, London, and beyond. David Solomon Sassoon (1880–1942) was a

4 Dating to 1884 *le-minyan shetarot* [= 1573].

5 The boy was born on Shabbat, *Parashat va-Yikra*, 3 *le-Ḥodesh Ge'ulim* (Nisan) 2088 *le-minyan shetarot* [= April 10, 1777]. בסימן טוב וברכה נולד הפרח הטוב הדומה לעץ רטוב גם ה' יתן לו הטוב יוסף ן' יוסף ן' מעוצ'ה אל מכונה האצ'רי ביום ש[בת] ק[ודש] ג' לחדש גאולים [=ניסן] בפ"ח [במניין השטרות (2088 שנים לשטרות); היא שנת התקל"ז ליצירה, היא שנת 1777 לסה"נ (לספירת הנוצרים)]. סדר ויקרא אל משה וידבר ה' אליו מאהל מועד לאמר כי ה' יצילה[ו] מפ"ח יקוש אנס"ו (=אמן נצח סלה ועד). The last few words are adapted from Psalm 91:3. I am indebted to Shaul Regev for help in deciphering this inscription.

6 David Solomon Sassoon, *Ohel Dawid: Descriptive Catalogue of the Hebrew and Samaritan Manuscripts in the Sassoon Library, London*, vol. 2 ([Oxford]: Oxford University Press; London: Humphrey Milford, 1932), 700 (no. 1013).

bibliophile and scholar who amassed a spectacular collection of thousands of manuscripts and early printed books. He published much, including on the Jews of Yemen, and owned numerous important manuscripts of Maimonidean texts, most notably a section of Maimonides's *Commentary on the Mishnah*, now housed in the National Library of Israel, which some scholars, including Sassoon, have argued was written by the author himself.[7]

Hartman MS 3 contains *Sefer Kedushah*, the fifth book of the *Mishneh Torah*, dealing with activities that diminish a person's holiness. It opens with *Isure Bi'ah*, discussing forbidden sexual relations in the context of *nidah* (a menstruant), incest, and adultery. The present manuscript consists mainly of the book's second section, *Hilkhot Ma'akhalot Asurot* (Laws of Forbidden Foods). However, the last two folios of the manuscript contain the beginning of the following section, *Hilkhot Sheḥitah* (Laws of Ritual Slaughter), indicating it was originally part of a larger manuscript.[8] The text begins on fol. 1v and is headed by a subtitle vocalized with superlinear pointing. Marginal notations in several hands appear throughout, including occasional corrections to the text as well as translations into Arabic (fol. 124r). A late inscription of 'אגלא' (fol. 1r) – a mystical acronym of אתה גיבור לעולם אדני, the opening words of the second paragraph of the *'Amidah* liturgy – indicates the growing influence of Kabbalah in Yemen in the eighteenth and nineteenth centuries. The manuscript bears the signatures of Yiḥye Kafiḥ (fols. 1r and 2r) and Solomon ben Saul (fol. 1v).

7 Jerusalem, National Library of Israel, Heb. 4° 5703. An additional section, not previously owned by Sassoon, is housed in the Bodleian Library, University of Oxford, MS. Pococke 295 (see Fig. 46). On the autograph, see Solomon David Sassoon, *A Comprehensive Study of the Autograph Manuscript of Maimonides' Commentary to the Mishnah* (Jerusalem, 1990).

8 From fol. 2r, pencil pagination labels the pages 45–132.

5

השגות הראב"ד על המשנה תורה
Hasagot ha-Rabad 'al ha-Mishneh Torah (Glosses of Rabad on the Repetition of the Law)
Abraham ben David of Posquières (Rabad)
[Italy, early 15th century]
MS 4. Manuscript on paper; 173ff.; 15.7 x 22.5 cm

In contrast to its wholesale acceptance by Yemenite Jewry, the *Mishneh Torah* faced criticism in Europe. Chief among Maimonides's immediate critics was Abraham ben David of Posquières (Rabad; ca. 1125–1198), who composed critical and incisive glosses to the innovative code. The leader of a vibrant intellectual culture in Provence,[1] Rabad authored many works, including responsa, glosses to Solomon ben Isaac (Rashi; 1040–1105) and the legal rulings of Isaac Alfasi (Rif; 1013–1103), and a commentary on the Talmud. He is considered a forerunner of Kabbalah, and, for his profound ability to clarify and elucidate difficult issues, he became known as the *Ba'al Hasagot* (Master of Scholarly Critique). His glosses to the *Mishneh Torah* elaborated and commented on the text, while exercising dissent as could only come from a peer and expert rabbinic scholar. Rabad did not comment on each section of the tome, but his glosses were wide-ranging and pointed. Criticism concerned interpretive matters, textual problems, and the importance of local customs. These appear alongside Rabad's comments that reconstruct Maimonides's textual explanations, identify sources otherwise absent from the *Mishneh Torah*, and demonstrate his process of formulating law.

In addition, Rabad addressed Maimonides's philosophical outlook. Rabad strongly opposed the construction of a system of dogma in Judaism, as well as Maimonides's reliance upon Aristotelian philosophy as a basis for Jewish theology. He clashed with Maimonides's assertion that even biblical accounts of sorcery, astrology, and divination are absurd and that practitioners deserved the death penalty. Rabad refused to judge the scriptural accounts of Eliezer (Genesis 24:14) and Jonathan (I Samuel 14:8–10), or various 'superstitions' contained within the Talmud, as heinous offenses. Instead, he declared that Maimonides himself warranted being subject to a ban of excommunication for denigrating their biblical ancestors.[2] In addition, Rabad challenged Maimonides's assertion that notions of God's corporeality are heretical, declaring that scholars greater and better than he had used such language based on their understanding of biblical verses and rabbinic homilies (Fig. 8).[3]

More generally, Rabad was critical of Maimonides's intent in writing his law code. He opposed the author's seemingly arbitrary manner of deciding law and his decision not to cite sources, as well as the codification of *halakhah* in general. Fearing that Maimonides sought to install his legal code as second only to the Bible, with its self-assured title 'Repetition of the Law,' Rabad concluded that while the author intended to improve upon the received halakhic system, he failed, 'for he forsook the way of all authors who preceded him.'[4]

1 On the place of *halakhah* in medieval Provence, see Pinchas Roth, *In This Land: Jewish Life and Legal Culture in Late Medieval Provence* (Toronto: Pontifical Institute of Medieval Studies, 2021). On Rabad, see Isadore Twersky, *Rabad of Posquières: A Twelfth-Century Talmudist* (Philadelphia: Jewish Publication Society of America, 1980).

2 *Mishneh Torah, Hilkhot 'Akum* 11:4.

3 *Mishneh Torah, Hilkhot Teshuvah* 3:7.

4 *Mishneh Torah*, last *hasagah* to the intro.; see also Twersky, *Rabad of Posquieres*, 131.

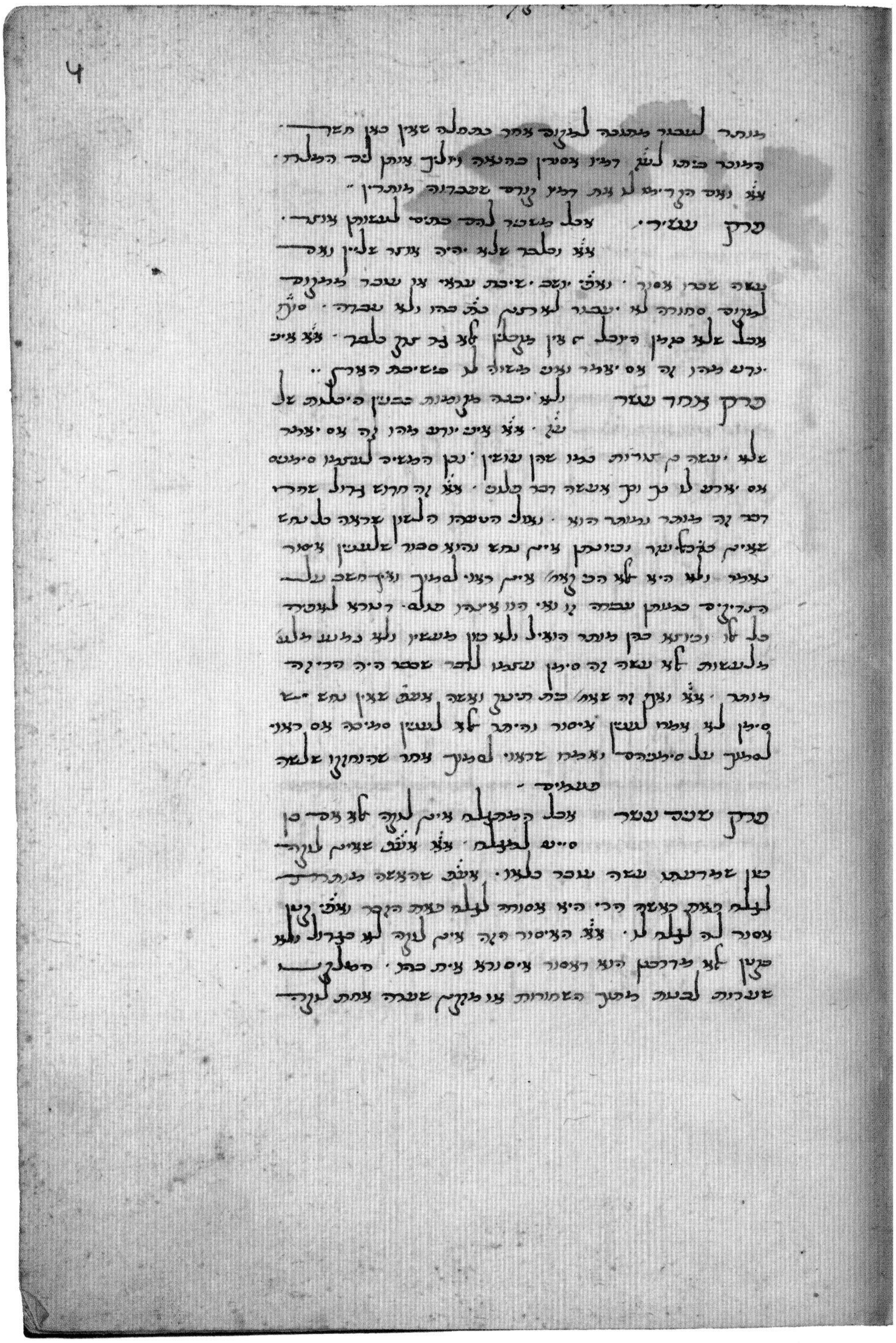

Fig. 8 Abraham ben David, *Hasagot ha-Rabad* [Italy, 15th century], MS 4, fol. 4r.

Despite his extensive criticism, Rabad nonetheless designated the *Mishneh Torah* a great achievement.[5] In fact, his *Hasagot* bolstered the work, for in seeking to prevent the *Mishneh Torah* from superseding the Talmud and becoming the final word on Jewish law, Rabad demonstrated its significance and the author's tremendous accomplishment. In turn, printers included his *Hasagot* in the Constantinople edition of 1509, which impacted subsequent commentaries and editions.

5 *Mishneh Torah*, *Kilayim* 6:2.

Fig. 9 Portrait and residence at Ramsgate of Sir Moses Montefiore (*The Illustrated London News*, November 3, 1883). Library of the Jewish Theological Seminary, PNT G1178.

This Hartman manuscript, beautifully written in semi-cursive Italian script in brown ink, includes a colophon devoid of specific information, but it is dated according to the script and the paper's horn watermark.[6] Originally, the volume had very large margins, as is clear from the cropped notations on fols. 11r and 30r. Bezalel Naor used this manuscript for variant readings in his critical edition of Rabad's glosses on the *Mishneh Torah*.[7]

Though the manuscript's earliest provenance is unknown, prominent individuals and institutions owned it in the last two hundred years. In the nineteenth century, it belonged to Salomon Halberstam (1832–1900), a merchant, scholar, and collector of hundreds of manuscripts.[8] The manuscript was acquired along with hundreds of others by the Judith Lady Montefiore College, a yeshiva founded by Sir Moses Montefiore (1784–1885),[9] the most influential Anglo-Jew in the modern period and a man of whom it was said, like Maimonides, 'From Moses to Moses, none arose like Moses' (Fig. 9).[10] In 1898, much of the yeshiva's collection was transfered to Jews' College in London, where it remained on loan for more than a century (see cat. nos. 2 and 33).

6 See Gerhard Piccard, *Wasserzeichen Fabeltiere* (Stuttgart: W. Kohlhammer, 1980), II:419.

7 Bezalel Naor (ed.), *Hasagot ha-Rabad le-Mishneh Torah: Mugah mi-Tokh 'Asarah Kitve-Yad* (Jerusalem: n.p., 1984).

8 See Halberstam, *Kohelet Shelomoh*, no. 410.

9 See Hirschfeld, *Descriptive Catalogue of the Hebrew Manuscripts of the Montefiore Library*, no. 96.

10 For a recent biography of Montefiore, see Abigail Green, *Moses Montefiore: Jewish Liberator, Imperial Hero* (Cambridge, MA: Harvard University Press, 2010). See also Louis Loewe (ed.), *Diaries of Sir Moses and Lady Montefiore: comprising their life and work as recorded in their diaries from 1812 to 1883 ...* (Chicago: Belford-Clarke Co., 1890). For an example of associating Montefiore with Maimonides, see Madison C. Peters, 'Famous Jews of the 19th Century,' *The Hebrew Standard*, September 24, 1909, 6.

[משנה] סדר נזיקין עם פירוש ... משה בר מיימון
[*Mishnah*] *Seder Nezikin ʿim Perush … Mosheh bar Maimon* (Order of Damages, with Commentary of Moses Maimonides)
[Yemen, 15th century]
MS 10. Manuscript on paper; 1 + 209ff.; 21.3 x 27.8 cm

[משנה] סדר טהרות עם פירוש ... משה בר מיימון
[*Mishnah*] *Seder Tohorot ʿim Perush … Mosheh bar Maimon* (Order of Purities, with Commentary of Moses Maimonides)
[Yemen, 15th century]
MS 13. Manuscript on paper; 245ff.; 18.5 x 26 cm

The innovation Maimonides displayed in both the *Mishneh Torah* and *Moreh Nevukhim* was presaged years earlier by his comprehensive *Commentary on the Mishnah*, the first of its kind. Composed in Judeo-Arabic, Maimonides authored what became known as *Kitab al-Siraj* (Book of the Lamp) between 1161 and 1168. The work explicated the readings of the Tana'im, condensed discussions of Amora'im found in the Talmud, and provided final halakhic decisions in each Mishnah. His interpretations of the Mishnah sometimes differed from those of the Talmud and he boldly offered conclusions to a number of unresolved debates found therein. Reflecting pedagogical objectives epitomized a decade later in his law code, Maimonides provided an aid for laymen who could not tackle the vagaries and complexities of the Talmud, and for advanced readers who could not master the entirety of the Mishnah without assistance.[1]

Beyond running commentary, Maimonides also composed lengthy introductions to the Mishnah that proved influential as independent compositions. His opening words to *Seder Zeraʿim* laid out a history of the Oral Law, from Moses until his own time. The foreword to *Avot*, known as *Shemonah Perakim* (Eight Chapters), is a philosophical and ethical treatise in which the author harmonized Aristotle's ethics with rabbinic teachings. The penultimate chapter of *Sanhedrin*, known as *Perek Ḥelek*, is preceded by Maimonides's famous 13 Principles of Faith (*ʿIkarim*). Though only part of the introduction, the *ʿIkarim* are arguably Maimonides's most widely recognized contribution. Popularized by liturgical poems (*piyutim*) such as *Yigdal* and often recited in an abridged form following prayer services, their entrance into standard liturgy meant that the majority of Jews could absorb rudimentary Maimonidean ideas. Still, subsequent Jewish thinkers offered differing enumerations, rejected the notion of dogma itself, and insisted that Maimonides himself did not abide by these beliefs.[2]

In keeping with his intention to educate a broad readership, Maimonides composed his commentary to the Mishnah in the vernacular Judeo-Arabic rather than the more scholarly Hebrew. Still, he regarded his work on the Mishnah as a triumph and seems to have wanted it translated into Hebrew to enable even greater, longer-lasting accessibility.[3] Several scholars in the thirteenth century, including Judah ben Solomon al-Ḥarizi and Samuel Ibn Tibbon, worked to translate the commentary into Hebrew. Although the translators for

1 See Maimonides's *Commentary on the Mishnah*, *ʿAvodah Zarah* 5:8 and *Ketubot* 1:6.

2 On the reception of the *ʿIkarim*, see Marc B. Shapiro, *The Limits of Orthodox Theology: Maimonides's Thirteen Principles Reappraised* (Oxford: Littman Library of Jewish Civilization, 2004); for *Yigdal* and the dilution of ideas, see 17–20.

3 Itzhak Shailat (ed.), *The Letters and Essays of Moses Maimonides* [Hebrew] (Jerusalem: Shailat Publishing, 1995), 409.

Fig. 10 [*Mishnah*] *Seder Nezikin* with Commentary of Maimonides [Yemen, 15th century], MS 10, fol. 199v.

Seder Mo'ed and *Seder Nashim* are known, the translator for *Seder Tohorot* remains a mystery.[4]

Hartman MS 10 consists of nearly the entire *Seder Nezikin* in Hebrew with Maimonides's Judeo-Arabic commentary.[5] The manuscript begins in the middle of the fifth chapter of *Bava Kama* (fol. 7r) and continues with *Bava Metsi'a* (fol. 21r), *Bava Batra* (fol. 47r), *Sanhedrin* (fol. 76r), *Makot* (fol. 119v), *Shevu'ot* (fol. 132r), *'Eduyot* (fol. 150v), and *'Avodah Zarah* (fol. 181v). A title in square script appears for *Avot* (fol. 199v), but the copyist omitted the Mishnaic text and commentary deliberately, perhaps because it was readily available (Fig. 10). The Yemenite scholar Yiḥye Kafiḥ added missing text, mostly at the beginning and end of the manuscript,[6] and his grandson, Yosef Kafiḥ, used this manuscript in his edition of Maimonides's *Commentary on the Mishnah*.

Yosef Kafiḥ noted that this particular manuscript is of special import because it constitutes an intermediate form of Maimonides's Mishnah commentary. Maimonides continuously edited his work, as clearly seen in fragments discovered in the Cairo Genizah (Fig. 11), and the scribe who copied this manuscript based his work on an early though not finalized recension of the *Commentary*. Yiḥye Kafiḥ's marginal notes, written in black ink, record variants of the *Commentary* found in other manuscripts at his disposal, and Yosef Kafiḥ's notes, added in blue ink, demonstrate how he assigned the various readings to the multiple recensions (see fol. 34v, for example). The manuscript includes numerous textual diagrams,[7] including a chart of the priestly blessing, *birkat kohanim* (fol. 199v).

4 See Davidson, *Moses Maimonides*, 165–66; Kraemer, *Maimonides*, 164.

5 Formerly Kafiḥ MS 65.

6 Yiḥye's additions appear on fols. 1r–6v, 52r–53v, 200r–201v, 208r–210v. A watermark (208r–208v) indicates the paper he used made its way to Yemen from Italy via Egypt. A Yemenite manuscript of Maimonides's commentary on *Seder Zera'im* held at the UC Berkeley School of Law bears the same watermark motif on a flyleaf (MS Robbins 271).

7 For instance, fols. 48v, 51r–52r, 58v, 65r, 67r.

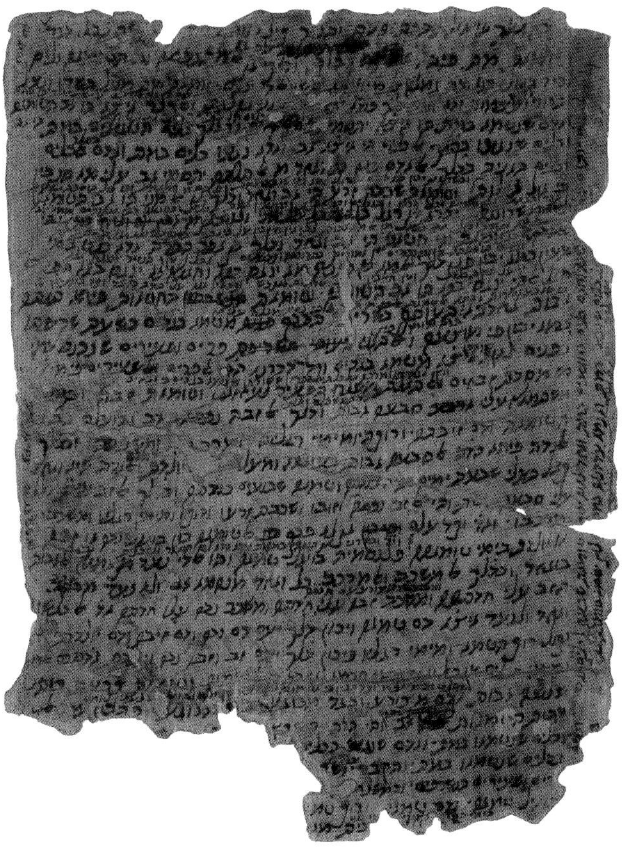

Fig. 11 *Commentary on the Mishnah* [Egypt, 12th century] (Autograph). Library of the Jewish Theological Seminary, MS 8254, fol. 3v.

Hartman MS 13 comprises *Seder Tohorot*, the most difficult of the Mishnah's six orders because of its obscure rules related to ritual purity, the near total absence of Talmudic commentary, and the abundant references to long-forgotten realia of Roman Judea.[8] Nevertheless, Maimonides maintained the same quality of commentary to this order as he did for the others and systematically treated all the rules and categories of ritual purity in a lengthy introduction. This manuscript is significant because of its status as an early Judeo-Arabic copy of Maimonides's *Commentary*. Various fragments identified in the Cairo Genizah have been published, including on the introduction to *Tohorot*, and autographs of Maimonides's *Commentary on the Mishnah* are held in the Bodleian Library in Oxford and the National Library of Israel, but the author's handwritten copy of *Tohorot* is no longer extant. In his edition, Kafiḥ utilized Hartman MS 13 – referring to it (and the above mentioned MS 10) as ק in the apparatus – to complement a complete manuscript that dates to 1223.[9] Missing folios from the original manuscript were replaced in 1904 by Kafiḥ's uncle Shalom ben Yiḥye Kafiḥ for Yosef ben Sa'id Pinhas ha-Kohen.[10] In addition, the manuscript includes a loose leaf consisting of prayers evoking the aid of angels for sustenance, Torah study, and repentance.[11]

8 Formerly Kafiḥ MS 68.

9 Bodleian Libraries, University of Oxford, MS. Pococke 97.

10 Folios 1–19 and 228–245. His full name is given in the additional colophon as Shalom ben Yiḥye ben Shelomoh ben Shalom ben Shelomoh ben Yosef (fol. 245v).

11 For such prayers variously ascribed to R. Ishmael the High Priest, the Tosafist R. Jacob Tam, or to the relatively unknown medieval rabbi Isaac ben Isaac of Chinon, see Ephraim Kanarfogel, *'Peering through the Lattices': Mystical, Magical, and Pietistic Dimensions in the Tosafist Period* (Detroit, MI: Wayne State University Press, 2000), 172–82; and Ḥayim Palache, *Ateret Ha-Ḥayim* (Salonika, 1841), sec. 9, 9b.

7

מורה נבוכים
Moreh Nevukhim (Guide of the Perplexed)
Translated by Samuel ben Judah Ibn Tibbon
[Italy, after 1465]
MS 1. Manuscript on paper; 167ff.; 20.3 x 29.8 cm

Maimonides's writings in both Jewish law and theology sparked immediate responses. His contemporaries and subsequent generations of scholars grappled with his ideas and the manner in which he presented them. The adoration and controversy he engendered varied, but his work remained relevant. By the time this manuscript was composed, about two and half centuries after his death, Maimonides's halakhic code, the *Mishneh Torah*, had proven more impactful than his philosophical magnum opus, *Moreh Nevukhim*. The legal corpus was pertinent and readable to a far wider Jewish public than an esoteric treatise designed for singular intellectuals. Extant fifteenth-century manuscripts of the *Mishneh Torah* far outnumber manuscripts of *Moreh Nevukhim*.

As such, this manuscript of *Moreh Nevukhim* is among the more impressive in the Hartman Collection. Although lacking a colophon, the Renaissance-era codex in all likelihood was commissioned by a wealthy Jew who desired an exceptional decorated manuscript. The translated Hebrew text of Samuel Ibn Tibbon was copied by a professional scribe onto quality paper with carefully ruled pages and wide margins. Judging by the script and the watermark of the paper, the manuscript was copied after 1465 but before the turn of the century.[1] It consists of 16 quires, mostly of ten folios, and the pages are pricked on the outer edges for ruling, very uncommon in paper manuscripts.[2] It also contains a decorative program that was never fully executed. The scribe left space for an initial word panel to commence the translator's introduction (fol. 7r) and penned an elegant initial word commencing part 3 of the *Guide* (fol. 108v). In addition, an illustration of Ezekiel's Account of the Chariot (*Ma'aseh Merkavah*) appears (at the foot of fol. 108v) and faint line drawings appear later in the manuscript (fols. 127v–128r). The depiction of *Ma'aseh Merkavah* diverged from explicit rabbinic restrictions prohibiting its portrayal, as well as Maimonides's more general prohibition of making images for decorative purposes (Fig. 12).[3] Hartman MS 1 is one of only three medieval or early modern Hebrew manuscripts of *Moreh Nevukhim* known to include such an image, though it also appeared in other manuscript genres like Bibles and *maḥzorim*.[4]

1 See C. M. Briquet, *Les Filigranes: Dictionnaire Historique des Marques du Papier dès Leur Apparition Vers 1282 Jusqu'en 1600. A Facsimile of the 1907 Edition With Supplementary Material Contributed by a Number of Scholars*, ed. Allan Stevenson (Amsterdam: Paper Publications Society, 1968), vol. 3, no. 3387. According to Briquet, paper with this watermark stemmed from Florence (1465), and similar watermarks appeared in several other cities, including Venice (1464–1473), Siena (1465–1469), and Augsburg (1469) (Briquet, vol. 1, 224).

2 See Malachi Beit-Arié, *Hebrew Codicology: Tentative Typology of Technical Practices Employed in Hebrew Dated Medieval Manuscripts* (Jerusalem: Israel Academy of Sciences and Humanities, 1981), 48–49.

3 See *Rosh ha-Shanah* 24b, *'Avodah Zarah* 43b, *Tosafot* on *Yoma* 54b; *Shulḥan 'Arukh*, *Yoreh De'ah* 141:4; and *Mishneh Torah, 'Avodah Zarah ve-Ḥukot ha-Goyim* 3:10–11. See also Sara Offenberg, 'The Human Face on the Divine Chariot: Jacob the Knight,' *TheTorah.com* (2022), https://www.thetorah.com/article/the-human-face-on-the-divine-chariot-jacob-the-knight (accessed November 9, 2022); Offenberg points out that Solomon Ibn Adret (Rashba; 1235–1310) permitted the depiction of each of the four faces of the Chariot's angelic being separately (n. 4). Thanks to Gabriel Wasserman and Sharon Liberman Mintz for references.

4 See Evelyn Cohen's essay in this volume.

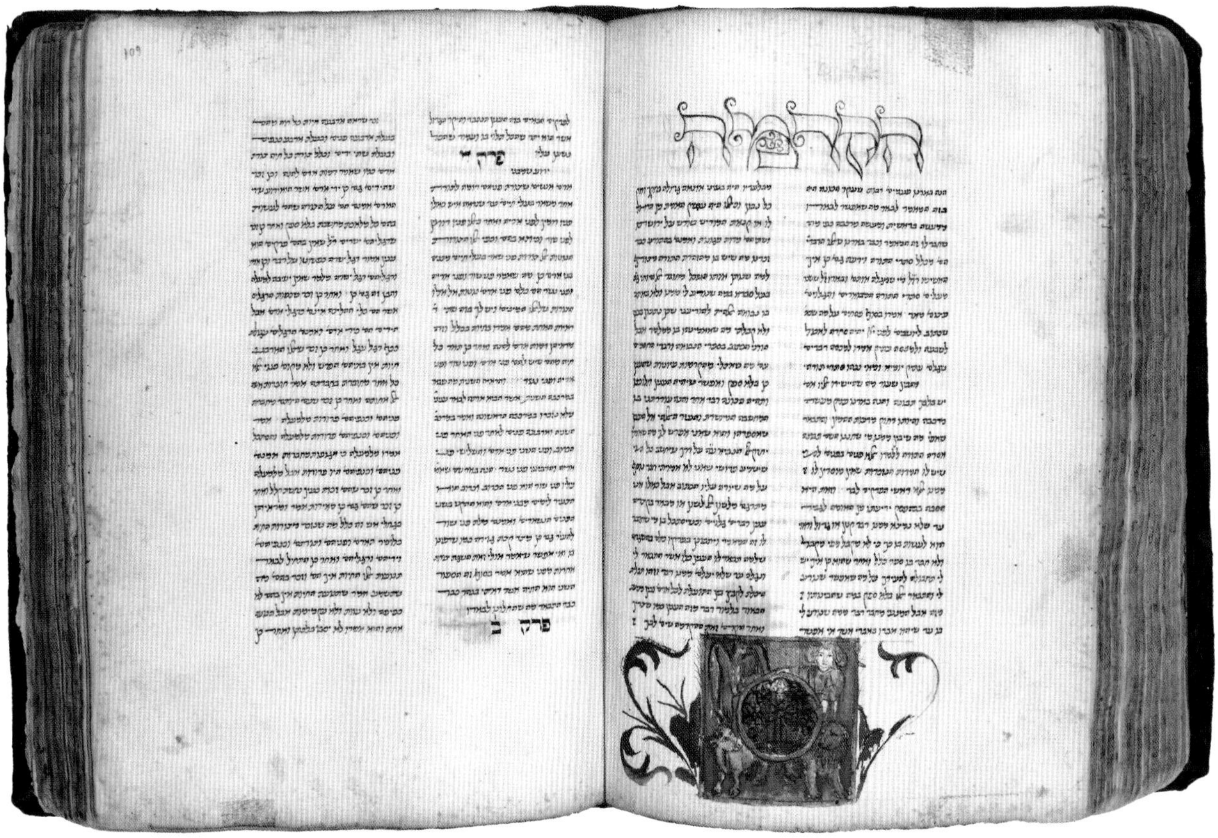

Fig. 12 *Moreh Nevukhim* [Italy, ca. 1465], MS 1, fols. 108v–109r.

There are many variants between this version of Ibn Tibbon's Hebrew translation and the subsequent printed versions. In fact, this text more closely parallels the original Judeo-Arabic compilation, and the table of contents and the register of biblical verses differ from those later found in printed editions. In addition, the codex contains marginalia on fols. 13v–23v. Fol. 5r includes a riddle from Maimonides's son, Abraham, and fol. 5v contains five poems concerning *Moreh Nevukhim* authored by various individuals, though most manuscripts of this work include only one or two poems.[5] Fol. 1v includes a note stating that a Father Basilio of Bologna donated the manuscript to a convent (*Cappuccini*) where he once served as lecturer.[6]

5 See Maud Kozodoy, 'Prefatory Verse and the Reception of the *Guide of the Perplexed*,' *Jewish Quarterly Review* 106, no. 3 (2016): 257–82. Four of the five poems in this manuscript are mentioned in Moritz Steinschneider, 'Moreh Mekom ha-Moreh,' *Kovets 'al Yad* 1 (1885): 1–31 (nos. 42, 60, 7, and 46); he lists only a few manuscripts that have more than two poems ('Moreh Mekom ha-Moreh,' 22). There are significant differences between the printed and manuscript versions of poem no. 7. For the fifth poem, which is attributed to R. Joseph Kimḥi, see Israel Davidson, *Thesaurus of Medieval Hebrew Literature*, 4 vols. (New York: Jewish Theological Seminary of America, 1924), 3:113, no. 978.

6 The inscription reads: 'Applicato alla Libreria de Cappuccini di Bologna dal P[adre] Basilio da Bologna ex-Lettore Cappuccini an. 1797.' Thanks to Martina Mampieri for help in deciphering the meaning of the inscription.

8

משנה תורה
Mishneh Torah (Repetition of the Law)
Printed by Solomon ben Judah and Obadiah ben Moses
[Rome?, ca. 1475]
2°. RB 1
Steinschneider, 6513,1; Freimann, A17; Goff, Heb-76; Dienstag, '*Mishneh Torah*,' no. 1; Offenberg, no. 87; Iakerson, no. 72; Vinograd, Rome no. 3

משנה תורה
Mishneh Torah (Repetition of the Law)
Printed by Gershom ben Moses Soncino
Soncino, 1490
2°. RB 2. 2 vols.
Steinschneider, 6513,2; Freimann, A55; Goff, Heb-77; Dienstag, '*Mishneh Torah*,' no. 2; Offenberg, no. 88; Iakerson, no. 43; Vinograd, Soncino no. 39

The printing press revolutionized the world of knowledge, perhaps matched only by the development of writing systems and the popularization of the Internet. Johannes Gutenberg is famous for having introduced into Europe printing with movable type, though block printing had been in use for centuries. He produced thousands of broadsheet indulgences in the early 1450s before issuing his most beautiful and celebrated work, a 42-line Latin Bible, in 1455.

Naturally, the form and appearance used by printers were based on manuscript production. Printers modeled their types on the scripts in use and hired artists to devise decorative woodcut initial words or letters as if they were embellishing a lustrous manuscript. Scholars estimate that some 30,000 titles in any and all languages were printed in Europe through the end of the year 1500. These books are called *incunabula* (sing. *incunabulum*). Of this enormous number of books, copies of fewer than 140 Hebrew titles from this period are extant. Despite this meager fraction, early Hebrew printing was extraordinary, with Jews wholeheartedly embracing the new technology as *melekhet ha-kodesh* (holy work). During these decades and into the beginning of the sixteenth century, Jews were forbidden from living in England and France, prohibited from printing in Germany, and expelled from the Iberian peninsula, Sicily, and the Kingdom of Naples. Yet Hebrew presses were the first to introduce printing in Portugal (Pentateuch, Faro, 1487), the Ottoman Empire (*Arba'ah Turim*, Constantinople, 1493), and the African continent (*Sefer Abudarham*, Fez, 1516). Jews printed Bibles, volumes of the Talmud, prayer books, law codes, and more.[1] Maimonides's famed *Mishneh Torah* was printed in whole or in part at least six times during the incunabula period, both in Iberia and the Italian peninsula. Despite all of these editions, it is noteworthy that printers of Hebrew books issued as many as ten editions of Jacob ben Asher's *Arba'ah Turim* in the same period.

The vagaries of early printing often make it difficult to determine precisely when and where, and even by whom, books were printed. The Hartman Collection includes a folio of one of the first printed Hebrew texts ever produced, and almost certainly the first printed edition of the *Mishneh Torah*. Consisting of chapters 3–7 of *Hilkhot Sanhedrin* in *Sefer*

1 For a general history of Hebrew printing in the fifteenth century, see A. K. Offenberg, *A Choice of Corals: Facets of Fifteenth-Century Hebrew Printing* (Nieuwkoop: De Graaf, 1992). For a survey of extant copies of Hebrew incunabula in public collections, see Offenberg, *Hebrew Incunabula in Public Collections: A First International Census* (Nieuwkoop: De Graaf, 1990). See also the British Library's 'Incunabula Short Title Catalogue': https://data.cerl.org/istc/_search (accessed November 9, 2022).

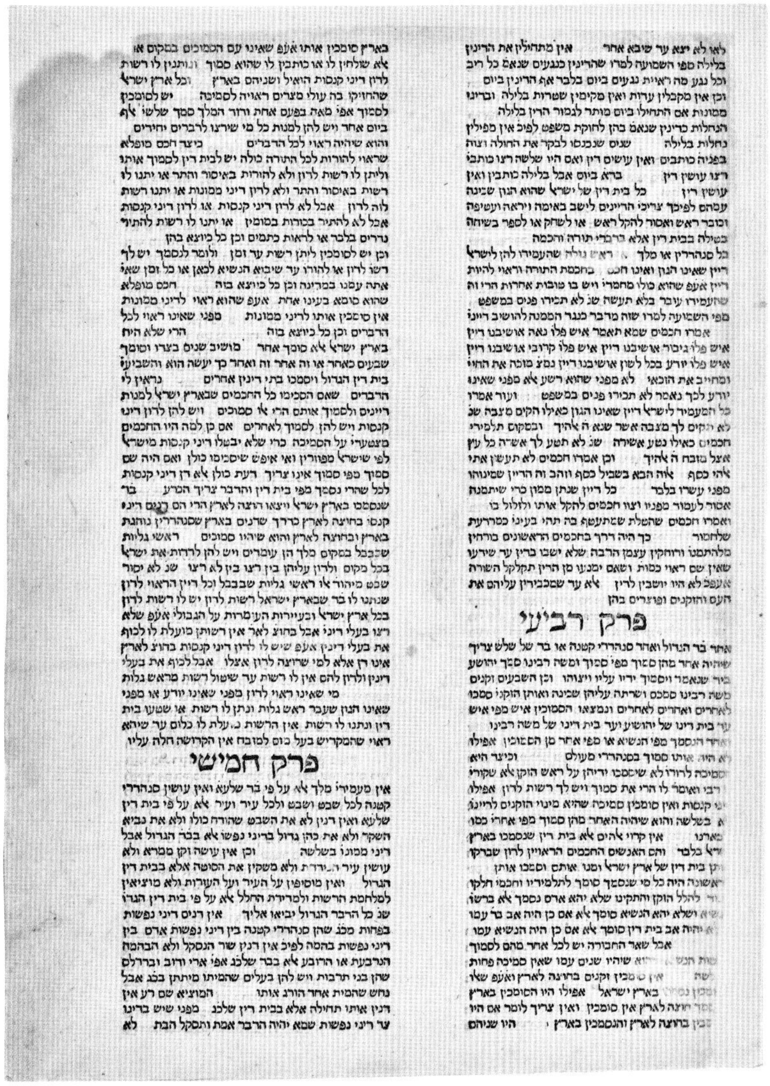
פרק חמישי

פרק רביעי

Fig. 13 *Mishneh Torah* ([Rome?]: Solomon ben Judah and Obadiah ben Moses, ca. 1475), RB 1.

Shofetim, without commentary or additional apparatus, it would be 19 folios from the end of a complete edition (Fig. 13). In the absence of any mention in the volume of a place of production, some scholars assert based on the paper stock that the book was produced in Rome, although the letter type is somewhat different from other Hebrew books known to have been printed in that city. Whereas most contemporary Hebrew imprints from Rome were printed in a square Italian-Ashkenazic type, the printers of this edition used a square Sephardic type, possibly an indication of their intent to export copies to Spain and Portugal, where Maimonides was the supreme halakhic authority. The printer mentioned in the colophon, Obadiah ben Moses, is usually associated with Obadiah of Rome, who together with a Manasseh and a Benjamin, also both of Rome, printed six (or eight) undated books considered to have been the first printed Hebrew books produced (ca. 1469 to 1475).[2]

In addition, the Hartman Collection includes a nearly complete copy of another *Mishneh Torah* printed during the incunabula period.[3] Scholars disagree as to whether manuscripts were used to prepare the text of this edition or whether it was produced on the basis of the

2 For a discussion of the earliest Hebrew printed books, see Shimon Iakerson, *Catalogue of Hebrew Incunabula from the Collection of the Library of the Jewish Theological Seminary of America* (New York and Jerusalem: Jewish Theological Seminary of America, 2004–2005), x–xiii (and literature cited).

3 The Hartman copy consists of 377 of 380ff., lacking only fol. 1 of vol. 1 and the final two leaves of vol. 2. For typographical differences in various copies of this edition, see Isaac Rivkind, 'Dikduke Sefarim,' *Kiryat Sefer* 4 (1927): 275–76, and Rivkind, 'Dikduke Sefarim,' in *Alexander Marx Jubilee Volume on the Occasion of His Seventieth Birthday*, 2 vols., ed. Saul Lieberman (New York: Jewish Theological Seminary of America, 1950), 404 (Hebrew volume).

או לא אבוש בהביטי אל כל מצותיך

כל המצות

שניתנו למשה בסיני בפירושן ניתנו שנאמר
ואתנה לך את לוחות האבן והתורה והמצוה
תורה זו תורה שבכתב והמצוה זו פירוש' וצונו
לעשות התורה על פי המצות ומצוה זו היא
הנקראת תורה שבעל פה כל התורה כתבה
משה רבינו קודם שימות בכתב ידו ונתן
ספר לכל שבט ושבט וספר אחד נתנוהו
בארון לעד שנאמר לקוח את ספר התור' הזה
ושמתם אותו וגו' והמצוה שהוא פירוש
התורה לא כתבה אלא צוה בה לזקנים
וליהושע ולשאר כל ישראל שנאמר את כל
הדבר אשר אנכי מצוה אתכם אותו תשמרו
לעשות וגו' ומפני זה נקראת תורה שבעל פה
אף על פי שלא נכתב' תורה שבעל פה למדה
משה רבינו כולה בבית דינו לשבעים זקנים
ואלעזר ופנחס ויהושע שלשתן קבלו ממשה
וליהושע שהוא תלמידו של משה רבינו מסר
תורה שבעל פה וצוהו עליה וכן יהושע כל
ימי חייו למד על פה וזקנים רבים קבלו
מיהושע וקבל עלי מן הזקנים ומפנחס
ושמואל קיבל מעלי ובית דינו ודוד קיבל
משמואל ובית דינו ואחיה השילוני מיוצאי
מצרים היה ולוי היה ושמע ממשה והיה קטן
בימי משה והוא קיבל מדוד ובית דינו

ואליהו קיבל מאחיה השילוני ובית דינו
ואלישע קיבל מאליהו ובית דינו ויהוידע
הכהן קיבל מאלישע ובית דינו זכריה קיבל
מיהוידע ובית דינו והושע קיבל מזכריה
ובית דינו ועמוס קיבל מהושע ובית דינו
וישעיה קיבל מעמוס ובית דינו ומיכה קיבל
מישעיה ובית דינו ויואל קיבל ממיכה ובית
דינו ונחום קיבל מיואל ובית דינו וחבקוק
קיבל מנחום ובית דינו וצפניה קיבל מחבקו'
ובית דינו וירמיה קיבל מצפניה ובית דינו
וברוך בן נריה קיבל מירמיה ובית דינו ועזרא
ובית דינו קבלו מברוך בן נריה ובית דינו
בית דינו של עזרא הם הנקראים אנשי כנסת
הגדולה והם חגי זכריה ומלאכי דניאל וחנני'
ומישאל ועזריה ונחמיה בן חכליה ומרדכי
בלשן וזרובבל והרבה חכמים עמהם תשלום
מאה ועשרים זקנים האחרון מהם הוא שמעון
הצדיק והוא היה מכלל המאה ועשרי' וקיבל
תורה שבעל פה מכולם והוא היה כהן גדול
אחר עזרא. אנטיגנוס איש סוכו ובית דינו
קיבלו משמעון הצדיק ובית דינו ויוסי בן
יועזר איש צרידה ויוסף בן יוחנן איש
ירושלים ובית דינם קבלו מאנטיגנוס ובית
דינו ויהושע בן פרחיה וניתאי הארבלי ובית

א ב

Fig. 14 *Mishneh Torah* (Soncino: Gershom ben Moses Soncino, 1490), RB 2, vol. 1, fol. 1r.

first printed edition (Rome?, ca. 1475).[4] Following manuscript tradition, each book in this imprint begins with a list of contents that details the various laws to be discussed and concludes with a list of subjects and their total number of chapters. The text was printed in two columns. Four different typefaces were used, including a square type distinctive of the Soncino imprints. In addition, the first page was printed with the Soncinos's famous elaborate woodcut border depicting three cherubs within a floral design, and large woodcut headings appear in several other places (Fig. 14).[5]

This imprint was the second book published by the great Hebrew printer Gershom Soncino. The Soncino family had left Speyer, in the southwest of modern-day Germany, as exiles in 1454 and settled in Soncino, in northern Italy. They adopted the toponymic surname of their new home, and in the early 1480s, Israel Nathan ben Solomon founded a printing business managed by his sons Moses and Joshua Solomon. Between 1483 and 1492, Joshua Solomon printed as many as 32 books in the towns of Soncino, Casalmaggiore, and Naples. In 1492, he issued the *editio princeps* of the Mishnah with nearly four dozen woodcut diagrams and the commentary of Maimonides.[6] In addition, three titles were published by 'Bene Soncino,' various family members who may have worked under the direction of Joshua Solomon.

Following the death of Joshua Solomon, his nephew, Gershom, perfected his craft and became the greatest of the pioneers of Hebrew printing. Gershom issued the first illustrated Hebrew book, *Meshal ha-Kadmoni* (Brescia, 1491); possibly the first Hebrew wall calendar (Barco?, 1496); the first non-Hebrew book printed by a Jew, *Abselmii Laurentii, Vita Epaminudae* (Fano, 1502); and the first Hebrew book with a title page, *Sefer ha-Roke'aḥ* (Fano, 1505). Gershom printed in at least a dozen cities, often signing his name *Ger-sham* (גר-שם; 'temporary sojourner,' following Exodus 2:22). In total, he printed nearly one hundred Hebrew titles and perhaps as many non-Hebrew titles.

The Hartman copy of the Soncino *Mishneh Torah* bears the stamps of Jews' College of London (fol. 2r) and its later incarnation, the London School of Jewish Studies Library (fol. 1v).

4 See M. Lutzky, afterword to *Mishneh Torah*, 5 vols. (New York: Shulsinger Bros., 1947), and S. Z. Havlin (intro.), *Rabbi Moshe ben Maimon (Maimonides) Code of Jewish Law (Mishne-Torah) Ed. Constantinople 1509*, 4 vols. (Jerusalem: Makor, 1972), 14–18.

5 Fols. 12v, 29v, 48v, 99v, 152r, 201r, 247v, and 253v. In addition, depictions of *tefilin* appear on fol. 37r.

6 Brad Sabin Hill, *Hebraica (saec. X AD saec. XVI): Manuscripts and Early Printed Books from the Library of the Valmadonna Trust: An Exhibition at the Pierpont Morgan Library, New York* ([London]: Valmadonna Trust Library, 1989), no. 15.

9

ספר המצות

Sefer ha-Mitsvot (Book of Commandments)
Scribe: Shalom ben Zechariah Eldani
[Yemen], 1492
MS 5. Manuscript on paper; 123ff.; 19.5 x 27.1 cm

Sefer ha-Mitsvot is Maimonides's rendering of the 248 positive and 365 negative commandments contained within the Torah. The idea that a total of 613 commandments permeate the Torah dates at least to the Amoraic period. A dictum of the third-century Palestinian sage R. Simlai delineates that number of positive and negative commandments,[1] though no one seems to have attempted to enumerate the individual mitzvoth until the Geonic work *Halakhot Gedolot*, attributed most often to Simeon Kayara. Over the next few centuries, several scholars detailed new lists of commandments in *Azharot* (exhortations) and in prose. Three of the most prominent authors were Sa'adiah Gaon (882–942), the first to group the commandments around the Decalogue; Solomon Ibn Gabirol, who wrote about the commandments both generally and specifically; and Ḥefets ben Yatsliaḥ (tenth century), who authored a work in Arabic.

Maimonides composed *Sefer ha-Mitsvot* between 1168 and 1170, perhaps as a survey of Jewish law prior to producing the *Mishneh Torah.*[2] Having completed his *Commentary on the Mishnah*, he set out to order the entire legal corpus of Judaism in his multi-volume tome, the *Mishneh Torah*. Along the way, he found previous listings of commandments unsystematic and inconsistent. He published his *Sefer ha-Mitsvot* with an introduction that presented 14 principles by which he identified and enumerated the commandments. In the main body of the work, the author listed each idea and cited several examples to support his opinion.

Although *Sefer ha-Mitsvot*, like so many other Rambam treatises, became the most authoritative work of its kind and one that required serious attention, it was not accepted without criticism. Most notably, Moses ben Naḥman (Naḥmanides or Ramban; 1194–ca. 1270) strongly disapproved of Maimonides's rendering, accusing him of inconsistencies and of unjustly disparaging earlier scholars for their compositions. Eliezer ben Samuel of Metz produced his *Sefer Yere'im* in the 1170s, based on the same *Halakhot Gedolot* that Maimonides criticized and Naḥmanides later defended.

Maimonides's account of the mitzvoth originally appeared in Arabic under the title *Kitab 'al-Farai'd* (Book of Divine Precepts). It was translated into Hebrew by Abraham Ibn Ḥasdai, whose version is no longer extant, as well as by the Provençal scholar and translator Moses Ibn Tibbon, whose version became the standard for printed editions. Yosef Kafiḥ, to whom this Hartman manuscript belonged,[3] also translated *Sefer ha-Mitsvot.*[4] The work first appeared in print in Constantinople as early as 1510,[5] and frequently accompanied printed editions of the larger and heavily in demand *Mishneh Torah.*

1 Talmud, *Makkot* 23b. See also Talmud, *Shabbat* 87a.

2 Halbertal, *Maimonides*, 108.

3 Formerly Kafiḥ MS 66.

4 Kafiḥ, *Book of Commandments: Arabic Original with New Translation and Commentary* (Jerusalem: Mossad Harav Kook, 1971).

5 On the dating, see Abraham Yaari, *Hebrew Printing at Constantinople: Its History and Bibliography* [Hebrew] (Jerusalem: Magnes Press, 1967), no. 80 (records the date as ca. 1510–1515); Steinschneider had earlier recorded it as ca. 1516–1518 (Steinschneider, no. 6513,62).

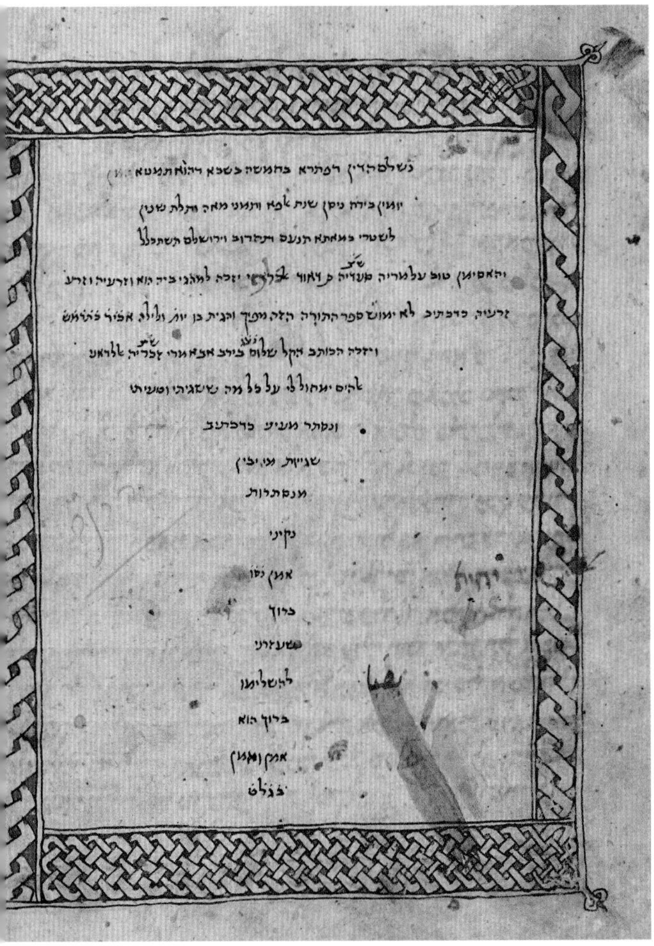

Fig. 15 (left) *Sefer ha-Mitsvot* ([Yemen], 1492), MS 5, fol. 123v.

Fig. 16 (right) *Sefer ha-Mitsvot* ([Yemen], 1492), MS 5, fol. 66v.

This manuscript is in the original Judeo-Arabic used by the author. According to the colophon, the manuscript was completed on Thursday, 8 Nisan 1803 *le-minyan shetarot* (= April 17, 1492). The scribe, Shalom ben Zechariah Eldani, copied the manuscript for Sa'adiah Ibn Daud 'al-Razi, and wished him and his offspring blessings (Fig. 15). The manuscript includes marginal notations throughout in three or four hands.

At the conclusion of the first section detailing the positive commandments, and just before the section commencing the negative commandments, a rectangular box in red and green ink is divided into rows and columns with Hebrew numbers in each box: 1–15, 19, 26, 32, 54, 73, 94, 143, 147, 149, 150, 152, 154, 155, 157–70, 172, 175, 184, 195, 197, 206–15 (Fig. 16). The numbers seem to indicate those positive commandments that are especially pertinent, including those surrounding devotion to God, piety, humility, and honor, and observance of Sabbath and festivals. Mitzvoth no longer germane, particularly those involving the Temple, appear in the manuscript text but are not specified in the chart. Curiously, the mitzvah of checking for the kosher signs of locusts, which appears between the commandments to inspect the signs of permissible birds and fish (nos. 150 and 152), is not noted in the graph, despite (or perhaps because of) a prominent tradition among Yemenite Jews permitting their consumption.

10

משנה תורה
Mishneh Torah (Repetition of the Law)
Edited by Abraham ben Joseph Ibn Ya'ish
Printed by David and Samuel Ibn Naḥmias
Constantinople, 1509
2°. RB 3. 4 vols.
Steinschneider, 6513,3; Yaari, *Constantinople*, no. 6; Dienstag, '*Mishneh Torah*,' no. 6; Vinograd, Constantinople no. 16

Although the *Mishneh Torah* appeared in print in its entirety at least four times during the incunabula period, no printer had embarked upon publishing the great code with any of its elucidating commentaries. This large edition, dubbed *Ha-Ḥibur ha-Gadol* (The Great Composition) by its printers, incorporated commentaries that became standard in subsequent editions, including the glosses of Abraham ben David of Posquières (Rabad); *Hagahot Maimoniyot* by Meir ha-Kohen of Rothenburg (thirteenth century), which aimed to attach the legal rulings of medieval Ashkenazic scholars to Maimonides's law code;[1] and *Magid Mishneh* by Vidal Yom Tov of Tolosa (fourteenth century).[2] In addition, an anonymous commentary, *Hilkhot Yesode ha-Torah* (Basic Principles of the Torah), accompanies the opening section of the work; *Migdal 'Oz*, by Yom Tov Ibn Gaon, is found with *Sefer Ahavah*; and a commentary by Obadiah ben David appears with *Hilkhot Kidush ha-Ḥodesh* (Laws of the New Moon) (Fig. 17).

In an afterword, the editor, Abraham Ibn Ya'ish, explained the purpose of this imprint and the reason for including these commentaries. Due to the catastrophic expulsions of Jews from Spain and Portugal, once home to great Jewish civilizations and some of the world's most important Hebrew printing houses, Jews lacked a corpus of Hebrew books from which to study. The brothers David and Samuel Ibn Naḥmias, refugees from the Iberian peninsula, sought to alleviate the deplorable decline of Torah study by printing Maimonides's great halakhic work with commentaries they deemed crucial.

The Naḥmias press in Constantinople was one of the most important and innovative presses of early Hebrew printing. Their first imprint, the *Arba'ah Turim*, appeared in 1493, soon after they arrived in Constantinople. With that publication, the Naḥmias brothers were the first to print with movable type in the Ottoman Empire, decades before members of the Armenian and Greek communities opened print shops and more than two centuries before Turkish-language printing commenced.[3] Over the next three decades, Naḥmias printers issued nearly 30 imprints – 20 between 1505 and 1515 – including Talmud tractates, many works on *halakhah*, ethical tracts, and the first edition of Isaac Abarbanel's commentary on the Haggadah, *Zevaḥ Pesaḥ*.

This imprint is noteworthy because it initiated the practice of foliation, whereby Hebrew letters, representing numerical values, appeared on the recto side of a given folio.[4] Blank

1 Efraim Urbach, *Ba'ale ha-Tosafot* (Jerusalem: Bialik Institute, 1955), 434–36. On the versions of *Hagahot Maimoniyot*, see David Davidetzky, 'The Composition of the "Notes on Maimonides"' [Hebrew], *Tsefunot* 1 (1988): 49–59; and Israel Mordechai Peles, 'Taglit: Ketav Yad Kadum shel Hagahot Maimoniyot—ke-Nusaḥ Defus Kushta,' *Yeshurun* 13 (2003): 744–87.

2 Jacob Spiegel, 'Sefer "Magid Mishneh" she-'al "Mishneh Torah" le-ha-Rambam,' *Kiryat Sefer* 46 (1971): 554–79.

3 On the dating of the imprint, see Adri K. Offenberg, 'The First Printed Book Produced at Constantinople,' *Studia Rosenthaliana* 3 (1969): 96–112, repr. in Offenberg, *A Choice of Corals*, 102–32; Offenberg, 'The Printing History of the Constantinople Hebrew Incunable of 1493: A Mediterranean Voyage of Discovery,' *The British Library Journal* 22 (1996): 221–35.

4 Marvin J. Heller, 'Earliest Printings of the Talmud,' in *Printing the Talmud: From Bomberg to Schottenstein*,

Fig. 17 *Mishneh Torah* (Constantinople: David and Samuel Ibn Naḥmias, 1509), RB 3, fol. 1r.

spaces appear within the text where diagrams illustrating *Hilkhot Kidush ha-Ḥodesh* should appear (end of vol. 1). The printers intended either to hand-press the diagrams after printing the text or to enable book owners to include their own sketches. Similar instances are found in Talmud tractates, such as *ʿEruvin* and *Sukah*, printed during this first half-century of Hebrew printing. The *Kidush ha-Ḥodesh* diagrams were subsequently printed in the Venice, 1574–1575 edition of the *Mishneh Torah* (see cat. no. 22).

Very few complete copies of this imprint are extant. Copies in the British Library, Cambridge, and Oxford are all imperfect.[5] The last few folios in vol. 4 of the Hartman copy, containing poems in praise of the *Mishneh Torah* and this edition in particular, are not found in the facsimile of this edition edited by Shlomo Zalman Havlin in 1973. This copy also contains marginal notations throughout, and Maimonides's famous section on the messiah is censored (vol. 4, fol. 258v), although no censor's signature appears in the volume.

The Hartman copy has several ownership signatures indicating its rich history. It is particularly interesting that the name of Yiḥye ben Joseph Tsaleḥ (Maharits; 1713–1805), one of the greatest Yemenite rabbis in recent centuries, is crossed out, while others remain.[6] The name Salim Ibn Said appears amid three separate extensive entries, including a formal text for an emissary's collection of charitable funds and an account of the assassination of the king of Yemen, Imam Yaḥya Ibn Muhammad, in 1948.[7] In addition, the manuscript contains elaborate signatures belonging to an Aaron (vol. 1, fol. 276v)[8] and Saʿadiah David Azulai (vol. 4, fol. 258r).[9]

ed. Sharon Liberman Mintz and Gabriel M. Goldstein (New York: Yeshiva University Museum, 2005), 61–78 (62).

5 A complete copy was sold at Christie's in May 1986; see Christie's, *Hebrew Printed Books: Duplicates from the Library of The Jewish Theological Seminary of America*, cat. Felix de Marez Oyens [New York, 1986], no. 51.

6 Vol. 2, fol. 1r. Although the inscription is crossed out, 'יחיא אלעד בן כמר"ר יוסף צאלח' is visible when viewing a manipulated digital image. It is possible that a later owner held Tsaleḥ in low esteem because of his relatively conservative position toward Kabbalah and the broader Sephardic influence.

7 Vol. 2, following fol. 98; vol. 4, fol. 2.

8 כתוב אדם שמו על סיסה ... אדם מן משוק ... על כן כתבתי שמי על הצעיר אהרן .... The signature includes a doodle of what appears to be part of a face, with a nose, mouth, and beard.

9 סעדיה דוד ס"ט (=סופו טוב / סיפיה טב) אזולאי (?).

11

תשובות שאלות ואגרות ... רבינו משה המיימוני
Teshuvot, She'elot ve-Igerot … Rabenu Mosheh ha-Maimoni (Responsa and Correspondence)
[Constantinople, ca. 1517]
4°. RB 12
Steinschneider, 6513,111; Yaari, *Constantinople*, no. 87; Vinograd, Constantinople no. 85

This imprint was the first to consist of a collection of Maimonides's correspondence and legal responsa, or *She'elot u-Teshuvot* (queries and responses).[1] The laudatory opening page of this thin volume states:

> Responsa and correspondence of the Great Luminary, the Western Light, our master, our teacher, our rabbi Moses Maimonides [of blessed memory], which came to him from the east and west, from north and south, from the sages of France, Spain, Yemen, and Babylonia (Fig. 18).

Publication information is lacking, but it is similar to other collections of responsa issued in Constantinople circa 1517, including those of Asher ben Yeḥiel (Rosh; 1250 or 1259–1327) and of Solomon ben Adret (Rashba; 1235–1310).[2] The imprint includes responsa concerning the reception of *Moreh Nevukhim*, and the final page (fol. 24v) contains two responsa from Maimonides's son, Abraham.

Maimonides's expertise in rabbinics, philosophy, medicine, and more appears in his cogent responses to questions posed from all over the world. More importantly, perhaps, this literature attests to the great thinker's role as a rabbinic authority for communities across the Jewish world and as a leader of Egyptian Jewry. At various points during his residency in Egypt, Maimonides served as *Nagid* (Prince) and *Ra'is 'al Yahud* (Head of the Jews), positions of leadership appointed by the supreme rabbinic authority (Gaon) and the Fatimid court, respectively.[3] The sheer number of letters, combined with evidence of his considerate and compassionate manner, speak to Maimonides's significance as both rabbi and communal leader.

The total number of responsa known to have been composed by Maimonides is 464, although this thin imprint contains far fewer. The responsa were composed in either Hebrew or Judeo-Arabic, depending upon the chosen language of the questioner. Identifying details related to the questions posed to Maimonides, such as date or place of composition, are often lacking, but extant responsa stem from about 1167 almost until his death in 1204. Prominent scholars from all over the Jewish world sent halakhic and ethical questions to the Great Eagle, as he was known, including the *dayanim* (rabbinic judges) Anatoli and

1 See the critical editions by Abraham H. Freimann (ed.), *Teshuvot ha-Rambam* (Jerusalem, 1934); and Joshua Blau (ed.), *Teshuvot ha-Rambam*, 4 vols. (Jerusalem: Meḳitse Nirdamim, 1957–1986). See also Abraham N. Zuroff, 'The Responsa of Maimonides' (Ph.D. diss., Yeshiva University, 1966).

2 For the opinion that Maimonides's *Teshuvot, She'elot ve-Igerot* was printed around the same time as the *Sefer Abudarham* (Constantinople, 1513), see Meir Benayahu, *Rabbi Eliyahu Capsali, of Crete* [Hebrew] (Tel Aviv: Tel Aviv University, 1983), 152.

3 On leadership, see Arnold E. Franklin, 'Jewish Religious and Communal Organization,' in *The Cambridge History of Judaism: Volume 5, Jews in the Medieval Islamic World*, ed. Phillip I. Lieberman (Cambridge: Cambridge University Press, 2021), 450–83. On the titles, see Elinoar Bareket, 'The Head of the Jews (ra'is al-yahud) in Fatimid Egypt: A Re-evaluation,' *Bulletin of the School of Oriental and African Studies* 67, no. 2 (2004): 185–97.

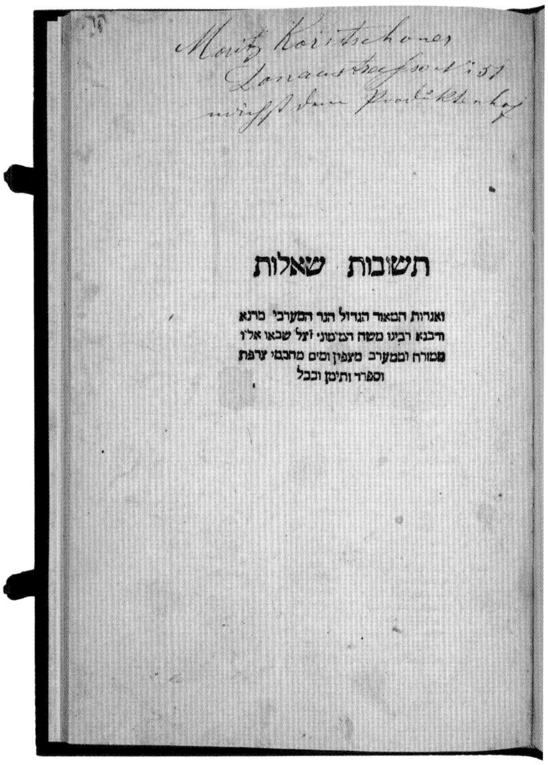

Fig. 18 *Teshuvot, She'elot ve-Igerot* [Constantinople, ca. 1517], RB 12, fol. 1r.

Meshullam of Alexandria, Jephthah ben Ali, Jonathan ha-Kohen of Lunel, Obadiah the Proselyte, Nissim of Damascus, Samuel Ibn Tibbon, and Samuel ben ʿAli Gaon of Baghdad.

Maimonides's responsa provide social and cultural context for twelfth-century life in the Mediterranean region, as well as insight into his own personality. They demonstrate, for instance, the waning of Babylonian cultural and religious hegemony. During an era of Jewish economic and geographical expansion, Maimonides challenged the authority of the Gaon, Samuel ben ʿAli, by permitting Jews to travel on the high seas on the Sabbath.[4] He also actively engaged in polemics to defend his own scholarship. His responsa to Jonathan ha-Kohen, a disciple of Abraham ben David of Posquières (Rabad), the great Provençal scholar and detractor of Maimonides, are essentially retorts to Rabad's criticisms.[5]

To be sure, the responsa demonstrate compassion as well. Despite having been subjected to the Almohad persecutions, Maimonides did not express rabid anti-Muslim sentiment, nor did he classify Muslims as idolaters (notwithstanding pagan origins associated with the Ka'aba stone in Mecca).[6] His response to an inquiry from Obadiah the Proselyte, a convert from Islam, is especially insightful. The latter inquired as to whether he was permitted to recite phrases such as 'Our God and God of *our* fathers' and 'Thou who has chosen *us*' in blessings and prayers. Maimonides assured the convert that the patriarch Abraham was his ancestor as well and that he was equal to all Jews and should therefore recite the standard prayers.[7]

The Hartman copy belonged to Moritz Koritschoner (d. 1912), director of the Imperial and Royal Länderbank in Vienna, Austria. The folios appear in quires of six, with printed pagination appearing only on the first biofolium of each quire (fols. 1 and 7). A later paginator rendered fols. 15 and 16 as יה and יו, in contrast to the tradition of utilizing טו and טז so as not to write forms of the divine name.

4 Blau (ed.), *Teshuvot ha-Rambam*, nos. 308–309.

5 Freimann (ed.), *Teshuvot ha-Rambam*, xliii–xliv; Blau (ed.), *Teshuvot ha-Rambam*, vol. 3, 42–43.

6 Salo W. Baron, 'Historical Outlook of Maimonides,' *Proceedings of the American Academy for Jewish Research* 6 (1934–1935): 5–113 (83–84); Freimann (ed.), *Teshuvot ha-Rambam*, no. 369; Blau (ed.), *Teshuvot ha-Rambam*, no. 448. See Ari Berman's foreword to this volume.

7 Freimann (ed.), *Teshuvot ha-Rambam*, no. 42; Blau (ed.), *Teshuvot ha-Rambam*, no. 293; Franz Kobler (ed.), *Treasury of Jewish Letters: Letters from the Famous and Humble*, 2 vols. (Philadelphia, PA: Jewish Publication Society of America, 1953), 1:194–96.

12

משנה תורה
Mishneh Torah (Repetition of the Law)
Edited by David ben Eliezer ha-Levi Pizzighettone and Jacob ben Ḥayim ben Isaac Ibn Adoniyahu
Printed by Daniel Bomberg
Venice, 1524–1525
2°. RB 4. 2 vols.
Steinschneider, 6513,4; Habermann, *Bomberg*, no. 91; Dienstag, '*Mishneh Torah*,' no. 7; Vinograd, Venice no. 96

[משנה] סדר טהרות עם פירוש ... משה בר מיימון
[Mishnah] Seder Tohorot 'im Perush ... Mosheh bar Maimon (Order of Purities, with Commentary of Moses Maimonides)
Printed by Daniel Bomberg
Venice, 1528
2°. RB 30
Steinschneider, 1968b; Habermann, *Bomberg*, no. 121; Vinograd, Venice no. 133

This sixth complete edition of the *Mishneh Torah*, published by the important printing house of Daniel Bomberg, served as the basis for subsequent editions (Fig. 19). It includes the previously published commentaries of the Constantinople edition – *Hasagot ha-Rabad*, *Hagahot Maimoniyot*, and *Magid Mishneh* – as well as the complete commentary of *Migdal 'Oz*, which had appeared in the first edition of 1509 only in part. While passages that appear in the former edition are absent from this edition, and vice versa, the wording of the *Hagahot Maimoniyot* in Bomberg's imprint is more complete and apparently less modified. Here, glosses often appear in the first person, while the 1509 imprint includes passages that end with the words 'thus far the language of R. M. K.' (R. Meir ha-Kohen, presumed author of *Hagahot Maimoniyot*), as well as the statement 'may the All-Merciful pardon Meir ha-Kohen.'[1]

Daniel Bomberg (ca. 1483–1553) was born in Antwerp to a Calvinist mercantile family. Wealthy and well educated, Bomberg settled in Venice as a young man to pursue commercial interests. Before long, he turned his deep appreciation for books into a business venture, establishing the first Hebrew press in the city and himself as the first non-Jewish printer of Hebrew titles. While the Soncino and Naḥmias families were the most prolific and important *Jewish* printers of their era, no Hebrew press came close to rivaling that of Daniel Bomberg.[2]

Between 1517 and 1549, the Bomberg press issued more than 250 titles. Among his many accomplishments was the printing of the *editio princeps* of the Babylonian Talmud (1519/20–1523), upon which nearly all subsequent editions of the Talmud were based. Having acquired the exclusive right to print the Talmud from the Venetian Senate, as well as the official endorsement of Pope Leo X, Bomberg issued two more complete editions of the Talmud, in 1526–1531 and 1543–1549, respectively. Bomberg also published the first *Biblia Rabbinica*

1 See *Hilkhot Zekhiyah u-Matanah* 11:19.

2 For an overview of Bomberg's life and work, see Bruce Nielsen, 'Daniel van Bombergen, a Bookman of Two Worlds,' in *The Hebrew Book in Early Modern Italy*, ed. Joseph R. Hacker and Adam Shear (Philadelphia, PA: University of Pennsylvania Press, 2011), 56–75, 230–52.

Fig. 19 *Mishneh Torah* (Venice: Daniel Bomberg 1524–1525), RB 4, vol. 2, fol. 1r.

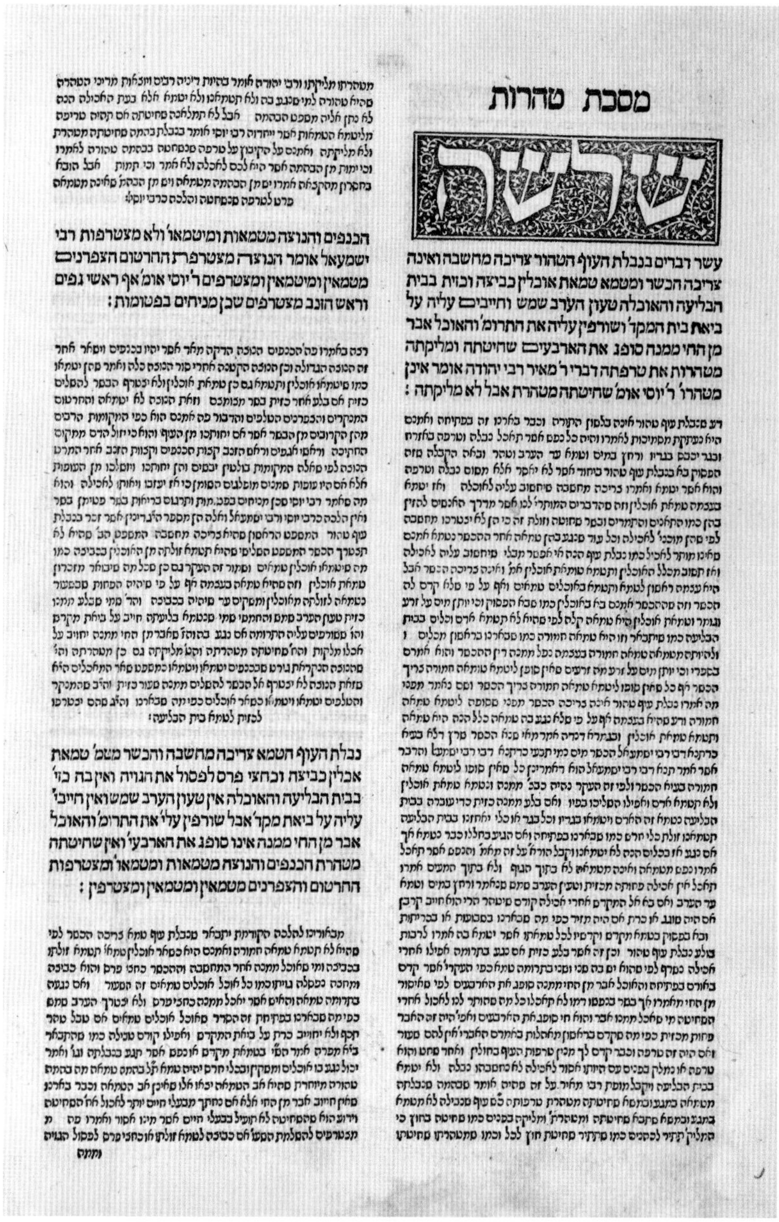

Fig. 20 [*Mishnah*] *Seder Tohorot* with Commentary of Maimonides (Venice: Daniel Bomberg, 1528), RB 30, fol. 53v.

(1515–1517),[3] the first Jerusalem Talmud (1522–1524),[4] and the first printed Karaite book, a four-volume prayer book for the Karaite communities in the eastern Mediterranean and the Crimean peninsula (1528–1529).

Bomberg's success as a printer of Hebrew books was dependent upon more than simply quality paper and type. He went to great lengths to hire first-rate scholars to direct his projects. Though the press's Talmud volumes were largely based on earlier printed editions, editors of other rabbinic texts consulted and often corrected the manuscripts they wished to publish. In an introduction to this *Mishneh Torah*, David ben Eliezer ha-Levi Pizzighettone, who had previously edited books for the Soncino Press, described his difficult job. 'I was forced to correct [the commentaries] on my own,' Pizzighettone remarked, 'for all I had was one book of *Magid Mishneh*, the edition printed in Turkey (תוגרמה) [in 1509], and one

3 See Jordan S. Penkower, 'Jacob Ben Ḥayyim and the Rise of the *Biblia Hebraica*' (Ph.D. diss., Hebrew University of Jerusalem, 1982); Penkower, 'The First Edition of the Hebrew Bible That Bomberg Published and the Beginning of His Publishing House' [Hebrew], *Kiryat Sefer* 58 (1983): 586–604, esp. 587, 601–02, nn. 8–9, 68; Penkower, 'Rabbinic Bible,' in *Dictionary of Biblical Interpretation*, ed. John H. Hayes, 2 vols. (Nashville, TN: Abingdon, 1999), vol. 2, cols. 361b–64a.

4 Yakov Z. Mayer, *Editio Princeps: The 1523 Venice Edition of the Palestinian Talmud and the Beginning of Hebrew Printing* [Hebrew] (Jerusalem: Magnes Press, 2022).

[manuscript of] *Migdal 'Oz*, which was full of mistakes' (fol. 2r). On the whole, however, he relied upon the manuscripts in front of him, even when disagreeing with their reading; only four times, each explained in the lengthy introduction, did he correct the actual text of the *Mishneh Torah* on his own initiative.[5]

The historian and physician Joseph ben Joshua ha-Kohen (1496–1575), born in Avignon to exiles from Spain, wrote: '[Bomberg] brought forth from darkness unto light many books in the holy tongue. Constantly there went in and out of his house many learned men and he never withdrew his hand from giving unto all in accordance with their demands and to the extent of the means with which God had endowed him.'[6] Intense social and intellectual interaction between Jews and Christians occasionally led to Jewish conversion to Christianity, as may have been the case with Pizzighettone's co-editor, Jacob ben Ḥayim Ibn Adoniyahu (ca. 1470–ca. 1538).

Ibn Adoniyahu served as proofreader and reviser for several Bomberg projects. He is best known for editing Bomberg's second edition of the *Biblia Rabbinica*, which was published at the same time as the *Mishneh Torah* and became the basis for all subsequent Rabbinic Bibles. Ibn Adoniyahu produced other significant works, such as this Mishnah with Maimonides's commentary (Fig. 20). Like Joshua Solomon Soncino before him, Bomberg included Maimonides's *Commentary on the Mishnah* at the end of each Talmud volume, along with the *Piske Tosafot* and the *Piske ha-Rosh* (halakhic rulings of the Tosafists and of Asher ben Yeḥiel) (see cat. no. 24).

5 For an example of correcting gone wrong, compare various manuscript and printed editions of *Mishneh Torah, Hilkhot Sefer Torah* 8:11; see Moshe Goshen-Gottstein, 'The Authenticity of the Aleppo Codex,' *Textus* 1 (1960): 17–58 (37–40). Maimonides's original text stated that the song of *Ha'azinu* (Deuteronomy 32) should consist of 67 lines, though printed books until recent scholarly editions have indicated 70 lines.

6 See David W. Amram, *The Makers of Hebrew Books in Italy: Being Chapters in the History of the Hebrew Printing Press* (Philadelphia, PA: Julius H. Greenstone, 1909), 183–84, citing Joseph ben Joshua ha-Kohen, *Divre ha-Yamim le-Malkhe Tsarfat u-le-Malkhe Bet Otoman ha-Togar* (Sabbioneta, 1554), fols. 137v.

13

אגרות להמאור הגדול ... רבינו משה המיימוני
Igerot le-ha-Ma'or ha-Gadol ... Rabenu Mosheh ha-Maimoni (Letters of the Great Light)
Printed by Cornelius Adelkind, at the press of Giovanni Dei Farri and Brothers
Venice, 1544
8°. RB 13
Steinschneider, 6513,112; Habermann, *Adelkind*, no. 5; Vinograd, Venice no. 211

[משנה] מסכת אבות עם פירוש ... משה בר מיימון
[*Mishnah*] *Masekhet Avot 'im Perush ... Mosheh bar Maimon* (Tractate *Avot*, with Commentary of Moses Maimonides)
Printed by Meir ben Ephraim of Padua and Jacob ben Naphtali ha-Kohen of Gazzuolo
Mantua, 1558
2°. RB 31
Steinschneider, 2581b; Vinograd, Mantua no. 42

Venice was home to several thousand Jews in the sixteenth century. Consisting of immigrants from Ashkenaz, Iberia, and throughout the Mediterranean, the city's vibrancy helped create a hotbed of Jewish cultural activity. The Hebrew printing house of Daniel Bomberg epitomized the strength and impact of Venetian Jewry's intellectual enthusiasm, but it was by no means the only source of printing. Jewish communities in cities and towns like Bologna, Ferrara, and Mantua boasted important presses.

In 1544, Cornelius Adelkind brought this collection of letters and responsa to press at the printing house of Giovanni Dei Farri and Brothers (Fig. 21). The Dei Farri press had just commenced Hebrew publishing, but a year later, after issuing some ten titles, the press

אגרות להמאור הגדול
הנר המערבי מרנא ורבנא רבינו משה המיימוני זצ"ל
שבאו אליו · ממזרח · וממערב · מצפון · ומים ·
מחכמי צרפת · וספרד · ותימן · ובבל · ודברי
מוסר וצוואה שצוה הרב הגדול ז"ל לבנו החכם רבי
אברהם ז"ל · ושאלות ששאלו מהרב הנזכר ז"ל
ותשובותיו עליהן · נדפס שנת לבריאה
חמשת אלפים ושלש וארבעה ·
בויניציאה ·
היא העיר הגדולה · המהוללה ·

Fig. 21 *Igerot le-ha-Ma'or ha-Gadol* (Venice: Giovanni Dei Farri and Brothers, 1544), RB 13, fol. 1r.

Fig. 22 [*Mishnah*] *Masekhet Avot* (Venice: Meir ben Ephraim of Padua and Jacob ben Naphtali ha-Kohen of Gazzuolo, 1558), RB 31, fol. 1r.

ceased operations.[1] It is difficult to ascertain why the press closed or its relationship with the dominant Bomberg press. Though loyal to Bomberg, Adelkind published Hebrew texts at several Venetian establishments.

This was just the second time that a collection of Maimonides's responsa was printed. The order of the letters differs from the first edition produced in Constantinople (see cat. no. 11), as does the title, which is slightly misleading because many of the letters post-date Maimonides. The volume contains material concerning the controversy over Maimonides's *Moreh Nevukhim*, as well as the ethical will of the Great Eagle. A year after the release of this imprint, Adelkind published Maimonides's responsa for the Giustiniani press. Collections of Maimonides's *She'elot u-Teshuvot* were printed twice more in Venice in the second half of the sixteenth century and again there in the mid-seventeenth century. Amsterdam was the origin of an edition by the renowned Proops press in 1712, and at least a dozen additional editions appeared throughout central and eastern Europe by the end of the nineteenth century.

This volume of Maimonides's commentary on tractate *Avot*, frequently translated as *Ethics of the Fathers*, appeared in Mantua as part of the two-volume prayer book known as *Maḥzor Roma*, published between 1557 and 1560 (Fig. 22). The separate title page, displaying the date [5]318 (= 1558), suggests the tractate was disseminated as a discrete unit. It was not uncommon for publishers in the early centuries of printing to produce smaller works to

1 Amram, *The Makers of Hebrew Books in Italy*, 200–201.

רשי הרמבם

משה כבר

משה

קבל תורה מסיני ומסרה ליהושע ויהושע
לזקנים וזקנים לנביאים ונביאים מסרוה לאנשי
כנסת הגדולה׃ הם אמרו שלשה דברים הוו
מתונים בדין׃ והעמידו תלמידים הרבה׃ ועשו
סייג לתורה׃ ב שמעון הצדיק היה משירי
כנסת הגדולה הוא היה אומר על שלשה דברים
העולם עומד על התורה׃ ועל העבודה׃ ועל
גמילות חסדים׃ ג אנטיגנוס איש סוכו קבל
משמעון הצדיק הוא היה אומר אל תהיו כעבדים
המשמשין את הרב על מנת לקבל פרס אלא
הוו כעבדים המשמשין את הרב על מנת שלא
לקבל פרס ויהי מורא שמים עליכם׃ ד

Fig. 23 [*Mishnah*] *Masekhet Avot* (Venice: Meir ben Ephraim of Padua and Jacob ben Naphtali ha-Kohen of Gazzuolo, 1558), RB 31, fol. 72v.

provide them with a source of income during the production of larger projects. In this case, they indicated that it was the first *Avot* in print to include the commentary of Rashi, referred to here as 'first among commentators, Rabenu Shelomoh' (ראש המפרשים רבינו שלמה ז"ל). The Mishnaic text appears in square font with vocalization, flanked by the commentaries of Maimonides on the right and Rashi on the left (Fig. 23). The imprint includes the so-called sixth chapter of *Avot*, known as *Kinyan Torah*, with the commentary of Rashi only. The Hartman copy contains the signatures of censors Dominico Irosolimitano and Giovanni Domenico Carretto (fols. 86v, 88r).

The separate nature of the work reflected its manuscript history as well. Buried within his commentary to the *Seder Nezikin*, Maimonides's eight introductory chapters to his explanation of *Avot* became known in Hebrew as *Shemonah Perakim* (Eight Chapters) and found an independent audience. He presented a philosophical introduction to ethics, combining rabbinic literature with Greek philosophy mediated through Arab philosophers. At least 25 complete or fragmentary manuscripts in Judeo-Arabic (primarily from Yemen) and at least 60 in Hebrew translation are extant. A volume of the Hebrew translation was printed as early as 1485 by Joshua Solomon Soncino.[2]

2 Goff, Heb-83.

14

משנה תורה עם ספר המצות
Mishneh Torah, with *Sefer ha-Mitsvot* (Repetition of the Law, with Book of Commandments)
Printed by Alvise Bragadini
Venice, 1550
2°. RB 5. 2 vols.
Steinschneider, 6513,5; Dienstag, '*Mishneh Torah*,' no. 8; Vinograd, Venice no. 408

משנה תורה עם ספר המצות
Mishneh Torah, with *Sefer ha-Mitsvot* (Repetition of the Law, with Book of Commandments)
Printed by Marco Antonio Giustiniani
Venice, 1550–1551
2°. RB 6. 2 vols.
Steinschneider, 6513,6; Habermann, *Adelkind*, no. 60; Dienstag, '*Mishneh Torah*,' no. 9; Vinograd, Venice no. 409

When Daniel Bomberg left Venice in 1549, the largest and most influential Hebrew printing press then in operation closed. Hoping to profit from the demand for Hebrew books, a number of Venetian aristocratic families established their own presses. Alvise Bragadini began his long and influential career as a Hebrew printer with an edition of the *Mishneh Torah* issued in 1550. It includes all the commentaries of the Bomberg edition (Venice, 1524–1525), as well as the glosses of the great halakhist and rabbinic leader Meir ben Isaac Katzenellenbogen (Maharam; 1473–1565) of Padua. In addition, for the first time the text of the halakhic code was accompanied by Maimonides's *Sefer ha-Mitsvot*, based on the Constantinople 1509 edition of Moses Ibn Tibbon's Hebrew translation and accompanied by a separate title page (Fig. 24).

Bragadini's *Mishneh Torah* embodies the care and intelligence expressed in sixteenth-century Hebrew printing. His printer's mark – three crowns set triangularly, symbolizing the diadem of royalty, priesthood, and Torah (see *Avot* 4:13)[1] – appears on the title page, as it would for more than 400 books printed over the next 160 years. At the top of the page, the verse 'Joyfully shall you draw water from the fountains of triumph' (Isaiah 12:3) is modified to highlight the author of the book, reading ממיימוני ('from Maimoni') rather than ממעיני ('from the fountains'). Maimonides is further alluded to by the circumvallating verses: 'And for all the great might (*Yad ha-Ḥazakah*) and awesome power that Moses displayed before all Israel' (Deuteronomy 34:12), and 'Moses alone shall come near the Lord; but the others shall not come near, nor shall the people come up with him' (Exodus 24:2).

That same year, Marco Antonio Giustiniani, an established Venetian printer who was then nearing completion of printing the entire Babylonian Talmud (1546–1551), issued the first volume of his own edition of the *Mishneh Torah* (Fig. 25). (The second volume appeared at the very beginning of the following year.) Giustiniani had established his press in Venice in 1545 and immediately impacted local printing business by publishing books previously issued by Bomberg, and hiring personnel, including Elijah Levita Ashkenazi (1469–1549) and Cornelius Adelkind (sixteenth century), who had hitherto worked at the Bomberg press.[2] His printer's mark depicted a Moorish edifice akin to the Dome of the Rock with

1 On the printer's mark, see Abraham Yaari, *Hebrew Printers' Marks, from the Beginning of Hebrew Printing to the End of the 19th Century* [Hebrew] (Jerusalem: Hebrew University, 1944), no. 18.

2 Marvin J. Heller, *The Sixteenth-Century Hebrew Book: An Abridged Thesaurus*, 2 vols. (Leiden: Brill, 2004), 1:287.

Fig. 24 *Mishneh Torah*, with *Sefer ha-Mitsvot* (Venice: Alvise Bragadini, 1550), RB 5, fol. 394r (beginning vol. 2).

הלכות שבועות הפלאה שצד

פרק ראשון

ארבעה

פרק ראשון

ארבעה

the words *Bet ha-Mikdash* (Holy Temple) emblazoned on it. Billowing above the structure is a banner with the inscription: 'The glory of this latter House shall be greater than that of the former one, said the Lord of Hosts' (Haggai 2:9),[3] which may have been aimed at the press of Daniel Bomberg, nearing its end by the mid-1540s.[4]

Giustiniani's greatest contribution to Hebrew printing was the aforementioned edition of the Talmud, printed between 1546 and 1551. Adelkind worked with editor Joshua Boaz ben Simon Barukh to create an innovative edition of the Talmud. A Spanish exile who decried the poor state of Jewish scholarship, Joshua Boaz sought to encourage and ease Talmud study by printing three indexes on the Talmudic page: *En Mishpat* indicates the location of pertinent legal topics in the *Mishneh Torah*, *Sefer Mitsvot Gadol* (*Semag*), and *Arba'ah Turim*; *Torah Or* identifies the sources for Scriptural texts embedded in the main text of the page; and *Masoret ha-Talmud* (or *Masoret ha-Shas*)[5] references parallel and related passages elsewhere in the Talmud. Boaz's contribution made the Talmud more user-friendly and hence rendered this edition of inestimable value, and indeed the indexes subsequently became standard elements of the printed Talmud.

Together, the Bragadini and Giustiniani editions of the *Mishneh Torah* proved surprisingly significant. As discussed in early entries, Maimonides's law code inspired glosses and commentaries already in the immediate generations after its composition. As it became increasingly entrenched as a core text of the halakhic canon in the ensuing centuries, scholars continued to author novel explanations pertinent to more contemporary developments. Meir Katzenellenbogen, who headed a council of regional rabbis in Venice

3 Marvin J. Heller, 'The Printer's Mark of Marco Antonio Giustiniani and the Printing Houses that Utilized It,' in *Studies in the Making of the Early Hebrew Book* (Leiden: Brill, 2008), 44–53.

4 An unusually large representation of this printer's mark appears on vol. 1, fol. 24v, and vol. 2, fol. 768v.

5 The word Talmud was placed on the *Index Librorum Prohibitorum* and it fell out of use due to censorship. *Shas* and *Gemara* were deemed suitable substitutes.

Fig. 25 *Mishneh Torah*, with *Sefer ha-Mitsvot* (Venice: Marco Antonio Giustiniani, 1550–1551), RB 6, vol. 2, fol. 1r.

and served the Ashkenazic community of nearby Padua, approached Giustiniani about including his glosses in the new edition of Maimonides's *Mishneh Torah*.[6] Unable to come to an agreement, the rabbi instead partnered with the rival Bragadini press. Unauthorized and unscrupulous, Giustiniani proceeded to issue the Katzenellenbogen glosses anyway, threatening to ruin the Bragadini venture. Seeking to preserve his financial investment, Katzenellenbogen wrote to Moses Isserles (Rema; d. 1572), who would later become among the most authoritative Ashkenazic rabbis of the early modern period. Though still a young man, Isserles already carried weight in his rabbinic capacity in Cracow. He responded by prohibiting the distribution of Giustiniani's edition and placing a ban on Jews who purchased it.[7] Faced with his own financial loss, Giustiniani appealed to Pope Julius III, who assigned a committee of six cardinals, the Congregation of the Inquisition, to investigate.

6 His name was among the heads of the seven Italian communities (Venice, Rome, Bologna, Ferrara, Mantua, Reggio, and Modena) that assembled in Ferrara on June 21, 1554 to enact *takanot* (ordinances).

7 *She'elot u-Teshuvot Rema* (Cracow, 1640), no. 10.

Led by Cardinal Giovanni Pietro Caraffa, the future Pope Paul IV, the committee concluded nothing about the issue at hand. What began as a business dispute and incidents of plagiarism led to a series of persecutions that irrevocably affected Italian Jewry, Hebrew printing, and the course of Jewish history. A papal bull issued on August 12, 1553 ordered owners of the Talmud to submit their copies to the authorities. Anyone found with a copy of the Talmud after the given deadline was subject to two years imprisonment for a first offense and five years for a second offense. Informers received a monetary reward.

On Rosh Hashanah, 1553, representatives of the Inquisition conducted a house-to-house search of the Jewish residences in Rome. After the collection of copies of the Talmud and other rabbinic texts, hundreds of books were ceremoniously burned in Campo di Fiori. Letters were sent by the Inquisition and the Pope to the heads of Italian states and papal nuncios in foreign capitals to enforce the prohibition of the Talmud. Conflagrations occurred throughout Italy. In Venice, more than a thousand complete books of the Talmud and hundreds of other Hebrew books were consigned to the flames in Piazza San Marco on a Sabbath in October 1553. R. Abraham Menaḥem ben Jacob ha-Kohen Rapa (1520–after 1594) related the events to the biblical text and branded the horror as Heaven-sent:

> [Regarding] the burning of the Oral Law in the year 1553/54 (בשנת שי"ד), 'the hand (יד) of the Lord was against' us.[8] The decree from Rome [called] for an inferno. In Venice – woe to the eyes that saw this – on the 13th and 14th of *Marḥeshvan* 5314 (= October 31 and November 1, 1553), with the fire burning continuously. So I established these days for myself for each and every year as days of fasting, weeping, and mourning. For this was as oppressive to me as the burning of the House of our God.[9]

The long-lasting effects of the confiscation and burning of the Talmud included Church censorship of Hebrew books.[10] In 1515, the Fifth Lateran Council had adopted the concept of a list of forbidden books, banning offensive or heretical works. The following year, Pope Leo X, who later granted Daniel Bomberg the right to print the complete Talmud, issued a papal bull establishing Church censorship. Although the Church was originally concerned with stamping out heresy within Christianity, Jewish books were soon threatened. The Talmud and its rabbinic offspring were placed on the *Index Librorum Prohibitorum* (Index of Prohibited Books) in 1559, and for decades to come Jews were required to submit their books for censorship. Rabbinic leaders, including Meir Katzenellenbogen, responded by establishing a formal process of self-censorship to detect passages or even entire works that could be deemed offensive to the Church: any book submitted for publication required at least three rabbinic approbations (*haskamot*) attesting to the text's value and suitability.

The Hartman copies of both the Giustiniani and Bragadini editions of the *Mishneh Torah* reflect this history of Church censorship. Volume 2 of the Giustiniani edition was repeatedly examined by Church officials in the late sixteenth and early seventeenth centuries, and it bears the signatures of no fewer than six censors, including Laurentius

8 Deuteronomy 2:15. Rapa amended the verse to refer to it more personally (בנו rather than the more removed בם of the biblical text).

9 *Minḥah Belulah* (Verona, 1594), fol. 203v. Additional accounts of the conflagrations appeared in Judah ben Samuel Lerma's *Leḥem Yehudah* (Sabbioneta, 1554), Joseph ben Joshua ha-Kohen's *Emek ha-Bakhah*, and Mattathias Deladrut's unpublished *Zikaron*. See Abraham Yaari, 'Burning the Talmud in Italy' [Hebrew], in his *Studies in Hebrew Booklore* (Jerusalem: Mossad Harav Kook, 1958), 198–234; and Marvin J. Heller, 'Sibling Rivalry: Simultaneous Editions of Hebrew Books,' *Quntres* 2, no. 1 (2011): 22–36 (and literature cited therein).

10 On censorship on the Italian peninsula, see Piet van Boxel, 'Hebrew Books and Censorship in Sixteenth-Century Italy,' in *Jewish Books and their Readers*, ed. Scott Mendelbrote and Joanna Weinberg (Leiden: Brill, 2016), 75–99; Amnon Raz-Krakotzkin, *The Censor, the Editor, and the Text: The Catholic Church and the Shaping of the Jewish Canon in the Sixteenth Century*, trans. Jackie Feldman (Philadelphia, PA: University of Pennsylvania Press, 2007); Meir Benayahu, *Copyright, Authorization, and Imprimatur for Hebrew Books Printed in Venice* [Hebrew] (Jerusalem: Mekhon Ben-Tsevi, Mossad Harav Kook, 1971).

Franguellus (1575), Allessandro Scipione (1597), Dominico Irosolimitano (1599), Luigi da Bologna (1599), Giovanni Domenica Vistorini (1609), and Giovanni Domenico Carretto (1617).[11] The frequent examinations probably stemmed from Church awareness that Jews regularly rewrote by hand that which had come under the pen of the censor.[12]

The Giustiniani edition in the Hartman Collection contains stamps of 'Moise Symion Pessah Grand Rabbin, Volo[s] 1882' and the 'Institutum Judaicum' at the University of Berlin, shedding light on its modern provenance. Volos, in modern-day Greece, was home to a small community of Romaniote Jews beginning in the fourteenth century, and Moise Pessah served as rabbi from 1892 until his death in 1955. The Institutum Judaicum was a special academic course for Protestant theologians in preparation for missionary work among Jews. The first of its kind was founded at the University of Halle in 1724, and similar programs were developed in 1886 at the University of Leipzig and the University of Berlin. The latter, once home to this volume, was led by Hermann L. Strack (1848–1922), professor of Talmudic and rabbinic literature, who studied under the great Jewish scholar Moritz Steinschneider.

But it is the Bragadini volumes that are especially notable for the more extensive and older trail of provenance documentation.[13] Both Bragadini volumes contain miscellaneous manuscript content in Hebrew and Italian, including family records and unpublished poems (Fig. 26).[14] The largest number of entries stem from members of the Katzigin family, who settled in the Piedmont region after migrating from Germany.[15] Much information is recorded about births, deaths, travels, accidents, illnesses, epidemics, robberies, and more, in locations including Carmagnola, Casale Monferrato, Cherasco, Turin, and Vercelli. A flyleaf at the beginning of volume 1 contains a record of several transactions regarding the borrowing of books.[16] Meanwhile, the title page of volume 1 includes entries from Abraham Pescarol, a printer of Hebrew books in Cremona in the sixteenth century,[17] and Gershon Concio, who acquired the book from R. Judah ben Abraham Segre of Chieri.[18]

11 On censors and censorship, see Popper, *The Censorship of Hebrew Books*. Franguellus, Irosolimitano, and Scipione were all Jewish converts to Christianity. Franguellus and Irosolimitano may have been censoring books in Ferrara when they signed these volumes, Luigi da Bologna was at this time active in Modena/Reggio Emilia, and Scipione and Carretto worked primarily in Mantua.

12 The Bragadini edition lacks censors's signatures, though it too displays extensive censorship; see vol. 1, fols. 16r, 26r, 27r, 28r, 51r, 69r, 183r; and vol. 2, fols. 359r, 491v, 512r, 648v, 763r.

13 There are six flyleaves, four of which include extensive writing. In vol. 1, a separate handwritten sheet is tipped into fol. 2r, and handwritten notes appear on fols. 2r and 3r.

14 An elegy by Nehemiah Katzigin for his wife, who succumbed to an epidemic in 1805 at the age of 35 while he was away in Turin (vol. 1, verso of first flyleaf); a poem honoring a Katzigin family member for bestowing a gift on the synagogue (vol. 1, recto of second flyleaf); and an elegy upon the death of Joseph Ḥayim Galico of Modena, composed in Turin on 14 Iyar 5535 (= May 14, 1775) (vol. 1, leaf tipped into fol. 2r).

15 For the Katzigin family, see Marco Mortara, *Mazkeret Ḥakhme Italiyah* (Padua: F. Sacchetto, 1886), 13; Jefim Schirmann, *Studies in the History of Hebrew Poetry and Drama* [Hebrew] (Jerusalem: Bialik Institute, 1979), vol. 2, 71–73; Israel Adler, 'Three Musical Ceremonies for Hoshana Rabba in the Jewish Community of Casale Monferrato (1732–1733, 1735)' [Hebrew], in *Yuval: Studies of the Jewish Music Research Centre, Volume 5: The Abraham Zvi Idelsohn Memorial Volume*, ed. Israel Adler et al. (Jerusalem: Magnes Press, 1986), 51–137 (esp. 94 for Katzigin family tree) (Hebrew section); Renata Segre, *The Jews in Piedmont*, vol. 3 (Jerusalem: Israel Academy of Sciences and Humanities, 1990).

16 Separate entries mention copies of the *Zohar*, *Hilkhot ha-Rif*, *Pirke Avot* with the commentary of Isaac Abarbanel, and Talmud tractates *Ketubot* and *Sanhedrin*. A list of ten books were returned to a R. Daniel Levi in 5529 (= 1768/69): אלשיך על התורה, נחלת שבעה, בית יוסף טור א[ורח] ח[יים], קונקורדנסיה, רב אלפס, גמרה כתובות, שפתי חכמים, זהר שמות, שני לוחות הברית, שערי ציון.

17 On Pescarol's activities, see Meir Benayahu, *Hebrew Printing in Cremona: Its History and Bibliography* [Hebrew] (Jerusalem: Mekhon Ben-Tsevi, Mosad ha-Rav Kuk 1971), 60–64.

18 Abraham Segre was a rabbi, poet, and book collector in Casale Monferrato, while Gershon Concio's son, Joseph, was a well-known poet, scholar, and printer in Chieri at the beginning of the seventeenth century.

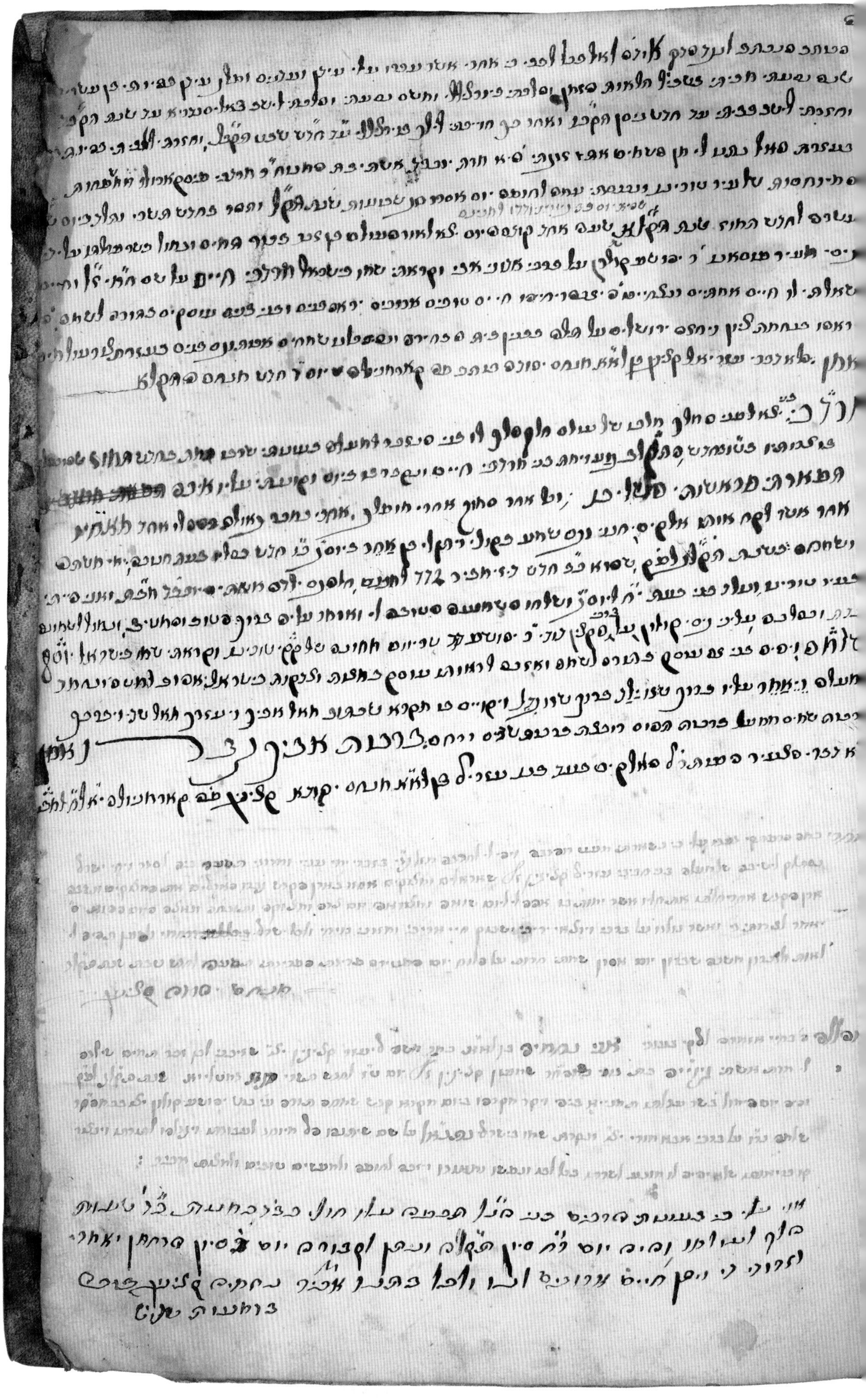

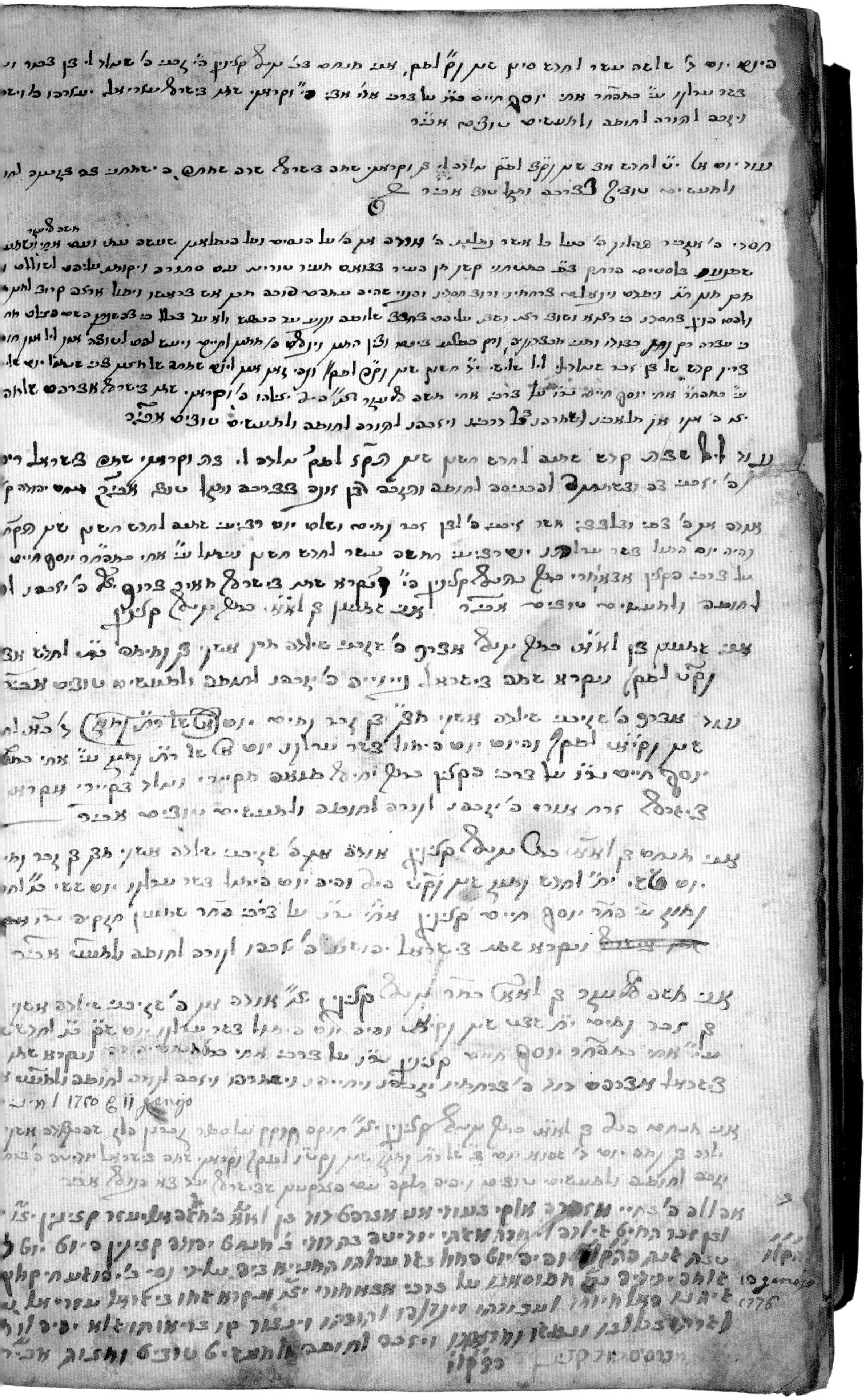

Fig. 26 *Mishneh Torah*, with *Sefer ha-Mitsvot* (Venice: Alvise Bragadini, 1550), RB 5. Records of the Katzigin family.

15

קרית ספר
Kiryat Sefer (City of the Scroll)
Moses ben Joseph di Trani (Mabit)
Printed by Alvise Bragadini
Venice, 1551
2°. RB 16
Steinschneider, 6577,3; Vinograd, Venice no. 427

Moses ben Joseph di Trani (Mabit; 1500–1580) was born in Salonika, the son of an Italian father of Spanish origin. As a young man, he immigrated to Safed where he studied under Jacob Berab (ca. 1474–1546), who himself authored a commentary on the *Mishneh Torah*.[1] Trani was active as a rabbi and rabbinic judge for fifty-four years. During his prodigious career, he produced ethical and philosophical texts, hundreds of responsa, and *Kiryat Sefer*, a commentary on the *Mishneh Torah* that focused on determining which commandments are of biblical origin and which are rabbinic enactments (Fig. 27).[2] During his lifetime, he published three books: the present volume; *Sefer ha-Teḥiyah ve-ha-Pedut* (Mantua, 1556), a commentary on chapters 7 and 8 of Sa'adiah Gaon's *Emunot ve-De'ot*; and *Bet Elohim* (Venice, 1576), a work on prayer, atonement, and the fundamentals of faith. The Bragadini press in Venice posthumously published a two-volume collection of his responsa in 1629–1630.

Trani was an integral part of one of the most creative, productive, and influential Jewish communities in the early modern period. Safed during the sixteenth century was home to legal scholars and mystical masters, including Moses Cordovero, Solomon Alkabetz (author of the Sabbath hymn *Lehkha Dodi*), Joseph Karo, Isaac Luria, and Elazar Azikri (author of *Yedid Nefesh*). Amid a flourishing of kabbalistic ideas and messianic hope, Berab sought to revive *semikhah*, the ancient form of rabbinical ordination that ceased to exist in the fourth or fifth century. In his *Mishneh Torah*, Maimonides stated that the Sanhedrin (great *bet din* or court) would be reestablished prior to the arrival of the messiah,[3] and he provided instructions for how to bring this about: the rabbis of the Land of Israel would nominate one from among themselves to be invested as the first *samukh* (ordained rabbi), who would in turn have the authority to ordain others, leading to the formation of a Sanhedrin.[4]

The tragedies of the Iberian expulsions and the elation over the ingathering of many Jews from across the diaspora into their ancient homeland were interpreted by some, including Berab, as portents of the imminent messianic redemption. Berab succeeded in convincing 25 rabbis, including Trani and Joseph Karo (1488–1575), author of the *Shulḥan 'Arukh* and a commentary on the *Mishneh Torah* entitled *Kesef Mishneh*, that they had the authority to initiate this process. Berab was designated the first *samukh* in 1538, after which a messenger was sent to Levi Ibn Habib in Jerusalem asking for his consent. Ibn Habib, who had previously clashed with Berab in various disputes, rejected the entire venture. He objected to the authority of the Safed rabbinate – arguing that the rabbis of Jerusalem were

1 Berab's comments are on all the parts of the *Mishneh Torah* that Vidal Yom Tov of Tolosa did not deal with in his *Magid Mishneh*, a part of which was published by J. L. Maimon, 'Akdamut Milin,' *Sinai* 36 (1955): 275–357. This volume of *Sinai* consists solely of articles related to Maimonides, as it was 'Dedicated to the 750th Anniversary of the Death of Maimonides.'

2 On the importance of this addition, see David Metzger, 'Hagahot ha-Mabit 'al Sifro Kiryat Sefer,' *Moriah* 8 (1979): 14–28.

3 *Mishneh Torah, Sanhedrin* 1:3.

4 *Mishneh Torah, Sanhedrin* 4:11.

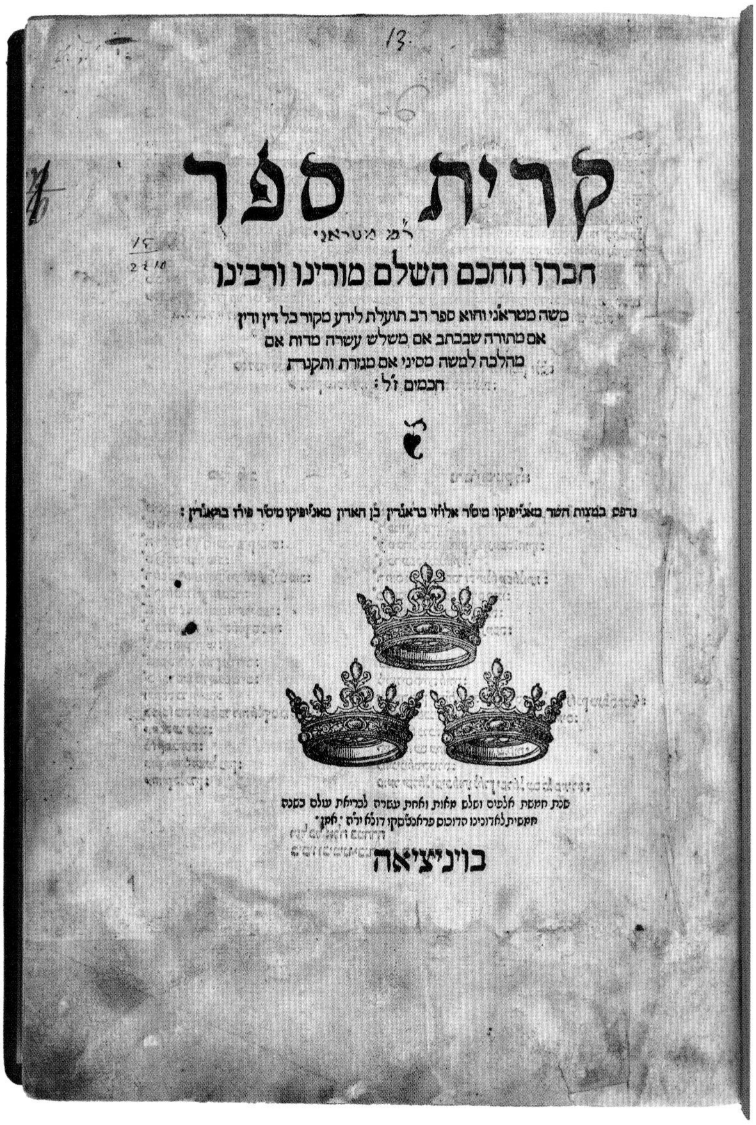
קרית ספר
ר׳מ מטראני
חברו החכם השלם מורינו ורבינו
משה מטראני והוא ספר רב תועלת לידע מקור כל דין ודין
אם מתורה שבכתב אם משלש עשרה מדות אם
מהלכה למשה מסיני אם מגזרת ותקנת
חכמים ז״ל:
נדפס במצות השר מאניפיקו מיסר אלויזי בראגדין בן הארון מאניפיקו מיסר פיר״ו בראגדין:
בויניציאה

Fig. 27 Moses ben Joseph di Trani, *Kiryat Sefer* (Venice: Alvise Bragadini, 1551), RB 16, fol. 1r.

by the nature of their location Jewry's highest spiritual leaders – and regarded Maimonides's statement about *semikhah* as merely an opinion rather than law itself.

Discussions about the matter continued for three months between the rabbis of Jerusalem and Safed, until Berab, having been denounced by enemies in a personal affair, was forced by Ottoman officials to leave the Land of Israel. As *semikhah* could not be granted outside the Land of Israel and fearful that his plans would fail if he never returned, Berab granted *semikhah* to four rabbis who lived in Safed, including Karo and Trani. Levi Ibn Habib objected publicly, writing a treatise on the illegality of Berab's actions (*Kunteres ha-Semikhah*) – it appeared in the printed edition of Ibn Habib's responsa (Venice, 1565), which also contained his own commentary on Maimonides's *Hilkhot Kidush ha-Ḥodesh* (Laws of the New Moon) – and gained support from the great scholar David ben Solomon Ibn Abi Zimra (Radbaz; ca. 1479–1573). With the authority of modern *semikhah* questioned, it did not gain the support it required to unite rabbinic Jewry, and the momentum to move forward gradually dissipated on its own within two generations.

The Hartman copy of *Kiryat Sefer* is censored on several folios but does not include a censor's signature.[5] Marginal notations in a sixteenth- or seventeenth-century hand appear on some pages. In addition, this volume includes three folios (lacking in most copies) with comments and corrections that were added to the end of the volume after the book was published.

5 For instance, see fols. 12r and 15r (גוי, מינות, משומד, מינין, עבודה זרה).

16

מורה נבוכים
Moreh Nevukhim (Guide of the Perplexed)
Edited by Meir Parenzo
Printed by Alvise Bragadini
Venice, 1551
2°. RB 9
Steinschneider, 6513,101; Habermann, *Parenzo*, no. 9; Vinograd, Venice no. 421

Maimonides's great philosophical work *Moreh Nevukhim* was one of the first Hebrew books ever printed (see cat. no. 1). Although the imprint contained no publication information, bibliographers have dated that book to about 1473 through analysis of the paper, type font, and format.[1] It was not printed a second time for more than seven decades. The reason may have been due to the difficulty of the content; a work intentionally composed for an intellectual elite was not in high demand, despite its importance, and was therefore a poor business investment. Certainly, printers, readers, and the rabbinic establishment deemed biblical, liturgical, Talmudic, and halakhic works to be of greater necessity than philosophical treatises in the early years of Hebrew printing.

By the middle of the sixteenth century, Hebrew printing was no longer in its infancy and Alvise Bragadini, a Venetian aristocrat seeking to break into the lucrative Hebrew printing business, released this novel edition of *Moreh Nevukhim* (Fig. 28). He employed Meir ben Jacob Parenzo, editor of several publications for the Bragadini press, who succeeded in producing Samuel Ibn Tibbon's Hebrew translation of the *Guide* complete with commentaries and indexes. Numerous medieval scholars produced full and partial commentaries on the work, most of which have remained unpublished. The commentaries and indexes contained here, however, became standard features of printed editions of *Moreh Nevukhim* and, consequently, integral to studying Maimonides's philosophical thought.

The older and more influential of the two commentaries printed here is the *Efodi*,[2] written by Isaac ben Moses ha-Levi, better known as Profiat Duran (d. ca. 1414). Duran's activities embodied the complexity of late fourteenth- and early fifteenth-century Sephardic Jewry. During the summer of 1391, preacher-inspired riots ravaged Jewish communities in Spain. Tens of thousands of Jews were murdered or driven from their homes, while tens of thousands more converted to Christianity to save their lives. Jewish property was confiscated, synagogues were seized and declared churches, and overall Jewish life in Spain was precarious.[3] In the early decades of the fifteenth century, still more thousands of Jews willfully heeded the call of conversion voiced by Dominican and Franciscan friars.

Still, a crypto-Judaism developed among some of the converts who sought to maintain a connection to their Jewish heritage. Duran was one such scholar who, having succumbed to forcible conversion in 1391, lived for several years as a Christian, even serving as astrologer to King Juan I of Aragon, before openly reverting to Judaism in the first decade of the fifteenth century. In 1396, he composed an ingeniously ambiguous anti-Christian polemic entitled *Al Tehi ka-Avotekha* (Be Not Like Your Fathers), which was praised and circulated

1 A. K. Offenberg, *Catalogue of Books Printed in the XVth Century Now in the British Library: BMC Part XIII Hebraica* (Leiden: Brill, 2004), 9–10.

2 Profiat Duran used the term *Efod* often. He called his book on grammar *Ma'aseh ha-Efod* and his book on the calendar *Ḥeshev ha-Efod*. The root (אפד), which refers to the priestly garments worn in the Temple, is an acronym for אני פרופיאט דורן or אמר פרופיאט דורן.

3 On the riots, see Benjamin Gampel, *Anti-Jewish Riots in the Crown of Aragon and the Royal Response, 1391–1392* (Cambridge: Cambridge University Press, 2016); on the following century, see Mark D. Meyerson, *A Jewish Renaissance in Fifteenth-Century Spain* (Princeton, NJ: Princeton University Press, 2004).

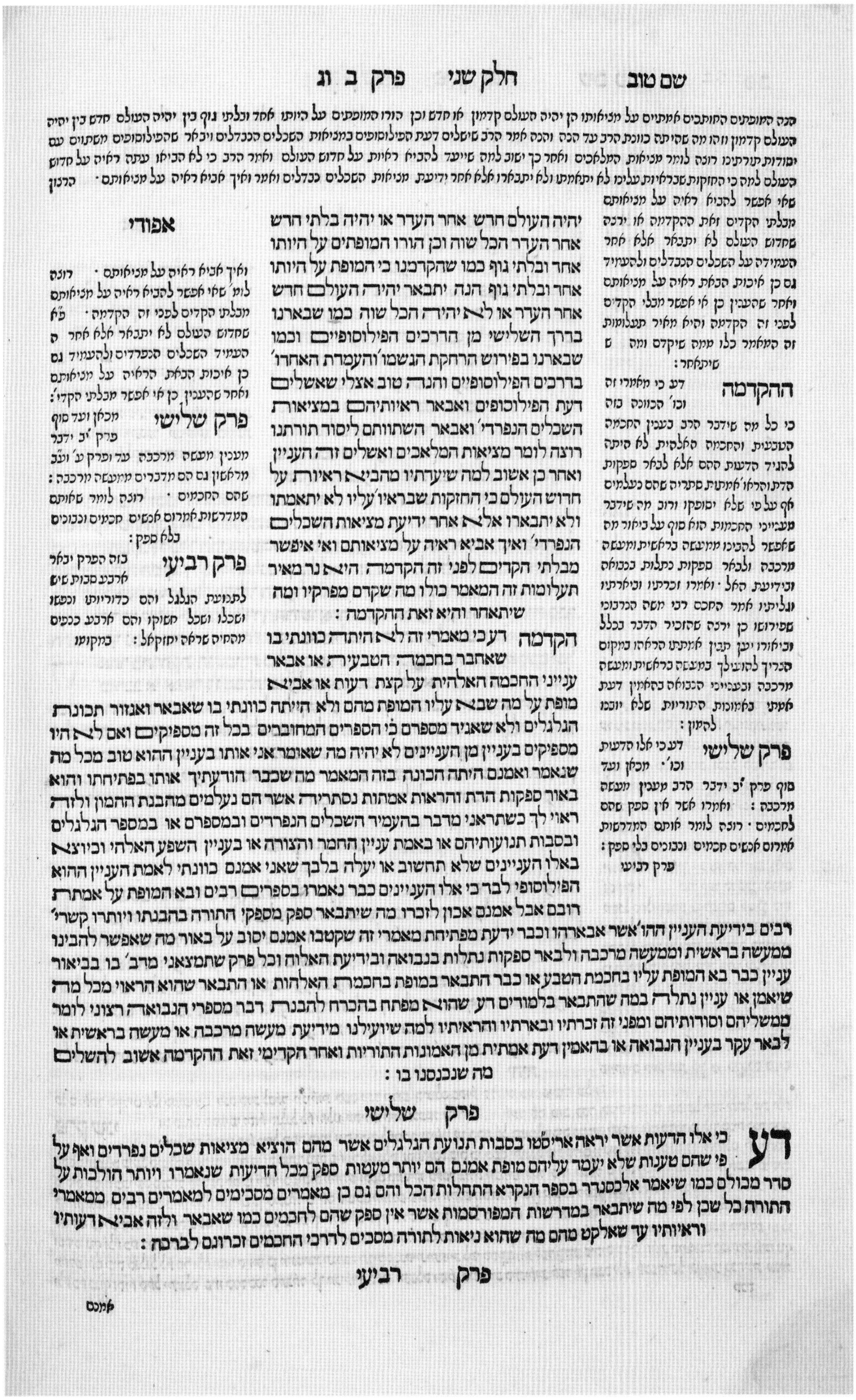

שם טוב　חלק שני　פרק ב וג

יהיה העולם חדש אחר העדר או יהיה בלתי חדש אחר העדר הכל שוה וכן הורו המופתים על היותו אחד ובלתי גוף כמו שהקדמנו כי המופת על היותו אחד ובלתי גוף הנה יתבאר יהיה העולם חדש אחר העדר או לא יהיה הכל שוה כמו שבארנו בדרך השלישי מן הדרכים הפילוסופיים וכמו שבארנו בפירוש הרחקת הגשמות והעמדת האחדו׳ בדרכים הפילוסופיים והנה טוב אצלי שאשלים דעת הפילוסופים ואבאר ראיותיהם במציאות השכלים הנפרדי׳ ואבאר השתוותם ליסוד תורתנו רוצה לומר מציאות המלאכים ואשלים זה העניין ואחר כן אשוב למה שיערתיו מהביא ראיות על חדוש העולם כי החזקות שבראיו׳ עליו לא יתאמתו ולא יתבארו אלא אחר ידיעת מציאות השכלים הנפרדי׳ ואיך אביא ראיה על מציאותם ואי איפשר מבלתי הקדים לפני זה הקדמה היא נר מאיר תעלומות זה המאמר כולו מה שקדם מפרקיו ומה שיתאחר והיא זאת ההקדמה :

הקדמה דע כי מאמרי זה לא היתה כוונתי בו שאחבר בחכמה הטבעית או אבאר עניני החכמה האלהית על קצת דעות או אביא מופת על מה שבא עליו המופת מהם ולא היתה כוונתי בו שאבאר ואגזור תכונת הגלגלים ולא שאגיד מספרם כי הספרים המחוברים בכל זה מספיקים ואם לא היו מספיקים בעניין מן העניינים לא יהיה מה שאומר אני אותו בעניין ההוא טוב מכל מה שנאמר ואמנם היתה הכונה בזה המאמר מה שכבר הודעתיך אותו בפתיחתו והוא באור ספקות הדת והראות אמתות נסתריה אשר הם נעלמים מהבנת ההמון ולזה ראוי לך כשתראני מדבר בהעמיד השכלים הנפרדים ובמספרם או במספר הגלגלים ובסבות תנועותיהם או באמת עניין החמר והצורה או בעניין השפע האלהי וכיוצא באלו העניינים שלא תחשוב או יעלה בלבך שאני אמנם כוונתי לאמת העניין ההוא הפילוסופי לבד כי אלו העניינים כבר נאמרו בספרים רבים ובא המופת על אמתת רובם אבל אמנם אכוון לזכרו מה שיתבאר ספק מספקי התורה בהבנתו ויותרו קשרי׳ רבים בידיעת העניין ההו׳ אשר אבארהו וכבר ידעת מפתיחת מאמרי זה שקטבו אמנם יסוב על באור מה שאפשר להבינו ממעשה בראשית ומעשה מרכבה ולבאר ספקות נתלות בנבואה ובידיעת האלוה וכל פרק שתמצאני מדב׳ בו בביאור עניין כבר בא המופת עליו בחכמת הטבע או כבר התבאר במופת בחכמת האלהות או התבאר שהוא הראוי מכל מה שיאמן או עניין נתלה במה שהתבאר בלמודים דע שהוא מפתח בהכרח להבנת דבר מספרי הנבואה רצוני לומר ממשליהם וסודותיהם ומפני זה זכרתיו ובארתיו והראיתיו למה שיועילנו מידיעת מעשה מרכבה או מעשה בראשית או לבאר עקר בעניין הנבואה או בהאמין דעת אמתית מן האמונות התוריות ואחר הקדימי זאת ההקדמה אשוב להשלים מה שנכנסנו בו :

פרק שלישי

דע כי אלו הדעות אשר יראה אריסטו בסבות תנועת הגלגלים אשר מהם הוציא מציאות שכלים נפרדים ואף על פי שהם טענות שלא יעמד עליהם מופת אמנם הם יותר מעטות ספק מכל הדיעות שנאמרו ויותר הולכות על סדר מבולם כמו שיאמר אלכסנדר בספר הנקרא התחלות הכל והם גם כן מאמרים מסכימים למאמרים רבים ממאמרי התורה כל שכן לפי מה שיתבאר במדרשות המפורסמות אשר אין ספק שהם לחכמים כמו שאבאר ולזה אביא דעותיו וראיותיו עד שאלקט מהם מה שהוא נאות לתורה מסכים לדרכי החכמים זכרונם לברכה :

פרק רביעי

Fig. 28 *Moreh Nevukhim* (Venice: Alvise Bragadini, 1551), RB 9, fols. 82v.

by Christians until it was recognized for its satirical nature and publicly burned. The epistle derided Christian doctrine (the irrationality of salvation through faith alone), Church affairs (the schism between Rome and Avignon), and zealous Jewish converts to Christianity. In contrast, Duran presented a philosophic view of Judaism, whereby salvation is attained through the harmonious melding of faith in the Divine, honest and inquisitive intellect, and performance of the commandments.

Although Duran's commentary to *Moreh Nevukhim* is literal and far-reaching, he may be considered a less extreme rationalist than the author of the companion commentary issued in this imprint. That commentary, by the fifteenth-century Spanish philosopher and preacher Shem Tov ben Joseph Ibn Shem Tov, was known more for its clarity and length than its profundity and originality. It essentially paraphrased the *Guide* and was composed with the intention of serving as an independent treatise. The author's grandfather and namesake, Shem Tov Ibn Shem Tov, had strongly opposed Maimonidean philosophy, claiming that Kabbalah was the true way of the Torah and that philosophy was a corrupting force. The elder Shem Tov's sons, however, rejected Kabbalah and grew to be moderate defenders of Aristotelian and Maimonidean philosophy. Joseph Ibn Shem Tov, who himself authored a commentary to Duran's *Al Tehi ka-Avotekha* (Constantinople, 1554), agreed with his father that philosophy was potentially harmful, but he refused to reject it outright. In *Kevod Elohim* (Ferrara, 1556), he argued that one who understood his faith rationally was superior to one who blindly practiced the religion. Joseph's son Shem Tov, the author of this commentary on the *Guide*, proved to be more fanatic. A staunch rationalist and a zealous supporter of Maimonides, he preached the Maimonidean tenet that only the man of intellect was created in the image of God. He wrote of *Moreh Nevukhim*: 'He who knows this book and observes it in purity is beloved above and cherished below, and he can be assured that he will be a son of the world to come.'[4]

The indexes included in this volume originate from the two Hebrew translators of the *Guide*. Samuel Ibn Tibbon compiled an alphabetical glossary of foreign words that he used in his translation, entitled *Perush ha-Milot ha-Zarot*. He organized the glossary into several classes of words, including Arabic, rare Mishnaic terms, and homonyms with special meanings. Judah ben Solomon al-Ḥarizi, meanwhile, produced a short description of each chapter and an explanation of difficult words, although the latter translation may have had its greatest impact among Christian readers.[5]

The Hartman copy, bound in seventeenth-century tooled leather, includes extensive notations in Italian in the *Perush ha-Milot ha-Zarot* section. It also contains a scrap of paper from a late nineteenth-century liturgical work, possibly a Yom Kippur *Maḥzor*,[6] as well as a stamp in blue ink from R. Yeḥiel Mikhl ha-Levi of Donetsk (Ukraine).[7]

4 והיודע זה הספר ומשמרו בטהר׳ הוא אהוב למעלה ונחמד למטה והוא מובטח שהוא בן העולם הבא (fol. 2r; Shem Tov intro.).

5 On the translations, see Yair Shiffman, 'The Differences Between the Translations of Maimonides' Guide of the Perplexed by Falaquera, Ibn Tibbon and Al-Harizi, and Their Textual and Philosophical Implications,' *Journal of Semitic Studies* 44, no. 1 (1999): 47–61.

6 One side of the folio, probably the recto, includes chapters from the Mishnah (*Masekhet Yadayim* and *Hilkhot Sha'atnez*), followed by instructions to recite the Torah sections of the Binding of Isaac and the Israelites receiving of manna, and the beginning of *Bakashot* (requests) that seem to continue to the other side.

7 יחיאל מיכל הלוי מ[ורה] צ[דק] דאניעצק (title page).

מורה נבוכים
Moreh Nevukhim (Guide of the Perplexed)
Edited by Cornelius Adelkind
Printed by Tobias Foa
Sabbioneta, 1553
2°. RB 10. 2 copies
Steinschneider, 6513,102; Yaari, *Foa*, Sabbioneta no. 4; Habermann, *Adelkind*, no. 113; Vinograd, Sabbioneta no. 8

Just two years after the Bragadini press in Venice issued the second edition of *Moreh Nevukhim*, Tobias Foa, a Hebrew printer in nearby Sabbioneta, published this impressive volume (Fig. 29). Like the previous edition, it includes the indexes of Samuel Ibn Tibbon and Judah ben Solomon al-Ḥarizi, as well as the commentaries of Profiat Duran and Shem Tov ben Joseph Ibn Shem Tov. It was supplemented with the brief commentary of Asher (Bonan) ben Abraham Crescas, linked on the title page to the other commentaries by the biblical verse 'A three-fold cord is not readily broken' (Ecclesiastes 4:12). In the view of the printers, the student of the *Guide*, armed with these three aids to Maimonides, would be equipped to face any intellectual challenge. Such confidence, however, is the way of a printer aiming to sell his product and not necessarily of the philosopher. Although Crescas believed that young students could benefit from his comments, he conceded in his preface that he did not always comprehend the *Guide* and that ultimately the depth of the author's wisdom was beyond the intellectual capacity of even the greatest minds of his generation.

Between 1551 and 1559, Tobias ben Eliezer Foa produced 26 Hebrew books in Sabbioneta, located in northern Italy. The press was regarded highly for issuing beautiful and significant books at a time when the Catholic Church had suppressed Hebrew printing in Venice and elsewhere. Foa hired experts to accomplish the work, including Cornelius Adelkind, editor of this *Moreh Nevukhim*, who had previously served as chief editor of the Bomberg press in Venice. Under Adelkind's direction, the Foa press issued the last Talmud tractate (*Kidushin*)[1] before the Talmud was banned, as well as an exemplary edition of *Hilkhot Rav Alfasi* (Laws of R. Isaac Alfasi), which was temporarily substituted for the Talmud as the primary text of study. Unfortunately, Foa's work in Sabbioneta was cut short when the ecclesiastical authorities deemed certain books he issued anti-Christian. At least two books he had started printing in Sabbioneta were completed elsewhere: a Maḥzor in Cremona in 1560 and a Mishnah in Mantua in 1563. After Foa ceased operations, his type fonts were purchased and used in Venice by Giovanni de Gara.

The intricate border of the title page of this edition of *Moreh Nevukhim* was also used by other printing presses, including in Salonika and Cracow.[2] The text appears within an ornate architectural form consisting of a large floral wreath overflowing with fruits and vegetables. It is guarded by two figures from Greek mythology: on the right, a man in Roman-style battle dress leans on a shield (Ares/Mars), on the left a woman wields a spear

1 It is unknown how many Talmud tractates Foa released. The extant *Kidushin* holds the additional distinction of being the only Talmud tractate ever printed with cantillation signs, for the aid of study and memorization. The actual editor of the volume was Joshua Boaz ben Simon Barukh, editor of the Giustiniani edition of the Talmud and compiler of three influential indexes contained therein. See Marvin J. Heller, *Printing the Talmud: A History of the Individual Treatises Printed From 1700 to 1750* (Leiden: Brill, 1999), 193–200.

2 Heller cites three additional books for which it was used: *Bereshit Rabah* with the commentary *Matenat Kehunah* (1595), *Sefer ha-Terumah* by Samuel ben Isaac Sardi (1596), and the responsa of Joseph Karo (1597).

Fig. 29 *Moreh Nevukhim* (Sabbioneta: Tobias Foa, 1553), RB 10, fol. 1r.

(Athena/Minerva).[3] Between them a wreath encircles the Foa coat of arms: a blossoming tree flanked by lions, the initial letters – *tet* (ט) and *peh* (פ) – of the printer's name, and the biblical verse 'The righteous bloom like a date-palm' (Psalm 92:13). The verse aptly fit the successful Foa family: descendants of Tobias Foa utilized various iterations of this emblem for centuries as they printed Hebrew books in Amsterdam, Venice, and Pisa until at least 1803.

The Hartman Collection includes two copies of this imprint. Copy 1 contains several ownership inscriptions, including that of Isaac Serra (1739–1818), an important lay leader of the Spanish-Portuguese community of London. Copy 2 serves as an example of the *Guide*'s broad impact. It contains extensive marginal notations from the Crimean Karaite Isaac ben Moses Mangubi (fol. 46r).[4] In addition, the book includes the names of Samuel ben Mordecai, who purchased it from a dealer in Constantinople in the spring of 1807 (fol. 174v),[5] and Abraham Barukh, who signed the book in the winter of 1867 and whose notes appear throughout (front paste-down endpaper).

In addition, copy 2 was censored, though without evidence of a censor's signature, and the brown ink used for censorship is comparable to that used in most of the volume's manuscript notations.[6] Some copies of this edition, including the two in the Hartman Collection, contain *Be'ur 'inyan shene kavim* by Rabbi Moses Provençal of Mantua, an illustrated commentary on *Moreh Nevukhim* I:73, which discusses the mathematical Theorem of Apollonius.[7]

3 See Heller, *Printing the Talmud*, 325.

4 See Daniel J. Lasker's essay in this volume.

5 ספר מורה נבוכים של שמואל בכ'ר מרדכי הישיש זצ"ל שקניתיו ממוכר ספרים בקוסדינא לכשריה פרושות שנת התקע"ז ... סיון.

6 For example: fol. 69v (end of part one, ch. 75), censorship of הנצרי' שהשם ג' ונחשוב אנחנו שהוא אחד; fol. 115v (in commentary of Shem Tov), ואתה תבון אל מי שהוא והוא אל השלוחים ואל התלמידי'...והתלמידים כן יהיה ענינם; fol. 118r, the word האל (God) is skipped over in a sentence otherwise censored so as not to desecrate God's name.

7 See Cecil Roth, *The Jews in the Renaissance* (Philadelphia, PA: Jewish Publication Society of America, 1964), 236–37. The folios appear in copy 1 after the title page, and in copy 2, with notes from Mangubi, between fols. 64 and 65. It seems likely that the two unpaginated folios and this *Moreh Nevukhim* were printed concurrently.

18

De Astrologia Rabbi Mosis filii Meimon epistola elegans (Maimonides's Epistle on Astrology)
Translated by Johannes Isaac Levita
Printed by Jakob Soter
Cologne, 1555
16°. RB 32
Steinschneider 6513,118; Vinograd, Cologne no. 4

סדר עולם זוטא ופרקי ר׳ משה בן מיימון על ענייני מלך המשיח
Chronicon Breve, et Capita R. Mose Ben Maïemon de rebus Regis Messie
(Brief Chronology, and Chapters by Maimonides on the Messiah)
Translated by Gilbert Génébrard
Printed by Martin le Jeune
Paris, 1572
8°. RB 37
Steinschneider 5873,13; Vinograd, Paris no. 59

Maimonides's writings reached far beyond the confines of Jewish communities. During his life, he gained repute within his larger Islamic environment, and Muslim scholars continued to extol his intellectual prowess for generations. Within decades of his death, outside his initial sphere of influence, Christian theologians took notice of his oeuvre and disseminated many of his works in Latin translation. Like other medieval scholars, such as Avicenna and Averroes, Maimonides provided a basis from which a religiously diverse readership could grapple with important philosophical questions.

The two present imprints, published in the third quarter of the sixteenth century, indicate the extent to which Christian scholars especially engaged with Maimonides's writings.[1] *De Astrologia Rabbi Mosis filii Meimon* is a Latin translation of Maimonides's *Epistle on Astrology*,[2] sent in 1194 to a circle of rabbis in Provence who had been enamored with his *Epistle to Yemen* (see cat. no. 1) but confused by passages on astrology and the messiah.[3] The missive to Montpellier addressed a variety of topics, but at its core Maimonides, who regarded astrology as a remnant of ancient idolatry, lambasted the foolishness of associating the movements and relative positions of celestial bodies with outcomes in the natural world and with human affairs. 'Any number of men, great in years but not in wisdom,' Maimonides wrote, 'wasted all their days in studying these books and imagined that these follies are science.'[4]

The *Epistle on Astrology* had an immediate impact and sparked a sustained correspondence between Maimonides and Provençal Jewish scholars. Its relevance persisted and even increased during the early modern period, when interest in astronomy featured prominently in the courts of Europe's ruling classes.

De Astrologia, published in Cologne in 1555, comprises Maimonides's original Hebrew text and a Latin translation by Johannes Isaac Levita (1515–1577) (Fig. 30). The bilingual text

1 See Joanna Weinberg's essay in this volume.

2 Alexander Marx, 'The Correspondence between the Rabbis of Southern France and Maimonides about Astrology,' *Hebrew Union College Annual* III (1926): 311–58; Ralph Lerner, 'Maimonides' Letter on Astrology,' *History of Religions* 8:2 (1968): 143–58; Isadore Twersky, *A Maimonides Reader* (Springfield, NJ: Behrman House, 1972), 463–73. See also Y. Tzvi Langermann, 'Maimonides' Repudiation of Astrology,' *Maimonidean Studies* 2 (1991): 123–58.

3 Davidson, *Moses Maimonides*, 494–501; Kraemer, *Maimonides*, 426–35.

4 Quoted in Halbertal, *Maimonides*, 75.

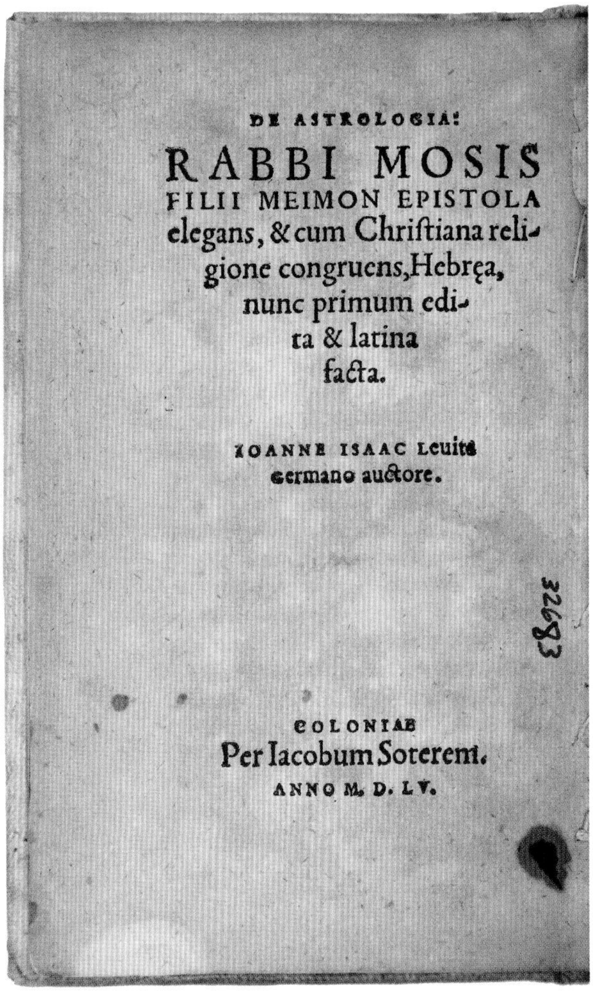

Fig. 30 Johannes Isaac Levita (trans.), *De Astrologia Rabbi Mosis filii Meimon epistola elegans* (Cologne: Jakob Soter, 1555), RB 32, fol. 1r.

appears on facing pages, with the volume reading right to left and including only a single, Latin title page. Levita supplemented Maimonides's words in both languages by embedding citations from Judah ha-Levi's *Sefer ha-Kuzari* (Book of the Khazar), Baḥya Ibn Pakuda's *Ḥovot ha-Levavot* (Duties of the Heart), *Sefer Yetsirah* (Book of Formation), Sa'adiah Gaon (882–942), and Levi ben Gershon (Gersonides or Ralbag; 1288–1344). The typesetters distinguished these texts from that of Maimonides by including them without vowels in the Hebrew and by setting them in italics in the Latin.

Born in 1515, Levita served as rabbi in Wetzlar before being baptized as a Protestant in 1546. He later adopted Catholicism upon assuming a position as professor of Hebrew at the University of Cologne, and produced numerous translations of important texts, many of which were published by Jakob Soter.[5] Despite or perhaps because of his conversion to Christianity, Levita celebrated Maimonides as a scholar, employing the accolade ממשה עד משה לא קם כמשה ('From Moses to Moses, none arose like Moses') in his introduction to *De Astrologia*. That same year, Levita published a translation of *Ru'aḥ Ḥen* (Spirit of Grace), an introduction to philosophy and an explanation of challenging concepts and terms found in Maimonides's *Moreh Nevukhim* (see cat. no. 20). In addition, Levita became embroiled in disputes over the authority and legitimacy of the biblical vowel points (*nekudot*). Protestant theologians and grammarians followed Elijah Levita Ashkenazi (1469–1549), who stated that they had been introduced into the Hebrew Bible at a date later than the closure of the Talmud, but Johannes Isaac Levita argued that the meaning of the *nekudot* in relation to the biblical text suggested a more ancient origin.[6]

5 Levita's most significant publication was the grammar *Absolutissimae in hebraicam linguam institutiones* (Cologne, 1553), republished several times.

6 Stephen G. Burnett, *From Christian Hebraism to Jewish Studies: Johannes Buxtorf (1564–1629) and Hebrew Learning in the Seventeenth Century* (Leiden: Brill, 1996), 206–207.

Fig. 31 Gilbert Génébrard, *Chronicon Breve, et Capita R. Mose Ben Maïemon de rebus Regis Messie* (Paris: Martin le Jeune, 1572), RB 37, fol. 1r.

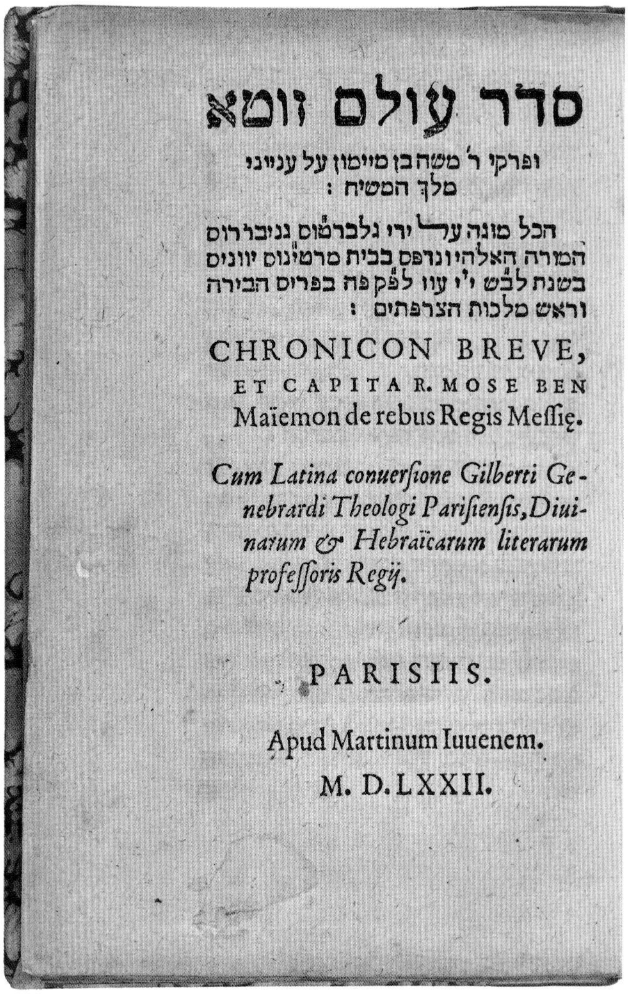

Maimonides's writings on science and philosophy were not his only contributions that Christian scholars deemed worthy of examination. In the seventeenth century, rising antiquarianism led to the study of the *Mishneh Torah*, particularly for what it revealed about ancient practices.[7] Isaac Newton utilized Maimonides in his work on the calendar and in the schematics of the Jerusalem Temple (see Appendix, Fig. 122).[8] Still others sought to appropriate or refute Maimonidean ideas in a bid to prove Christological readings of biblical texts.

Less than two decades after Soter printed Levita's translations of the *Epistle on Astrology* and *Ru'aḥ Ḥen*, Gilbert Génébrard (1537–1597) translated into Latin a short but evocative passage from the *Mishneh Torah*, using it to present a messianic culmination (Fig. 31). Printed by Martin le Jeune, a pioneer of printing Latin books with Hebrew type in Paris, *Chronicon Breve* consists of sections of *Seder 'Olam Zuta* (Abridged Order of the World) and Abraham Ibn Daud's *Sefer ha-Kabalah* (Book of Tradition), as well as the final two chapters of Maimonides's law code (*Sefer Shofetim*, *Hilkhot Melakhim* 11–12) – here entitled *Kabalat Rabi Mosheh* – and a listing of verses intended to support Christian messianic claims.[9] A heading notes that the *Mishneh Torah* text in this imprint was based on that

7 Marcello Cattaneo, 'Between Law and Antiquarianism: The Christian Study of Maimonides' Mishneh Torah in Late Seventeenth-Century Europe,' in *The Mishnaic Moment: Jewish Law Among Jews and Christians in Early Modern Europe*, ed. Piet van Boxel, Kirsten Macfarlane, and Joanna Weinberg (Oxford: Oxford University Press, 2022), 237–54.

8 Matt Goldish, *Judaism in the Theology of Sir Isaac Newton* (Dordrecht: Kluwer Academic, 1998), *passim*.

9 Jacob I. Dienstag, 'Christian Translators of Maimonides' "Mishneh Torah" into Latin: A Bio-Bibliographical Study,' in *Salo Wittmayer Baron Jubilee Volume*, ed. Saul Lieberman and Arthur Hyman, vol. 1 (Jerusalem: American Academy for Jewish Research, 1974): 287–309 (no. 10).

Fig. 32 Gilbert Génébrard, *Chronicon Breve, et Capita R. Mose Ben Maïemon de rebus Regis Messie* (Paris: Martin le Jeune, 1572), RB 37, quire 5, fol. 3r.

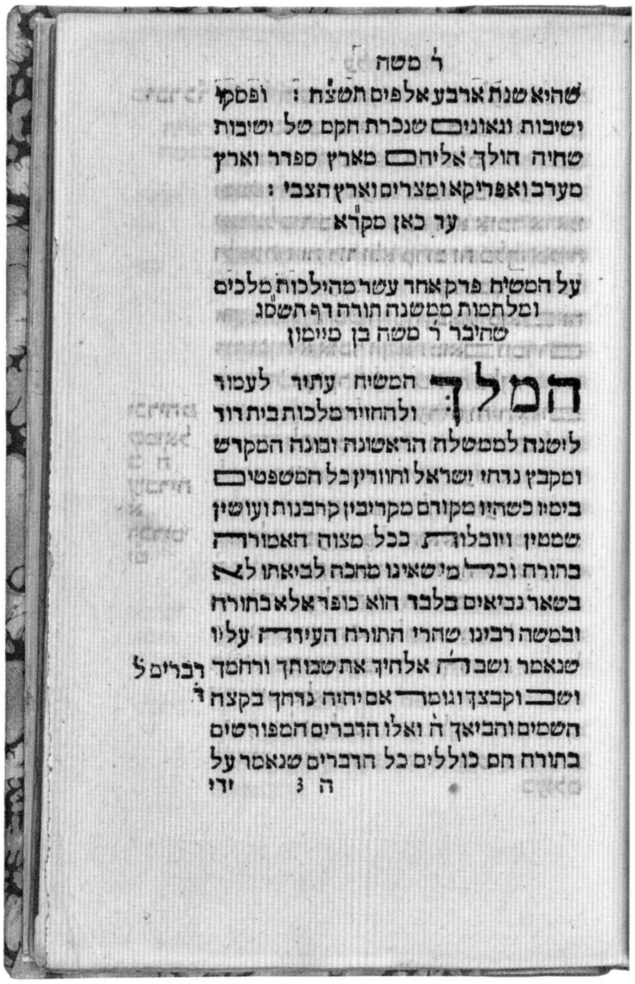
ר׳ משה
שהיא שנת ארבע אלפים תשצ״ח : ופסקו
ישיבות וגאונים שנכרת חקם של ישיבות
שחיה הולך אליהם מארץ ספרד וארץ
מערב ואפריקא ומצרים וארץ הצבי :
עד כאן מקרא

על המשיח פרק אחד עשר מהילכות מלכים
ומלחמות ממשנה תורה דף תשס״ג
שחיבר ר׳ משה בן מיימון

המלך המשיח עתיד לעמוד
ולהחזיר מלכות בית דוד
ליושנה לממשלה הראשונה ובונה המקדש
ומקבץ נדחי ישראל וחוזרין כל המשפטים
בימיו כשהיו מקודם מקריבין קרבנות ועושין
שמטין ויובלות ככל מצוה האמורה
בתורה וכל מי שאינו מחכה לביאתו לא
בשאר נביאים בלבד הוא כופר אלא בתורה
ובמשה רבינו שהרי התורה העידה עליו
שנאמר ושב ה׳ אלהיך את שבותך ורחמך דברים ל
ושב וקבצך וגומר אם יהיה נדחך בקצה
השמים והביאך ה׳ ואלו הדברים המפורשים
בתורה הם כוללים כל הדברים שנאמר על
ה 3 ידי

found on ‘fol. 763’ (דף תשס״ג), which refers to the edition published by Daniel Bomberg in Venice in 1524–1525 (see cat. no. 12). As such, *Chronicon Breve* follows a censored version of Maimonides’s text that replaced explicit references to Jesus with more generalized discussions of a false messiah (Fig. 32).

In contrast to Soter’s publication, Martin le Jeune’s separated the Hebrew and Latin sections into two parts, each preceded by its own title page. Le Jeune produced numerous scholarly texts in the middle of the sixteenth century and worked with Génébrard frequently. Génébrard was a French Catholic theologian and Hebraist who had studied under Abraham de Lunel, a Provençal Jew who converted to Christianity. Génébrard served as professor of Hebrew and Bible at Collège de France and was later appointed archbishop of Aix-en-Provence. He translated several Hebrew texts into Latin, including the Travels of Eldad ha-Dani (Paris, 1562–63), Song of Songs (Paris, 1570), *Seder ‘Olam Rabah* (Paris, 1578), and *Symbolum fidei Judaeorum* (Paris, 1569), based on Maimonides’s *Moreh Nevukhim*.

19

ספר האמונות
Sefer ha-Emunot (Book of Faiths)
Shem Tov Ibn Shem Tov
Printed by Abraham Usque
Ferrara, 1556
4°. RB 18
Steinschneider, 7126; Vinograd, Ferrara no. 37

השגות שהשיג ... משה אל אשקר ז"ל על מה שכתב רבי שם טוב בספר האמונות שלו נגד הרמב"ם
Hasagot she-hesig ... Mosheh Al-Ashkar ... 'al mah she-Katav Rabi Shem-Tov be-Sefer ha-Emunot she-lo Neged ha-Rambam (Moses Alashkar's Critique of Shem Tov's anti-Maimonidean *Sefer ha-Emunot*)
Moses ben Isaac Alashkar
Printed by Abraham Usque
Ferrara, 1556
4°. RB 19
Steinschneider 6424,2; Vinograd, Ferrara no. 46

In *Sefer ha-Emunot*, the Spanish kabbalist Shem Tov Ibn Shem Tov (ca. 1390–ca. 1441) criticized the philosophical works of Abraham Ibn Ezra (1089–1167), Levi ben Gershon (Gersonides or Ralbag; 1288–1344), and especially Maimonides. Although he revered Maimonides for his rabbinic writings, he held the Great Eagle's Aristotelianism responsible for the ease with which masses of Jews in late fourteenth- and early fifteenth-century Spain succumbed to conversionary pressures and apostatized. To Shem Tov, philosophy corrupted with its emphasis on the intellect and its denial of any and all literal readings found in the Bible. Adherence to the Talmud and the spiritualism of Kabbalah was the true way of the Torah. Perhaps because he did not offer an alternate system of thought to Maimonides, other than upholding faith in tradition, Shem Tov failed to inspire many adherents. His sons Joseph and Isaac increasingly identified with Maimonidean philosophy, and his grandson, Shem Tov ben Joseph, composed one of the most oft-studied commentaries on the *Guide* (see cat. no. 16).

To be sure, *Sefer ha-Emunot* gives voice to the dynamic decades of Shem Tov's lifetime. While criticizing philosophical interpretations of the Torah, the book's 11 'gates' describe various kabbalistic concepts, including the *Sefirot* (heavenly spheres) and the transmigration of souls, and detail mystical readings of angels, miracles, paradise, and prophecy. The work was apparently never finished, for at the end of this volume, printed by Abraham Usque, the editor stated: 'No more was found of this gate, nor of this book, for the author, of blessed memory, did not complete it' (fol. 111v). Through it all, one senses Shem Tov's anguish and anger. He lived during the aftermath of the disputation of Tortosa (1413–1414), which had seen Jewish leaders humiliated by Church officials and the willing conversion of thousands of Jews to Christianity. In his introduction to the volume, Shem Tov wrote of ongoing Jewish travails and offered this work as a way to uplift his brethren (Fig. 33).

Interestingly, the volume concludes with two leaves of text from the *Zohar* on *Parashat Va-Yera*, which, according to the printer, had been found with various manuscripts of *Sefer ha-Emunot*. Whether or not Shem Tov himself appended this section, Usque's decision may make these pages the earliest portion of the *Zohar* ever printed. It was not until 1558–1560,

Fig. 33 Shem Tov Ibn Shem Tov, *Sefer ha-Emunot* (Ferrara: Abraham Usque, 1556), RB 18, fol. 1r.

when printers in Cremona and Mantua issued competing editions, that the *Zohar* was first printed in full.[1]

Within a year of printing Shem Tov Ibn Shem Tov's critique of philosophy, Abraham Usque issued a defense of philosophy by Moses ben Isaac Alashkar (1466–1542). In these *Hasagot*, Alashkar vehemently defended the philosophical ideas of Maimonides, Gersonides, and other philosophers (Fig. 34). Shem Tov had condemned Maimonidean Aristotelianism as a corrupting influence and argued for faithfully upholding the traditions as portrayed in Kabbalah. Alashkar himself was familiar with Kabbalah but opposed its widespread diffusion, though his opposition to Kabbalah and support of Maimonides did not equal dogmatic rationalism. Early modern use of *Moreh Nevukhim* was quite different than it had been in the thirteenth century. In fact, the first translation of the *Guide* into a vernacular language, the Italian *Erdizione de' Confusi*, was completed by Amadeo (Jedidiah) Recanati and dedicated to the kabbalist and Talmudist Menaḥem Azariah da Fano (1548–1620).

1 On the reception of the *Zohar*, see Boaz Huss, *The Zohar: Reception and Impact*, trans. Yudith Nave (London: Littman Library of Jewish Civilization, 2016).

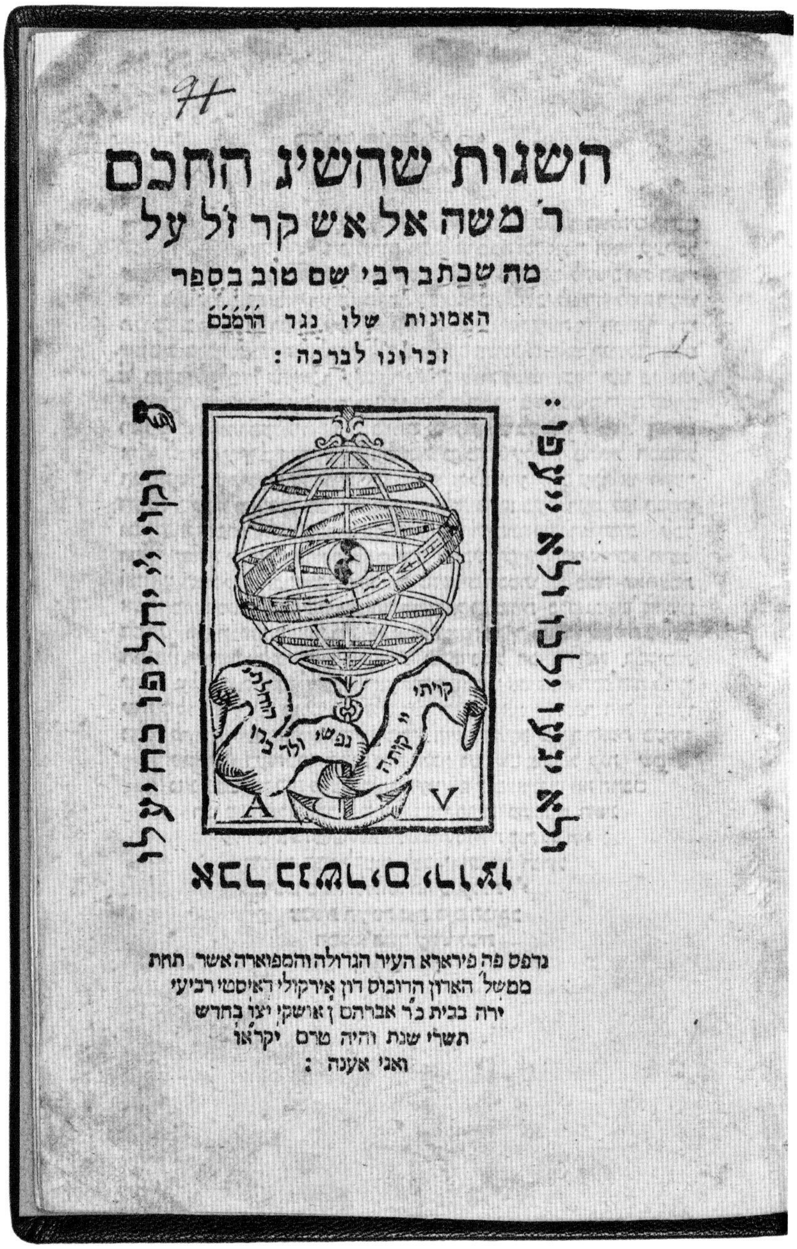
השגות שהשיג החכם
ר׳ משה אל אשקר ז״ל על
מה שכתב רבי שם טוב בספר
האמונות שלו נגד הרמב״ם
זכרונו לברכה :

נדפס פה פירארא העיר הגדולה והמפוארה אשר תחת
ממשל הארוך הדוכוס דון אירקולי ד׳איסטי רביעי
ירה בבית כ״ר אברהם ן׳ אושקי יצו בחדש
תשרי שנת והיה טרם יקראו
ואני אענה :

Fig. 34 Moses ben Isaac Alashkar, *Hasagot ... Mosheh Al-Ashkar* (Ferrara: Abraham Usque, 1556), RB 19, fol. 1r.

Alashkar's *Hasagot* in defense of Maimonides first appeared in print with his responsa, published by Tobias Foa in Sabbioneta in 1554. His *teshuvot* demonstrate that he consulted a wide range of halakhic sources, including the responsa of Maimonides and his son Abraham. During his career, Alashkar was a widely respected Talmudist, and he corresponded with several outstanding rabbis, including Elijah Capsali, Levi Ibn Ḥabib, and Jacob Berab. Born and raised in Spain, Alashkar, like so many Sephardic exiles, lived in several places in the Mediterranean region including Tunisia, Greece, and Egypt. He composed and published several poems, with one, '*Ba-Mah Akadem*,' describing his near-fatal experience on board a ship that foundered while transporting Jewish refugees in 1492.[2]

Born and raised in Portugal to crypto-Jewish parents, Abraham ben Salomon Usque, also known as Duarte Pinel (Pinhel), fled the Inquisition in the 1540s for Ferrara, Italy. There he worked with the Spanish ex-*converso* Yom-Tov ben Levi Athias, also known as

2 Five liturgical poems composed by Alashkar are appended to his printed responsa. Two more appeared in Yehudah Zarki's anthology *Yefeh Nof* (Sabbioneta, 1575), which, incidentally, was the first time that the teachings of Isaac Luria appeared in print. It is primarily through Alashkar's poetry that we know of his kabbalistic leanings.

Jerónimo de Vargas, to produce Jewish texts for former *converso* Jews wishing to practice Judaism openly. The most significant work they published was the so-called Ferrara Bible, the first translation of the entire Bible into Ladino.[3] Various iterations appeared: one listed the printer and publisher as Duarte Pinel and Jerónimo de Vargas, was dedicated to the Duke of Ferrara, and bore the Julian date (March 1, 1553); another presented their Hebrew names, was dedicated to the Jewish philanthropist Doña Gracia Nasi (Beatriz de Luna), and bore a Hebrew date (14 Adar 5313), some ten days following the former and on the holiday of Purim, no less.

That same year, Abraham Usque and Yom-Tov ben Levi Athias published Samuel Usque's *Consolaçam as tribulaçoens de Israel*, a wrenching depiction of Jewish history as a series of calamities up to and including the earth-shattering events of the Iberian expulsions. Samuel was probably a kinsman of Abraham, but the exact relationship has not been clarified. He may have worked with Doña Gracia Nasi in Ferrara to convince *conversos* to return completely to Judaism.[4] Perhaps due to the fury of the Counter-Reformation, Usque and Athias ceased to publish books in Spanish or Portuguese after 1555, and the press closed in 1558.[5]

Usque utilized an interesting printer's device, expressing his Jewish religious spirit and contemporary scientific interest. An astrolabe, used by astronomers in navigation and to predict the location of the celestial bodies, is adorned with a scroll that reads: 'I await the Lord, my soul waits, and in His word do I hope' (Psalm 130:5).[6]

The Hartman copy of Alashkar's *Hasagot* includes the signatures of two of the most active Church censors of the late sixteenth and early seventeenth centuries. Jews in Italy at that time were required to submit their books, at their own expense, to censors for verification that they were not offensive to the Church. Passages deemed insulting were usually concealed with the use of a quill and an ink well. Giovanni Domenico Carretto censored books in Mantua between 1607 and 1628, and his signature appears in countless Hebrew books, including in this volume.[7] Dominico Irosolimitano (ca. 1552–1621 or later), meanwhile, was a Jewish convert to Christianity who literally wrote the book on censorship. Born in Jerusalem and educated in Safed, he studied Jewish texts and the sciences and was active as both a rabbi and a physician. After converting to Christianity in the early 1590s, Irosolimitano joined the Inquisition as a censor of Hebrew books, a not uncommon role filled by converts. To ease the task of censors less proficient in Hebrew language and literature, Irosolimitano published a censorship manual called *Sefer ha-Zikuk*, which detailed objectionable passages to be expurgated in 420 Hebrew books. According to his own accounts, he censored upwards of 20,000 books.[8]

3 David Sandler Berkowitz, *In Remembrance of Creation: Evolution of Art and Scholarship in the Medieval and Renaissance Bible* (Waltham, MA: Brandeis University Press, 1968), no. 194; Stanley Rypins, 'The Ferrara Bible at Press,' *The Library* s5–X (1955): 244–69.

4 Published in English as *Consolation for the Tribulations of Israel*, trans. Martin A. Cohen (Philadelphia, PA: Jewish Publication Society of America, 1965). For biographical information on Samuel Usque, see Maria Teresa Guerrini, 'New Documents on Samuel Usque, the Author of the *Consolaçam as tribulaçoens de Israel*,' *Sefarad* 61:1 (2001): 83–89.

5 Cecil Roth, 'The Marrano Press at Ferrara, 1552–1555,' *Modern Language Review* 38:4 (1943): 307–17.

6 See Yaari, *Hebrew Printers' Marks*, no. 22; and Isaac Yudlov, *Hebrew Printers' Marks: Fifty-four Emblems and Marks of Hebrew Printers, Publishers and Authors* [Hebrew] (Jerusalem: Y. Yudlov, 2001), 25–26.

7 Censorship on fol. 6r; subtitle on fol. 1r was vocalized by hand in light brown ink that might match the pen of censor Carretto, as if he tested his pen before signing his name on the final page.

8 Gila Pribor, '"*Sefer ha-Zikuk" shel Dominico Yerushalmi*,' *Italia* 18 (2008): 7–302.

רוח חן
Ru'aḥ Ḥen (Spirit of Grace)
[Attributed to Judah ben Saul Ibn Tibbon]
Printed by Vincenzo Conti
Cremona, 1565
4°. RB 20
Steinschneider, 4039; Benayahu, *Cremona*, no. 36; Yudlov, *Ginze Israel*, no. 1187; Vinograd, Cremona no. 44

מלות ההגיון
Milot ha-Higayon (Treatise on Logic)
Translated by Moses Ibn Tibbon
Printed by Vincenzo Conti
Cremona, 1566
4°. RB 33
Steinschneider 6513,92; Benayahu, *Cremona*, no. 35; Vinograd, Cremona no. 43

These two books of philosophy were issued by the same press within a few months of each other in 1565 and 1566. The latter, Maimonides's *Milot ha-Higayon*, served as a fundamental source for understanding philosophical concepts and appeared with two early commentaries whose authors are unknown (see cat. no. 3). The former, *Ru'aḥ Ḥen* (Spirit of Grace),[1] was composed as an introduction to philosophy and an exposition of difficult concepts and terms found in *Moreh Nevukhim*.[2] With the 'spirit of grace of the esteemed *Guide of the Perplexed* wafting over' him (fol. 1v), the author found himself compelled to explore and reveal what he could of its opacity. The work expresses an ethical lifestyle attained through intellectual enlightenment. In so doing, traditional Jewish virtues like honoring one's parents, giving charity, and returning a lost object are contrasted with vices such as murder, theft, and vengeance. By conducting oneself through use of the 'practical intellect' – termed *ḥokhmah* (wisdom) and *da'at* (knowledge) – the intelligent, God-fearing Jew might reach the ultimate 'active intellect' (*intellectus agens*) and knowledge of the inner workings of the universe.

Ru'aḥ Ḥen has been most often attributed to Judah ben Saul Ibn Tibbon (ca. 1120–ca. 1190), known as the 'father of the translators.' Born in Granada, Ibn Tibbon left Spain for southern France, where he served as a physician and was active in the vibrant scholarship then emanating from Provence. He translated several treatises from Arabic to Hebrew, including Baḥya Ibn Pakuda's *Ḥovot ha-Levavot* (Duties of the Heart), Judah ha-Levi's *Sefer ha-Kuzari* (Book of the Khazar), and Sa'adiah Gaon's *Sefer ha-Emunot ve-ha-De'ot* (Book of Beliefs and Opinions). His work, and the work of his descendants, including Samuel Ibn Tibbon, translator of the *Guide of the Perplexed*, enabled the brilliance of Arabic-speaking Jewry to reach Jewish communities dwelling in Christendom. Judah's only surviving original composition is an ethical testament to his son. Famously, he stressed the importance of books:

> My son! Make thy books thy companions, let thy cases and shelves be thy pleasure-grounds and gardens. Bask in their paradise, gather their fruit, pluck their roses, take their spices and their myrrh. If thy soul be satiate and weary, change from garden to garden, from furrow to furrow

1 Zechariah 12:10.

2 See Ofer Elior, *A Spirit of Grace Passed Before My Face: Jews, Science and Reading, 1210–1896* [Hebrew] (Jerusalem: Mekhon Ben-Tsevi, 2016).

Fig. 35 [Judah Ibn Tibbon], *Ru'aḥ Ḥen* (Cremona: Vincenzo Conti, 1566), RB 20, fol. 1r.

> from prospect to prospect. Then will thy desire renew itself, and thy soul be filled with delight![3]

Authorship of *Ru'aḥ Ḥen* has also been attributed to another member of the Ibn Tibbon family, Jacob ben Abba Mari ben Samson Anatoli (ca. 1194–1258). A son-in-law of Samuel Ibn Tibbon, Anatoli was a scholar, translator, and outspoken supporter of Maimonides. Originally from Provence, he made his way to Naples to serve as physician to the emperor and devote himself to scholarship. He primarily translated scientific works from Arabic into Hebrew, including Ptolemy's *Almagest* and Averroes's works on Aristotle's Logic. His collection of homilies, *Malmad ha-Talmidim*, which was organized according to the weekly Torah portion, praised Maimonides enthusiastically and was widely read during the thirteenth century. It earned condemnation when Solomon ben Abraham Adret (Rashba; 1235–1310) issued his ban against the study of philosophy in 1305 (see cat. no. 1).

By the time Tobias Foa issued the *Guide* in 1553, approximately eight decades after the inception of Hebrew printing, three editions of *Moreh Nevukhim* had appeared in print. It would not appear again for almost two centuries. However, between 1544 and 1565, when Vincenzo Conti released these imprints in Cremona, *Ru'aḥ Ḥen* was printed four times. The popularity it enjoyed may have stemmed from the fact that, as an introduction to and exposition of Maimonidean philosophy, it was easier for readers to comprehend than the *Guide* itself. The first and second editions of the book appeared in Venice in 1544 and 1549, respectively.[4] The third edition appeared in Cologne in 1555; issued by Jacob Soter, the same year he published *De Astrologia Rabbi Mosis filii Meimon*, the Hebrew text was accompanied by the Latin translation of the Jewish apostate Johannes Isaac Levita (see cat. no. 18).

3 Israel Abrahams, *Hebrew Ethical Wills* (Philadelphia, PA: Jewish Publication Society of America, 1926), 63.

4 Francesco Brucioli printed the first edition. He succeeded in printing only one other Hebrew book in his career, also in 1544.

מלות ההגיון
שחבר הרמב״ם ז״ל עם שני פירושים
קרימונה

Fig. 36 Moses Ibn Tibbon, *Milot ha-Higayon* (Cremona, 1566), RB 33, fol. 1r.

Vincenzo Conti printed these volumes in Cremona at the end of 1565 and beginning of 1566.[5] He followed in the footsteps of other Christian businessmen, such as Daniel Bomberg, Marco Giustiniani, and Alvise Bragadini. Between 1556 and 1567, Conti published more than 40 books, often decorating his title pages with beautiful woodcut borders. He used this particular frame, which depicts winged putti amid a colonnaded structure, in at least three other books, and an additional two woodcuts to adorn several other title pages – a common practice in the Hebrew book trade since the incunabula period (Fig. 35).[6] Among his most important imprints was the *Zohar* (1559–1560); a competing edition was issued almost simultaneously in Mantua. Conti printed during one of the most difficult periods in the history of Italian Jewry, and certainly of Hebrew printing. A papal bull issued in 1553 ordered the confiscation and burning of the Talmud, and Cremona itself was the site of a conflagration of many thousands of Hebrew books in 1559. Conti generally printed books that had been sanctioned by the Inquisition, but it appears that he ceased operations in 1567 due to obstacles placed before Hebrew print houses by Church authorities.

Two ownership signatures appear on the title page of *Milot ha-Higayon*: one belonged to an Abraham Ephraim Shapira; the other to Jedidiah Tiah Weil (1722–1806), chief rabbi of Karlsruhe in the latter decades of the eighteenth century (Fig. 36). Weil succeeded his father Nathaniel Weil, author of *Korban Netanel*, a commentary on Jacob ben Asher's *Arba'ah Turim*. Prior to assuming rabbinic positions, the younger Weil studied under the great Talmudist, halakhist, and accused Sabbatian Jonathan Eybeschütz (1690–1764). A handwritten index appears at the end, though without attribution and seemingly without matching either of the signatures preserved on the title page.

5 Following the text of *Ru'aḥ Ḥen*, Conti included a paragraph by Abraham Pescarol, a fellow printer in Cremona, describing the difficulties of the printing trade and detailing the corrigenda (errors) in the text. See cat. no. 14 for a book in the Hartman Collection once owned by Pescarol.

6 See Solomon Ibn Adret, *Ve-Zot Torat ha-Bayit* (Cremona, 1565), and Eliezer ben Elijah Ashkenazi, *Yosef Lekaḥ* (Cremona, 1576). For a responsum about decorating Hebrew books with images of putti, see Samuel Aboab, *Sefer Devar Shemu'el She'elot u-Teshuvot* (Venice, 1702), no. 247.

תורת העולה
Torat ha-'Olah (Law of the Burnt Offering)
Moses ben Israel Isserles (Rema)
Printed by Mordecai ben Gershom Katz (Kohen)
Prague, 1569
2°. RB 21
Steinschneider, 6483,22; Vinograd, Prague no. 36

The author of *Torat ha-'Olah*, Moses Isserles (Rema; d. 1572), was considered by his contemporaries to be the 'Maimonides of Polish Jewry.' A scholar of rabbinic literature, philosophy, science, and Kabbalah, Isserles was a prolific writer and a man of humility and decisiveness. He served as chief rabbi of Cracow, founded a yeshiva there, and trained a generation of pioneering Ashkenazic scholars. He produced several profound works, including the monumental halakhic compendium *Darkhe Mosheh* and the more condensed *Mapah* (Tablecloth), which served as glosses to Joseph Karo's *Shulḥan 'Arukh* (Set Table). In detailing and codifying customs from areas in Europe otherwise excluded from Karo's work, Isserles effectively formed an Ashkenazic Jewry out of countless halakhically independent communities in central and eastern Europe.[1]

Besides producing some of the most influential halakhic works in early modern Jewish history, Isserles also developed a unique and influential philosophy.[2] Most significantly, he identified Maimonidean Aristotelianism and Kabbalah as one and the same. Both, he argued, expressed the inner meaning of the Torah; ostensible differences were in fact only differences of language and nomenclature. *Torat ha-'Olah* serves as Isserles's philosophical conception of Judaism (Fig. 37). Based on *Moreh Nevukhim* and the *Bet ha-Beḥirah* (The Chosen Temple) section of the *Mishneh Torah*, the treatise explores and expounds upon the Temple and its services. The book is divided into three parts: the first, entitled 'Mountain,' deals with the form of the Temple, the altar and other Temple furnishings and utensils, and the Temple Mount; the second, entitled 'Field,' explains the sacrifices in general, the incense and libation offerings, and the priestly duties; and the third and final section, the 'House,' details the purpose of sacrifices more specifically. Isserles explained that the entire Temple apparatus, including the form, dimensions, and number of each component part, corresponded to the divinely ordained world. The women's courtyard and its four chambers, for instance, corresponded to the active intellect and the four kingdoms (mineral, vegetable, animal, and rational).[3]

Throughout the work, Maimonides's influence is clear. The active intellect was a primary feature of Aristotelian and medieval philosophy and featured prominently in *Moreh Nevukhim*. Additionally, Isserles agreed with Maimonides that angels were not concrete material bodies but rather 'messengers,' powers of God, between the First Cause and the thing caused or created.[4] Nevertheless, Isserles did not unreservedly follow all Maimonidean teachings. For instance, he followed Joseph Albo's *Sefer ha-'Ikarim* in fixing the number of articles of faith at three, in contrast to Maimonides's 13.

1 The first edition of the *Shulhan 'Arukh* appeared in Venice in 1564–1565; the *Mapah* first appeared already in the second edition, printed in Cracow in 1569–1571. See Joseph Davis, 'The Reception of the *Shulhan 'Arukh* and the Formation of Ashkenazic Jewish Identity,' *AJS Review* 26:2 (2002): 251–76.

2 See Jonah Ben-Sasson, *The Philosophical System of R. Moses Isserles* [Hebrew] (Jerusalem: Israel Academy of Sciences and Humanities, 1984).

3 *Torat ha-'Olah*, vol. 1, chs. 4, 6, 8.

4 *Torat ha-'Olah*, vol. 2, ch. 24; vol. 3, ch. 17. See *Moreh Nevukhim* II:6.

Fig. 37 Moses Isserles, *Torat ha-'Olah* (Prague: Mordecai ben Gershom Katz, 1570), RB 21, fol. 1r.

Fig. 38 Moses Isserles's gravestone (Kraków). Includes the statement 'From Moses to Moses, none arose like Moses.' Photo © Paweł Mazur.

Isserles composed several other works of philosophy and Kabbalah, including *Meḥir Yayin* (Price of Wine) (Cremona, 1559), a commentary to the book of Esther that treats it as an allegory for human life; *To'afot Re'em* (Horns of a Wild Ox), which includes glosses to *Moreh Nevukhim* and the commentaries of Shem Tov ben Joseph Ibn Shem Tov and Profiat Duran; and commentaries on the *Zohar* and the *agadot* of the Talmud.[5] In addition, this copy of *Torat ha-'Olah* includes Isserles's commentary on the daily prayer *Barukh she-Amar* (fols. 172r–172v). For his philosophical reflection, Isserles faced vehement opposition from his elder cousin, the great Talmudist and halakhic decisor Solomon Luria (Maharshal; 1510–1574), but he was so deeply revered that his tombstone bears the inscription 'From Moses to Moses, none arose like Moses' (Fig. 38).

The 1569 edition of *Torat ha-'Olah* was printed by Mordecai Katz, a member of a printing family that established Prague as one of the centers of Hebrew printing in the sixteenth century. His father, Gershom, began printing in Prague in 1515, just three years after the publication of the first, and at that time only, Hebrew book to have been produced north of the Alps. Over the next decade, Gershom published several more books, and in 1526, with his brother Gronim (Jerome), he issued an illustrated Passover Haggadah that established

5 See Pinchas Giller, *Reading the Zohar: The Sacred Text of the Kabbalah* (Oxford: Oxford University Press, 2001), 27–28.

the press as one of the most outstanding in Europe. The following year, Gershom obtained a printing privilege from King Ferdinand I of Bohemia, which upon his death in 1545 was similarly granted to his son Moses and in 1598 to his great-grandson Gershom ben Bezalel. In the two decades following the publication of this edition of *Torat ha-'Olah*, Mordecai ben Gershom Katz issued nearly twenty Hebrew books. But he did not rest on the success of his father, choosing instead to embrace innovations in book publishing. For instance, in this volume, Mordecai provided citations in the margins,[6] an indispensable apparatus made famous by Giustiniani's Babylonian Talmud (Venice, 1546–1551).

Mordecai's printer's mark, depicted on the elaborate title page, consisted of a pair of hands presented in the manner of the priestly benediction, an allusion to the printer's priestly lineage.[7] His edition of *Torat ha-'Olah* includes other striking woodcuts: a portrait with beard and cap, flanked on each side by an angel in contemporary central European dress, appears at the bottom of the title page;[8] depictions of the Temple, similar but not identical to those used by the Giustiniani press,[9] appear at the conclusion of the first two parts of the volume (fols. 33v and 69r); and putti blowing horns surround the words *Perek Rishon* at the commencement of parts 2 and 3 (fols. 34v and 70r).

6 A superscript circle appears by the Rema's citation, while the book and chapter source are provided in the margin.

7 See Yaari, *Hebrew Printers' Marks*, nos. 37–38, 40.

8 This same border was used by Moses ben Bezalel Katz in his *Maḥzor mi-Kol ha-Shanah ... ke-Minhag Pehm Polin ve-Germanya* (Prague, 1606). For a suggestion that the portrait depicted Isserles himself, see Ilia Rodov, *The Torah Ark in Renaissance Poland: A Jewish Revival of Classical Antiquity* (Leiden: Brill, 2013), 87.

9 The banner at the top of the Temple in both Mordecai's and Giustiniani's works is emblazoned with the same biblical verse: גדול יהיה כבוד הבית הזה אמר יי' צבאות (Haggai 2:9).

משנה תורה
Mishneh Torah (Repetition of the Law)
Printed by Meir Parenzo for Alvise Bragadini
Venice, 1574–1575
2°. RB 7. 4 vols.; 3 copies
Steinschneider, 6513,7; Habermann, *Parenzo*, no. 16; Vinograd, Venice no. 600

This edition of the *Mishneh Torah* was the first to include Joseph Karo's important commentary, *Kesef Mishneh*.[1] Karo composed the work to complete and complement the *Magid Mishneh* of Vidal Yom Tov of Tolosa, which had originally covered the *Mishneh Torah* in its entirety but which, by Karo's time, was extant for only six of the 14 books. Karo's comments on the remaining eight books, and his additions to the extant six sections of Vidal's work, became indispensable for their elucidation of sources and alternate opinions, which Maimonides had notably omitted. In the course of his commentary, Karo noted textual difficulties that marred the early modern printings of the *Mishneh Torah*. Many of the passages with these difficulties were emended in the first edition to carry his commentary.

This carefully edited text was printed under the supervision of Meir ben Jacob Parenzo. Parenzo probably learned the printing trade at the press of Daniel Bomberg, where he worked with Cornelius Adelkind in 1545. He published five works on his own between 1546 and 1548, and he labored for some time as a typesetter and corrector at the press of Carlo Querini, for whom he published a Mishnah with the commentary of Obadiah Bertinoro in 1548. From about 1550, however, Parenzo worked at the press of Alvise Bragadini. He edited the first three volumes of this 1574–1575 edition of the *Mishneh Torah* until his death in 1575. The fourth volume was edited by Meir Parenzo's brother, Asher, who also worked for the Venetian printer Giovanni de Gara.

This edition includes *Hasagot ha-Rabad*, *Magid Mishneh*, and the commentary of Levi Ibn Ḥabib on *Hilkhot Kidush ha-Ḥodesh* (Laws of the New Moon), replete with illustrations. In addition, the printers included the index by Samuel Attia (first printed in the Constantinople edition) and the *alef-bet* index of the school of Barukh Uziel Ḥazak. Meir Parenzo's printer's mark – Venus standing over and pointing an arrow at a hydra – appears on the verso of the title pages of each of the volumes (Fig. 39), while his brother Asher's device of a mountain rising from the sea appears in the final volume. Bragadini's famed three crowns appear on the title pages of all four volumes.[2]

Some volumes of the Hartman copies are notable for having been issued on blue paper (all of copy 2; copy 3, vol. 4).[3] Printers often produced an extremely limited number of

1 The year of this imprint is sometimes mistakenly stated as 1576, but the colophon of vol. 4 records that work was completed on 29 Ḥeshvan [5]366 (= November 2, 1575); the first two volumes were completed in 1574.

2 See Yaari, *Hebrew Printers' Marks*, nos. 14, 18, 35, 36; and Ruthie Kalman, 'What is Venus Doing in the 1574–1576 Hebrew Edition of Maimonides's *Mishneh Torah*?' [Hebrew], *Pe'amim* 120 (2009): 61–91. The motif of Venus rising from the waters appeared in the printer's mark of Alessandro Gardoni (Venice, 1577–1578).

3 For a study on Hebrew books printed on colored paper, see Brad Sabin Hill, 'Hebrew Printing on Blue and Other Coloured Papers,' in *Treasures of the Valmadonna Trust Library: A Catalogue of 6th-Century Books and Five Centuries of Deluxe Hebrew Printing*, ed. David Sclar (London and New York: Valmadonna Trust Library, 2011), 84–111. For another complete copy of this edition on blue paper, which was then the only one known, see Brad Sabin Hill, *Hebraica (saec. X AD saec. XVI): Manuscripts and Early Printed Books from the Library of the Valmadonna Trust: An Exhibition at the Pierpont Morgan Library, New York* ([London]: Valmadonna Trust Library, 1989), no. 43.

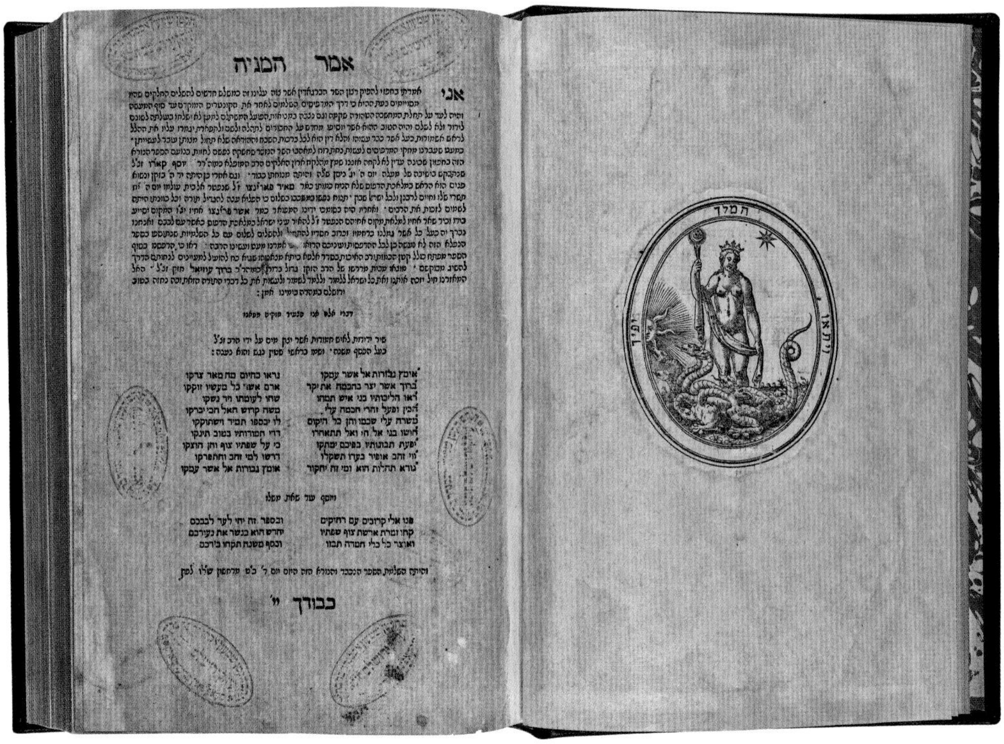

Fig. 39 *Mishneh Torah* (Venice: Alvise Bragadini, 1574–1575), RB 7, copy 3, vol. 4. Meir Parenzo's printer's mark.

special deluxe copies on colored paper, silk, linen, or vellum – the latter was most frequently used as the support in these deluxe copies, generally for a major or expensive work. Deluxe copies were presented to nobility or patrons or sold at a premium to collectors. Such sales could potentially finance an entire print run.

When producing deluxe copies, printers of Hebrew books used blue paper far more than any other colored paper and almost as much as vellum. While blue paper cost considerably less than vellum to manufacture, this may have reflected a fascination with the color blue in Jewish religious tradition.[4] Following frequent productions from the sixteenth-century Italian print houses, deluxe blue-paper Hebrew books continued to be issued by presses in the new printing centers of Holland and central Europe in the mid-seventeenth and early eighteenth centuries. Amsterdam printers, such as David de Castro Tartas, Solomon Proops, Isaac ben Solomon Raphael Judah Leon Templo, and Moses Frankfurt, produced biblical and liturgical works (as opposed to rabbinic texts) on deep blue paper, reflecting the tastes and interests of their clientele. David Oppenheim (1664–1736), chief rabbi of Prague and Bohemia and owner of the largest and most comprehensive collection of Hebrew books and manuscripts until the twentieth century, regularly ordered special copies printed on blue paper.[5] In 1721, Samson Wertheimer, a Viennese court Jew and a relative of Oppenheim, sponsored the famous Amsterdam Talmud (1715–1721), of which blue-paper copies were printed.[6]

The Hartman Collection contains one blue-paper volume (copy 3, vol. 4) that belonged to R. Samuel Salant (1816–1909), a renowned scholar from Lithuania who served as the Ashkenazic chief rabbi of Jerusalem for seven decades (Figs. 39, 40). Beyond his intellectual

4 See *Menaḥot* 43b, which states 'the *tekhelet* (blue dye on *tsitsit*) is like the sea, the sea is like the firmament, and the firmament is like the Heavenly Throne.'

5 Joshua Teplitsky, *Prince of the Press: How One Collector Built History's Most Enduring and Remarkable Jewish Library* (New Haven, CT: Yale University Press, 2019), 142–43.

6 Hill, 'Hebrew Printing on Blue and Other Coloured Papers,' 86. The Library of the Jewish Theological Seminary houses a blue-paper copy of *Shitah Mekubetset, Bava Metsi'a* (Amsterdam, 1721), once owned by Wertheimer (BM506.B33 A82 1721 c.2).

Fig. 40 *Mishneh Torah* (Venice: Alvise Bragadini, 1574–1575), RB 7, copy 3, vol. 4. Signature of R. Samuel Salant.

output, he encouraged Jewish settlement outside the Old City walls and helped establish communal institutions as the community grew by the tens of thousands.[7]

The other Hartman copies of the 1574–1575 *Mishneh Torah* likewise indicate exceptional provenance. Each changed hands repeatedly and includes signatures, stamps, and occasional dates of acquisition. The volumes of copy 1 contain the names of Isaac Tsarfati (vol. 4, title page), Raḥamim Aripol (vol. 4, title page),[8] Moshe Kalesher (vol. 1, flyleaf),[9] and Aryeh Leib (vol. 1, flyleaf), and stamps from M. E. Zuckermann, Posen (vols. 1 and 3, title page), *Yeshivat Torat Ḥayim*, Jerusalem (vol. 4, endpaper), and *Yeshivat Moshav Zekenim ben Pinḥas* (vol. 4, title page). Meanwhile, copy 2 passed through the hands of Aurelia bat Moses me-Rovigo,[10] David Volterra (probably of Rome), and the twentieth-century philanthropist Ivan Salomon.[11]

In addition, censorship appears throughout all four volumes of copy 2, especially sections on *ʿakum* (vol. 1) and the messianic era (vol. 4). Censors included Dominico Irosolimitano, Alessandro Scipione, Giovanni Domenico Vistorini, and Giovanni Antonio Costanzi (vol. 4, fol. 219r). Vistorini, whose signature appears in another book in the Hartman Collection (see cat. no. 24), checked and signed the famous Sarajevo Haggadah, and Constanzi renewed the confiscation and repression of Hebrew literature on the Italian peninsula in the 1730s.

7 For ownership markings, see fols. vii, 1r, 14r, 59r, 111r, 136v, 147, 161r, 248v, 297r.

8 אני הצעיר רחמים אריפול.

9 שייך ... משה קאלעשער ... י"א לחודש מרחשבן תרס"ו .... The inscription indicates that he acquired the book(s) on 11 Marḥeshvan [5]666 (= November 9, 1905).

10 זה קנית כספי ארילה בת כבר (=כבוד רבי) ומרים ראשי רכב ישראל אדוני אבי ה"ה כמה"ר משה מיראויגה (front flyleaf of each volume). See Psalm 3:4; *Bayit Ḥadash, Yoreh Deʿah* 242. Thanks to David Wachtel for help with the inscription.

11 In 1956, Salomon encouraged the surviving Orthodox rabbis of Europe to form a Conference of European Rabbis (CER), which has served as European Jewry's prime umbrella organization. In appreciation, the CER honored him by bestowing upon him the rabbinical title of *Ḥaver*; for the invitation to the ceremony, see American Sephardi Federation at the Center for Jewish History, ASF AR-8, *Papers of Abraham and Irma Lopes Cardozo*, Box 7, folder 43.

23

מגילת אסתר
Megilat Ester (Book of Esther)
Isaac Leon Ibn Tsur
Printed by Giovanni de Gara
Venice, 1592
4°. RB 34
Steinschneider, 5441,1; Habermann, *De Gara*, no. 136; Vinograd, Venice no. 770

ספר המצות
Sefer ha-Mitsvot (Book of Commandments), with Commentary of *Megilat Ester* (Book of Esther) by Isaac Leon Ibn Tsur
Printed by Aaron ben Moses Rofe
Berlin, 1733
2°. RB 35
Vinograd, Berlin no. 127

As a precursor to the *Mishneh Torah*, Maimonides composed *Sefer ha-Mitsvot*, enumerating and describing the rabbinic reckoning of 613 commandments found in the Torah (see cat. no. 9).[1] Several lists preceded that of Maimonides, including the *Halakhot Gedolot*, most often attributed to Simeon Kayara, and Sa'adiah Gaon's *Sefer ha-Mitsvot*. Maimonides's contribution had an even greater impact, with subsequent scholars being compelled to address his perspective and methodology. The Sephardic rabbi, kabbalist, and communal leader Moses ben Naḥman (Naḥmanides or Ramban; 1194–ca. 1270) disagreed with his predecessor, making the task of expositors of the laws all the more challenging.

Apart from the *editio princeps*, published in Constantinople as early as 1510, Maimonides's *Sefer ha-Mitsvot* was issued through the sixteenth century as a supplement to large volumes of the *Mishneh Torah*. These two books, issued in Venice in 1592 and in Berlin in 1733, respectively, speak to specific scholarly engagement with Maimonides's enumeration of the commandments. The earlier publication, issued by Giovanni de Gara, featured the commentary *Megilat Ester* by Isaac Leon ben Eliezer Ibn Tsur, which sought to support Maimonides in response to challenges posed by Naḥmanides (Fig. 41).[2] Though the quarto volume does not include an actual list of mitzvoth, it does consist of Maimonides's 14 principles (*shorashim*) that introduced his account, as well as Naḥmanides's response and Ibn Tsur's rejoinder. The introduction includes a section concerning Naḥmanides's comments on Maimonides's *Sefer ha-Mitsvot* that did not appear in subsequent editions, as noted in the margins by a previous owner. By commencing the title page with the words *Sefer zeh ḥadash hu*, the printer clearly indicated that the publication was new, a first edition.[3] The Venetian edition was funded by Simon Copio, father of the poet and salonierre Sarra Copio Sulam, in memory of his father Abraham Copio.[4]

Nearly a century and a half later, Aaron ben Moses Rofe issued an edition of Maimonides's *Sefer ha-Mitsvot* supplemented by Ibn Tsur's *Megilat Ester* (Fig. 42). The imprint included

1 *Makot* 23b.

2 Jacob I. Dienstag, *En Ha-Mizwot: Bio-Bibliographical Lexicon of the Scholarship Pertaining to the Sefer Ha-Mizwot of Moses Maimonides* [Hebrew] (New York: Yeshiva University, 1968), no. 34.

3 The editors appended texts discussing an 'androgenous' (intersex) individual and the so-called 'seven wisdoms' to the end of the imprint.

4 See Lynn Lara Westwater, *Sarra Copia Sulam: A Jewish Salonnière and the Press in Counter-Reformation Venice* (Toronto: University of Toronto Press, 2020); this includes Simon's last will and testament and an inventory of the contents of his house at the time of his death.

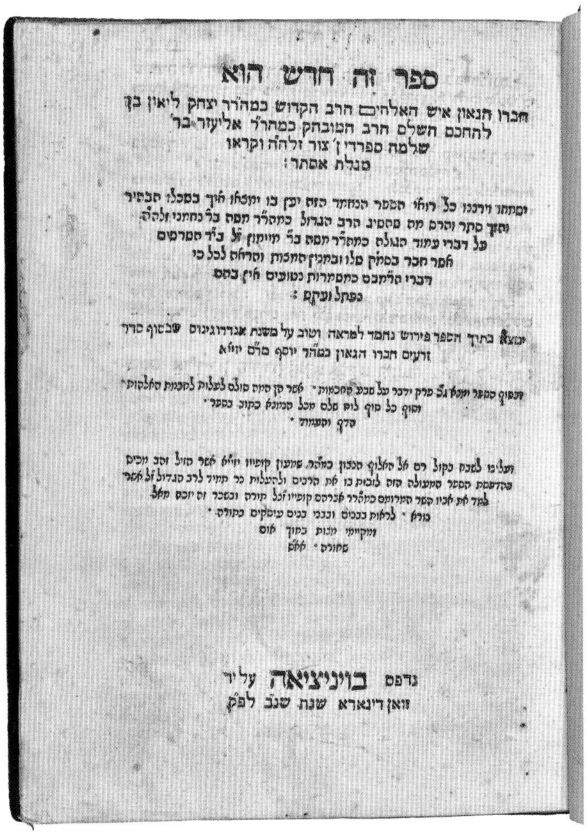

ספר זה חדש הוא

נדפס בוויניציאה על יד

זואן דינארא שנת שנב לפ"ק

ספר המצות

שחבר הנשר הגדול רבינו משה בן

מיימון ז"ל

נדפס פה קק ברלין

תחת ממשלת אדונינו המלך האדיר פרידריך ווילהעלם

Fig. 41 (left) Isaac Leon Ibn Tsur, *Megilat Ester* (Venice, 1592), RB 34, fol. 1r.

Fig. 42 (right) Isaac Leon Ibn Tsur, *Sefer ha-Mitsvot* with *Megilat Ester* (Berlin: Aaron ben Moses Rofe, 1733), RB 35, fol. 1r. Stamp of R. Samson Raphael Hirsch.

the introductions of Maimonides, Naḥmanides, and Ibn Tsur, and detailed each commandment with accompanying responses, frequently flanking the main text as if it were a page of Talmud. Incidentally, the Berlin edition mistakenly attributed the authorship of *Megilat Ester* to Isaac de Leon, the fifteenth-century Sephardic rabbi, despite the fact that the author's introduction presents his name as Isaac Leon.

Both books in the Hartman Collection have special provenance. The Venice imprint stayed on the Italian peninsula for centuries before making its way to the Valmadonna Trust Library, one of the most impressive private Judaica collections assembled during the second half of the twentieth century. The Berlin imprint stayed in Germany and bears the stamp of Rabbi Samson Raphael Hirsch, one of the premier architects of Orthodox Jewry in the nineteenth century.

משנה תורה: ספר נשים
Mishneh Torah: Sefer Nashim (Repetition of the Law: Book of Women)
Scribe: Shalom ben Me'oded ben Benayah ben Abraham ben Me'oded
Salf Banei al-Qadi, Yemen, 1559
MS 16. Manuscript on paper; 119ff.; 20 x 27 cm

משנה תורה: ספר נזיקין, ספר קנין, ספר משפטים, ספר שופטים
Mishneh Torah: Sefer Nezikin, Sefer Kinyan, Sefer Mishpatim, Sefer Shofetim (Repetition of the Law: Book of Damages, Book of Acquisition, Book of Civil Laws, Book of Judges)
Darb al-Ḥanashat, Yemen, 1594
MS 18. Manuscript on paper; 3 vols.: 304ff.; 22.3 x 32 cm

משנה תורה: ספר זרעים, ספר עבודה, ספר קרבנות
Mishneh Torah: Sefer Zera'im, Sefer 'Avodah, Sefer Korbanot (Repetition of the Law: Book of Seeds, Book of Divine Service, Book of Offerings)
Scribe: Me'oded ben R. David ben R. Benayah Musaya
Guran, Yemen, 1596
MS 17. Manuscript on paper; 232ff.; 19.5 x 30.2 cm

[משנה] מסכת נידה עם פירוש ... משה בר מיימון
[*Mishnah*] *Masekhet Nidah 'im Perush ... Mosheh bar Maimon* (Tractate *Nidah*, with Commentary of Moses Maimonides)
[Yemen, ca. 1600]
MS 23. Manuscript on paper; 6ff.; 27.2 x 38.3 cm

[משנה] מסכת חולין עם פירוש ... משה בר מיימון
[*Mishnah*] *Masekhet Ḥulin 'im Perush ... Mosheh bar Maimon* (Tractate *Ḥulin*, with Commentary of Moses Maimonides)
[Yemen, ca. 1600]
MS 24. Manuscript on paper; 7ff.; 27.2 x 38.3 cm

Jews generally adopted the print medium with enthusiasm. Despite or because of frequent and extensive migration, printing presses often reflected a significant presence of Jewish stability and culture. Early centers in Lisbon, Rome, and Fez gave way to Venice, Prague, and Constantinople in the sixteenth century, followed by Amsterdam in the eighteenth century and Vilna in the nineteenth. Jews in Yemen, however, never established Hebrew presses, necessitating the importing of printed books from elsewhere and the preservation of manuscript traditions. These manuscripts, produced toward the end of the sixteenth and beginning of the seventeenth centuries, attest to the care Yemenite scribes exercised in perpetuating the work of Maimonides.

Hartman MS 16, *Sefer Nashim* of the *Mishneh Torah*, consists of laws concerning marriage, divorce, levirate marriage, *na'arah betulah* (an unmarried woman seduced or raped), and *sotah* (a wife accused of infidelity). Yosef Kafiḥ used this manuscript, along with the accompanying MS 17 and MS 18, in producing his edition of the *Mishneh Torah*.[1] The script in this manuscript is noteworthy for the manner in which the scribe formed the

1 Formerly Kafiḥ MS 67; see Kafiḥ (ed.), *Mishneh Torah, Sefer Nashim*, vol. 5, intro.

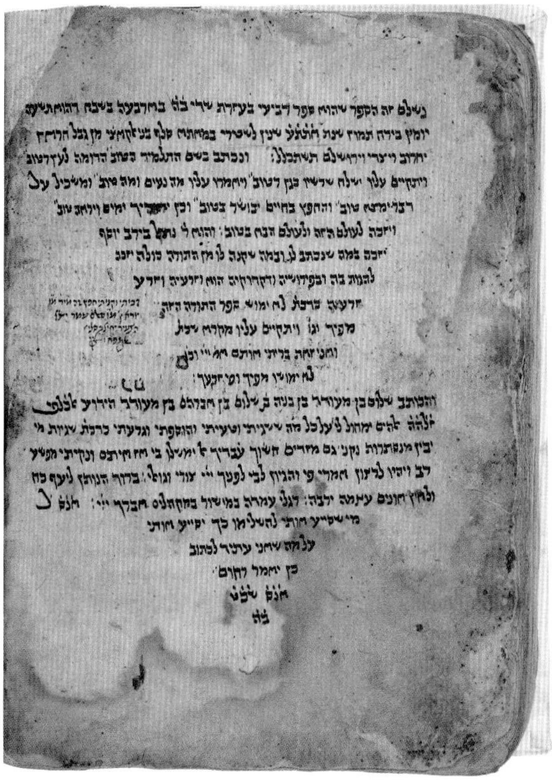

Fig. 43 *Mishneh Torah* (Yemen, 1559), MS 16, fol. 119v.

letters *alef* and *shin*, a style that largely fell out of use by the fifteenth century (Fig. 43).[2] Decorated catchwords appear at the end of each quire, with a decorated quire number at the top of each new gathering of pages. The manuscript's first folio consists of a micrographic design: on the recto is a design of Psalm 104 and Psalm 7, and on the verso is a lattice-shaped design of Psalm 119:145–168. The copyists of MS 16 and MS 17 (see below) may have belonged to the same family of scribes.[3] Before passing into the hands of Yihye Kafiḥ, it belonged to Saʿadiah ben Shalom (fol. 1v) and Shalom ben David (fol. 1v).

Hartman MS 18, in three volumes, consists of the last four books of the *Mishneh Torah*, covering commercial law, crime, and the legal system. Prior to Maimonides's law code, select topics were given monographic treatments in Judeo-Arabic, such as Hai Gaon's treatise on business transactions, *Sefer ha-Mekaḥ ve-ha-Memkar.* As with other areas of *halakhah*, Maimonides created a conceptually ordered and easily navigable one-stop shop. His contribution to civil and criminal law, for layman and judge alike, was so well accepted that in Toledo in 1305 rabbinic legislation mandated the adjudication of monetary suits in accordance with the *Mishneh Torah.*[4] Records for medieval Yemenite rabbinic courts are lacking, but material from later periods indicates how Maimonides's rulings were utilized in practice.[5]

In fact, MS 18 was commissioned by David ben Solomon and his brother Moses for the synagogue of Darb al-Ḥanashat (fol. 69r), possibly signifying that Yemenite communities held their own copies of the *Mishneh Torah* to be consulted by a local court.[6] In his edition,

2 See Malachi Beit-Arié, Edna Engel, and Ada Yardeni (eds.), *Specimens of Hebrew Medieval Hebrew Scripts*, vol. 1: *Oriental and Yemenite Scripts* [Hebrew] (Jerusalem: Israel Academy of Sciences and Humanities, 1987), nos. 118 (Sanaʿa, 1320), 121 (Tanʿam, 1338), 122 (unknown, 1343), 123 (At-Tawilah, 1356), 125 (Saʿdah, 1382), 128 (Sanaʿa, 1386). The present script is most similar to no. 121.

3 Moshe Gavra, *Entsiklopediyah le-Ḥakhme Teman*, 2 vols. (Bene Berak: ha-Makhon le-Ḥeker Ḥakhme Teman, 2001–2003), 1:315–16, and Gavra, *Shemot ha-Mishpaḥah shel ha-Yehudim be-Teman* (Bene Berak: ha-Makhon le-Ḥeker Ḥakhme Teman, 2014), 407.

4 See Fritz Baer, *Die Juden im Christlichen Spanien: Urkunden und Regesten*, vol. 1 (Berlin: Akademie Verlag, 1929), 949 and 955.

5 See Aharon Gaimani, *Changes in the Heritage of Yemenite Jewry* [Hebrew] (Ramat Gan: Bar-Ilan University, 2005), 235–61 (esp. 258).

6 Daniel Tabak, in his initial cataloguing of this manuscript, noted that Moshe Gavra mistakenly claimed

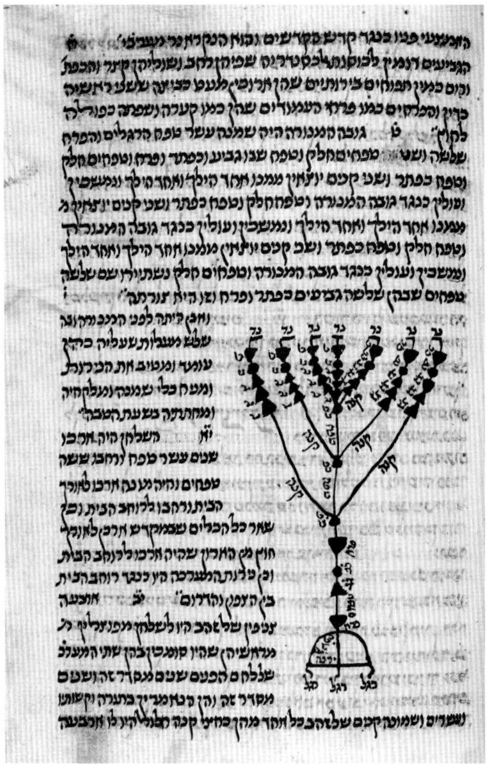

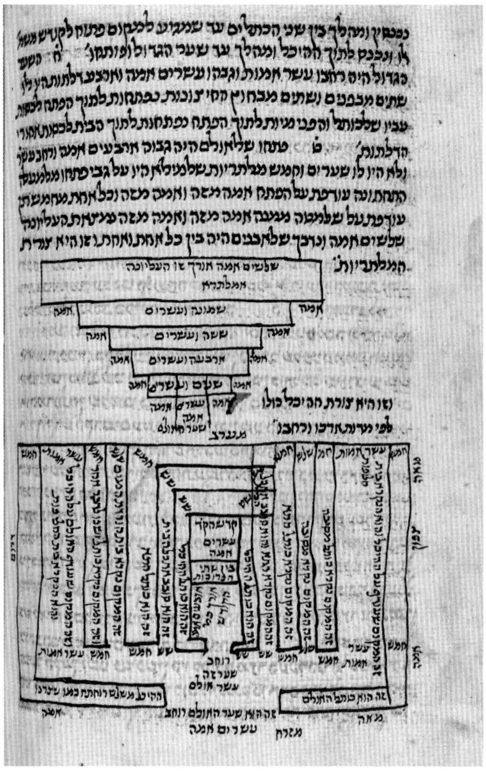

Fig. 44 (above left) *Mishneh Torah* (Yemen, 1596), MS 17, fol. 102r.

Fig. 45 (above right) *Mishneh Torah* (Yemen, 1596), MS 17, fol. 103v.

Fig. 46 (right) *Commentary on the Mishnah* (Autograph), The Bodleian Libraries, University of Oxford, MS. Pococke 295, fol. 184v.

Kafiḥ listed this as the second complete manuscript he used, and reproductions of the colophons appear in his first volume of *Sefer Shofetim*.[7] The scribe utilized six-pointed stars to denote chapter headings.[8] Yiḥye Kafiḥ filled in several folios at the end of volume 3. The manuscript contains a loose leaf of a seventeenth-century responsive poem by R. Saʿadiah

a different name for the synagogue, perhaps following the name of the David who commissioned the copy; see Gavra, *Entsiklopediyah le-kehilot ha-Yehudiyot be-Teman*, 2 vols. (Bene Berak: ha-Makhon le-Ḥeker Ḥakhme Teman, 2004), 1:164–65.

7 Formerly Kafiḥ MS 93; see Kafiḥ (ed.), *Mishneh Torah*, *Sefer Shofetim*, vol. 22, 10–11.

8 On the six-pointed star in Jewish material culture, see Gerbern S. Oegema, 'The Uses of the Shield of David on Heraldic Seals and Flags, on Bible Manuscripts, Printer's Marks, and Ex Libris,' *Jewish Studies*

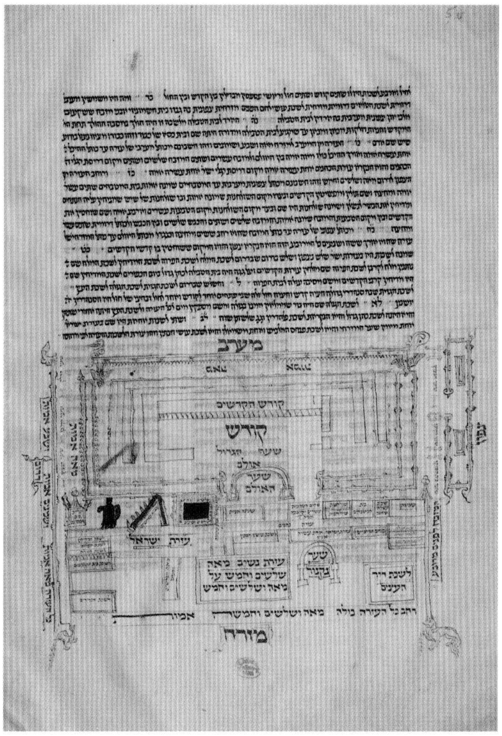

Fig. 47 *Mishneh Torah* (Northeastern France, 1296), MS Kaufmann A 77, vol. III, 5v, by courtesy of the Oriental Collection of the Library of the Hungarian Academy of Sciences.

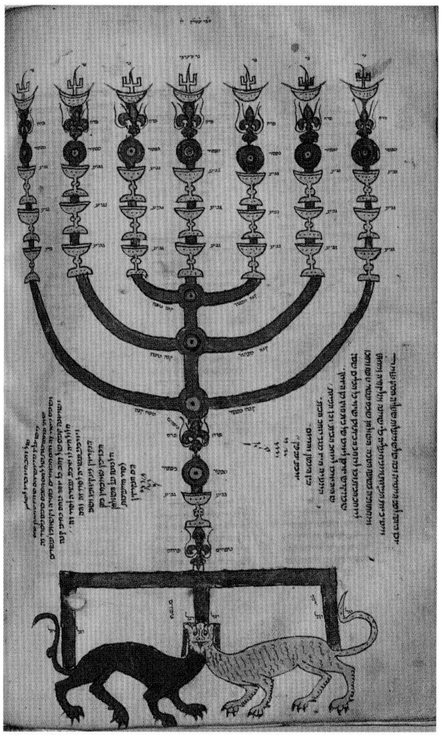

Fig. 48 *Mishneh Torah* [Ashkenaz, late 13th century]. Library of the Jewish Theological Seminary, MS 8282 / R350, fol. 277v.

ben Shlomo Dhmarmari, which incorporates stanzas from Daniel ben Judah Dayan's *Yigdal Elohim Ḥai*, a liturgical poem (*piyut*) based on Maimonides's 13 Principles of Faith.[9]

Hartman MS 17 consists of the *Mishneh Torah*'s books 7, 8, and 9, containing some of the most difficult sections of Jewish law in Maimonides's law code.[10] The laws governing agriculture codified in *Sefer Zera'im* lost most of their relevance when Jews left the Land of Israel, while the laws in *'Avodah* and *Korbanot*, concerning Temple implements and service, no longer bore any practical significance. Maimonides's presentation of these books distinctly demonstrates his intentional and well-ordered conception of *halakhah*, for the laws concerning the slaughter of animals and their kosher signs, treated in tractate *Ḥulin* in *Seder Kodashim* (the Mishnaic texts dealing with sacrifices and the Temple), do not appear here in accordance with the Talmudic order, but instead follow the laws of forbidden foods in *Sefer Kedushah* as per Maimonides's revolutionary reconception.

The primary contribution of this manuscript may be its diagrams, specifically of the altar (101r), Menorah (102r) (Fig. 44), Temple (103v, 105v) (Fig. 45), and ephod, a priestly vestment (118r). The Menorah is especially noteworthy as it conforms to the straight-armed Menorah sometimes attributed to Maimonides himself in a manuscript housed in Oxford's Bodleian Library (Fig. 46).[11] Although now a ubiquitous symbol due to its adoption and propagation by Chabad Hasidim, this straight depiction of the Menorah was part of a limited tradition, appearing in only about a half-dozen Yemenite manuscripts.[12] Such

Quarterly 5:3 (1998): 241–53; for the star in Yemenite culture, see Ingrid Hehmeyer, 'Water and Sign Magic in al-Jabin, Yemen,' *The American Journal of Islamic Social Sciences* 25:3 (2008): 94 nn. 22, 26.

9 Israel Davidson, *Thesaurus*, 4:67, no. *951; and Yosef Tobi, *Yemenite Jewish Manuscripts in the Ben-Zvi Institute* [Hebrew] (Jerusalem: Ben-Zvi Institute, 1982), 244–45, no. 334(a). For the poem, as well as a similar one by Dhmarmari's brother David, see Tobi, 'Shir Ma'aneh 'al 'Yigdal Elohim Ḥai' le-R. David ben Shlomo ha-Levi Dhmarmari,' *Afikim* 111–12 (Tishre 5758/October 1997): 40–42.

10 Formerly Kafiḥ MS 94; see Kafiḥ (ed.), *Mishneh Torah, Sefer Zera'im*, vol. 10, intro.

11 Bodleian Libraries, University of Oxford, MS. Pococke 295, fol. 184v.

12 Steve Fine, *The Menorah: From the Bible to Modern Israel* (Cambridge, MA: Harvard University Press,

schematized renderings were intended to demonstrate halakhic understanding rather than the scribe's creativity. In contrast, medieval European manuscripts emphasized the beautification of the Temple and its implements at the expense of proportionality, with depictions executed by commissioned Christian artists, like those in the Kaufmann *Mishneh Torah* (northeastern France, 1296) (Fig. 47) and an Ashkenazic manuscript housed in the Library of the Jewish Theological Seminary (Fig. 48).[13]

Of course, the *Mishneh Torah* was not the sole Maimonidean work regularly copied in sixteenth- and seventeenth-century Yemen. Hartman MS 23 and MS 24 consist of *Mishnayot* with Maimonides's commentary (Fig. 49). They do not contain colophons, marginal notations, or ownership marks, but it is clear that they were produced together by a professional scribe working off of Bomberg's second Talmud edition (1526–1531) (see cat. no. 12). The scribe differed from his model by adding the full Mishnaic text where the Venetian press had provided just headings, likely due to the expense and laboriousness of producing a separate Mishnah (Fig. 50). Regardless, the manuscripts indicate that printed Hebrew books made their way to Yemen from abroad despite or because of the absence of a local print market. For all the scholarly and cultural value of manuscript traditions, advances in technology provided greater access and affordability that would have been valued in Yemen as anywhere. Certainly, by the late nineteenth century, European and British collectors successfully procured manuscripts from communities in North Africa, the Middle East, and elsewhere by offering new printed books as replacements.[14]

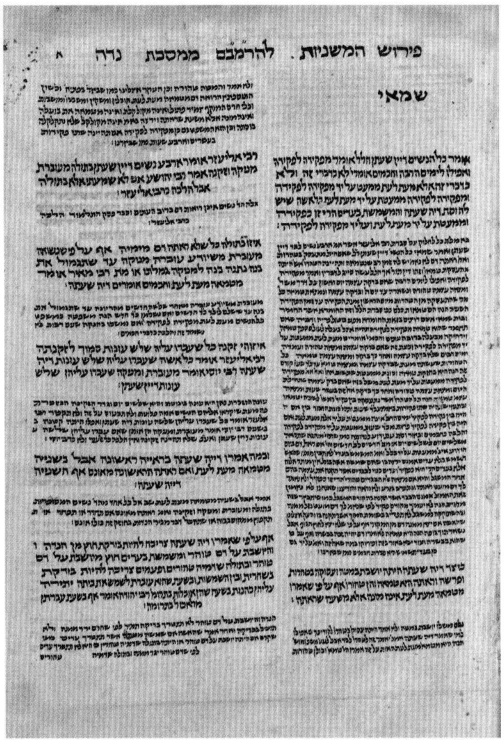
פירוש המשניות. להרמב״ם ממסכת נדה

Fig. 49 [*Mishnah*] *Masekhet Nidah* with Commentary of Maimonides [Yemen, ca. 1600], MS 23, fol. 1r.

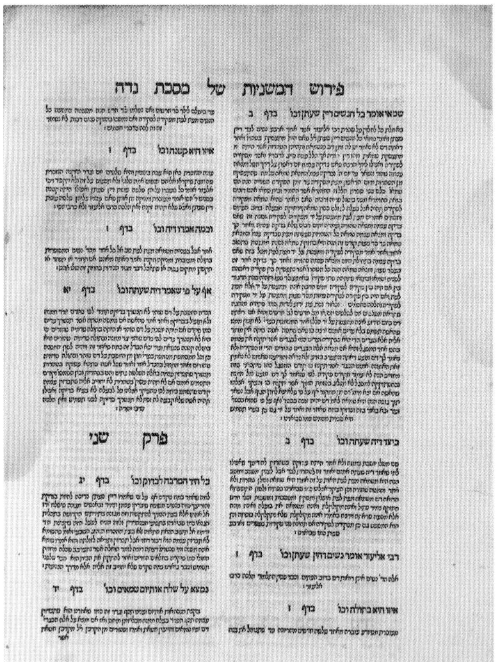
פירוש המשניות של מסכת נדה

Fig. 50 [*Mishnah*] *Masekhet Nidah* with Commentary of Maimonides (Venice: Daniel Bomberg, 1530), fol. 74v. Library of the Jewish Theological Seminary.

2016), 80–85. For a discussion of the shape of the Menorah, and a reproduction of this manuscript's Menorah, see Kafiḥ (ed.), *Mishneh Torah, ʿAvodah, Bet ha-Behirah*, 7:54–58 (56).

13 Budapest, Hungarian Academy of Sciences, MS A77, fol. III.5v; New York, Jewish Theological Seminary, MS R350, fol. 277v.

14 On the rise and practices of Western antiquities collectors and dealers in the nineteenth century, see Rebecca J. W. Jefferson, *The Cairo Genizah and the Age of Discovery in Egypt: The History and Provenance of a Jewish Archive* (London: I. B. Tauris, 2022).

פירוש משה בר מיימון על מסכת ראש השנה
Perush Mosheh bar Maimon ʿal Masekhet Rosh ha-Shanah (Commentary of Moses Maimonides on Tractate *Rosh ha-Shanah*)
[Middle East, ca. 1600]
MS 12. Manuscript on paper; 8ff.; 11 x 16.2 cm

Yemen was not alone in sustaining a manuscript culture after the invention of printing with movable type. Though devoid of a colophon, this slim manuscript of Maimonides's Commentary on the Talmudic tractate *Rosh ha-Shanah*, which includes nine illustrations, was likely copied in the Middle East around the turn of the seventeenth century (Fig. 51).

Although less well known and influential than his *Commentary on the Mishnah*, Maimonides authored a Talmud commentary covering at least the Orders of *Moʿed*, *Nashim*, and *Nezikin*. He himself said as much in his *Commentary on the Mishnah*, and a later responsum suggests additional commentary on difficult passages elsewhere in the Talmud.[1] Very little of the commentary has survived, perhaps because Maimonides engaged in composing this work while still in Córdoba and did not invest in perfecting the text while in North Africa. In later decades, he criticized the manner in which the Talmud was studied,[2] making a commentary a less valuable endeavor than his pioneering *Mishneh Torah*.

Extant manuscripts of the commentary appear in Hebrew, though sources do refer to a text in Judeo-Arabic.[3] Manuscripts like this one, which is not mentioned by the scholar Israel Ta-Shma in his list of the relevant manuscripts,[4] offer scholars a way, along with medieval citations and genizah fragments,[5] to reconstruct the nature of Maimonides's early understanding of the Talmud. The best-known manuscript of his commentary on *Masekhet Rosh ha-Shanah* is that housed in the Bibliothèque Nationale de France (MS Héb. 336), exceptional for recording Maimonides's place and year of birth.[6] Most of the related (and incomplete) manuscripts stem from the fourteenth and fifteenth centuries and are written in Byzantine script. Yeḥiel Brill printed an edition based on a fifteenth-century copy of a thirteenth-century Cretan manuscript, but scholars have doubted its authenticity.[7]

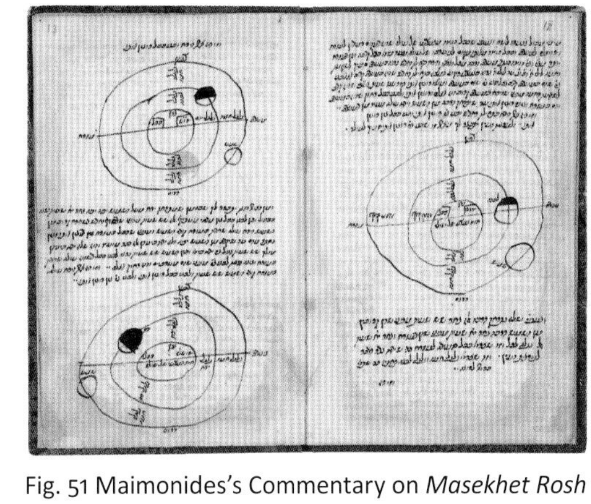

Fig. 51 Maimonides's Commentary on *Masekhet Rosh ha-Shanah* (Oriental, ca. 1600), MS 12, 12–13.

1 Moses Maimonides, *Mishnah ʿim Perush Rabenu Mosheh ben Maimon: Makor ve-Targum*, ed. and trans. Yosef Kafiḥ, *Vol. 1: Seder Zeraʿim* (Jerusalem: Mosad Harav Kook, 1963), 47 (intro.); Blau (ed.), *Teshuvot ha-Rambam*, no. 251. For a view against Maimonides's authorship, see Davidson, *Moses Maimonides*, 140–46.

2 Shailat, *Letters and Essays*, 256.

3 Simha Assaf, 'Mi-Perusho shel ha-Rambam le-Masekhet Shabbat,' *Sinai* 6 (1940): 103–10.

4 Israel Ta-Shma, *Studies in Medieval Rabbinic Literature* [Hebrew], vol. 2 (Spain) (Jerusalem: Bialik Institute, 2004), 314–15 (and n. 12). See also David Henshke, 'Maimonides as His Own Commentator' [Hebrew], *Sefunot* 8 (23) (2003): 117–63 (appendix 1).

5 See M. J. L. Sachs, *Ḥidushe ha-Rambam la-Talmud* (Jerusalem: Mekhon ha-Talmud he-Yisra'eli ha-Shalem, 1963).

6 Davidson, *Moses Maimonides*, 5–6 nn. 2, 10. The year recorded works out to be 1135.

7 Yeḥiel Brill (ed.), *Perush ʿal Masekhet Rosh ha-Shanah* (Paris, 1865).

לחם משנה
Leḥem Mishneh (Two Loaves of Bread)
Abraham ben Moses de Boton
Edited by Isaac Gershon
Printed by Daniel Zanetti
Venice, 1604–1606
2°. RB 17. 2 vols.
Steinschneider, 4195,2; Vinograd, Venice no. 973

This is the first edition of *Leḥem Mishneh*, a commentary on Maimonides's *Mishneh Torah* by the Talmudist Abraham de Boton (d. after 1592).[1] De Boton was born to the rabbinic scholar Moses de Boton and studied under Samuel de Medina before becoming rabbi of Salonika's Italian congregation, which included many Sephardim. He was noted for his breadth of knowledge and was consulted throughout the Sephardic diaspora on a wide range of halakhic matters. His numerous responsa were published posthumously by his grandson as *Leḥem Rav* (Smyrna, 1660).

De Boton's *Leḥem Mishneh* focused mainly on harmonizing Maimonides's apparent contradictions with the Talmud. He noted relevant Talmudic passages, which Maimonides intentionally absented from the *Mishneh Torah*, and commented on Vidal Yom Tov of Tolosa's *Magid Mishneh*. The *Leḥem Mishneh* became one of the most widely consulted commentaries on the *Mishneh Torah* and it has been included in most subsequent editions.

This imprint was brought to press by the scholar and editor Isaac ben Mordecai Gershon Treves (d. after 1620), usually referred to simply as Isaac Gershon (Fig. 52).[2] Gershon was born in Safed, where he studied under the renowned Bible commentator Moses Alshekh. He immigrated to Venice by 1576 and worked as a proofreader for many years, helping to publish numerous important works, including Moses da Trani's *Bet Elohim* (1576), Elijah de Vidas's *Reshit Ḥokhmah* (1579), Solomon Alkabetz's *Manot ha-Levi* (1585), Israel Najara's *Zemirot Yisrael* (1599–1600), Eleazar Azikri's *Sefer Ḥaredim* (1601), Alshekh's commentary on the Pentateuch (1601–1607), and the responsa of Moses Galante (1608). He also authored many works, including a commentary on the book of Esther, halakhic responsa, and supplementary material, such as an introduction or index, to works he brought to press.

The imprint includes introductions from the publisher, Joseph di Novis, and the author's son, Abraham, a scholar and prestigious rabbi in his own right. Through the seventeenth and eighteenth centuries, Hebrew texts, especially large-format volumes like this, were accompanied by introductions and approbations admiring and supporting the work. The final leaf of the first volume includes two poems by Moses Tarfon in praise of the book, which were reprinted in the Amsterdam, 1703 edition of *Leḥem Mishneh*.[3] The volumes include beautifully decorated title pages characteristic of the Zanetti printing house, which

1 See Meir Benayahu, 'Defuse Zaneti,' *Asufot* 12 (1999): 9–178 (130–45, no. 71); Benayahu, 'Reshimat ha-Sefarim she-Hadpis ve-she-Hagayah Rabi Yitsḥak Gershon,' *Asufot* 13 (2000): 65–90 (86, no. 50); Menahem Ben-Sasson, W. Z. Harvey, Y. Ben-Naeh, and Z. Zohar (eds.), *Studies in a Rabbinic Family: The de Botons* (Jerusalem: Misgav Yerushalayim, 1998).

2 Not to be confused with Isaac ben Mordecai Gershon or Isaac ben Gershon Treves. See Isaac Yudlov, 'R. Isaac Gershon and R. Isaac Treves' [Hebrew], *Kiryat Sefer* 59 (1984): 247–51; Mordecai Samuel Ghirondi, *Toledot Gedole Yisrael u-Ge'one Italyah* (Trieste, 1853), 145; David Conforte, *Koreh ha-Dorot* (Piotrków: Aharon Valden, 1895), 48.

3 Israel Davidson, *Thesaurus*, 1:196, no. 4280, and 3:258, no. 25.

Fig. 52 Abraham ben Moses de Boton, *Leḥem Mishneh* (Venice: Daniel Zanetti, 1604–1606), RB 17, vol. 1, fol. 1r.

Fig. 53 Abraham ben Moses de Boton, *Leḥem Mishneh* (Venice: Daniel Zanetti, 1604–1606), RB 17, vol. 1, fol. 2r. Signature of R. David Oppenheim.

produced several dozen Hebrew books in Venice during the late sixteenth and early seventeenth centuries.[4]

Volume 1 of the copy in the Hartman Collection belonged to David Oppenheim (1664–1736), chief rabbi of Prague and Bohemia and an avid collector and patron of Hebrew books (Fig. 53).[5] Notably, the frames of the title pages of the two volumes are identical, but the frame for volume 2 was printed upside-down.

4 See Yudlov, *Hebrew Printers' Marks*, 27–31.

5 For signatures, see vol. 1, fols. 2r and 3r. On Oppenheim as a collector, see Teplitsky, *Prince of the Press*.

27

משנה תורה: ספר מדע, ספר אהבה, ספר זמנים, ספר נשים, ספר קדושה, ספר הפלאה
Mishneh Torah: Sefer Mada, Sefer Ahavah, Sefer Zemanim, Sefer Nashim, Sefer Kedushah, Sefer Hafla'ah (Repetition of the Law: Book of Knowledge, Book of Love, Book of Times, Book of Women, Book of Holiness, Book of Separation)
Scribe: Joseph ben Amram ben ʿOded ben Zechariah ben Judah al-ʿAdawi
ʿAmran, 1651
MS 19. Manuscript on paper; 4 vols.: 404ff.; 20 x 30 cm

Although of a relatively late date, Kafiḥ used this manuscript in his edition of the *Mishneh Torah*.[1] Its significance lay in the apparatus supporting the Maimonidean text. Marginal notations in numerous hands appear throughout in both Hebrew and Judeo-Arabic. A running commentary, coeval with the original manuscript, is the most prominent addition; in one place it is actually embedded within the main text block (fols. 180v–183r). The glosses and comments vary in kind, with נ"א marking a נוסח אחר (variant reading), 'פ signifying פירוש (commentary), and 'שנ indicating שנאמר (biblical verses and Talmudic quotations) in the margins. There are also comments that attempt to explain Maimonides's formulations, like the use of a particular halakhic principle or the adoption of one rabbinic position over another. The comments avoid discussions that appear in standard commentaries and generally do not indicate the source of their citations,[2] though it appears they relied heavily upon Vidal Yom Tov de Tolosa's *Magid Mishneh*. A third type of gloss extrapolates the ethical import and quasi-mystical depth of Maimonides's precise formulations.[3]

Taken all together, the manuscript expresses a deep reverence for Maimonides and his written word. The first type of gloss was meant to assist the reader in understanding the *Mishneh Torah* as a standalone text within the context of biblical and Talmudic sources. The second set of glosses are likewise explanatory, while the third, comprising deeper comments, demonstrate the singular status of Maimonides in Yemenite thought (see cat. no. 1).

In addition, the manuscript included influences beyond Maimonides. There are statements from Joseph Karo's *Kesef Mishneh* and Moses di Trani's *Kiryat Sefer*,[4] demonstrating the penetration of printed halakhic literature – from Safed no less – into Yemenite Jewish culture in the seventeenth century (see cat. nos. 24 and 32). References to *Hagahot Maimoniyot* and Jacob ben Asher's *Arbaʿah Turim* likewise appear, reflecting an infusion of medieval Ashkenazic thought. Moreover, the commentary includes the texts of *The Alphabet of Rabbi ʿAkiva* and *Sefer Yetsirah*, both unusually juxtaposed with Maimonides, though known and copied in Yemen before the advent of Safed Kabbalah.

The glosses also contain unidentified citations, some of which run counter to the *Magid Mishneh*.[5] Daniel Tabak, in his initial cataloguing of this manuscript, determined that the glosses possibly preserve lost Yemenite customs, including one to burn all *ḥamets* on the night of the 14th of Nisan so as not to be concerned about having to search again (Fig. 54).[6]

1 Formerly Kafiḥ MS 98 and MS 99; referred to as ק in Kafiḥ's edition of the *Mishneh Torah*. Foliation is as follows: vol. 1, fols. 1–114 (*Sefer Mada, Sefer Ahavah*); vol. 2, fols. 115–228 (*Sefer Zemanim*); vol. 3, fols. 1–72 (*Sefer Nashim*); vol. 4, fols. 73–176 (*Sefer Kedushah, Sefer Hafla'ah*).

2 Compare the short comment in vol. 2, 180v, *Hilkhot Ḥamets u-Matsah* 1:6, to the pages of discussion in any standard commentary, which were all available in manuscript or print form prior to 1651.

3 See examples at vol. 2, fol. 180v, on *Ḥamets u-Matsah* 1:4, and fol. 181r, on 2:2.

4 See vol. 2, fols. 129v, 180r.

5 See vol. 2, fol. 182v, on *Ḥamets u-Matsah* 3:3.

6 See vol. 2, fol. 182r, on *Ḥamets u-Matsah* 3:1. The custom was a minority practice of R. Judah of Speyer. Tabak noted that this custom is absent from Yosef Kafiḥ, *Halikhot Teman*, ed. Yisrael Yeshayahu

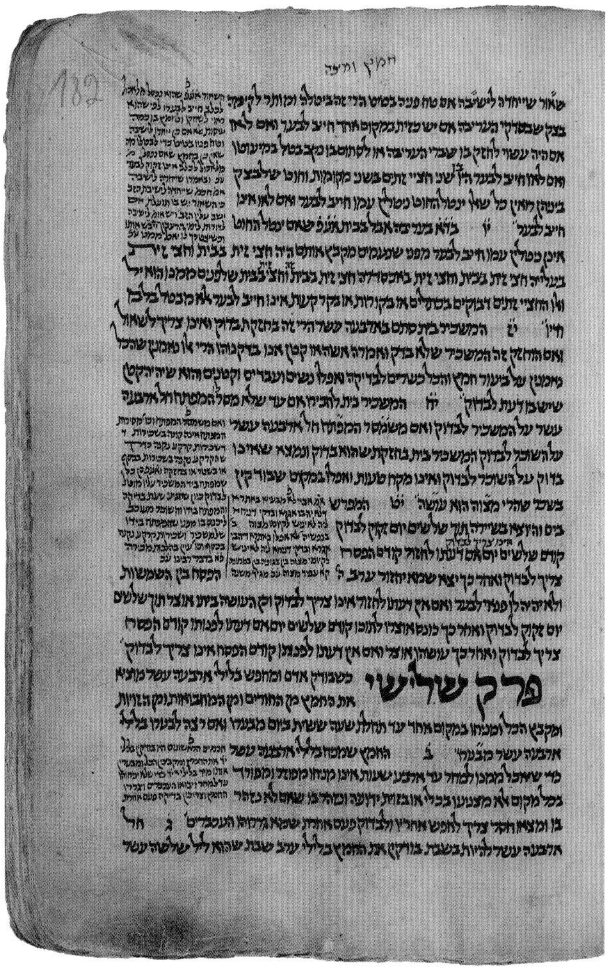

Fig. 54 *Mishneh Torah* (Amran, 1651), MS 19, vol. 2, fol. 182r.

Although scholars have long praised Yemenite Jewry's manuscript tradition, the texts here, along with others in the Hartman Collection, indicate that scholars had access to an impressive array of printed books, broadening our understanding of seventeenth-century Yemenite Jewry (see cat. no. 24).

The manuscript was copied by Joseph ben Amram ben ʿOded ben Zechariah ben Judah al-ʿAdawi (אלעדוי).[7] The colophons he provided at the conclusion of each book make it possible to note the pace at which he labored: working out of order but at a fast clip, al-ʿAdawi concluded *Sefer Zemanim* on 2 Nisan 1962 *le-minyan shetarot* (= March 24, 1651), *Sefer Mada* on 19 Iyar 1962 (= May 10, 1651), *Sefer Ahavah* on 1 Sivan 1962 (= May 21, 1651), *Sefer Kedushah* on 13 Sivan 1962 (= June 2, 1651), and *Sefer Nashim* on 27 Sivan 1962 (= June 16, 1651).[8] The Institute for Microfilmed Hebrew Manuscripts lists al-ʿAdawi as the copyist of several other texts in the same place at approximately the same time, including a copy of the Yemenite prayer book (*tiklal*) and another manuscript of the *Mishneh Torah*. Prior to Yiḥye and then Yosef Kafiḥ, the volumes belonged to Shelomoh ben Saʿadiah al-Fakʿah (vol. 1, fol. 1r), Dawud al-Dhmarmar and later his sons Saʿid and Musa, and Yiḥye ben Dawud al-Javre. A record of the sale between the sons and al-Javre, with the names of three witnesses, appears opposite the title page of volume 1.

(Jerusalem: Ben-Zvi Institute, 2002), 39; Ovadia Melamed, *Masoret ha-Tefilah ve-Shoresh ha-Minhag* (Jerusalem: Ovadia Melamed, 2000), 339; and Moshe Gavra, *Meḥkarim be-Sidure Teman*, vol. 3 (Bene Berak: ha-Makhon le-Ḥeker Ḥakhme Teman, 2010), 6–13.

7 See Gavra, *Entsiklopediyah le-Ḥakhme Teman*, 1:422–23. As with the scribes of Hartman MS 16 and MS 17 (see cat. no. 24), this scribe may have come from a line of copyists; see Gavra, *Entsiklopediyah le-Ḥakhme Teman*, 1:423–24, and Gavra, *Shemot ha-Mishpaḥah*, 547–48.

8 There is no colophon for *Sefer Haflaʿah*, because the manuscript lacks al-ʿAdawi's final folio (it was replaced at a later date).

מדע, אהבה, זמנים מהיד החזקה להרמב"ם
[*Mishneh Torah*] *Mada, Ahavah, Zemanim* (Book of Knowledge, Book of Love, Book of Times)
Printed by Domenego Vedelago
Venice, 1665
4°. RB 27
Steinschneider 6513,13; Vinograd, Venice no. 1374

In the 1660s, a massive messianic movement brought Jews to emotional heights not imagined in the history of the diaspora. When the charismatic Sabbatai Tsevi was endorsed by the young and well-connected kabbalist Nathan of Gaza in the spring and summer of 1665, news spread rapidly and enthusiastically that the long-awaited messiah had arrived. For more than a year, Jews far and wide, from the Dutch Republic to Poland to Yemen, celebrated the news and anticipated the coming redemption with bated breath. Ordinary people prophesied in the streets, while others sold their property anticipating the messiah's imminent invitation from Jerusalem. The ecstatic hope was shattered when Sabbatai, faced with a challenge to perform miraculous acts or be executed, converted to Islam in the fall of 1666. Still, belief in Sabbatai's messiahship persisted, and various forms of Sabbatian heresy challenged mainstream Jewish communities into the nineteenth century.

This very rare volume speaks to the prevalence of messianic sentiment in the 1660s, in part explaining the rapid and fervent spread of the movement (Fig. 55).[1] The book was funded by Joseph Cividale Zemel, whose son Menaḥem donated a magnificent Torah Ark to Venice's *Scuola Tedesca*, and printed by Domenego Vedelago, who had worked in the Venetian print houses of Bragadini and Vendramin. Vedelago ordinarily issued books with decorated title pages, but this otherwise modest page includes a rudimentary engraving of a bearded man miraculously riding a lion, incongruously placed above the main text. With production nearly finished, the printers seem to have gotten word of the messiah's arrival and hastened to commission the unusual engraving as an enthusiastic response. The colophon, which indicates the work was completed in mid-June, heralds the arrival of the 'anointed prince' (משיח נגיד) (Daniel 9:25).

Scholars have long assumed that the movement was ignited by Nathan of Gaza's epistle to Raphael Joseph in Alexandria, sent in September or October of 1665.[2] The missive, copied and sent throughout Europe and the Ottoman Empire, described Sabbatai astride a fire-breathing lion holding reins made of a seven-headed snake. The engraving on this title page indicates that Nathan proclaimed Sabbatai as messiah months earlier and that the image of a messiah atop a tamed lion evolved.

Fantastical news aside, the messiah's arrival had no bearing on the authority of Maimonides or the inviolability of his text. Beyond the engraving and chronogram, this *Mada, Ahava, Zemanim* does not contain additional messianic references. Consisting of just the first three books of the *Mishneh Torah*, the printers clearly sought to sell the book to a growing lay readership. The imprint lacks standard commentaries but contains a marginal apparatus that provides biblical citations, references to the halakhic codes *Sefer Mitsvot Gadol* and *Arba'ah Turim*, and correlating passages in Maimonides's *Moreh Nevukhim*. Likewise, the chapter in *Zemanim* on sanctification of the new moon is absent – because, says the introduction, few people grasped the concept or desired to learn it – while laws of *kashrut* and *sheḥitah* appear at the end of the volume.

1 See Barry Walfish, *'As it is Written': Judaic Treasures from the Thomas Fisher Rare Book Library* (Toronto: University of Toronto, 2015), no. 54.

2 Gershom Scholem, *Sabbatai Sevi: The Mystical Messiah*, trans. R. J. Z. Werblowsky (Princeton: Princeton University Press, 1973), 267–90.

מדע
אהבה זמנים
מהיד החזקה להרמב״ם ז״ל
עם כראה מקום מהפוסקים והפסוקים ומפתחות כללי הלכותיו
ועם הגהות וביאורים לתועלת כל החוגים
ואלה מוסיף על הראשונים בהלכות מאכלות אסורות
בחסיד ויתיר והליף וכאשר בהקדמה יראה הקורא
מקרוב באו לא שערום הדפוסים הקודמים עד עצם
היום הזה
באותיות חדשות ונייר מופה ורוב הגהה
בוויניציאה
במצות השר הגדול
אנדריאה מורישיני
שנת אמור לחכמה אחותי את

Appresso Domenego Vedelago.
Con licenza de' Superiori, e Priuilegio.

Fig. 55 *Mada, Ahavah, Zemanim* (Venice: Domenego Vedelago/Andrea Morisini, 1665), RB 27, fol. 1r.

29

משנה תורה
Mishneh Torah (Repetition of the Law)
Printed by Immanuel Athias
Amsterdam, 1702
2°. RB 8. 4 vols.
Steinschneider, 6513,8; Dienstag, '*Mishneh Torah*,' no. 11; Fuks and Fuks-Mansfeld, no. 418; Vinograd, Amsterdam no. 744

פאר הדור
Pe'er ha-Dor (Splendor of the Generation)
Translated by Mordecai ben Isaac Tama
Printed by Gerard Johann Janson and Israel Mondovi
Amsterdam, 1765
4°. RB 14
Steinschneider, 6513,122; Enelow, 'Belinfante,' no. 9; Vinograd, Amsterdam no. 1856

These two imprints were each issued in the great Jewish printing center of Amsterdam. Individually, the books reflected the continued impact of Maimonides and the cultural import of the local communities. The earlier publication, a four-volume *Mishneh Torah*, appeared in a print run of 1,150 copies (Fig. 56).[1] The project began under the direction of Joseph Athias (ca. 1635–1700),[2] who had founded a press in Amsterdam in 1658 and printed hundreds of Hebrew and vernacular titles during his career. Joseph's son Immanuel, who directed many of the press's activities from 1685 onward, brought the project to completion after his father's death. The imprint contains all of the standard commentaries previously used in editions of Maimonides's magnum opus: *Hasagot ha-Rabad*, *Magid Mishneh*, *Kesef Mishneh*, *Migdal 'Oz*, and *Hagahot Maimoniyot*. Abraham de Boton's *Leḥem Mishneh* does not appear here, perhaps because the Athias press intended to publish it separately the following year.[3]

Born on the Iberian peninsula around 1635, little is known of Joseph Athias's early years. This is often the case with *conversos* (also known by the derogatory term *marranos*, meaning pigs) who emigrated from Spain or Portugal in order to practice Judaism in more tolerant lands. After possibly spending time in Dutch Brazil, Athias settled in Amsterdam, home to the largest and most influential community of these newly practicing Sephardic Jews. Amsterdam had by then become Europe's wealthiest and most tolerant city. Two factors proved crucial to the prosperity of the Dutch Republic and its Jews. First, the Reformed religion, often known as Calvinism after the influential Christian theologian John Calvin (1509–1564), permitted religious freedom to a large extent. Jews were permitted to congregate for prayers, build synagogues and study halls, and print religious material. Secondly, the economic theory of mercantilism, in which the prosperity of a nation depended upon the

1 L. Fuks and R. G. Fuks-Mansfeld, *Hebrew Typography in the Northern Netherlands 1585–1815: Historical Evaluation and Descriptive Bibliography* (Leiden: Brill, 1987), part 2, 331–33.

2 As *The Golden Path* went to press, the Hartman Collection acquired a very rare single-folio prospectus issued by Joseph Athias in 1699 seeking subscribers to fund this *Mishneh Torah*.

3 Immanuel's imprint of *Leḥem Mishneh* was just its second edition, making it a first in Amsterdam as well. He published three of four volumes; the fourth was issued by Solomon Proops in 1714, the year of Immanuel's death. Interestingly, the fourth part looks just like the first three; Proops included Immanuel's distinct printer's mark and even used the same verse for the chronogram, updating it by enlarging two additional letters.

supply of capital, promoted the settlement of wealthy Jews with connections along trade routes and in port cities.

A network of Sephardim spread from Amsterdam, Hamburg, London, and Bordeaux to New Amsterdam (later, New York), the Caribbean, the Italian peninsula, and the Ottoman Empire. Sephardim who had practiced a clandestine and fractured form of Judaism while living nominally as Catholics in Spain or Portugal were able to embrace Judaism openly. The desire for Jewish cultural life, combined with the economic prosperity of the Dutch Republic, enabled Amsterdam's Jewish community to develop into one of the most important centers of Jewish learning and activity in the early modern period.[4]

Nowhere is this more evident than in the production of books by and for Jews in Amsterdam. Basing themselves on the great Christian print shops, the Jews of Amsterdam produced books in Hebrew and several vernacular languages, cast new fonts and type, and replaced Venice as the major center of Jewish printing. Joseph Athias and many others followed the lead of Manasseh ben Israel (1604–1657), founder of the first Jewish-owned Hebrew printing house in Amsterdam in 1627. Hundreds of Hebrew titles, and many dozens more of non-Hebrew titles, were issued by several Hebrew presses belonging to both Sephardim and Ashkenazim. Print runs consisted of thousands of copies, supplying Jewish communities all over Europe with Bibles, Talmuds, prayer books, legal codes, and more.

These beautiful gilt and goffered volumes of the *Mishneh Torah* exemplify the glory of Amsterdam printing (Fig. 57). The great Hebrew bibliographer and historian Moritz Steinschneider called it 'one of the most elegant and beautiful Hebrew editions ever to have appeared.'[5] One need only to view the frontispieces or the title page – a fine copperplate engraving of an architectural motif with the figures of Moses, Aaron, and cherubs – to appreciate Steinschneider's comment and glimpse the grandeur of Amsterdam Jewry at its height. The title page includes Immanuel's printer's device used for folio volumes: a mirror-image of his initials, MJA, for Manuel ben Joseph Athias.[6] The three-page dedication in Portuguese to Moses Machado, army purveyor for King William III of England and the press's economic patron, is indicative of Athias's good relations with Christians. Joseph Athias issued many titles for the Christian public and employed the distinguished professor Johannes Leusden (1624–1699) as editor of a Hebrew Bible, replete with the scholar's Latin commentary.[7] Joseph and Immanuel Athias, in fact, like other Jewish printers, were members of the Amsterdam Bookprinters Guild – a far cry from the inception of printing, when Jews were denied the privilege of printing in some places and were expelled from others.

One touching note about memory and martyrdom in the Athias family: Joseph's 75-year-old father, Jorge Mendez de Castro, was burned alive at the stake during an *auto-da-fé* in Córdoba on June 29, 1665. The Sephardic poet Daniel Levi de Barrios composed a long poem memorializing the victims of that particular *auto-da-fé*, giving the Jewish name of Jorge Mendez de Castro as Abraham Athias. Immanuel Athias honored his grandfather in the colophon of the final volume of this *Mishneh Torah*, stating that he died

4 On the community, see Miriam Bodian, *The Hebrews of the Portuguese Nation: Conversos and Community in Early Modern Amsterdam* (Bloomington: Indiana University Press, 1997); Yosef Kaplan, *An Alternative Path to Modernity: The Sephardi Diaspora in Western Europe* (Leiden: Brill, 2000).

5 Moritz Steinschneider and David Cassel, 'Jüdische Typographie und Jüdischer Buchhandel,' in *Allgemeine Encyclopädie der Wissenschaften und Künste*, ed. Johann Samuel Ersch and Johann Gottfried Gruber, Section 2, part 28 (Leipzig: F. A. Brodhaus, 1851), 21–94 (66).

6 Yaari, *Hebrew Printers' Marks*, no. 81; and Heller, 'Mirror-Image Monograms as Printers' Devices on Title Pages of Hebrew Books Printed in the Seventeenth and Eighteenth Centuries,' in *Studies in the Making of the Early Hebrew Book*, 38–39.

7 Fuks and Fuks-Mansfeld, *Hebrew Typography*, part 2, 292; Theodor Dunkelgrün, 'Like a Blind Man Judging Colors: Jospeh Athias and Johannes Leusden Defend Their 1667 Hebrew Bible,' *Studia Rosenthaliana* 44 (2012): 79–115.

Fig. 56 *Mishneh Torah* (Amsterdam: Immanuel Athias, 1702), RB 8, vol. 1, fol. 1r.

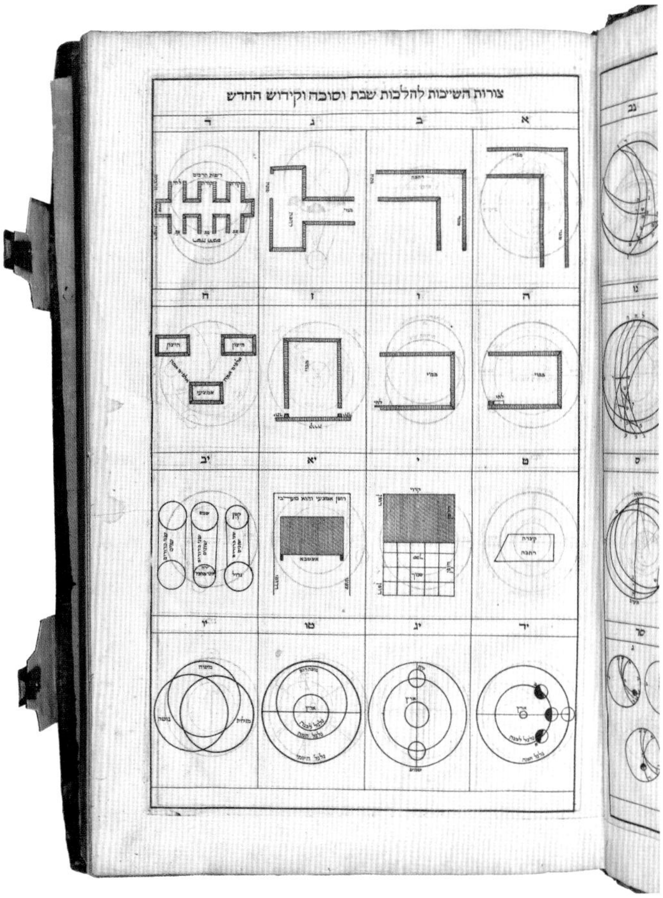

Fig. 57 *Mishneh Torah* (Amsterdam: Immanuel Athias, 1702), RB 8. Images concerning the laws of Shabbat, Sukkot, and the New Moon.

as a martyr for the sanctification of God's name.[8] So too did he honor his father Joseph, upon the latter's death in 1700, by choosing for that year's chronogram the quotation וימת יוסף ('And Joseph died'; Genesis 50:26).

A half-century later, Mordecai Tama traveled from his native Hebron to Amsterdam with the intention of publishing his grandfather's commentary on *Midrash Mekhilta*. As a major print center and port city, Amsterdam regularly attracted visitors seeking to make their mark through an impactful publication. Still others sent their manuscripts to Amsterdam from abroad, hoping to reach a wider and more prestigious audience than if they had been printed locally. Tama did not succeed in bringing his ancestor's work to fruition, but he did build connections with local Portuguese scholars. As others had before him, Tama recognized the impressive institutions established in Amsterdam, from the Esnoga to the Ets Haim Yesiba and library to the variety of Jewish print shops. In turn, Portuguese rabbis, scholars, and publishers valued Tama's rabbinic learning and knowledge of Arabic.

In 1765, Tama brought to press *Pe'er ha-Dor*, the first collection of Maimonides's correspondence to appear entirely in Hebrew (Fig. 58).[9] The Great Eagle had written most of his letters in Judeo-Arabic, the vernacular language used by the vast majority of Jews in the twelfth century. With the shift of Jewish cultural centers over several centuries, few Jews could read such texts in their original. Tama used a manuscript consisting of 155 responsa that had once belonged to Jacob Sasportas (1610–1698), a native of North Africa who finished

8 Fuks and Fuks-Mansfeld, *Hebrew Typography*, part 2, 291–92. The poem was printed in Amsterdam by David de Castro Tartas without mention of a date; see Meyer Kayserling, *Biblioteca Española-Portugueza-Judaica: Dictionnaire Bibliographique des Auteurs Juifs, de Leurs Ouvrages Espagnols et Portugais et des Oeuvres sur et Contre les Juifs et le Judaïsme* (Strasbourg: Charles J. Trubner, 1890), 17.

9 On Tama and this edition, see G. Margoliouth, 'Responses of Maimonides in the Original Arabic,' *Jewish Quarterly Review* 11 (1899): 533–50; and Oded Cohen, 'Eager to Belong: A Palestinian Jew in Eighteenth-Century Amsterdam,' *Studia Rosenthaliana* 46 (2020): 211–28.

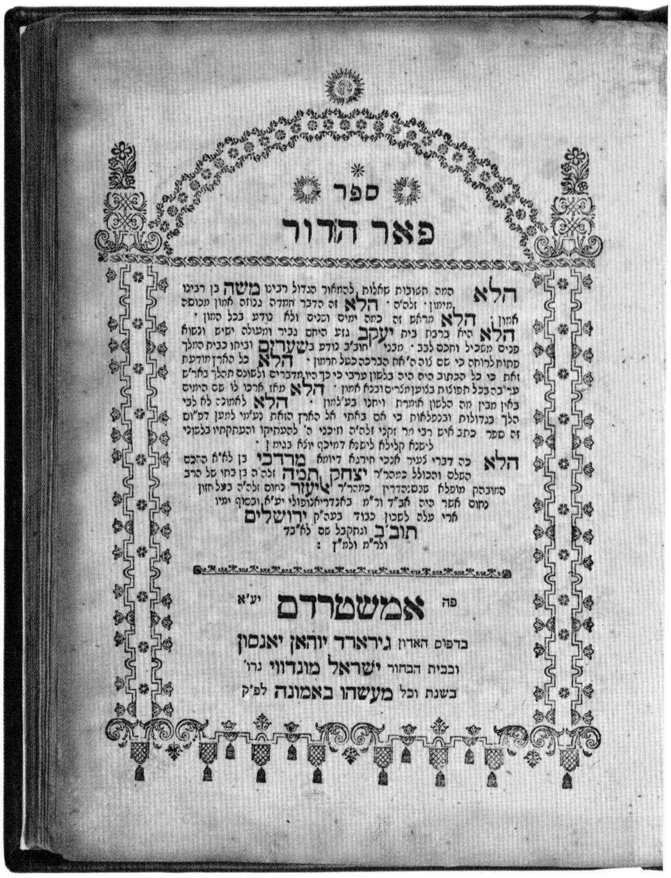

Fig. 58 Mordecai ben Isaac Tama, *Pe'er ha-Dor* (Amsterdam: Gerard Johann Janson and Israel Mondovi, 1765), RB 14, fol. 1r.

his career as chief rabbi to Amsterdam's Portuguese Jews.[10] The imprint contains an impressive array of paratexts, including introductions, *haskamot* (rabbinic approbations), poems, and a subject index. Paratexts provide cultural and social context of an imprint, and the large amount contained herein speaks volumes. Tama provided an introduction, while the publisher Gerard Johan Janson included a Spanish-language introduction previously composed by Sasportas. Several *haskamot*, from all over the world and across the cultural spectrum, extol the work, while poems from the Sephardic community of Amsterdam praise Tama even more than Maimonides and stress the importance of the Hebrew language.[11]

10 On Sasportas, see Yaacob Dweck, *Dissident Rabbi: The Life of Jacob Sasportas* (Princeton, NJ: Princeton University Press, 2019).

11 The *haskamot* are from the chief rabbis of both the Sephardic and Ashkenazic communities of Amsterdam and rabbis in The Hague, Rotterdam, Halberstadt, Safed, and Constantinople. The poems were written by Moses Raphael Hezekiah da Veges, David Franco Mendes, and Isaac ben Elijah Hezekiah ha-Kohen Belinfante. Tama is mentioned several times by Ḥayim Yosef David Azulai (Ḥida; 1724–1806) in his travelogue *Maʿagal Tov* (Livorno, 1879); see Aron Freimann (ed.), *Sefer Maʿagal Tov ha-Shalem* (Jerusalem, 1934).

ישועה בישראל והוא פירש ... על הלכות קדוש החדש ... [ל]משה בר מיימון
Yeshu'ah be-Yisrael ve-Hu Perush ... 'al Hilkhot Kidush ha-Ḥodesh ... [le-] Mosheh bar Maimon (Salvation in Israel, a Commentary on Maimonides's Laws of the New Moon)
Jonathan ben Joseph of Ruzhany
Printed by Johann Kölner
Frankfurt am Main, 1720
2°. RB 25
Steinschneider, 6513,36; Vinograd, Frankfurt no. 366

ישועה בישראל והוא פירש ... על הלכות קדוש החדש ... [ל]משה בר מיימון
Yeshu'ah be-Yisrael ve-Hu Perush ... 'al Hilkhot Kidush ha-Ḥodesh ... [le-] Mosheh bar Maimon (Salvation in Israel, a Commentary on Maimonides's Laws of the New Moon)
Jonathan ben Joseph of Ruzhany
[Central Europe, mid-18th century]
MS 9. Manuscript on paper; 58 ff.; 21.2 x 32 cm

At the age of 23, Maimonides composed a treatise in Arabic on the Jewish calendar. He later incorporated an expanded version into his *Mishneh Torah* under the title *Hilkhot Kidush ha-Ḥodesh*. Maimonides's computation (*computus* or *'ibur*) was one of three such works produced by twelfth-century Sephardic rabbis. It was preceded by the *Sefer ha-'Ibur* of Abraham bar Ḥiya ha-Nasi (Savasorda) (1065–ca. 1136), written around 1123, and a composition with the same title by Abraham Ibn Ezra (1092–1167), completed in 1146.[1] Each of these treatises sought to establish a definitive calendrical cycle and eradicate variation between communities.

During the previous few centuries, outlying communities deferred to the rulings of either the authorities in Babylonia or in the Land of Israel. In 921 CE, a controversy between the two spiritual centers flared up over their differing calculations, and as a result the communities that looked to the respective rabbinic centers celebrated Passover that year on different days. The Babylonian computation prevailed within the year, however, largely due to the towering personality of Sa'adiah Gaon. He published a *computus* entitled *Kitab al-'Ibur* to undermine the authority of the Jerusalem rabbinate and to rebut Karaite criticism of the irregularities of the rabbinic calendar. Yet Sa'adiah's work on the calendar did not circulate widely in the following centuries, perhaps because of the obscurity of the subject matter, making the twelfth-century Sephardic works, including that of Maimonides, all the more important. Although the *computus* treatises of Abraham bar Ḥiya and Abraham Ibn Ezra were popular in Italy and Byzantium, Maimonides's calendrical system made the greatest impact because it was embedded in the *Mishneh Torah*.

Sefer Yeshu'ah be-Yisrael, published in Frankfurt am Main in 1720, treated Maimonides's *Hilkhot Kidush ha-Ḥodesh* (and the third chapter of his *Hilkhot Yesode ha-Torah*) as a distinct treatise, as had been Maimonides's original intention (Fig. 59). The imprint consists of Maimonides's text in the center of each page, surrounded by the standard commentaries of Abraham ben David of Posquières (Rabad), Joseph Karo, Levi Ibn Habib, and Mordecai ben Abraham Jaffe (*Levush*; 1530–1612). The work was assembled by Jonathan ben Joseph of

1 Elisheva Carlebach, *Palaces of Time: Jewish Calendar and Culture in Early Modern Europe* (Cambridge, MA: Belknap Press of Harvard University Press, 2011), 14–24.

Fig. 59 (left) Jonathan ben Joseph of Ruzhany, *Yeshu'ah be-Yisrael ve-Hu Perush ... 'al Hilkhot Kidush ha-Ḥodesh* (Frankfurt am Main: Johann Kölner, 1720), RB 25, fol. 1r.

Fig. 60 (opposite left) Jonathan ben Joseph of Ruzhany, *Yeshu'ah be-Yisrael ve-Hu Perush ... 'al Hilkhot Kidush ha-Ḥodesh* (Frankfurt am Main: Johann Kölner, 1720), RB 25, fol. 39v.

Fig. 61 (opposite right) Jonathan ben Joseph of Ruzhany, *Yeshu'ah be-Yisrael ve-Hu Perush ... 'al Hilkhot Kidush ha-Ḥodesh* [Central Europe, mid-18th century], MS 9, fol. 39v.

Ruzhany (or Rozana),[2] who added his own commentary and drew several dozen diagrams to illustrate the astronomical concepts discussed in the text. His grandfather, Jacob ben Samuel Bunim Koppelman (1555–1594), had been a student of Jaffe and authored several works in his own right, including a commentary on Joseph Albo's *Sefer ha-'Ikarim*.

In the introduction, Jonathan ben Joseph explained the impetus for this publication. He served the community of Ruzhany as rabbi during a period of intense suffering. The first decade of the eighteenth century constituted years of civil war in Poland, coupled with invasions by two foreign powers. 'Many tribulations affected the countries in succession,' he wrote. 'Plague, famine, the sword of nations warring against each other, to the point where we became impoverished, the face of the honorable people of the city and country became diminished, and people lost their possessions, I and my family among them.'[3] When cholera broke out in Ruzhany, most of the city's residents perished. The survivors relocated to the banks of the nearby river and settled in booths or tents. Jonathan vowed that if he survived and was able to return as rabbi of Ruzhany, he would travel on foot to Frankfurt am Main in order to publish this book and spread the knowledge of astronomy among Jews.

In 1720, despite the blindness that afflicted him in his later years, Jonathan succeeded in publishing *Yeshu'ah be-Yisrael* at the press of the Christian printer Johann Kölner. That same year, Jonathan edited and commented upon Abraham bar Ḥiya's astronomical work *Tsurat ha-Arets*, and in the following years he produced commentaries on other scientific works. Jews could not obtain printing licenses in Frankfurt, so Christian firms, using Jewish personnel and finances, acted as fronts for Jewish publishers. Kölner printed more than one hundred Hebrew books in Frankfurt am Main between 1708 and 1728, about half of the city's publishing output in that period. Among Kölner's most important publications were a five-volume *Arba'ah Turim* (1712–1716) and a Talmud edition (1720–1723) that was almost immediately confiscated and not released for thirty years.

Yeshu'ah be-Yisrael contains dozens of woodcut diagrams, with two images of particular importance. The decorative device used at the end of the introduction depicts a bearded man at the top and a woman at the bottom, representing the sun and moon, respectively.[4] The title

2 Spelled ראזנאי or ראיזנאי, Ruzhany is between Grodno and Brest in Belarus. On the Jewish community there, see Yosef Kohen-Tsedek, '*Ve-nitsdak kodesh*,' *Ha-Eshkol* 3 (Cracow, 1900), 214–16.

3 Translation by David Wachtel in his initial cataloguing of this book.

4 For more on Kölner's press and an image of his printer's mark, which does not appear in this edition, see Yudlov, *Hebrew Printers' Marks*, 64.

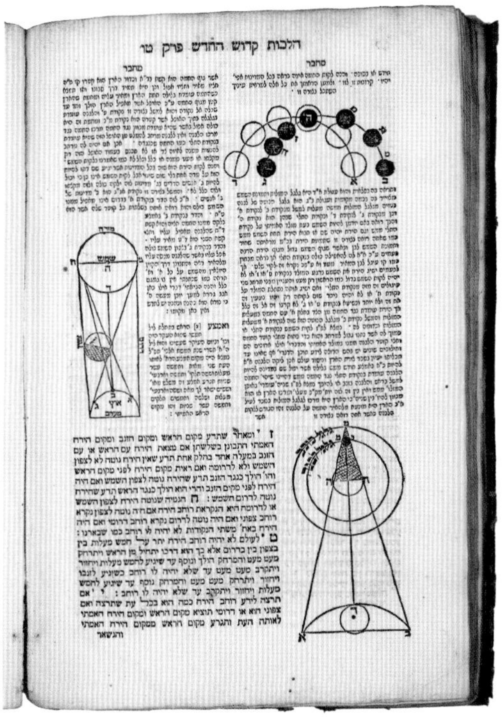

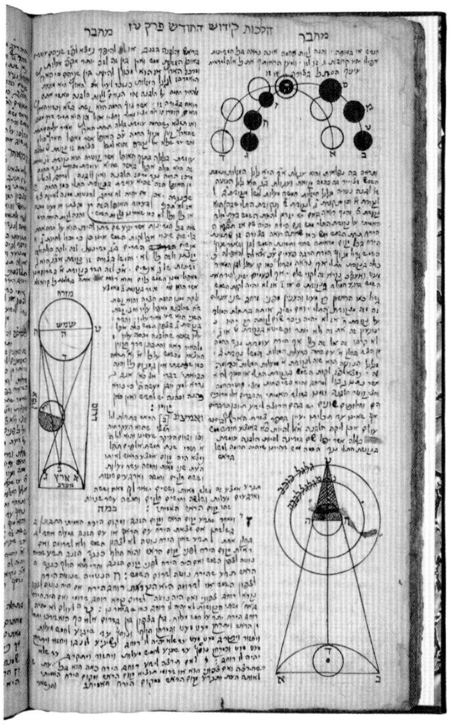

page includes depictions of the biblical figures of Moses, Aaron, David, and Jonathan. Moses and Aaron often flanked the text of Hebrew title pages, and it was common, although not as much, to include David with his harp. The appearance of Jonathan, however, is unique, having been included in honor of the author. Jonathan appears here holding a bow and arrow, illustrating how he alerted David to the threat of his father King Saul (I Samuel 20:20–22).

The last few folios of the book consist of calendrical tables of various astronomical works, including those of Maimonides's *Hilkhot Kidush ha-Ḥodesh* (fols. 54v–55r) and the fourteenth-century Toledo scholar Isaac Israeli ben Joseph's *Yesod 'Olam* (fols. 55v–56r). The earliest charts printed were those of the Sephardic astronomer, mathematician, and historian Abraham Zacuto (1452–1515), in his *Ha-Ḥibur ha-Gadol*. Translated into both Castilian and Latin and published as *Almanach Perpetuum* (Leiria, 1496), the work may have influenced European sailing expeditions, including those by Christopher Columbus and Vasco da Gama.[5]

The information covered in Maimonides's *Hilkhot Kidush ha-Ḥodesh* is extremely specialized even by scholarly standards. Esoteric in nature, publishers omitted it from an otherwise complete edition of *Mada, Ahava, Zemanim* printed in Venice in 1665 due to a lack of interest and intellectual capacity among potential readers (see cat. no. 28). Nevertheless, increased interest in science and mathematics in the eighteenth century meant that select students and scholars found the subject relevant.

Hartman MS 9 is a contemporary manuscript copy of the 1720 printed edition of Jonathan ben Joseph's *Yeshu'ah be-Yisrael*. It contains exact reproductions of the calendrical tables and dozens of text illustrations found in the Frankfurt imprint (figs. 60, 61).[6] Although the scribe is unknown, it is clear that the manuscript was copied by an individual well versed in both Judaism and science. Only one illustration contained in the printed edition does not appear in this manuscript; in its place the scribe noted that the image was also found in the astronomical and mathematical treatise *Sefer Neḥmad ve-Na'im* by astronomer and historian David Gans (1541–1613). Presumably, the scribe possessed a copy of that work as well, indicating that he was an erudite scholar with a keen interest in science.

5 José Chabás and Bernard R. Goldstein, *Astronomy in the Iberian Peninsula: Abraham Zacut and the Transition from Manuscript to Print* (Philadelphia, PA: American Philosophical Society, 2000).

6 For another example in the Hartman Collection of a scribe copying a printed book, see cat. no. 24.

31

מורה נבוכים
Moreh Nevukhim (Guide of the Perplexed)
Edited by Meshulam Solomon ben Ḥayim Segal
Printed by Israel ben Abraham
Jessnitz, 1742
2°. RB 11
Vinograd, Jessnitz no. 48

Three editions of *Moreh Nevukhim* were issued during the first eighty-five years of Hebrew printing. After Tobias Foa's 1553 edition in Sabbioneta, however, Maimonides's great philosophical treatise did not appear in print in Hebrew again for nearly two hundred years. During the sixteenth century, Jewish intellectual thought shifted from philosophy to Kabbalah, and printers either had little interest or did not find it financially viable to publish the work.

The present edition encouraged the study of Maimonides's philosophical magnum opus among members of the Jewish Enlightenment movement, or *Haskalah*, which originated in Germany during the mid-eighteenth century (Fig. 62). Many *maskilim* (proponents of *Haskalah*), including Moses Mendelssohn (1729–1786), utilized Maimonides's philosophical writings while developing complex and compartmentalized modern Jewish identities.[1] The philosophical inquiry prominent among medieval Sephardic scholars appealed to central European Jews engaged with rational thought and seeking advancement in larger European societies. Mendelssohn, like the Ashkenazic halakhist Moses Isserles and the Italian kabbalist Moses Ḥayim Luzzatto, came to be linked to Maimonides through the adage 'From Moses to Moses, none arose like Moses.' In jest, he attributed his crooked posture to the hours of his youth spent studying the *Guide*.[2] Mendelssohn's famous *Be'ur*, a Hebrew commentary accompanying his German translation of the Pentateuch, unreservedly adopted a Maimonidean approach.[3]

This edition was published by Israel ben Abraham, a proselyte who had reputedly been a Christian clergyman. He authored a Yiddish–Hebrew grammar entitled *Mafteaḥ Leshon ha-Kodesh*, printed by the Proops press in Amsterdam in 1713. Between 1707 and 1744, Israel ben Abraham established printing houses in Berlin, Jessnitz, Wandsbeck, and elsewhere, and issued more than seventy Hebrew books. He had acquired the typographical equipment previously used by the Amsterdam printer Moses ben Avraham Avinu, also a convert to Judaism as his name suggests (see cat. no. 34).[4]

Based largely on Foa's edition of *Moreh Nevukhim*, Israel ben Abraham's own edition includes the commentaries of Shem Tov ben Joseph Ibn Shem Tov, Profiat Duran, and Asher (Bonan) ben Abraham Crescas. It was edited by Meshulam Solomon ben Ḥayim Segal of Jessnitz, who also incorporated the indexes of *Kelale Pirke ha-Moreh*, *Perush ha-Milot ha-Zarot*, and *Moreh Mekom ha-Pesukim* as found in the Venice 1551 edition. However, previously published poems and Crescas's introduction were not included.

1 Irene E. Zwiep, 'From Moses to Moses…? Manifestations of Maimonides in the Early Jewish Enlightenment,' in *Moses Maimonides (1138–1204): His Religious, Scientific, and Philosophical* Wirkungsgeschichte *in Different Cultural Contexts*, ed. Görge K. Hasselhoff and Otfried Fraisse (Würzburg: Ergon, 2004), 323–36.

2 Alexander Altmann, *Moses Mendelssohn: A Biographical Study* ([n.p.] University of Alabama Press, 1973), 12.

3 Adrian Sackson, 'From Moses to Moses: Anthropomorphism and Divine Incorporeality in Maimonides's *Guide* and Mendelssohn's *Bi'ur*,' *Harvard Theological Review* 112, no. 2 (2019): 209–34.

4 Marvin J. Heller, 'Observations on the Worker to Book Production Ratio in an Eighteenth Century Hebrew Printing-House,' in *Studies in the Making of the Early Hebrew Book*, 257–63; and Heller, 'Israel ben Abraham, His Hebrew Printing-Press in Wandsbeck and the Books He Published,' in *Further Studies in the Making of the Early Hebrew Book* (Leiden: Brill, 2013), 169–93.

Fig. 62 *Moreh Nevukhim* (Jessnitz: Israel ben Abraham, 1742), RB 11, fol. 2r.

סדר סדור התפילה
Seder Sidur ha-Tefilah (Order of Prayers)
Sana'a, 1826
MS 27. Manuscript on paper; 2 vols.: 322ff.; 16.6 x 23.1 cm, 17.1 x 23.6 cm

מורה נבוכים
Moreh Nevukhim (Guide of the Perplexed)
[Yemen, 19th century]
MS 25. Manuscript on paper; 2 vols.: 280ff.; 21.6 x 30.6 cm

With Ottoman expansion in the sixteenth century, rabbinic emissaries from the Land of Israel traveled south to Yemen, and Yemenite Jews made their way north. New schools of thought and previously unknown halakhic and kabbalistic writings, including those printed in Europe, arrived in Yemen and influenced local practices and approaches. Shalom Shabazi (1619–1720), a prolific poet, disseminated Lurianic Kabbalah, and Sar Shalom Sharabi (1720–1777), author of a kabbalistic prayer book and eventual head of *Yeshivat Bet El* in Jerusalem, deepened its influence. Concurrently, Shalom Iraqi al-Kohen (1685–1780), a rabbi and community leader who worked in a financial capacity for the Yemenite political authorities for decades, worked to change local liturgical traditions to conform with the prominent kabbalistically infused Ottoman rites. He donated printed books to various communities and successfully convinced 19 of the 22 synagogues in Sana'a, the spiritual and cultural center of Yemenite Jewry, to change their rite.[1]

The conflict between those who maintained the local rites (*baladi*) and those open to influences from the Levant (*shami*) was somewhat mediated by Yiḥye Tsaleḥ (Maharits; 1713–1805).[2] He promoted Yemenite traditions in law and liturgy, citing earlier authorities to reinforce established practice. But he did not entirely reject outside influences, honoring kabbalists from Safed and elsewhere and even incorporating certain Sephardic and kabbalistic practices, such as the recitation of Kabbalat Shabbat Friday evening before the night-time service and the repetition of the final words of the *Shema* prayer.

Tsaleḥ's commentary on the prayer book, *'Ets Ḥayim*, proved especially influential in formulating Yemenite traditions. The Hartman Collection contains a pair of manuscripts featuring Tsaleḥ's commentary: volume 1 includes prayers for Rosh Hashanah, Yom Kippur, fast days, and penitential prayers, while volume 2 consists of prayers for the Festivals and the Passover Haggadah (Fig. 63). The set probably included one additional volume devoted to daily and Sabbath prayers. The scribe based his work on Maimonides, Amram Gaon, Tsaleḥ, and the Safed kabbalist Isaac Luria, though the latter, wrote the scribe, was largely misunderstood. Other kabbalistic influences – including *Tikun Ḥatsot*, with liturgical poems (*piyutim*) by Moses Alshekh (1508–1593), Ḥayim ha-Kohen of Aleppo (1585–1655), and Moses Zacut (1625–1697) – indicate the widespread connections Yemenite Jews secured and preserved with foreign communities in the early modern period. In addition, volume 1 includes an anonymous elegy (*kinah*) from Jerusalem, meant to be chanted to a local wedding tune of *Kol Ḥatan*, and a prayer recited when a community fasted in times of drought. Nevertheless, the work as a whole did not indicate a wholesale adoption of *shami* liturgy, for the manuscript lacks other prominent kabbalistic customs, including *Tikun Lel Shavu'ot* and the welcoming of celestial guests (*ushpizin*) on Sukkot.

1 Yosef Tobi, *'Iyunim be-Megilat Teman* (Jerusalem: Magnes Press, 1986), 151–80.
2 See cat. no. 10 for a printed book in the Hartman Collection once in the possession of Yiḥye Tsaleḥ.

Fig. 63 (left) *Sidur ha-Tefilah* (Sana'a, 1826), MS 27, vol. 1, fol. 1v.

Fig. 64 (right) *Sidur ha-Tefilah* (Sana'a, 1826), MS 27, vol. 1, fol. 57r.

In addition, the volumes include Tsaleḥ's explanations of particular *halakhot*, a verbatim account of a sermon he gave on the Sabbath before Passover (vol. 1, fols. 2r–4r), and a compilation of laws relating to Passover entitled *Zevaḥ Pesaḥ* by his brother Suleiman Tsaleḥ. The section of Torah readings for Festivals appears in a square script used in writing Torah scrolls, though with vowel points, and each verse is followed by its Aramaic translation (*targum*), as per the Yemenite custom of publicly reading the *targum* following the recitation of each biblical verse. The scribe was conscious of aesthetics, however, so the Aramaic texts to the Song of the Sea (Exodus 15) and Song of David (II Samuel 22) appear adjacent to the biblical text and do not disturb the traditional brick-pattern layout copied from ritual scrolls (Fig. 64). It is clear, both from the careful layout and the scribe's explicit reference on the title page, that the manuscripts were intended to serve as a guide for a printed publication. Where and how this might have been accomplished is not clear, as print technology was not available locally to Yemenite Jews at the time.

The Hartman Collection contains another two-volume set that speaks to attempts among Yemenite Jews to maintain tradition in the nineteenth century. This *Moreh Nevukhim* in the original Judeo-Arabic was illustrated on almost every page. The title pages, dozens of headings, and hundreds of words throughout the volumes are decorated in red, green, and purple ink, each unique and in multiple pigments (Fig. 65). The first volume, consisting of part 1 of the *Guide* and home to the vast majority of decoration, was penned by a single scribe. The second volume, which contains only minor rudimentary pen illustration at the beginning of part 3, was composed by several scribes and may have been produced in separate parts.

פצל ד'

ליס פרצֿא מן ד'כר כל מעני יקֿץ עליה וֹלך טֿאהֿס
לאן ליסֿת הֹדֹב ֹאמֿטֿלֹה אלכֿבֿ פי טֿלֹגֹֿב כל נֹדֿכר מן תֿלֹך
אלמעאני מֿא כֹאן מֿחֹתֿאגֿין ֹאיֹה פי בֹרֹדֿנֹא לֹא גֿיר פֹמן וֹלך

ירֹד וֹעלֹה פי טֿלֹגֹֿב ֹאלֿעֹברֹחֹנֹייֹה ללֹהֹבֿוֹט וֹטֿוֹלֹע

פֿאמֿא ֹאנֹתֹֿקֹל ֹאלֹגֹֿסֿם מן מוֹצֹֿע מֹלֹא שֿי מֿוֹצֹֿע ֹאֹקֹפֿל מֹנֹדֿ
קֿיֹל ירֹד" וֹאדֿי ֹאנֹתֹֿקֹל מן מוֹצֹֿע מֹא שֿי מֿוֹצֹֿע מֿעֹל מֿי
וֹאֹך ֹאלֹמוֹצֹֿע קֿיֹל עֹלֹה " הֹס ֹאסֿתֹֿעֿיר הֹדֹֿא ֹן ֹלֹאסֿמֿאֹן צ
בֿלֹמֿלֹאֹה וֹללֹעֹצֹֿמֿה חֿתֿי אֹדֿי ֹמֿחֹטֹֿת מֹגֹֿלֹה' ֹאֹטֹֿבֿך קֿיֹל
ירֹד " וֹאֹדֿי עֹלֹה מֹגֹֿלֹתֹֿה פי ֹאֹגֹֿלֹאֹה קֿיֹל עֹלֹה " ֹקֹֿל הֹב
הֹבֿוֹ חֹֿסֿר בֹֿקֹֿרֹבֹך יֿעֹלֹה עֹלֹיך וֹגֿו' וֹאֹהֹה הֹֿרֹד וֹגֹֿו' וֹקֹֿל וֹנֹתֹֿן
יֿי ֹאֹלֹיֹך עֿלֹיֿם עֿל כל גֿֿויֿי הֹאֹרֹץ " וֹקֹֿל ויֿגֹֿדֹל יֿי ֹאֹרֿת
ֹשֿלֹמֹה לֿמֹעֹלֹה " וֹקֹֿד עֹֿלֹמֹה כֹהֹֿרֹת ֹאֹקֹתֹֿעֿמֿטֿלֹהֹס מעֹֿלֹיֹן ב
בֹֿקֹֿדֹם וֹלֹא מורֿיֿדֿין "   **וֹעֹלֹי יֿֿֿֿהֿֿֿ אֹפֿֿֿֿ וֹ אֹֿֿֿ**

יֿקֿתֹֿעֿמֿל פֿי ֹאנֹחֹטֹֿוֹט
ֹאֹנֹ"ֹד וֹכֿוֹן ֹאֹאנֹסֹֿאֹן וֹהֹגֹֿה בֹֹפֹֿדֹֿרֹה נֹחֹו אֹמֿר לֹֿסֹֿיֹס גֿרֿֿש
וֹיֹֹֹרֹד הֹנֹה ירֹד " וֹכֹֿרֹֹך מֹן ֹאֹגֹֿגֹֿב בֹֿפֹֿכֹֿרֹה נֹחֹו אֹמֿר עֿאֹל
גֹֿיֹכֹֿן יֹֹֹקֹֿל עֹלֹה "   **וֹֹבֿלֿמֿאֹ בֹֿנֿאֿ מֿעֿֿשֿֿֿה**

ֹסֹֿאהֹֿדֿֿֿיֿיֿ פֿי חֹֿפֹֿל
שֿי ֹאֹסֹֿאֹפֹֿלֹֿיֹן בֹֿאֹמֹֿוֹצֹֿע וֹבֹֿמֹֿדֹֿרֹֿגֹֿה וֹֹגֹֿוֹד בֹֿאֹלֹֿאֹפֹֿה
שֿי ֹאֹמֹֿחֹֿיֹֿט וֹכֹֿאֹן הֹו הֹֹע פֿי הֹעֹל ֹשֹֿעֹלֹֿיֹֿן עֹלֿי חֹֿנֹֿירֿֿ'
וֹֹבֹֿוֹרֹדֹה וֹגֹֿלֹֹלֹֿתֹֿה וֹעֹצֹֿמֹֿהֹֿ לֹֿא עֹֿלֹו מֹֿכֹֿאֹן וֹשֹֿא תֹֹֹֿ כֹֿמֹֿי שֹֿא
חֹֿיֹֿצֹֿא עֹֿלֹם מֹֿנֹֿה וֹאֹפֹֿאֹֿצֹֹֿ' וֹחֹֿי עֹלֹי בֹֿעֹ גֹֿגֹֿא פֹֿעֹֿבֹֿר ֹאֹורֹֿחֹֿי
עֹלֹֹ' ֹאֹלֹֹבֹֿי' ֹאֹו בֹֿחֹֿלֹוֹל סֹֿבֹֿיֹֿנֹה פֹי מֹֿוֹצֹֿע בֹֿירֹֿידֹֿה וֹעֹֿבֹֿר בֹֿאֹֿרֹתֹֿפֹֿאֹע
תֹֹֿלֹך ֹאֹהֹֿצֹֿה' ֹאֹלֹֿבֹֿוֹֿייֹֿה עֹֿן ֹאֹשֹֿבֹֿך ֹאֹו חֹֿנֹֹֿטֹֿה' ֹאֹסֹֿבֹֿיֹֿנֹה עֹֿן ֹאֹמֹֿוֹצֹֿע
בֹֿעֹֿלֹֹייֹֿך " פֹֿכֹֿל עֹֿלֹֹיֹֿך וֹירֹֿיֹדֹה ֹאֹגֹֿרֹהֹא מֹֿנֹֿסֹֿוֹבֹֿך לֹֿו לֹֿבֹֿחֿֿֿֿ
תֹֿע ֹאֹחֹֿכֹֿמֹֿי ֹאֹמֹֿרֹֿחֹֿו בֹהֹא הֹרֹי ֹטֹֿמֹֿעֹֿנֹֿי "   **וֹכֹֿֿֿֿֿדֿֿֿֿ רֿֿ יֿֿֿצֹֿאֿֿֿ**

ֹאֹרֹֹֿי ֹנֹֿלֹה מֹֿכֹֿר בֹֿאֹֿמֹֿה" ֹאֹו כֹֿאֹקֹֿלֹֿיֹם "
ב

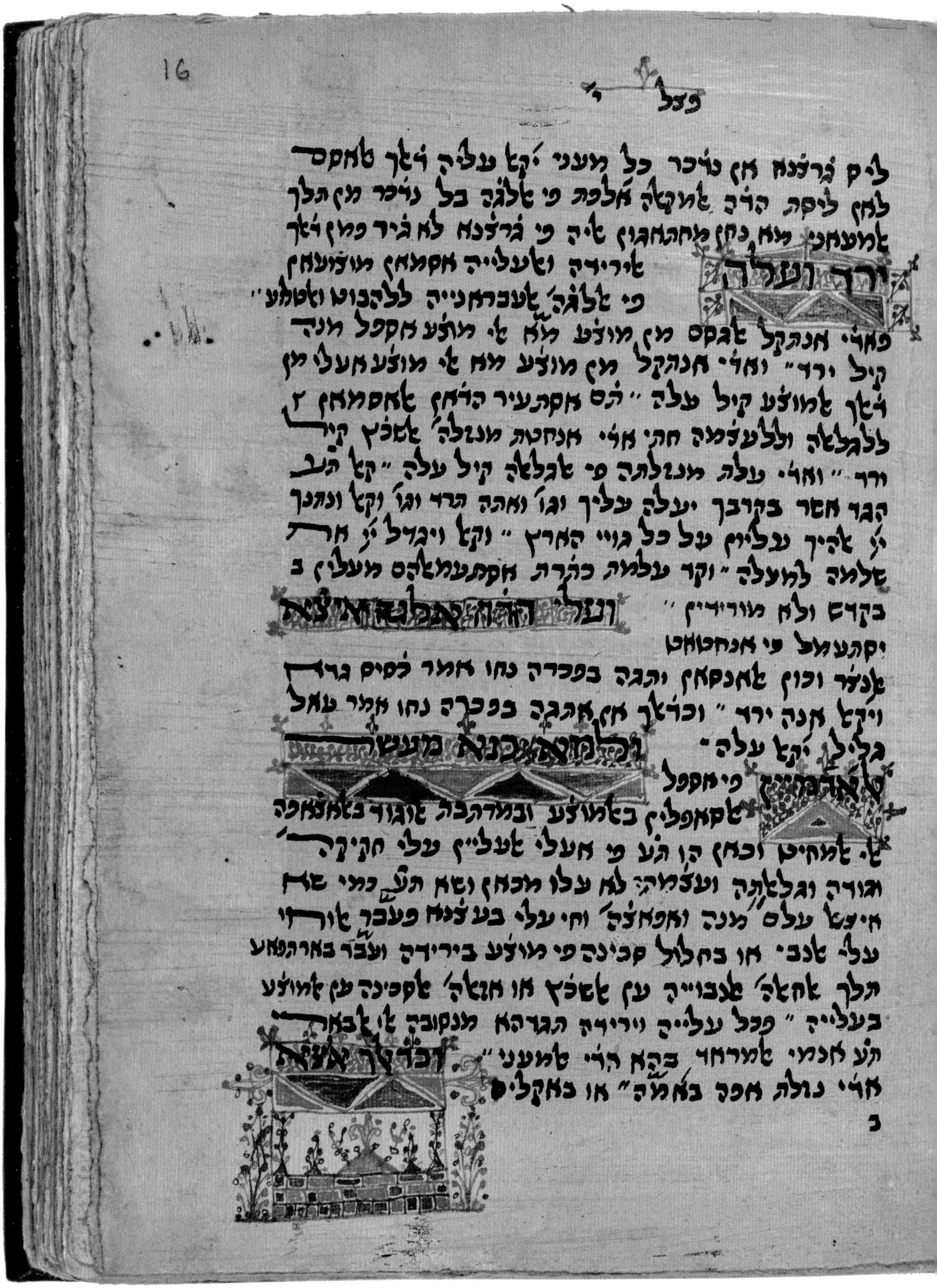

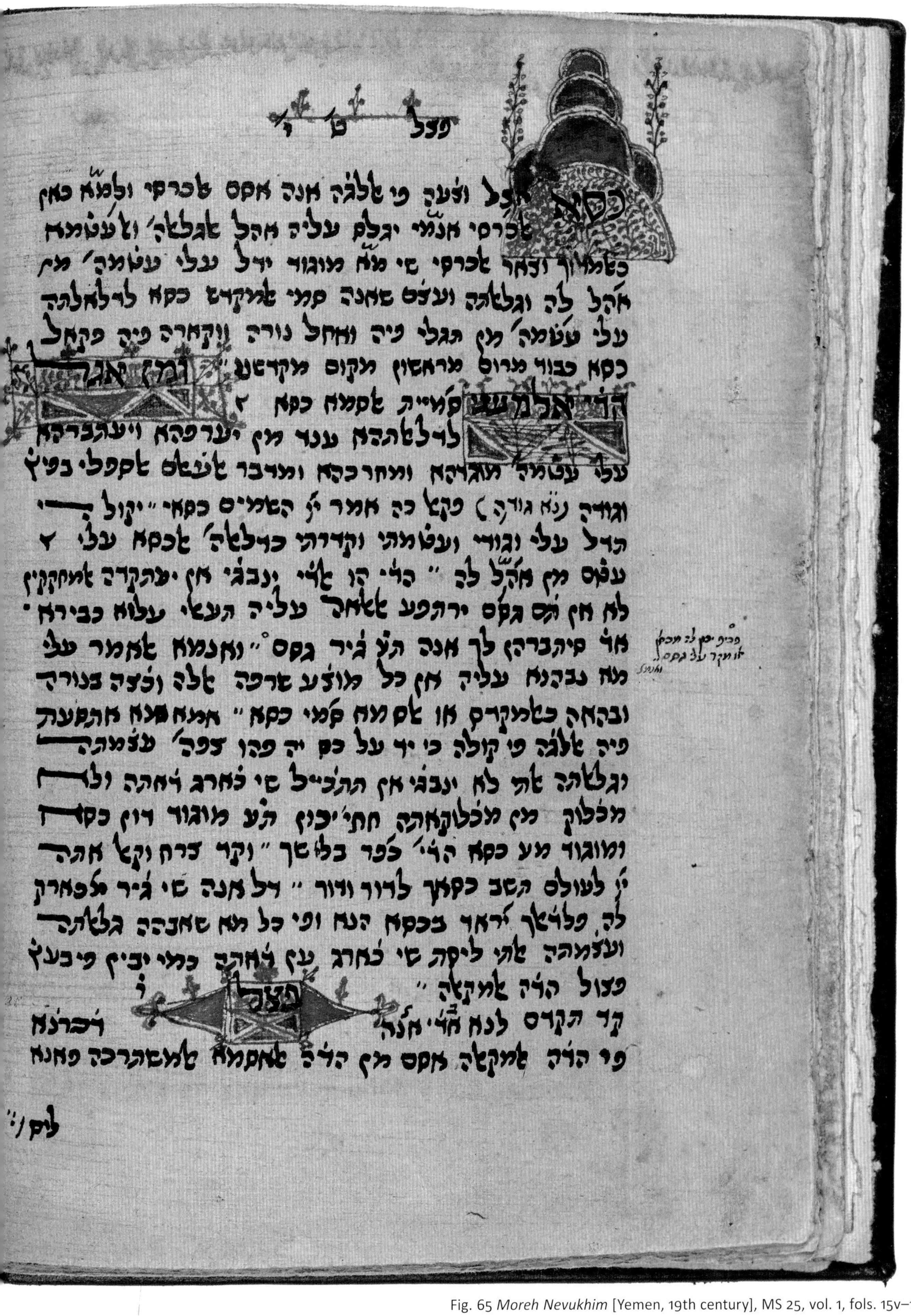

Fig. 65 *Moreh Nevukhim* [Yemen, 19th century], MS 25, vol. 1, fols. 15v–16r.

33

[שאלות ותשובות]
[*She'elot u-Teshuvot*] (Responsa)
[Oxford, mid-19th century]
MS 8. Manuscript on paper; 102ff.; 16.8 x 21.7 cm

This volume is a nineteenth-century copy of a sixteenth-century manuscript of Maimonides's responsa found in the Bodleian Library in Oxford (Fig. 66).[1] The manuscript consists of 221 responsa and differs significantly from all printed editions of Maimonides's correspondence. The responsa reproduced here are less extensive than the published renditions, which is unusual as manuscripts are generally older, and therefore deemed more authoritative, than printed editions. This manuscript was heavily edited, probably by Moritz Steinschneider (1816–1907), and contains notes marking the corresponding responsa found in *Pe'er ha-Dor* (Amsterdam, 1765). The copyist also supplemented the manuscript version of a given responsum by including information contained in that printed edition.

In addition to its textual importance, this manuscript is significant for its composition and its ownership. According to a note on fol. 1r, the copy was made between 1854 and 1858 by an unnamed student of Steinschneider, a pioneer of the *Wissenschaft des Judenthums* (Science of Judaism) movement in Germany that promoted academic study of Jewish history and culture (Fig. 67).[2] During those years, Steinschneider was hard at work on his *Catalogus Librorum Hebraeorum in Bibliotheca Bodleiana* (Berlin, 1852–1860), a multi-volume, Latin-language catalogue of the Hebrew printed books housed in the Bodleian Library. The Bodleian had instantly become the world's most important repository of Hebrew printed books when it acquired the collection of David Oppenheim.[3] Although Steinschneider managed to compile much of the catalogue while in Berlin by using existing catalogues and with help from the Bodleian Library staff, he also spent five summers in Oxford in order to complete the project. Stemming largely from this magnum opus, which raised Hebrew bibliography to an unprecedented scholarly level, he became universally regarded as the father of modern Hebrew bibliography.[4]

Steinschneider helped lay the foundation for modern Jewish scholarship to such an extent that it may be said that all contemporary students of Jewish history and culture are his academic progeny. To be sure, he was not merely a bibliographer. Throughout his scholarly career, Steinschneider published more than 1,400 books and articles on a wide array of subjects, including literature, philosophy, science, and booklore, in languages such as German, Italian, French, English, Hebrew, and Latin. Defined equally by his Jewishness and his modernity, Steinschneider sought to contextualize all of Jewish culture within a global scheme. To Steinschneider, the medieval ancestors of modern Jewry were anything but solitary and separate from Christian and Muslim societies. He demonstrated how Jews served as conduits between traditions and how they reflected the trends in the dominant cultures. As a preliminary step toward composing a complete cultural history, Steinschneider

1 For the source manuscript, see Bodleian Libraries, University of Oxford, MS. Oppenheim Add. 4° 143; and Adolf Neubauer, *Catalogue of the Hebrew Manuscripts in the Bodleian Library and in the College Libraries of Oxford*, 2 vols. (Oxford: Clarendon Press, 1886–1906), no. 2359. See also Hirschfeld, *Descriptive Catalogue of the Hebrew Manuscripts of the Montefiore Library*, no. 97, where Hirschfeld misidentified Oxford, MS. Pococke 280b (Neubauer 2218) as the volume upon which it was based. See also Halberstam, *Kohelet Shelomoh*, no. 130.

2 See Irene Zwiep's essay in this volume.

3 See cat. no. 26 for a printed book in the Hartman Collection once in the possession of David Oppenheim.

4 See Reimund Leicht and Gad Freudenthal (eds.), *Studies on Steinschneider: Moritz Steinschneider and the Emergence of the Science of Judaism in Nineteenth-Century Germany* (Leiden: Brill, 2012).

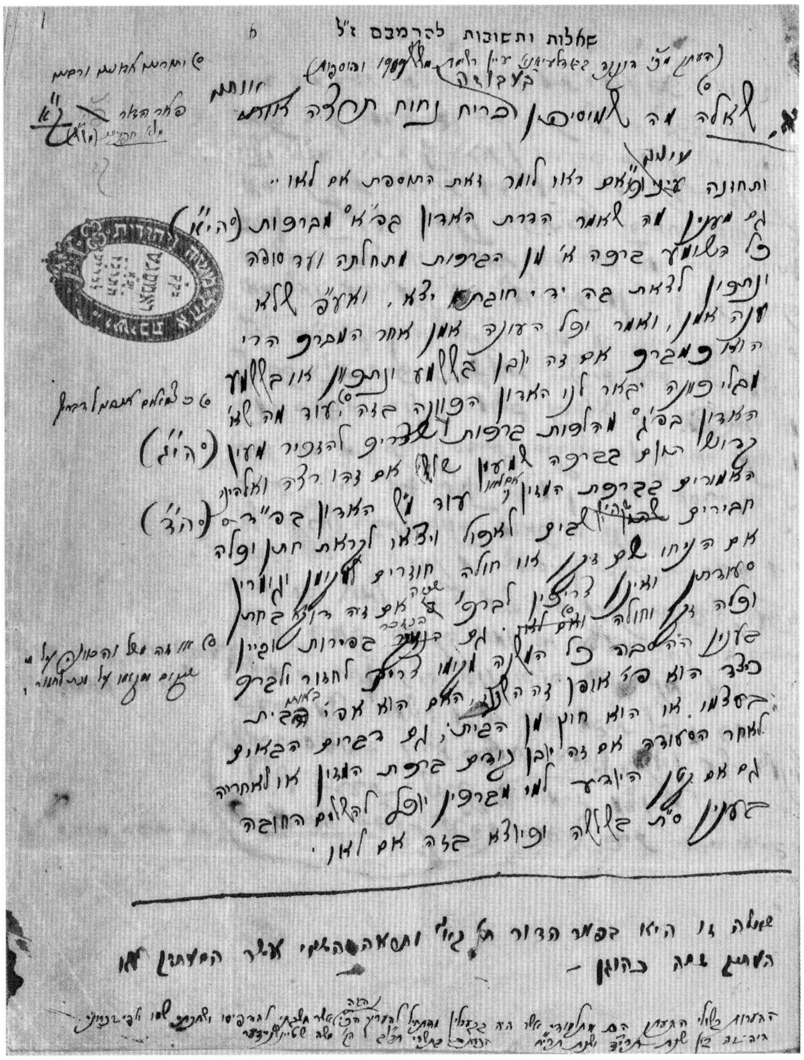

Fig. 66 [Responsa] [Oxford, mid-19th century], MS 8, fol. 1r.

undertook a thorough and scientific study of all the available literary material. Thus, he devoted himself to the preparation of bibliographies, producing catalogues of Hebrew manuscript collections in Leiden (1858), Munich (1875; 2nd ed., 1896), Hamburg (1878), Berlin (1878–1897), and elsewhere, enabling scholars to publish literary and cultural histories to the present day.

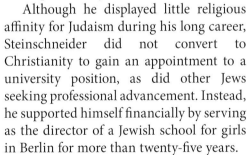

Although he displayed little religious affinity for Judaism during his long career, Steinschneider did not convert to Christianity to gain an appointment to a university position, as did other Jews seeking professional advancement. Instead, he supported himself financially by serving as the director of a Jewish school for girls in Berlin for more than twenty-five years.

As with other volumes in the Hartman Collection, the present manuscript once belonged to Salomon Halberstam and Moses Montefiore (see cat. nos. 2 and 5).

Fig. 67 Portrait of Moritz Steinschneider. Library of the Jewish Theological Seminary, PNT G1495.

פרקי משה הוא ספר הרפואות
Pirke Mosheh hu Sefer ha-Refu'ot (Aphorisms of Moses)
[Printed by Chava Grossman]
Lviv, [ca. 1830]
4°. RB 15
Steinschneider, 6513,148; Zedner, 579; Roest, 858; Vinograd, Lemberg no. 493

Pirke Mosheh was Maimonides's best-known medical treatise. Originally composed in Arabic, like nearly all of his writings, two thirteenth-century Hebrew translations survive in manuscript. The predominant version, by the Italian translator Nathan ben Eliezer ha-Me'ati, appears in a manuscript in the Hartman Collection and was used in this first printing of *Pirke Mosheh* in 1830 (see cat. no. 2).[1]

The dating of the imprint has been a matter of scholarly interest. The title page states: 'Gedruckt bei Jides Rosanes 1804' (Printed by Judith Rosanes 1804). Judith Rosanes (fl. 1788–1805) was the first Jewish woman to operate a Hebrew printing press for an extended period of time. Her press, originally in Zolkiew (in modern-day Ukraine) during her husband's lifetime and then in nearby Lviv (Lemberg) after his death, employed more than twenty people and produced more than fifty books. In the mid-nineteenth century, long after she had died, printers occasionally placed her name with an earlier date on the title page instead of their own name and the correct date in order to circumvent printing bans established by government authorities.[2] This book was one such case; the '04' of the year appears in a different font, and bibliographers almost universally attribute the book to the 1830s (Fig. 68).[3]

Judith's extended family made up one of the preeminent Jewish printing dynasties of eastern Europe. Her great-grandfather, Uri Phoebus, had opened a printing press in Zolkiew in 1691 after successfully printing books for several years in Amsterdam. Judith and her husband, David Mann, printed in Zolkiew until the latter's death, but she established a new press in Lviv in 1782. Their son, Naftali Hertz Grossman, set up his own press in Lviv in 1797, and at least two cousins and their wives and children printed for decades in both Zolkiew and Lviv. After Naftali's death in 1827, his wife Chava continued running the press until 1849, and their daughter Feige took over operations until at least 1857. The majority of books falsely attributed to Judith, such as this imprint, were probably issued by Chava.

Women have played a rich and prominent role in Hebrew printing from its inception.[4] In 1477, less than a decade after the first printed Hebrew books were issued in Rome, the

1 The final section of this compilation is incomplete in this edition. It was published from a manuscript by Senior Sachs in *Ha-Teḥiyah* 1 (1850): 35–38, with notations.

2 Sara Fraenkel, 'Who was the Falsificator of Judith Rozanis in Lemberg?' [Hebrew], *Proceedings of the Ninth World Congress of Jewish Studies*, Division D, vol. 1 (Jerusalem, 1985): 175–82.

3 Abraham Yaari, 'Judith Rosanes' Hebrew Press at Lwów' [Hebrew], *Kiryat Sefer* 17 (1940), 108, no. 48. According to Yaari, the books falsely attributed to Rosanes were issued between 1830 and 1850. Many bibliographers date the printing of *Pirke Mosheh* to 1834, although Steinschneider put it at 1835. The basis for the dating is the book's accompanying *haskamah* (rabbinic approbation) of Eleazar Landau, which is signed יום ג' ד"ג אדר פרקי משה לפרט (Tuesday, 23 Adar 5730 = March 18, 1830) (with a ד, not a כ); a single dot above the letters *kof* and another above the *mem* in the chronogram indicate that they are not to be counted, while a dot above the letter *heh* designates its numerical value as five thousand rather than merely five.

4 For women and printing, see Abraham M. Habermann, *Nashim 'Ivriyot be-Tor Madpisot Mesadrot Motsi'ot la-Or ve-Tomkhot ba-Meḥaberim* (Berlin: R. Mas., 1933); Abraham Yaari, 'Women in the Holy Endeavor (of Printing)' [Hebrew], in *Studies in Hebrew Booklore*, 256–302; Abraham Karp, *From the Ends of the Earth: Judaic Treasures of the Library of Congress* (Washington, DC: Library of Congress, 1991), 167–71; Brad Sabin Hill, 'A Catalogue of Hebrew Printers,' *British Library Journal* 21 (1995): 34–65 (42, 45);

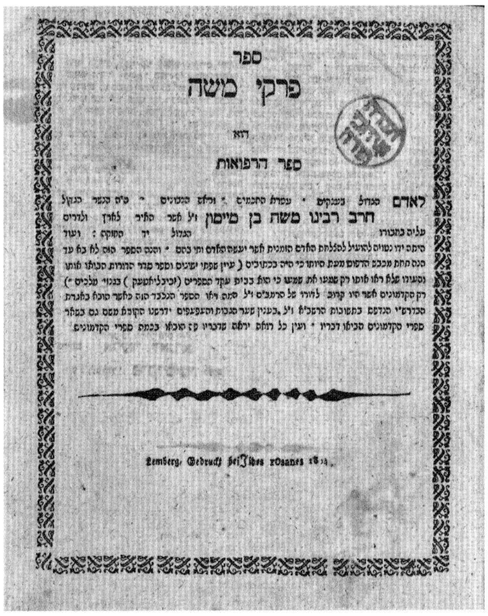
ספר
פרקי משה
הוא
ספר הרפואות
הרב רבינו משה בן מימון

Fig. 68 *Pirke Mosheh* (Lemberg: [Chava Grossman,] 1830), RB 15, fol. 1r.

ethical work *Beḥinat 'Olam* was edited or typeset by Estellina Conat. Doña Reyna Mendes (ca. 1539–1599), daughter of the philanthropist Doña Gracia Mendes, established a press (the first Jewish woman to do so) in Constantinople and released about fifteen volumes, including prayer books and a Talmud tractate.[5] Through the nineteenth century, the names of more than fifty women appeared on title pages or in colophons of Jewish books. Some were mentioned specifically, like Estellina and Reyna, while others appeared anonymously, such as 'Widow and Orphans Proops' (Amsterdam) and 'Widow and Brothers Romm' (Vilna), two of the most active and influential Hebrew presses of the eighteenth and nineteenth centuries, respectively.

Young girls were often put to work as *zetserins* (typesetters) in family print shops.[6] The sisters Ella and Gella, daughters of a convert named Moses ben Avraham Avinu who printed in several cities at the end of the seventeenth and the beginning of the eighteenth centuries, even left testimonials. In 1696, a prayer book issued by the press in Dessau closed with the statement:

> These Yiddish letters I set with my own hand.
> Ella, daughter of the Honorable Rabbi Moses from Holland.
> My years are no more than nine.
> I am the only daughter among six children.
> Therefore if you should find an error,
> This text was set by a child, remember.[7]

Just three years later, at the age of 12, Ella hinted in the colophon of *Masekhet Nidah* – one volume of the near-complete edition of the Talmud issued by the press in Frankfurt an der Oder (1697–1699) – that she was in search of a husband.[8]

and Jennifer Breger, 'Printers,' in *The Shalvi/Hyman Encyclopedia of Jewish Women* (December 31, 2009, Jewish Women's Archive), http://jwa.org/encyclopedia/article/printers (accessed November 8, 2022).

5 See cat. no. 22 for a *Mishneh Torah* (Venice, 1574–1575), once in the possession of an Italian Jewish woman named Aurelia bat Moses (from Rovigo).

6 Chava Turniansky, 'Meydlekh in der altyidisher literatur,' in *Jiddische Philologie. Festschrift für Erika Timm*, ed. Walter Röll and Simon Neuberg (Tübingen: Niemeyer, 1999), 7–20.

7 Kathryn Hellerstein, *A Question of Tradition: Women Poets in Yiddish, 1586–1987* (Stanford, CA: Stanford University Press, 2014), 61–69 (62). Evidently, Gella was born after the publication of this book.

8 The colophon, with its explicit chronogram, reads: על ידי הפועל במלאכת הקודש באמונה הזעציר ישראל בן לא"א כהר"ר משה שלי"ט / וע"י אחותו הבתולה עלה בת כהר"ר משה שלי"ט : בשנת **נ**קבה **תסבב גבר** לפ"ק -- 'By the hand of the faithful typesetter in this holy work, Yisrael ben Moshe / And by the hand of his maiden sister Ella bat Moshe, in the year *Nekevah* ***tesovev gaver*** [a woman shall go after a man]' [Jeremiah 31:22].

35

מאמר תחיית המתים
Ma'amar Teḥiyat ha-Metim (Treatise on the Resurrection of the Dead)
Scribe: Sebastiano Solari
[Rome (Vatican City?), ca. 1835]
MS 26. Manuscript on paper; 20ff.; 21.8 x 31 cm

Beyond his monumental literary contributions, Maimonides composed numerous letters, essays, and treatises on a variety of topics. His writings on medicine appeared initially as responses to specific queries, often posed by members of the Fatimid or Ayyubid political elite. Likewise, his responsa attended to halakhic challenges of the moment, and were only later compiled in book form and treated as a unit. Larger discourses, like *Igeret ha-Shemad* (Epistle on Forced Conversion) and *Igeret Teman* (Epistle to Yemen), composed in 1165 and 1172, respectively, were penned to bolster Jews facing a host of spiritual, social, and political challenges.

The essay eliciting the longest-lasting interest may have been his *Ma'amar Teḥiyat ha-Metim*.[1] In 1191, Maimonides learned that Samuel ben 'Ali Gaon of Baghdad, with whom he had clashed previously, had written an epistle of his own accusing his rival in Egypt (though not by name) of denying the rabbinic tenet that the souls of the deceased would be materially resurrected.[2] The allegation itself was not new, as Maimonides's short references to the belief – as part of his 13 Principles of Faith and in the *Mishneh Torah* – had already elicited doubt and criticism.[3] In response to Maimonides's outline of angelic life in the World-to-Come, Abraham ben David of Posquières (Rabad; ca. 1125–1198) remarked, 'This man's words, it seems to me, are akin to one who states that the resurrection of the dead refers not to bodies but to souls alone.'[4] In the years preceding Samuel ben 'Ali's attack, Maimonides had heard reports of philosophically inclined men arguing erroneously that his views on the subject were purely allegorical.

Maimonides opened his Treatise on the Resurrection of the Dead by panning his detractors for misconstruing what he regarded as clear, equating their accusations against him with trinitarian readings of Deuteronomy 6:4 (*Shema Yisrael*). Defensiveness aside, Maimonides sought to articulate more fully his thoughts on a subject that he had only pithily acknowledged previously. He argued that the concept of resurrection entailed accepting the Creator's omnipotence, which in turn allowed for the possibility of miracles. His commitment to rationality notwithstanding, Maimonides insisted on a straightforward, if succinct, reading of the concept of resurrection.[5] However, he emphatically distinguished between the temporary eschatological period in which souls would return to bodily life and the more ethereal World-to-Come, when the righteous would exist in pure spirit without evil or bodily concerns.

As with much of Maimonides's other work, the essay was translated into Hebrew soon after it circulated in its original Judeo-Arabic.[6] The first printed edition of *Ma'amar*

1 See Davidson, *Moses Maimonides*, 513–37; Kraemer, *Maimonides*, 407–25.

2 Ezekiel 37; Daniel 12:2-3; Mishnah, *Sanhedrin* 10:1. On the epistle from Samuel ben 'Ali, see Tzvi Langermann, 'Igeret R. Shemu'el ben 'Ali be-'Inyan Teḥiyat ha-Metim,' *Kobez al Yad* 15 (2001): 39–94. See also Herbert A. Davidson, 'Maimonides and Samuel Ben Ali,' in *Studies in the History of Culture and Science: A Tribute to Gad Freudenthal*, ed. Resianne Fontaine et al. (Leiden: Brill, 2011), 171–88.

3 *Mishneh Torah, Hilkhot Teshuvah* 3:6.

4 Rabad gloss on *Mishneh Torah, Hilkhot Teshuvah* 8:2.

5 Tzvi Langermann, 'Maimonides and Miracles: The Growth of a (Dis)belief,' *Jewish History* 18, nos. 2/3 (2004): 147–72.

6 See Jacob I. Dienstag, 'Maimonides' Treatise on Resurrection: Bibliography of Editions, Translations and

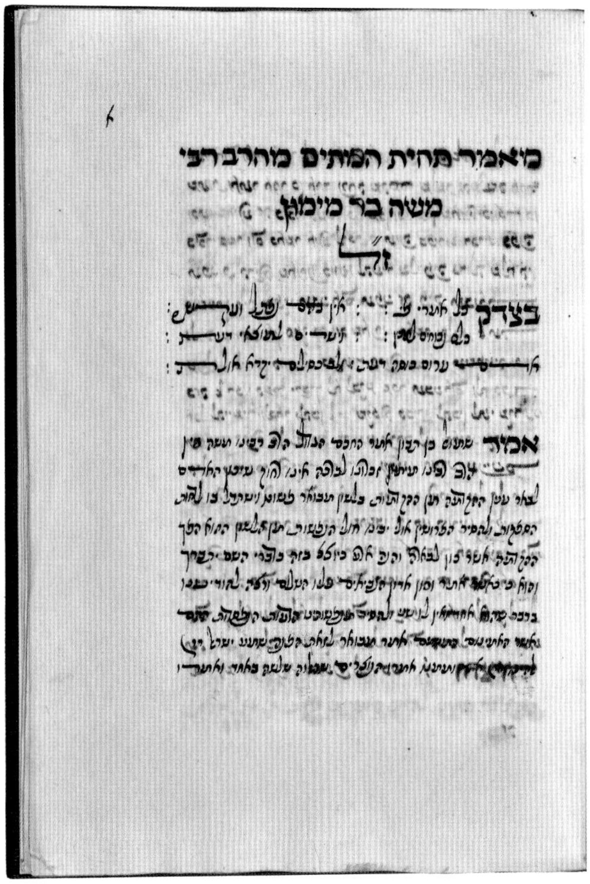

Fig. 69 *Ma'amar Teḥiyat ha-Metim* [Rome, ca. 1835], MS 26, fol. 1r.

Teḥiyat ha-Metim, published in Constantinople in 1569, reproduced the translation of Samuel Ibn Tibbon, while Judah ben Solomon al-Ḥarizi's rendition remained in manuscript.[7] In the fifteenth century, Flavius Mithridates, a Jewish convert to Catholicism, produced a Latin translation for the Renaissance philosopher Giovanni Pico della Mirandola (1463–1494).

The Hartman Collection is home to a nineteenth-century manuscript of Ibn Tibbon's translation (Fig. 69). It was copied by Sebastiano Solari, a convert to Christianity originally named Raḥamim Hezekiah Mizraḥi. Solari copied several manuscripts between 1833 and 1836 that now reside in the Vatican Library, including a miscellany of kabbalistic treatises and an ornamental multicolored sheet of biblical verses.[8] In the latter, Solari referred to himself as a 'former rabbi of Babylon (Baghdad) and Professor of Hebrew language.' Where he taught Hebrew is unknown, but he was baptized on Sunday, July 17, 1831, at the age of 45, in the Church of Santi Domenico e Sisto in Rome.[9] He produced this *Ma'amar Teḥiyat ha-Metim* for Andrea Molza (1783–1851), a principal scholar and custodian of the Vatican Apostolic Library over the course of three decades in the first half of the nineteenth century.[10] Solari's artistry and professionalism as a scribe are evident in each of his extant manuscripts, though the iron gall ink he used has eroded the present manuscript's fine paper.

Studies, Revised Edition,' in his *Eschatology in Maimonidean Thought: Messianism, Resurrection and The World to Come* (New York: Ktav, 1983), 226–41.

7 Jerusalem, National Library of Israel, Heb.8° 3941; see Abraham Halkin, 'Ma'amar Teḥiyat ha-Metim le-Rambam be-Targumo shel R. Yehudah al-Ḥarizi,' *Kobez al Yad* 9 (1980): 129–50.

8 Benjamin Richler (ed.), *Hebrew Manuscripts in the Vatican Library: Catalogue* (Studi e testi 438), Palaeograph. and Codicolog. Malachi Beit-Arié and Nurit Pasternak (Vatican City: Biblioteca Apostolica Vaticano, 2008), 459 (Vat. ebr. 544), 464–65 (Vat. ebr. 547), 474 (Vat. ebr. 557), 525–26 (Borg. ebr. 20).

9 *Diario di Roma*, part 3, no. 59 ([Rome]: Stamperia Cracas, 1831), 2. Thanks to Martina Mampieri for the reference.

10 On Molza, see Emma Abate, Judith Olszowy-Schlanger, and Delio Vania Proverbio, 'Giovanni Giorgi e Andrea Molza Scriptores: Due Volti dell'Orientalistica Romana,' *Miscellanea Bibliothecae Vaticanae* 25 (2019): 264–90 (esp. 277 for Solari and reference to this manuscript).

שני המאורות ... לשני המאורות הגדולים, ה"ה מאמר הייחוד להרמ"בם
Shene ha-Me'orot ... li-Shene ha-Me'orot ha-Gedolim, h"h Ma'amar ha-Yiḥud le-ha-Rambam / Schene ha-meoroth enthält Maamar ha-Jichud
(The Two Luminaries ... Treatise on the Unity of God)
Edited by Moritz Steinschneider
Published by Aryeh Leib Zarenzanski
Berlin, 1847
4°. RB 23
Steinschneider, 7271,4; Vinograd, Berlin nos. 654, 659

שני מאמרי המשגל
Shene Ma'amare ha-Mishgal / Ein Beitrag zur Geschichte der Medizin des XII. Jahrhunderts (Two Essays on Cohabitation / A Contribution to the History of Twelfth-Century Medicine)
Edited by Hermann Kroner
Printed by Zvi Hirsh ben Isaac Itzkowsky
Berlin, 1906
4°. RB 22

There was nary a topic that Maimonides did not address in his decades of writing. More than two dozen anonymous treatises on philosophy and medicine have been attributed to him, though the authorship's authenticity is difficult to verify. *Ma'amar ha-Yiḥud* is one such lesser-known tract of questionable authorship.[1] While it is generally consistent with Maimonides's thought, it expresses a trend toward Sufism more in line with his descendants than with the Great Eagle himself.[2] The editor of this edition, the historian and father of modern Hebrew bibliography Moritz Steinschneider, identified it as a true work of Maimonides.

Translated into Hebrew by Isaac ben Nathan in the fourteenth century, *Ma'amar ha-Yiḥud* first appeared in print in 1846.[3] Steinschneider had edited the text, provided notations mainly on the Arabic original, and included German and Hebrew introductions. In addition, he had included a letter of commentary and corrections from Solomon Judah Rapoport of Prague (Shir; 1808–1880). When the original financier failed to pay the printer, however, operations ceased and the imprint was circulated in just a few copies. In 1847, the printing venture was rescued and expanded (utilizing the same printing establishment) by Aryeh Leib Zarenzanski. Steinschneider republished the treatise with the notes of Rapoport and himself, and he added a section of three responsa on astronomy and the New Moon by Abraham Ibn Ezra accompanied by the annotations and emendations of the Italian scholar Samuel David Luzzatto (Shadal; 1800–1865). Steinschneider dubbed the volume *Shene ha-Me'orot*, the 'two luminaries,' referring to the great medieval Sephardic scholars, Maimonides and Ibn Ezra (Fig. 70).

1 Y. Tzvi Langermann, 'A New Look at *Ma'amar ha-Yiḥud*, Attributed to Moses Maimonides' [Hebrew], *Tarbiz* 65 (1996): 109–28.

2 See Paul B. Fenton, 'Maimonides—Father and Son: Continuity and Change,' in *Traditions of Maimonideanism*, ed. Carlos Fraenkel (Leiden: Brill, 2009), 103–37; Fenton, 'Abraham Maimonides (1186–1237): Founding a Mystical Dynasty,' in *Jewish Mystical Leaders and Leadership in the 13th Century*, ed. Moshe Idel and Mortimer Ostow (Northvale, NJ: Jason Aronson, 1998), 127–54; and S. D. Goitein, 'A Jewish Addict to Sufism: In the Time of the Nagid David II Maimonides,' *Jewish Quarterly Review* 44:1 (July 1953): 37–49.

3 *Maamar Ha-Jichud (Abhandlung über die Einheit)* (Berlin: Hirsch Markus Sew, 1846).

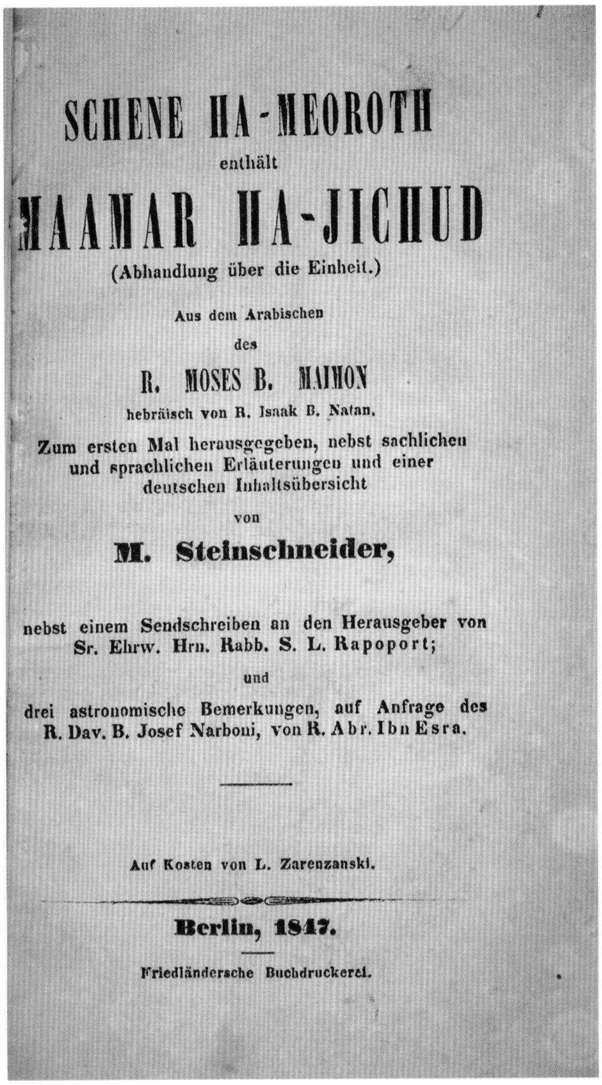
SCHENE HA-MEOROTH
enthält
MAAMAR HA-JICHUD
(Abhandlung über die Einheit.)
Aus dem Arabischen
des
R. MOSES B. MAIMON
hebräisch von R. Isaak B. Natan.
Zum ersten Mal herausgegeben, nebst sachlichen
und sprachlichen Erläuterungen und einer
deutschen Inhaltsübersicht
von
M. Steinschneider,
nebst einem Sendschreiben an den Herausgeber von
Sr. Ehrw. Hrn. Rabb. S. L. Rapoport;
und
drei astronomische Bemerkungen, auf Anfrage des
R. Dav. B. Josef Narboni, von R. Abr. Ibn Esra.

Auf Kosten von L. Zarenzanski.

Berlin, 1847.

Friedländersche Buchdruckerei.

Fig. 70 *Shene ha-Me'orot* (Berlin: Aryeh Leib Zarenzanski, 1847), RB 23.

Ma'amar ha-Yiḥud was originally composed in Arabic and may have been known as *Makalah fi al-Taḥid*. As it quotes *Moreh Nevukhim*, it must have been written after the year 1200. Although the title suggests that the treatise concentrates on the unity of God, the author addressed many more subjects, including the creation of the world, the levels and types of angels, the four classical elements (fire, air, water, and earth), the immortality of the soul, prophecy, and hygiene. The copy in the Hartman Collection belonged to Michael Friedländer (1833–1910), translator of an eminently readable and oft-republished English edition of *Moreh Nevukhim*.[4]

Many of the smaller treatises from or attributed to Maimonides concern medicine. Some were commissioned by a sultan or other aristocrat for a specific purpose, while others are more general. Extant manuscripts reveal Maimonides's views on hemorrhoids, asthma, psychology, poison, and sexual activity. His *Fi Tadbir al-Sihha* (Guide to Good Health), a treatise composed in 1198 for the Egyptian Sultan Al-Afdal Nur al-Din Ali, taught that personal well-being depended upon several physical and psychological factors, including proper relations in work and family, as well as good diet, exercise, and aesthetically pleasing surroundings.

Shene Ma'amare ha-Mishgal consists of two essays on cohabitation attributed to Maimonides, never before printed. It was edited by the German physician and rabbi Hermann Kroner, who utilized as many as six manuscripts in preparing the texts. The first

4 Warren Zev Harvey, 'Michael Friedländer's Pioneering English Translation of the Guide,' in *Maimonides' 'Guide of the Perplexed' in Translation: A History from the Thirteenth Century to the Twentieth*, ed. Josef Stern, James T. Robinson, and Yonatan Shemesh (Chicago: University of Chicago Press, 2019), 209–24.

essay, entitled *Fi al-Jima'a*, is the better-known of the two and was composed for Sultan Omar Ibn Nur 'al-Din, nephew of Saladin the Great. The sultan wanted to learn new ways to increase his sexual capacity, for which Maimonides supplied dietary and medicinal suggestions. It was included here in two translations: the first by Zeraḥiah ben Isaac ben She'altiel Ḥen of Barcelona (thirteenth century), known for his translation of *Pirke Mosheh*, and the second without attribution.[5] The second essay is a more extensive warning against excessive cohabitation, which Kroner erroneously ascribed to Maimonides.[6]

Maimonides's views on sexuality appeared in both the *Mishneh Torah* and *Moreh Nevukhim*. To Maimonides, 'No prohibition in all the Torah is as difficult to keep as that of forbidden unions and illicit sexual relations.'[7] Preventive measures, such as barring *yiḥud* (being alone with a member of the opposite sex), were put in place in the Talmud and legal codes to keep Jews from even the temptation to sin. In *Moreh Nevukhim*, Maimonides explained the rite of circumcision as symbolizing man's need for moderation, as the act itself helped to weaken a man's sex drive.[8] Hoping to broaden and intensify man's concern, elsewhere in the *Mishneh Torah* he labeled sexual relations before marriage as harlotry, based on the biblical verse 'Thou shalt not profane thy daughter to make of her a harlot' (Leviticus 19:29).[9] In other words, not only should man watch over himself, but he should watch over his children, for a laxness in one could possibly lead to the sin of the other.

5 Zeraḥiah translated the Arabic title as *Ma'amar 'al Ribui ha-Tashmish*, while the anonymous author entitled his translation *Ma'amar ha-Mishgal*. On the erroneous attribution to Maimonides, see Süssman Muntner, 'Rabenu Mosheh ben Maimon Ma'amar 'al Ḥizuk Ko'aḥ ha-Gavra,' in *Ketavim Refu'iyim*, 4 vols. (Jerusalem. 1965), 4:44–45.

6 See Fred Rosner (ed.), *Maimonides' Treatises on Poisons, Hemorrhoids and Cohabitation* (Haifa: Maimonides Research Institute, 1984), 153–82.

7 *Mishneh Torah, Isure Bi'ah* 22:18.

8 *Moreh Nevukhim* III:49.

9 *Mishneh Torah, Ishut* 1:4.

מלחמות השם
Milḥamot Ha-Shem (Wars of the Lord)
Yiḥye Kafiḥ
Scribe: Shalom ben Abraham Uzaryi
[Yemen], 1933
MS 21. Manuscript on paper; 4 + 91ff.; 18.2 x 24.5 cm

The Hartman Collection includes numerous manuscripts once owned by the Yemenite scholar Yosef Kafiḥ, best known as a translator and editor of Maimonides (Fig. 71). Some of these previously belonged to his grandfather Yiḥye Kafiḥ (1850–1931), the chief rabbi of Sana'a and an important figure in Yemen in the late nineteenth and early twentieth centuries (Fig. 72). In his early years, the elder Kafiḥ studied under Ḥayim Koraḥ, a kabbalist and student of the influential kabbalist Yiḥye Tsaleḥ. With the Ottoman conquest of Yemen in 1872, Kafiḥ was exposed to new ideas and broader perspectives. He corresponded with Jewish scholars from elsewhere, came to challenge the prominence of Kabbalah as an only recently imported phenomenon, and developed a belief that Yemenite Jewry should go back to a beginning point of intellectual and cultural purity. Kafiḥ encouraged strict adherence to *halakhah* as formulated in the *Mishneh Torah* and founded the *Dor De'ah* (enlightened generation) movement.

The opponents of the *darda'im*, as they became known, were labeled *'ikeshim*, from *dor 'ikesh* (the stubborn generation; Deuteronomy 32:5), or those avowedly clinging to their established convictions. Rifts developed, with families on either side of the divide refusing to marry the other. The *'ikeshim* regarded the *darda'im* as heretics and excommunicated the entire group, formally accusing them of capital offenses, such as treasonous relationships with foreign powers and selling alcohol to Muslims. In 1914, the *'ikeshim* turned to rabbinic authorities in Ottoman Palestine for support. Bans were signed and denunciations were pasted on Jerusalem's walls. Many of the city's most prestigious rabbis condemned Kafiḥ and placed him under a ban.

For his part, Kafiḥ authored polemical treatises. In *Milḥamot Ha-Shem*, Kafiḥ sought to combat the influence of Lurianic Kabbalah and restore the prestige of the rational thought of Maimonides and Sa'adiah Gaon. He denied the authenticity of the *Zohar*, disputing its attribution to the Tannaitic sage Shimon bar Yoḥai. Earlier rabbinic scholars like Leone de Modena (1571–1648) and Jacob Emden (1697–1776) had questioned the antiquity of the *Zohar*, but Kafiḥ's critique had social implications. He labeled Lurianic Kabbalah as idolatrous and irreconcilable with true monotheistic Judaism. A group of rabbis in Sana'a composed a rejoinder entitled *Emunat Ha-Shem*, and ultimately Muslim authorities sought a compromise by ruling that Jews should neither denigrate nor be forced to study Kabbalah.[1]

Although Kafiḥ's attack on Kabbalah did not succeed, his *Dor De'ah* movement elevated the status of Maimonides in Yemen. The *darda'im* and their spiritual descendants are largely responsible for the widespread assumption that the Jews of Yemen have been entirely loyal to Maimonides since the twelfth century. Certainly, Yosef Kafiḥ linked Maimonides's rulings and Yemenite practises and utilized early manuscripts in their Judeo-Arabic

1 See Yosef Tobi, 'Who Was the Author of *Emunat ha-Shem*?' [Hebrew], *Daat: A Journal of Philosophy & Kabbalah* 49 (2002): 87–98; and Danny Bar-Maoz, 'Beḥinah Historit shel Tarbut ha-Mahaloket ve-ha-Palganut be-Kehilat Yehude Teman' (Ph.D. diss., Bar-Ilan University, 2001), 217–29. *Emunat ha-Shem* did not appear in print until 1938 (in Jerusalem), accompanied by *haskamot* (approbations) from the *yishuv*'s greatest rabbinic authorities, including Abraham Isaac Kook, Ben-Tsiyon Meir Ḥai Uziel, Tsevi Pesah Frank, and Isaac Halevi Herzog.

Fig. 71 Portrait of Yosef Kafiḥ. Collection of Tsofit Tsachi.

Fig. 72 Portrait of Yiḥye Kafiḥ. The Pritzker Family National Photography Collection, The National Library of Israel.

original to reproduce the Great Eagle's texts. Followers of Yosef Kafiḥ are behind various endeavors that have made the works, ideas, and positions of Maimonides accessible to the public.

The Hartman manuscript of *Milḥamot Ha-Shem* opens with an index to all Talmudic statements 'contra the *Zohar* and the new kabbalists' (מפתח מאמרי רז״ל נגד הזהר והמקובלים החדשים). Emphasizing the *novelty* of kabbalists contrasted with and thereby substantiated the traditionalism Kafiḥ espoused. His decision to write the work in Hebrew, rather than Judeo-Arabic, may have stemmed from a desire to reach an audience outside of Yemen, arguing with and hoping to convince rabbinic and intellectual leaders of the illegitimacy of Kabbalah.

חדושי רבינו חיים הלוי: חדושים וביאורים על הרמב"ם
Ḥidushe Rabenu Ḥayim ha-Levi: Ḥidushim u-Ve'urim 'al ha-Rambam / Chiduszej Rabejnu Chaim Halejwi (Novel Interpretations and Explanations on Maimonides)
Ḥayim Soloveitchik
Printed by J. Klein
Brisk, 1936
2°. RB 24

Maimonides's *Mishneh Torah* has served scholars and laypeople alike for eight centuries. For generations, readers have delved into its clear prose in search of wisdom and guidance about Jewish life in ever-changing circumstances. The modern epitome of this phenomenon is the present volume, consisting of the posthumously published insights on Maimonides's law code by R. Ḥayim Soloveitchik (1853–1918).[1]

Known as Reb Ḥayim Brisker, after the Yiddish name of the city (Brest) in which he and his father acted as rabbis, Soloveitchik is credited with initiating the intense, highly analytical study of the Talmud known as the 'Brisker method.' Soloveitchik's technique developed over many years, while serving as rabbi in Brisk and as lecturer in the famed Volozhin yeshiva, and stressed methodological understanding of the Talmud and its commentators. Rather than rely on a single medieval rabbinic authority or interpret texts to match others with which they conflicted, students were taught to break down rabbinic opinions or halakhic concepts into their composite parts. Thereupon, arguments could be reconstructed and novel ideas applied to halakhic problems.

Yeshivat 'Ets Ḥayim in Volozhin was founded in 1803 by Soloveitchik's great-great-grandfather, Ḥayim of Volozhin (Fig. 73). The elder Ḥayim had been the primary student of the great halakhist, kabbalist, and unofficial head of Lithuanian Jewry, Elijah Gaon of Vilna (Gra; 1720–1797).[2] His yeshiva initiated a program of Talmudic study that spread throughout Lithuania in the nineteenth century.[3] Lithuania became a great center of Jewish learning and has proven to be the progenitor of much of today's non-Hasidic Ashkenazic Orthodox community.

Ḥayim Soloveitchik was a member of perhaps the most influential, innovative, and prolific rabbinic family in modern times. His father, Yosef Dov Soloveitchik (1820–1892), lectured at the Volozhin yeshiva, served as rabbi in several towns, and came to be known as the *Bet ha-Levi*, the title of his responsa and of his commentary on the Pentateuch.. Ḥayim married the granddaughter of Naphtali Tsevi Yehudah Berlin (Netsiv; 1816–1893) and daughter of Rafael Shapiro, both former heads of the Volozhin yeshiva. Ḥayim's sons, Moshe (1879–1941) and Yitzḥak Ze'ev (Reb Velvel; 1886–1959), each authored works on Maimonides and established major centers of Torah learning outside of Lithuania. The latter fled the Holocaust for the British Mandate of Palestine, and his descendants founded

1 R. Ḥayim's novellae on the Talmud were also published posthumously (3 vols., 1952–1966). See Marc B. Shapiro's essay in this volume.

2 On the Gra, see Eliyahu Stern, *The Genius: Elijah of Vilna and the Making of Modern Judaism* (New Haven, CT: Yale University Press, 2013); on his opposition to *Moreh Nevukhim*, due to its adoption among *maskilim*, see Allan Nadler, 'The "Rambam Revival" in Early Modern Jewish Thought: Maskilim, Mitnagdim, and Hasidim on Maimonides' *Guide of the Perplexed*,' in *Maimonides After 800 Years: Essays on Maimonides and His Influence*, ed. Jay M. Harris (Cambridge, MA: Harvard University Press, 2007), 50.

3 Shaul Stampfer, *Lithuanian Yeshivas of the Nineteenth Century: Creating a Tradition of Learning*, trans. Lindsay Taylor-Guthartz (Oxford: Littman Library of Jewish Civilization, 2012).

Fig. 73 Photograph of the Volozhin Yeshiva. Courtesy of the Leiman Library.

several 'Brisker' yeshivas in Jerusalem. The former immigrated to America in 1929 and was appointed as head (*rosh yeshiva*) of the Rabbi Isaac Elchanan Theological Seminary (RIETS), today affiliated with Yeshiva University. Each of Moshe's sons was distinguished in his own right, but none was as prestigious as Joseph B. Soloveitchik (the Rav; 1903–1993), who succeeded his father as *rosh yeshiva* of RIETS for nearly half a century and established a model for Modern Orthodox Judaism in America.

ESSAYS

MAIMONIDES ON 'ANECDOTAL EVIDENCE' IN MEDICINE AND SCIENCE

Tzvi Langermann

Maimonides received his medical education as a young man in Spain and North Africa. He did not train for a career; rather, he pursued the study of medicine for his personal edification. Nonetheless, he was very diligent, even traveling to interview famous physicians whose controversial treatments were the talk of the profession. It was only much later, after he had relocated to Egypt, that circumstances compelled him to practice medicine for a livelihood. Maimonides had made his living from commerce, investing, together with his brother David, in a consortium of traders. David was charged with traveling to India to bring back the goods. On one fateful journey, David perished in a shipwreck, and Maimonides had no choice but to put his medical training into practice.

One often reads that Maimonides served the king, sultan, or wazir of Egypt. In fact, none of those offices existed when Maimonides practiced medicine. The ruler, Salaḥ al-Din (Saladin), was a military commander who seized power. Maimonides served the state's most powerful administrator, a cleric known by the epithet al-Qadi al-Fadil, who was Maimonides's personal friend as well as his patient. Maimonides also maintained a private clinic in his residence. Every morning he would ride to al-Qadi al-Fadil's home to treat members of the household. When he returned later in the day, Maimonides would find his waiting room full. The duties were so exhausting that Maimonides would receive patients while lying on his back.[1]

Maimonides wrote quite a few medical texts, all of them in Arabic.[2] They can be grouped under three rubrics. 1) Commentaries and annotated digests of the great Greek authorities, Hippocrates and Galen. The best known of this group is his commentary on Hippocrates's *Aphorisms.* 2) Monographs, usually written at the behest of private patients and with regard to their particular medical issues. Maimonides carefully crafted these treatises, filling them with general information on the topic at hand, so that the end product would be useful to the profession at large and not just the individual for whom it was written. The *Regimen of Health* is the outstanding representative of this group. 3) The voluminous *Moses's Chapters*, consisting mainly of excerpts from the books of Galen, supplemented by information drawn from Arabic medical writers and his own observations. The material for this book was drawn from notes that Maimonides jotted down in the course his practice; toward the end of his life, he edited the notes and prepared them for publication.

Maimonides's medicine – physiology, etiology, pathology, therapeutics – derives in its entirety from the Galenism that held sway for more than a millennium throughout Europe and the Islamic world. Other than some advice for wholesome living, with regard to diet, sleep, and exercise, and which he saw fit to include in his great halakhic code, the *Mishneh*

1 My translation from Itzhak Shailat (ed.), *The Letters and Essays of Moses Maimonides* [Hebrew] (Jerusalem: Shailat Publishing, 1995), 550–51. The passage is found near the end of Maimonides's letter to his translator Samuel Ibn Tibbon, dissuading the latter from traveling to Egypt.

2 Gerrit Bos, along with a number of collaborators on individual volumes, has published the entire corpus in his series, *The Medical Writings of Maimonides.* Seventeen volumes have appeared, providing accurate editions of the original Arabic text, as well as those Hebrew and/or Latin translations that exist for any given work, along with annotated English translations and extensive glossaries.

Torah, his medical teachings are of no professional use today. However, one theoretical question that Maimonides addressed at length has been reopened in the wake of the COVID pandemic.

In the early months of the COVID pandemic medical professionals were desperately searching for a medication that could cure, or at least ameliorate, the condition of the many thousands of people suffering from the virus. Two critical questions had to be answered before any drug could be approved: Is the drug effective? Is the drug safe? The currently accepted testing protocols are very lengthy, requiring three phases of trials, from initial laboratory experiments to tests on human volunteers, before a new drug can be authorized. With a pandemic raging, hospitals and staff buckling under the crush of patients, and an increasingly worried general population and their even more stressed elected leaders, it was pretty clear to everyone that one would have to fast track the process for any promising remedy. Nonetheless, there was a loud outcry about employing a drug for whose efficacy one had at best only 'anecdotal evidence.'

The dilemma was not new to medical science. Galen had to deal with this issue, as did Moses Maimonides and hundreds of other medieval and early modern physicians in Europe, North Africa, the Middle East, and India. To be sure, pre-modern medicine had an entirely different view of health, disease, therapeutics, and pharmacology than those held today to be authoritative. However, pre-modern physicians too had to grapple with the fact that several medical substances whose efficacy was not established according to the science of the day had nevertheless been accepted into the pharmacopoeia. There was no science of statistics in Maimonides's day, nor did medical science at the time ask for any rigorous quantitative evidence. 'Anecdotal' evidence was nothing more than the claim that 'many' had tried the drug and found it be effective. On the other hand, the science of the day did demand a clear explanation of the mode of action of the drug, something today that serves only to support the statistical evidence (and assuage a skeptical public). But here too, doctors could not explain how these substances worked.

Maimonides was not entirely comfortable with the necessity of accepting drugs whose efficacy could not be explained rigorously. This was not just because of his personal preference for 'hard' science; it seems that other factors came into play as well. In a revealing letter to his Hebrew translator, Samuel Ibn Tibbon, Maimonides explained that every evening, exhausted though he was from the day's activities, he would review certain topics in the medical literature because he wanted to be able to provide a sound justification for any treatment he might endorse or oppose. He wrote: 'For you know how long and difficult this art [medicine] is for someone who is conscientious and fastidious, and who does not wish to say anything without first knowing its proof, its source [in the literature], and the type of reasoning [involved].'[3] To whom would he need to provide a reasoned scientific explanation? Maimonides served al-Qadi al-Fadil, arguably the most powerful individual in Saladin's Egypt, someone who could impose his will on Saladin himself. However, he was just one of a coterie of physicians. Potentates at that time kept several physicians on retainer, who would often decide by committee on the treatment to administer. In order to hold his own against colleagues, who at times were quite bumptious, it would be best to cite chapter and verse from authoritative texts.

It seems that Maimonides was also wary that giving credence to drugs solely on the basis of a purported 'case series' of successful treatments would open the door for any quack to advertise his wares as potions that had been shown to be efficacious. This is one of the points raised by Maimonides in his most sustained discussion of medical 'experience' (Arabic *tajriba*), which was the contemporary classification accorded to scientific claims that had no theoretical justification. The science of his day asked for a proof of a drug's 'mode of action'; for example, that the drug was 'dry' and hence would desiccate a disease that was classified as 'wet.' A claim to truth that rested solely on the purported causal connection repeatedly

3 The original document is cited in note 1 above. The translation here is taken from Yitzhak Tzvi Langermann, 'Maimonides' Repudiation of Astrology,' *Maimonidean Studies* 2 (1991): 123–58 (137–38).

linking a drug to a subsequent cure was considered to be weak. The passage is found in chapter 13 of Maimonides's monograph *On Asthma*:

> It is known to anyone who has tried to practice the art of medicine … that it is an art which requires experience and analogical reasoning. And the things which are known through experience are far greater in number than those known through reason. Since people know this, they rely so much on experience that the multitudes have a well-known saying; 'Ask the experienced [practitioner] rather than the physician.'

That adage – *is'al al-mujarrab wa-la tis'al al-ḥakim* – is still widely cited. Maimonides now takes note of the danger I alluded to above: 'Any cheating, impudent and insolent person can gain access [to this art] by saying "I have remedies which I have tested."' But the experience accepted in scientific medicine is not that claimed by any one physician:

> The greatest mistake is that the experience which is mentioned and referred to in medicine is only the experience of the physician in his own era. But this is not so. Rather, [medical] experience is the sum of the experience acquired over the course of past generations [even] before the time of Galen – namely, those things that have been written down in medical books. Some of the drugs and compound remedies were tested for hundreds of years and were [only then] written in books … in our times, experience is claimed only by pseudo-physicians, who make people believe in something which has not been proven only in order to cover up their [own] shortcoming.[4]

A remedy whose efficacy had been shown through experience was said to act by means of a special property (Arabic *khassa*). This was just a way of filling in the blank for 'mode of action' when none of the scientific modes accepted at that time seemed to apply. Clearly, Maimonides was suspicious of remedies that worked by means of a 'special property.' These were also called occult properties, because their mode of action was concealed (Latin *occelere*). Many – but not all – such remedies would be considered today to be magical. Nonetheless, if a physician with an impeccable reputation for caution and precision had tested an 'occult' remedy in his own clinical experience, Maimonides would be confident in its efficacy and recommend it. Such was the case with Abu Marwan Ibn Zuhr (d. 1161), known in the west as Avenzoar, one of the greatest medical doctors to practice in Islamic Spain. Maimonides knew his son and heard from him stories of his father's great dedication in verifying 'anecdotal evidence' for remedies. In Book 22 of his *Medical Aphorisms* Maimonides reproduces a long list of such drugs. Quite a few of these are hard for us to accept as scientifically validated, such as the claim that looking into the eyes of a wild ass is beneficial for vision and the prevention of cataracts. No less suspicious is the claim that wearing the fur of hares strengthens the bodies of adults, including the elderly, whereas wearing lambskin strengthens the bodies of children. Others sound more reasonable, such as the advice that eating peaches is good for the stomach, and bathing in lukewarm olive oil is helpful for alleviating all pains in the body.[5]

But this is not the only place that Maimonides allows such questionable remedies into medical practice on the basis of anecdotal evidence for their efficacy. Strange as it seems to modern sensibilities, Maimonides justifies ostensibly superstitious practices endorsed by

4 Gerrit Bos, *Maimonides: On Asthma. A Parallel Arabic-English Text Edited, Translated, and Annotated* (Provo, UT: Brigham Young, 2002), 95–99, translation slightly modified. Concerning Galen's views on the subject, see Philip J. van der Eijk, 'Galen on the Use of the Concept of "Qualified Experience" in his Dietetic and Pharmacological Works,' in Philip J. van der Eijk, *Medicine and Philosophy in Classical Antiquity* (Cambridge: Cambridge University Press, 2005), 279–98.

5 Gerrit Bos, *Maimonides: Medical Aphorisms: A Parallel Arabic-English Edition. Treatises 22–25* (Provo, UT: Brigham Young, 2017), 11–16.

the Talmud by arguing that 'in those times' such practices were thought to derive from experience. He writes about this in his *Guide of the Perplexed* III:37:

> You must not consider as a difficulty certain things that they have permitted, as for instance 'the nail of one who is crucified and a fox's tooth' [Shabbat 67a]. For in those times these things were considered to derive from experience and accordingly pertained to medicine and entered into the same class as the hanging of a peony upon an epileptic and the giving of a dog's excrements in cases of the swelling of the throat and fumigation with vinegar and marcasite in cases of hard swellings of the tendons. For it is allowed to use all remedies similar to these that experience has shown to be valid even if reasoning does not require them. For they pertain to medicine and their efficacy may be ranged together with the purgative action of aperient medicines.[6]

I am confident that Maimonides had scammony in mind when he mentioned 'the purgative action of aperient medicines.' The purgative action of that plant (of the morning glory family) has been well known since antiquity. Scammony served as the example *par excellence* of a medicinal substance whose efficacy was demonstrated by experience alone; the ancients had no clue concerning its mode of action.

Medical theory could suggest a treatment which would then be validated by experience. In a passage from Galen's *De methodo medendi* cited in Book 8 of the *Medical Aphorisms*, we learn that theory and experience together indicate that the body should be rid of superfluities (e.g., undigested food) before administering a heating agent to an affected organ. Otherwise, the heat will attract superfluities, thus exacerbating the condition.[7] Modern medicine thinks along similar lines: theoretical reasoning suggests a particular compound and/or a course of action, which is then put to the test. The critical difference lies in the value of testing in an era when the science of statistics was unknown. And, one should add, there were no regulatory bodies to insure that only remedies that had passed rigorous clinical testing would be on the market. A medical doctor would experiment on his own patients and even his own family members, something that in our own day is unthinkable. He would then advertise the drug on the basis of his self-proclaimed successful experimentation.

Finally, Maimonides's discomfort with the anecdotal evidence supplied by experience as a source of knowledge was not limited to the field of medicine. It is very likely that his famous repudiation of astrology rests in part on this posture. Astrologers claimed that particular configurations of stellar bodies were repeatedly witnessed to accompany human events such as the emergence of a new religion or a new world political order, but they could not explain why this was so. Whereas only a small part of medicine relied upon anecdotal evidence, astrology in its entirety rested upon that rickety epistemological foundation. Empirical evidence (shaky to begin with) could not alone validate astrology.

In sum, remedies verified by 'anecdotal evidence' alone were a fixed and accepted feature of the pre-modern pharmacopoeia. I would not be surprised if today's manuals still include tried and tested remedies that have never been subjected to rigorous clinical trials. Some such remedies accepted by Maimonides had been in use for centuries and authorized by ancient authorities. Others had been employed over a shorter period of time but verified by towering medical writers, and Maimonides accepted those as well. On the other hand, quacks who advertised uncorroborated remedies abounded, leading Maimonides to extend words of caution that still ring true today.

6 Moses Maimonides, *The Guide of the Perplexed*, trans. Shlomo Pines (Chicago: University of Chicago Press, 1963), 544.

7 Gerrit Bos, *Maimonides: Medical Aphorisms: A Parallel Arabic-English Edition. Treatises 6–9* (Provo, UT: Brigham Young, 2007), 52–53.

MAIMONIDES AND THE JEWS OF YEMEN[1]

YOSEF YUVAL TOBI

It is common knowledge that Rabbi Moses Maimonides (1138–1204) and his writings have a special place in the hearts of Yemenite Jews. But that is only half the story. While Maimonides has certainly been venerated and his halakhic and theological positions adopted, his thought also aroused controversy in Yemen during his lifetime and his legacy generated an enduring rift among Yemenite Jews. The arc of this fluctuating relationship will be traced below across three distinct periods: Maimonides's own lifetime, the thirteenth to fifteenth centuries, and the sixteenth century to today.

In Maimonides's Lifetime: A Relationship Tested

The special connection between Yemenite Jewry and Maimonides was not initially formed due to his standing as a celebrated halakhist or theologian. In 1172, the Jews of Yemen found themselves in a terrible quandary. A Muslim had proclaimed himself Mahdi (a messianic figure within Islam) and tried to forcibly convert the Jews with the support of a Jewish convert. At the same time, a Jew declared himself the messiah who had come to redeem his people. These developments imperiled Jewish souls and bodies alike; Jewish messianism could be perceived as political agitation that needed a good quelling.

The Nagid (chief representative of Jews to the sultanate) of Yemenite Jewry at the time, Rabbi Jacob ben Nathaniel, sought advice on how to best handle the messianic pretender from the Nagid of Egyptian Jewry – none other than Maimonides. Jacob ben Nathaniel turned to Maimonides as his political counterpart, who possessed great learning, astuteness, and contacts. Maimonides served as Nagid to the Ayyubid sultanate in the 1170s and again from 1196 until his death in 1204. Beginning in 1185, he was also a physician at the sultan's court.

Their correspondence seemingly constitutes the first direct contact between the Jews of Yemen and Maimonides, and it was very cordial. Jacob ben Nathaniel lavishes praise on Maimonides, who responds with modesty: 'I am the most insignificant of the Spanish sages.' He, in turn, praises the Nagid of Yemen and his entire community with exceedingly poetic descriptions, emphasizing their generosity, study of Torah, and religious observance. Turning to the matter at hand, Maimonides denounces the would-be messiah and says that the community should treat him as a madman.

The young Cairene leader then wrote an epistle to the Yemenite Jewish community called *Igeret Teman*, a comprehensive treatment of various issues raised by the appearance of a false messiah. This only deepened the appreciation of the Yemenite Jews for Maimonides and fostered a sense of mutual understanding and brotherhood.

However, this warm relationship was soon cooled by the controversy concerning Maimonides's purported disbelief in the resurrection of the dead. His *Mishneh Torah*, the comprehensive halakhic code, was completed in 1177, and Maimonides stated in a letter to the sages of Lunel in Provence that it received a warm reception among Yemenite Jews. After about a dozen years though, suspicions were voiced that the great Maimonides did not

1 Translated from Hebrew by Daniel Tabak.

believe that the soul would be returned to the dead for resurrection in the messianic era. This led some to reject a spiritual afterlife altogether and interpret any explicitly contradictory sources from Scripture or the rabbinic canon allegorically, a mode of reading often championed by Maimonides himself.

Amid this theological chaos, the Jews of Yemen decided to solicit clarity from the very source of the controversy. In 1189, they wrote to Maimonides, and the response they received read: 'Resurrection of the dead is a Torah tenet, namely, the return of the soul to the body. One may not remove this matter from its straightforward sense.' This statement did not allay the concerns of some Yemenite Jews, who sent a letter critical of Maimonides to Rabbi Samuel ben Eli Gaon, head of the yeshiva in Baghdad, a Jewish spiritual center of the Islamicate that rivaled Maimonides's in Egypt.

Until now, Maimonides had been under the impression that his response to the inquiry from Yemenite Jewry had put the matter to rest. One can imagine his shock and displeasure at receiving a letter from none other than Samuel ben Eli in 1191. Not only had Yemenite Jews publicized the matter for the entire Jewish world, but they had sent their criticism to a rival. R. Samuel polemicized against Maimonides in his letter, but he also tried to calm inflamed passions by referring to his 'many good qualities, leadership, and humility.'[2] In response, Maimonides thanked R. Samuel for this, and then went on to denigrate his critics. Even R. Samuel did not escape his condemnation in the end.

Subsequently, Maimonides set out again to put an end to the accusations and misunderstandings in a discourse dedicated to resurrection, *Ma'amar Teḥiyat ha-Metim*. In the work, he declared that he did not reject belief in resurrection but believed it to be a temporary state that would precede an eternal, disembodied life.

This episode clearly rocked the respectful and peaceable relationship that had prevailed between Maimonides and the Jews of Yemen. In a letter penned to the sages of Lunel ca. 1200, Maimonides contrasted the impressive Talmudic erudition of Jews in Provence with the lack thereof among Arabian Jewry. In all the cities of Yemen, he wrote, 'few study the Talmud intensively ... for they are on the periphery.'[3] Only his own *Mishneh Torah* corrected the error of their ways, inspiring greater attention to *halakhah* and religious practice. These unflattering remarks about the Jews of Yemen stand in stark contrast to the praise expressed in their initial correspondence. It is difficult to believe that he truly meant them, for the accusation was not true;[4] more likely, the Yemenite decision to involve Samuel ben Eli in the affair still rankled. Mordechai Akiva Friedman has argued that Maimonides experienced a 'personal tragedy' upon learning that Yemenite Jews had reported to R. Samuel that 'many have despaired of redemption' on Maimonides's account.[5]

Even if the Yemenite community had lost respect in Maimonides's eyes, he did not fail to come to their aid. In 1199, the Ayyubid ruler of Yemen, Al-Malik Al-Mu'izz Isma'il, forced the Jews of his domain to convert to Islam, and for his entire rule he did not allow Egyptian Jewish leaders to intercede on behalf of their Yemenite brethren. After the tyrant's death, however, Maimonides fought for his coreligionists to be able to openly revert to Judaism, on the grounds that Islam does not recognize religious coercion of *dhimmis*. It worked. In 1202, the decree was revoked, two years before Maimonides's death.

The Thirteenth to Fifteenth Centuries: A Legacy Embraced

Despite the tension created by the resurrection controversy, Yemenite Jews looked to Maimonides (and his descendants) as their lodestar for Jewish living. His oeuvre served as the foundation for Yemenite literary productivity for nearly three hundred years and cast its

2 Moses Maimonides, *Teshuvot ha-Rambam*, ed. Joshua Blau (Jerusalem: Meḳitse Nirdamim, 1960), 2:570.
3 Itzhak Shailat (ed.), *The Letters and Essays of Moses Maimonides* [Hebrew] (Jerusalem: Shailat Publishing, 1995), 559.
4 See Yosef Tobi, *The Talmud in Yemen* [Hebrew] (Tel Aviv: Afikim, 1973).
5 Mordechai Akiva Friedman, *Maimonides, the Yemenite Messiah, and Apostasy* [Hebrew] (Jerusalem: Ben-Zvi Institute, 2002), 5, 136–41.

long shadow even into later centuries. Yemenite Torah scholars composed many commentaries on Maimonides's writings, and followed his halakhic and philosophical positions in their own original compositions.[6]

In this period, the *Mishneh Torah* to all intents served as the exclusive source for halakhic determinations in Yemen, something that was not true of any other Jewish community. Even after Maimonides's passing, Yemenite Jews sent halakhic queries to his successors – his son R. Abraham and his grandson R. Joshua. One can get a sense of the didactic role of Maimonides's works from the fact that five dictionaries were compiled by Yemenite Jews for the Hebrew terminology of the *Mishneh Torah* and the Judeo-Arabic of his *Commentary on the Mishnah*. Even the Torah scrolls in Yemen were corrected according to the Torah scroll that Maimonides had copied for himself from the 'Keter of Ben-Asher,' the so-called Aleppo Codex.

There also seems to be a link between the liturgical rite of Yemenite Jewry and the one recorded by Maimonides in the *Mishneh Torah*. In his halakhic treatment of various issues concerning prayer, he cites the widespread rite of Spanish communities, but at the end of his discussion he includes an entire liturgical rite that is quite close to the ancient Yemenite one. R. Joseph Kafiḥ concluded from this that Maimonides adopted the Yemenite rite, which he could have learned from Yemenites in Cairo.[7]

Maimonides very often rejected the straightforward reading of rabbinic homilies, and even stated his intention to compose a special work, *Sefer ha-Derashot*, dedicated to this. He never managed to produce this, but his son R. Abraham did write a brief treatise applying this hermeneutic, titled *Ma'amar 'al ha-Derashot*. Yemenite Jewish thinkers developed this Maimonidean method of interpreting rabbinic homilies, which incidentally played a role in further iterations of the resurrection controversy. While most Yemenite Jews had accepted Maimonides's word in his *Ma'amar Teḥiyat ha-Metim* as final, one fifteenth-century scholar claimed that Maimonides had read all passages about resurrection allegorically and that the treatise was a forgery. A different writer living around the same time dedicated a work to defending Maimonides from his detractors.[8] Echoes of the controversy surrounding Maimonides's true position on resurrection reached even Islamic scholars in Yemen.[9]

The Sixteenth Century to Today: Decline and Division

It was only in the latter half of the fifteenth century, with the introduction of the *Zohar* and kabbalistic literature to Yemen, that Maimonides's predominance in Yemenite Jewish thought and practice began to wane. This slow decline was accelerated in the sixteenth century as Safedian Kabbalah began making inroads into Yemen, influencing theology, customs, and prayer. The old *baladi* (local) liturgical rite, which as we have seen might have been adopted by Maimonides, was being replaced by the kabbalistically inflected *shami* (Land of Israel) rite.

6 See Yitzhak Tzvi Langermann, *Yemenite Midrash: Philosophical Commentaries on the Torah* (New York: Harper Collins, 1996); Zechariah ben Solomon ha-Rofeh, *Midrash ha-Ḥefets 'al Ḥamishah Ḥumshe Torah*, ed. Meir Havatzelet (Jerusalem: Mossad Harav Kook, 1981); Meir Havatzelet and Yosef Tobi (eds.), *Sho'el u-Meshiv: Perush Midrashi Alegori 'al ha-Torah ve'al ha-Aftarayot: Teman ha-Me'ah ha-15* (Tel Aviv, 2006); Eliezer Schlossberg, 'Yemenite Midrashic Literature: Between Old and New' [Hebrew], *Jewish Studies* 54 (2019): 215–44.

7 Yosef Tobi, 'Nusaḥ ha-Tefillah shel Yehude Teman,' *Tema* 7 (2001): 29–64.

8 Yosef Tobi, 'Ketav Haganah mi-Teman 'al Shitat ha-Rambam be-'Inyan Teḥiyat ha-Metim,' *Tema* 6 (1998): 29–57.

9 The last such scholar of note, Muḥammad al-Shawkani (1760–1834), composed a treatise against Maimonides, charging that the Jewish thinker did not deny resurrection but rejected the corporeal delights of the afterlife, of the sort that Islam promises its righteous. An anonymous Jewish scholar responded with his own brief tract. See Paul B. Fenton, 'A Muslim Polemic in Yemen Against Maimonides' [Hebrew], in *Le-Rosh Yosef: Texts and Studies in Judaism*, ed. Yosef Tobi (Jerusalem: Afikim, 1995), 409–34; and Yehuda Ratzaby, ''Inyene dat be-fulmus ben Muslemim li-Yehudim be-Teman,' *Yeda 'Am* 14 (1970): 12–21.

R. Zechariah al-Ḍahiri (d. 1608) brought back teachings and customs from Safed, at a time when the teachings of rabbis like Joseph Karo, Moses Cordovero, and Isaac Luria still echoed in its narrow alleys. First editions of Karo's *Shulḥan 'Arukh* and kabbalistic treatises began arriving via bookdealers to Yemen, a famously good market for distribution. Emissaries (*shadarim*) of the Holy Land sent out to collect funds facilitated this shift away from local rites, customs, and laws to those radiating from Ottoman Palestine. Karo's *Shulḥan 'Arukh* was slowly but surely edging out Maimonides's *Mishneh Torah*.[10]

In the eighteenth century, Shalom 'Iraki, a Jewish political figure of Egyptian extraction, tried to hasten this transition. Using his political power as the Nasi of Yemenite Jewry and governor of the mint, he tried to force all Yemenite Jews to adopt the *shami* liturgical rite and the rulings of *Shulḥan 'Arukh*. Pent-up tensions that had been growing over centuries suddenly exploded. Stalwart proponents of the 'indigenous' mode of Yemenite Jewish living, which accorded with Maimonidean *halakhah* and philosophy, fiercely opposed this abuse of power. In the end, the great Rabbi Yiḥye Tsaleḥ (1713–1805) arrived at a compromise of sorts.

If we fast-forward a century to the 1870s, we find a solitary Yemenite figure trying to turn back the clock on these centuries of change. R. Yiḥye Kafiḥ in Sana'a sought to thoroughly excise kabbalistic influence and the rulings of *Shulḥan 'Arukh* from Yemenite Judaism. Simmering tensions between opponents and proponents of Kabbalah again burst into the open, and the conflict followed them to Israel, where it continues to divide the Yemenite community to this day.[11] One positive externality of this conflict is that R. Yiḥye Kafiḥ and his grandson and successor R. Joseph Kafiḥ initiated a renaissance of sorts in the study of Maimonides's life and writings, not only among Yemenite Jews but among denizens of the bet midrash and professors of academe the world over.

10 Yosef Tobi, 'Shulḥan 'Arukh le-R. Yosef Karo le-umat "Mishneh Torah" le-ha-Rambam be-Teman,' *Tema* 12 (2012): 5–30.

11 Yosef Tobi, 'Tenu'at "Dor-De'ah" mi-Teman u-vikorato shel R. Mosheh Tsarum 'al Minhage ha-Kabalah,' *Deḥak* 6 (2016): 604–22.

ON THE CITATION OF MAIMONIDES IN MEDIEVAL ASHKENAZ

Ephraim Kanarfogel

Maimonides's major halakhic work, the *Mishneh Torah*, was completed in Egypt in 1178 and reached southern France no later than 1194.[1] By the end of the twelfth century, the *Mishneh Torah* was the subject of intense study from Provence to Castile, and at least one major collection of glosses, those of Abraham ben David (Rabad) of Posquieres, had already been composed. Even Meir ha-Levi Abulafia (Ramah) of Toledo, an avowed critic of the *Mishneh Torah* who wrote in the early years of the thirteenth century, could not help but notice the rapidity with which the *Mishneh Torah* had become a focus of study and discussion in Iberia and Provence.[2]

However, the use of the *Mishneh Torah* among the rabbinic elite of northern Europe appears to have proceeded at a much slower pace. Students of the leading northern French Tosafist, Isaac ben Samuel (Ri) of Dampierre, barely cited the *Mishneh Torah* at the turn of the thirteenth century, and when they did it was only to confirm their own approaches.[3] Moreover, the standard *Tosafot* glosses to the Babylonian Talmud, redacted for the most part during the second half of the thirteenth century, refer to rulings by Maimonides only twice.[4]

The first work by a northern French Tosafist to make significant use of the *Mishneh Torah* was *Sefer Mitsvot Gadol* (*Semag*) by Moses ben Jacob of Coucy, but it is important to place *Semag* – completed during the 1240s, more than sixty years after the composition of the *Mishneh Torah* – into its proper literary and historical contexts.[5] During a campaign to preach the observance of Jewish law, Moses of Coucy traveled throughout France and into Spain, perhaps even establishing an academy for those who wished to strengthen their Torah study and observance.[6] R. Moses undoubtedly came to appreciate the *Mishneh Torah* during his stay in Spain, where this work was utilized by both learned and less learned Jews, with the latter cohort relating to it as a primer of Jewish law.

Given his stated intention to speak to a Spanish Jewish audience as well, it is hardly surprising that Moses of Coucy strayed from the pattern of his French teachers and colleagues and made extensive use of the *Mishneh Torah*, to frame and inform his presentation of biblical precepts and halakhic concepts. At the same time, however, Moses of

1 See Isadore Twersky, 'The Beginnings of *Mishneh Torah* Criticism,' in *Biblical and Other Studies*, ed. Alexander A. Altmann (Cambridge, MA: Harvard University Press, 1963), 161–82 (167–68).

2 See Twersky, 'The Beginnings of *Mishneh Torah* Criticism,' 171–77; and Bernard Septimus, *Hispano-Jewish Society in Transition* (Cambridge, MA: Harvard University Press, 1982), 39–43.

3 See Ephraim Urbach, *Ba'ale ha-Tosafot* (Jerusalem: Bialik Institute, 1980), 263, 272, 311 (n. 117), 327; and Ephraim Kanarfogel and Moshe Sokolow, 'Rashi and Maimonides Meet in a Genizah Fragment: A Reference to "Mishneh Torah" in a Letter from a Tosafist' [Hebrew], *Tarbiz* 67 (1998): 411–16.

4 See *Tosafot Berakhot* 44a, s.v. *'al*; *Tosafot Menaḥot* 42b, s.v. *tefilin*; and Urbach, *Ba'ale ha-Tosafot*, 618 (n. 99).

5 See *Sefer Mitsvot Gadol*, vol. 2 (Jerusalem: Makhon Yerushalayim, 2003), editor's introduction, 17–24.

6 See Ephraim Kanarfogel, 'Rabbinic Attitudes toward Nonobservance in the Medieval Period,' in *Jewish Tradition and the Non-traditional Jew*, ed. J. J. Schacter (Northvale, NJ: Jason Aronson, 1992), 9–10, 18, 24–25; and Israel Ta-Shma, *Studies in Medieval Rabbinic Literature* [Hebrew], vol. 2 (Spain) (Jerusalem: Bialik Institute, 2004), 149–54.

Coucy did not cite the *Mishneh Torah* uncritically. He ruled against Maimonides in favor of the Tosafists, just as he occasionally lamented (as others did) the absence of source citations in the *Mishneh Torah*.[7]

On the other hand, the much briefer and more widely copied *Sefer ʿAmude Golah* (known also as *Sefer Mitsvot Katan*) by Isaac ben Joseph of Corbeil (composed ca. 1265, with glosses added by Perets ben Elijah of Corbeil) makes little use of the *Mishneh Torah*.[8] Isaac of Corbeil and Rabenu Perets were both students of the Tosafist academy led by the brothers of Evreux, and Isaac was the son-in-law of the prominent Tosafist, Yeḥiel of Paris.[9] This finding accords with the minimal presence of the *Mishneh Torah* in the contemporaneous standard northern French *Tosafot* to the Talmud.

The situation in Germany was similar. The pietistic preambles (*Hilkhot Ḥasidut, Hilkhot Teshuvah*) with which Eleazar of Worms (d. ca. 1230) began his halakhic work, *Sefer Rokeaḥ*, appear to owe something to the form of the *Mishneh Torah*, which starts in *Sefer ha-Mada* with matters or rules for philosophical thought, ethics, and comportment before proceeding to deal with more traditional Jewish legal topics.[10] Mention should also be made of the remarkable encomium found in the Torah commentary of an associate of Eleazar of Worms, Ephraim ben Samson, which maintains that the last verse of the Torah – ולכל היד החזקה ולכל המורא הגדול אשר עשה משה (Deuteronomy 34:12) – alludes to the two major works of Moses ben Maimon: his *Mishneh Torah*, known also as *Yad ha-Ḥazakah* based on its fourteen organizational sections, and his *Moreh Nevukhim*, represented by the similar Hebrew word, *ha-mora*.[11]

Nonetheless, the earliest Germanic rabbinic scholar to make significant use of the *Mishneh Torah* in Talmudic and halakhic contexts was Isaac *Or Zaruʿa* of Vienna, a contemporary of Moses of Coucy. R. Isaac, who hailed from the Slavic lands, studied with the German Tosafists Rabiah of Cologne and Simḥah ben Samuel of Speyer, and with Judah Sirleon in Paris.[12] Another student of Simḥah of Speyer, Isaiah di Trani (Rid, d. ca. 1240), cites Maimonides's *Guide of the Perplexed* in several places in his Torah commentary, *Nimuke ha-Rid*, which he completed around 1200 while still a student in Ashkenaz or just after his return to Italy. However, R. Isaiah did not cite the *Mishneh Torah* with any frequency in his *Tosafot Rid* or collected halakhic rulings, except in his *pesakim* to tractate *Shevu'ot*.[13]

These *pesakim* contain some twenty-five references to the *Mishneh Torah*. Although Rid endorsed the view of Rambam in a number of instances,[14] he strongly disagreed with Maimonides's position in quite a few others.[15] At one point, R. Isaiah cited both Alfasi and Rambam for an overview of how to balance the technical requirements for the swearing of oaths in a range of situations.[16] Impressed by Rambam's systematic treatment of the oaths

7 See Judah Galinsky, 'The Significance of Form: R. Moses of Coucy's Reading Audience and His Sefer ha-Miẓvot,' *AJS Review* 35 (2011): 293–321; and Isadore Twersky, *Introduction to the Code of Maimonides* (New Haven, CT: Yale University Press, 1980), 188–95, 259–72, 325–36.

8 See Galinsky, 'The Significance of Form,' 311 n. 85.

9 See Urbach, *Baʿale ha-Tosafot*, 571, 576.

10 See Urbach, *Baʿale ha-Tosafot*, 393, 408; Ivan Marcus, *Sefer Ḥasidim and the Ashkenazic Book in Medieval Europe* (Philadelphia, PA: University of Pennsylvania Press, 2018), 138 (n. 62).

11 See *Perush Rabenu Efrayim ben R. Shimshon ʿal ha-Torah* (Jerusalem: Julius Klugmann, 1992), pt. 1, 282 (to Exodus 25:36); and Ephraim Kanarfogel, *The Intellectual History and Rabbinic Culture of Medieval Ashkenaz* (Detroit, MI: Wayne State University Press, 2013), 23 n. 83, end.

12 See Urbach, *Baʿale ha-Tosafot*, 436–38; and Uziel Fuchs, 'Iyunim be-Sefer Or Zaruʿa le-R. Yitsḥak ben Mosheh me-Vienna' (M.A. thesis, Hebrew University, Jerusalem, 1993), 11–20.

13 See Israel Ta-Shma, *Creativity and Tradition: Studies in Medieval Rabbinic Scholarship, Literature and Thought* (Cambridge, MA: Harvard University Press, 2006), 177–78; and Kanarfogel, *Intellectual History*, 515–18. On Rid's *Nimuke Ḥumash* and its Ashkenazic origins, see Kanarfogel, *Intellectual History*, 238–40.

14 See *Piske ha-Rid ʿal Masekhet Shevu'ot*, ed. A. Y. Wertheimer (Jerusalem: Mekhon ha-Talmud ha-Yisra'eli ha-Shalem, 1996), 77, 79, 104, 108–09, 111–12, 145.

15 See *Piske ha-Rid*, 70, 73–74, 83–84, 88–91, 96–98, 125, 134, 146. On 152–53 and 158–60, Rid cites Rambam approvingly, but then proceeds to argue with his view in related matters.

16 See *Piske ha-Rid*, 163.

and their halakhic underpinnings, Rid felt that Maimonides's view had to be taken into account even when he did not agree. Indeed, in one of the three references to the *Mishneh Torah* found in *Tosafot Rid*, R. Isaiah praised Maimonides's unusual knowledge (*hokhmot nora'ot ve-nifla'ot*) concerning the questions that were put to witnesses who came forward to report having seen the new moon, asserting that no scholar can fathom (or perhaps verify) Maimonides's teachings in this matter (*ve-'en hakham ba-'olam she-yukhal la'amod 'al devarav*).[17]

Isaac *Or Zaru'a*'s use of the *Mishneh Torah* is much broader (with the total number of citations exceeding 160), although for the most part these citations are few and far between and merely note Rambam's view on the matter at hand.[18] However, in three distinct areas of Jewish law, passages from the *Mishneh Torah* are cited on numerous occasions and discussed in detail. These are *Hilkhot Shabat ve-'Eruvin* (laws of Sabbath and Sabbath boundaries); the laws of *gitin* and *'agunot* (divorce and 'chained' women); and a large swath of *Piske Bava Metsia* (covering chapters dealing with a range of monetary laws and contractual obligations), along with the fourth chapter of tractate *Sanhedrin* on judicial procedures. The intense focus in *Sefer Or Zaru'a* on very specific parts of the *Mishneh Torah* is similar to what has been noted for *Piske ha-Rid* in the area of oaths.

In order to account for these discrete usages, it is helpful to briefly review a theory proposed by Israel Ta-Shma that focuses on another suggestive datum about how the standard northern French *Tosafot* to the Talmud cited medieval predecessors from the Sephardic (Islamic) orbit. *Tosafot* cited the *Halakhot* of Isaac Alfasi (Rif, d. 1103 in Lucena) more than fifty times. At the same time, *Tosafot* cited Ḥananel ben Ḥushiel of Kairouan (d. 1056) tenfold, or nearly six hundred times. Although Rif was cited by *Tosafot* with great respect, it is difficult to account for this large disparity in the number of citations from these two Sephardic scholars, whom the *Tosafot* considered (somewhat imprecisely) to be teacher and student.

Ta-Shma suggests that the Tosafists cited the Talmudic commentary of Rabbenu Ḥananel much more frequently than they did Alfasi's *Halakhot* because of the fundamental differences between these works in both form and function. Rabbenu Ḥananel provided a running commentary on the text of the Talmud itself, consistently (albeit briefly) deciding the *halakhah* from among the views presented by the Talmud. Although Alfasi's *Halakhot* emerge from the text of the Talmud, this work is geared much more single-mindedly to deciding Jewish law and is far less concerned with interpreting the Talmudic discussion as it unfolds. As such, the Tosafists viewed Rabbenu Ḥananel's work as much closer to their own mission and methodology of Talmudic interpretation. *Tosafot* glosses or comments deconstruct and interpret the Talmudic *sugya* closely, often following up these analyses with the implications for Jewish law. On the other hand, the Alfasi's *Halakhot*, also known as *Hilkhot ha-Rif*, is much more code-like.[19]

Maimonides's *Mishneh Torah* posed the same difficulties for the Tosafists, only more so. It certainly does not provide an ongoing commentary to the text of the Talmud, even as it

17 See *Tosafot ha-Rid 'al Masekhet Rosh ha-Shanah*, ed. Y. Hirschfeld (Jerusalem: Mossad Harav Kook, 2016), 66–67 (23b); and Jacob Dienstag, 'Yaḥasam shel Ba'ale ha-Tosafot le-ha-Rambam,' in *Sefer ha-Yovel li-Khevod Shemu'el Kalman Mirski*, ed. Simon Bernstein and Gershon Churgin (New York: Va'ad ha-Yovel, 1958), 350–79 (365). Note that the other two references to the *Mishneh Torah* in *Tosafot Rid* are found in the first chapter of tractate *Nedarim* (12a), regarding the properties of vows.

18 In *Sefer Or Zaru'a*, ed. Y. Farbstein (Jerusalem: Makhon Yerushalayim, 2010), pt. 1, these include *Hilkhot Tsedakah* (sec. 19); *Keri'at Shema* (25); *Netilat Yadayim* (68); *Se'udah* (158); *Shevi'it* (332); *Nidah* (341); and in a responsum (sec. 745, fol. 632). In *Sefer Or Zaru'a*, pt. 2, see *Hilkhot Pesaḥim* (sec. 248); *Megillah* (370–71), *'avelut* (430, 432). In *Sefer Or Zaru'a*, pt. 3, see *Piske Bava Metsia* (ch. 1), secs. 20, 48; *Piske Bava Batra*, 104, 252, 260; *Piske Shevu'ot*, 17, 19.

19 See Israel Ta-Shma, *Studies in Medieval Rabbinic Literature* [Hebrew], vol. 1 (Germany) (Jerusalem: Bialik Institute, 2004), 43–61. Ta-Shma proposes a secondary explanation, which also applies to the *Mishneh Torah*. The Tosafists believed that Rabbenu Ḥananel was of Italian origin. Since Italy was the *ursprung* of Ashkenazic rabbinic culture, an Italian 'passport' provided a rabbinic work in the eyes of the Tosafists with additional credibility, an imprimatur that did not exist for either Alfasi's work or the *Mishneh Torah*.

often supplies clear Hebrew translations for Talmudic passages within its halakhic formulations. Maimonides, like Alfasi, may well have been a great rabbinic scholar in the eyes of the Tosafists, but they remained fundamentally unattracted by his monolithic code. The absence of citations from the *Mishneh Torah* in the literature of the *Tosafot* of northern France was not about settling the score with Maimonides for his philosophy or his dislike of certain rabbinic approaches to *agadah*.[20] Rather, it was about the different Talmudic and halakhic methodologies embraced by Rambam, as compared to those that were at the heart of the Tosafist enterprise.

But if this was so, why did Isaac *Or Zaru'a* cite the *Mishneh Torah* so frequently and consequentially in the three areas of Jewish law outlined, just as Isaiah di Trani did regarding the assignment of oaths and related matters? My suggestion is that Isaac *Or Zaru'a* utilized the *Mishneh Torah*'s *Hilkhot Shabbat* because he found especially useful definitions, structures, and rulings in Maimonides's presentation (as Rid did). The laws of the Sabbath, as found in earlier Ashkenazic codes to which R. Isaac had access, such as *Sefer Yere'im* by Eliezer of Metz (d. 1198) and *Sefer ha-Terumah* by Barukh ben Isaac (d. ca. 1210), were treated as a series of cases and details with little cohesion or overarching approach to the categories of permitted and prohibited activities. Isaac *Or Zaru'a* wished to present an approach that would also include explanations and conceptualizations of the Sabbath laws in a more comprehensive way.[21] To accomplish this, he made extensive use of two sources – Maimonides's *Mishneh Torah* and Rashi's Talmudic commentary to tractate *Shabbat*. Rashi's commentary was seen as an excellent means of explaining the laws of the Sabbath, while Maimonides's extensive treatment of these laws (over the course of thirty chapters in the *Mishneh Torah*) provided the quintessential categorization and conceptualized presentation of these laws in an integrated whole.[22]

In short, Isaac *Or Zaru'a* used the *Mishneh Torah* in his *Hilkhot Shabbat* because he felt that it was necessary and valuable to do so. He did not wish to rely solely on the Tosafist rulings and interpretations that he received from his teachers in northern France and Germany, as he did in other areas of ritual and religious law where he barely mentioned Maimonides. Moreover, there are more than a few instances in *Hilkhot Shabbat* in which Isaac *Or Zaru'a* cited Maimonides's treatment and adopted his rulings where there was no analogous formulation from among his Tosafist teachers and predecessors.[23] There are others in which he singled out the *Mishneh Torah* as representative of a particular approach,[24] and several more where he explained why he did not understand Rambam's ruling, showing that Maimonides's views had to be reckoned with and treated.[25]

Similar considerations animate *Or Zaru'a*'s use of the *Mishneh Torah* in the areas of divorce law and monetary law. An effective presentation of the laws of divorce, including resolving (or preventing) problems associated with *'agunot*, must ideally consider all the ways that a marriage can be retracted according to Jewish law. Isaac *Or Zaru'a* was well versed in matrimonial law based on his extensive Tosafist training and background and did not feel the need for additional assistance from the *Mishneh Torah*. However, innovative suggestions about how to deal with the thorny dimensions of divorce law could be taken from any reliable quarter. Thus, Maimonides is cited, often at length, about instances in which a woman is permitted to remarry on the basis of the testimony of one witness, about the responsibilities of a messenger who transports a bill of divorce,[26] and about contracts

20 See Avraham Grossman, 'From Andalusia to Europe: The Attitude of Rabbis in Germany and France in the Twelfth-Thirteenth Centuries towards the Halakhic Writings of Alfasi and Maimonides' [Hebrew], *Pe'amim* 80 (1999): 14–32 (26–27).

21 Cf. Haym Soloveitchik, '*Mishneh Torah*: Polemic and Art,' in *Maimonides 800 Years After: Essays on Maimonides and his Influence*, ed. Jay M. Harris (Cambridge, MA: Harvard University Press, 2007), 327–43 (333), on *Semag*'s use of Rambam's *Hilkhot Shabbat*.

22 See *Sefer Or Zaru'a*, pt. 2, *Hilkhot Shabbat*, secs. 22, 28, 29, 54–56, 58, 60, 63, 68, 75, 83, 131, 178, 188, 191–92.

23 See *Sefer Or Zaru'a*, pt. 2, *Hilkhot Shabbat*, secs. 35, 44, 64, 116, 121, 126–27, 149, 184.

24 See *Sefer Or Zaru'a*, pt. 2, *Hilkhot Shabbat*, secs. 36, 42, 45, 120, 130, 150, 156, 170, 190.

25 See *Sefer Or Zaru'a*, pt. 2, *Hilkhot Shabbat*, secs. 57, 89, 122, 129.

26 See *Sefer Or Zaru'a*, pt. 1, *Hilkhot 'Agunah/Gitin*, secs. 693, 700; and see also 711, 721.

that are signed by non-Jews. In addition, his unique views about the validity of a bill of divorce that was (in effect) produced by the wife, or of a *get* prepared on a defective writing surface, are also included.[27] In one instance, Isaac *Or Zaru'a* appears to favor the approach of Rambam over that of Rashbam,[28] although in another, R. Isaac challenges Rambam's ruling as well intentioned (since it was aimed at avoiding *'iggun*, where a woman was stuck in a marriage) but overly lenient.[29]

Halakhic logic and clear reasoning are often the leading determinants, with few variations tied to regional traditions or customs, in formulating Jewish monetary law. This category is far less prescriptive than ritual law or other areas of *halakhah* that deal with permitted and prohibited acts based solely on Torah precept, for which logic alone cannot suffice. As such, Isaac *Or Zaru'a* again felt at ease exploring creative and insightful Maimonidean approaches. R. Isaac often began the discussion of a topic in monetary law with a citation from the *Mishneh Torah* followed by his own analysis, sometimes introducing parallel Ashkenazic positions and discussions. It is not uncommon for Maimonides's view to be used to support that of a Tosafist, but there are times when Isaac *Or Zaru'a* subscribed to the view of Maimonides rather than to that of his Tosafist predecessors.[30] In any case, Maimonides's formulations were fully engaged by *Sefer Or Zaru'a* in many of these passages, just as they were by R. Isaac's colleague Isaiah di Trani in his *Piske Shevu'ot*, another dimension of Jewish economic law in which creative well-based ideas could easily be included.[31]

In sum, Isaac *Or Zaru'a*'s approach to the *Mishneh Torah* was consistent with that of other Tosafists only up to a point. Although the *Mishneh Torah* may not have been similar to *Sefer Or Zaru'a* in its style of presentation or analytical method, Isaac of Vienna held that it should be used when needed (and did not otherwise detract from the perceived hegemony of Ashkenazic Talmudism). The gloss-like standard *Tosafot* to the Talmud did not have the same aims or discursive format as the large halakhic compendium that was *Sefer Or Zaru'a*, which, despite its Tosafist loyalties, sought to provide a greater degree of halakhic completeness.

These observations can explain more than the particular usage patterns of the *Mishneh Torah* in *Sefer Or Zaru'a*. As noted above, Isaiah di Trani had no difficulty citing Maimonides's *Moreh Nevukhim* in his Torah commentary, as was the case for other non-Talmudic disciplines where Ashkenazic dominance was not a concern. Indeed, while the teachings of the *Mishneh Torah* are largely absent in the Talmudic and halakhic literature of thirteenth-century Tosafists, a series of Tosafist Torah commentaries compiled in the middle of that century cite relevant passages from the *Mishneh Torah* and even from the *Guide of the Perplexed*.

For example, *Sefer ha-Gan*, composed in northern France ca. 1240 by Aaron ben Joseph ha-Kohen,[32] begins its comment on Genesis 1:26[33] by presenting (without attribution) the essence of the interpretation of the Tosafist and *peshat* exegete, Joseph ben Isaac *Bekhor Shor* of Orleans. Since it is inappropriate to refer to the form of the Creator as indicated by

27 See *Sefer Or Zaru'a*, pt. 1, *Hilkhot 'Agunah/Gitin*, secs. 705, 716, 719–20, 737.

28 See *Sefer Or Zaru'a*, pt. 1, *Hilkhot 'Agunah/Gitin*, sec. 712.

29 See *Sefer Or Zaru'a*, pt. 1, *Hilkhot 'Agunah/Gitin*, sec. 696, and see also sec. 713.

30 See, e.g., *Sefer Or Zaru'a*, pt. 3, *Piske Bava Metsia*, secs. 66–67, 76, 90, 101, 115–17, 128, 133, 171, 183, 194, 237, 329. See also *Piske Sanhedrin*, sec. 75.

31 See *Piske Bava Metsia*, secs. 48, 54, 57, 71, 73, 84–85, 88, 91–92, 120–21, 129, 131–32, 175, 191, 362. See also *Piske Sanhedrin*, secs. 50, 77, 79, 91. Cf. Haym Soloveitchik, 'The Halakhic Isolation of the Ashkenazic Community,' *Simon Dubnow Institute Yearbook* 8 (2009): 41–47 (44); and Jeffrey Woolf, 'Admiration and Apathy: Maimonides' *Mishneh Torah* in High and Late Medieval Ashkenaz,' *Be'erot Yitzhak: Studies in Memory of Isadore Twersky*, ed. Jay M. Harris (Cambridge, MA: Harvard University Press, 2005), 427–53 (435–36).

32 See S. A. Poznanski, *Mavo 'al Ḥakhme Tsarefat Mefarshe ha-Mikra* (Warsaw: Mekitse Nirdamin, 1913), xcviii–civ; *Sefer ha-Gan*, ed. J. M. Orlian (Jerusalem, 2009), 19–29; and Kanarfogel, *Intellectual History*, 268–69, 287–89, 356–58.

33 'And the Almighty said, let us make man in our image.'

a series of biblical verses, *Bekhor Shor* maintains that references to divine eyes or speech are a metaphor to convey the notion that God can communicate, akin to the scriptural comparison of God's voice to the sound of rushing water. Thus, the claim that man is made in God's image refers only to man's ability to intimidate; the fear of man, like the fear of God, will be placed over other creatures.[34] *Sefer ha-Gan* follows with a description of the punishment according to 'the book of Maimonides' for one who believes that God has a physical image, in what appears to be a paraphrase of *Hilkhot Teshuvah* 3:6–7. *Sefer ha-Gan* also links Rashbam's interpretation of the verse – that the form attributed to humans corresponds to the form of the angels – to the category of angels (*ishim*; *anthropos*) found in Maimonides's *Hilkhot Yesode ha-Torah* 2:7. However, these *ishim* and the people to whom they appeared, including Hagar, Joshua, and Manoah, are not mentioned in the passage from the *Mishneh Torah*. They are found only in *Moreh Nevukhim* (II:42), suggesting that Aaron ha-Kohen made use of this work as well.[35]

This perceived shift in the use of Maimonides's writings by the Tosafists as they moved between different areas of Torah study is readily understood. Nahmanides and other leading thirteenth-century Spanish Talmudists referred to the Tosafists at several points as the leading lights of Talmudic interpretation in their day,[36] a role and responsibility that the Tosafists took quite seriously. They consulted (and deferred to) few non-Ashkenazic contemporaries in Talmudic studies and allied fields, except when those outside teachings could be helpful in providing halakhic definitions and other insights, as the citations of Maimonides by Isaac *Or Zaru'a* and Isaiah di Trani demonstrate. On the other hand, in areas of study other than Talmud and *halakhah*, such as biblical interpretation and *piyyut* composition, the Tosafists were more open to outside influences.[37] Indeed, these same considerations can also explain why the standard *Tosafot* to the Talmud barely mentioned Abraham ben David (Rabad) of Posquieres,[38] even as Rabad frequently referred to the teachings of Rabbenu Tam.[39]

The consensus of modern scholarship is that a significant change occurred regarding the citation of the *Mishneh Torah* during the latter part of the thirteenth century in the study hall of Meir of Rothenburg (Maharam; d. 1293). For the first time in Ashkenaz – and nearly a century after it was composed – the *Mishneh Torah* was cited freely in the context of halakhic studies (along with Alfasi's *Halakhot*), although there is some debate about the intentions of programmatic statements made by Maharam concerning the *Mishneh Torah*. Nonetheless, several of his students allied themselves with the halakhic works of Alfasi and Maimonides: *Piske ha-Rosh* and *Sefer Mordekhai* are arrayed according to the order of Rif's *Halakhot*; and Meir ha-Kohen, the author of *Hagahot Maimuniyot*, produced systematic glosses to the *Mishneh Torah*.[40]

34 See *Perushe R. Yosef Bekhor Shor 'al ha-Torah*, ed. Y. Nevo (Jerusalem: Mossad Harav Kook, 1994), 6. See also *Tosafot ha-Shalem*, ed. Jacob Gellis, vol. 8 (Jerusalem: Mif'al Tosafot ha-Shalem, 1990), 119 (sec. 5).

35 See MS. Nuremberg 5, recorded in *Tosafot ha-Shalem*, ed. Gellis, vol. 1 (Jerusalem: Mif'al Tosafot ha-Shalem, 1982), 1:65–66 (sec. 26). *Sefer ha-Gan* on Leviticus 21:4 (ed. Orlian, 283) cites the *Mishneh Torah* in a halakhic context. Similarly, while Abraham Ibn Ezra's biblical interpretations are barely mentioned in *Tosafot* texts (see *Tosafot Rosh ha-Shanah* 13a, s.v. *de-akrivu*; *Tosafot Kidushin* 37b, s.v. *mi-moḥarat*; and the commentary of Ibn Ezra to Leviticus 23:11), several Tosafists, including Joseph *Bekhor Shor* of Orleans, Moses of Coucy, and Yeḥiel of Paris, are quite supportive of Ibn Ezra's interpretations in their commentaries to the Torah. See Ta-Shma, *Studies in Medieval Rabbinic Literature*, 1:276–77; and Kanarfogel, *Intellectual History*, 141, 178–79, 286, 301, 326, 334–35, 495. For literary contacts between Ibn Ezra and Rabbenu Tam on matters of syntax and poetry, see Urbach, *Ba'ale ha-Tosafot*, 68, 108–109.

36 See Ephraim Kanarfogel, 'Between Ashkenaz and Sefarad: Tosafist Teachings in the Talmudic Commentaries of Ritva,' in *Between Rashi and Maimonides: Themes in Medieval Jewish Thought, Literature, and Exegesis*, ed. Ephraim Kanarfogel and Moshe Sokolow (New York: Ktav, 2010), 237–73.

37 See Kanarfogel, *Intellectual History*, 382–87, 393 n. 74, 412, 436–37, 442–43, 495.

38 See Isadore Twersky, *Rabad of Posquieres: A Twelfth-Century Talmudist* (Philadelphia: Jewish Publication Society of America, 1980), 53 n. 42; and Urbach, *Ba'ale ha-Tosafot*, 615–16.

39 See Israel Ta-Shma, *Ha-Sifrut ha-Parshanit la-Talmud*, vol. 1 (Jerusalem: Magnes Press, 1999), 202–203.

40 See Urbach, *Ba'ale ha-Tosafot*, 548–49; Grossman, 'From Andalusia to Europe,' 27–29; Woolf, 'Admiration and Apathy,' 436–38; Soloveitchik, 'The Halakhic Isolation of the Ashkenazic Community'; and my entry

In short, the reception of Maimonides's writings in medieval Ashkenaz depended not on his philosophy or beliefs, but on what he had to offer its rabbinic figures, a calculation that depended largely on the genre and aim of each project.[41] Leaving aside the study hall of Maharam, which effectively closed out the Tosafist period, Maimonides was neither friend nor foe in Ashkenaz. Reception of his work there depended solely on the disciplinary context in which it was being viewed.

in the *Yale Companion to Jewish Writing and Thought in German Culture, 1096–1996*, ed. Sander L. Gilman and Jack Zipes (New Haven, CT: Yale University Press, 1997), 27–34.

41 See Ephraim Kanarfogel, 'The Popularization of Jewish Legal and Customary Literature in Germanic Lands during the Thirteenth Century,' in *Jüdische Kultur in den SchUM-Städten*, ed. Karl E. Grözinger (Weisbaden: Harrassowitz, 2014), 233–45. For additional sources and further discussion of these issues, see Ephraim Kanarfogel, 'Assessing the (Non-) Reception of *Mishneh Torah* in Medieval Ashkenaz,' in *'In the Dwelling of a Sage Lie Precious Treasures': Essays in Jewish Studies in Honor of Shnayer Z. Leiman*, ed. Yitzhak Berger and Chaim Milikowsky (Brooklyn, NY: Ktav, 2020), 123–45.

ILLUMINATING MAIMONIDES: ILLUSTRATING THE *MOREH NEVUKHIM* IN MANUSCRIPTS FROM THE MIDDLE AGES AND THE RENAISSANCE*

EVELYN M. COHEN

It may come as a surprise to find that medieval and Renaissance copies of the writings of Maimonides – his *Mishneh Torah*, a codification of Jewish law, in particular – were at times embellished with precious pigments and gold leaf; sometimes they included scenes of daily life that related to the text. It might come as an even greater surprise to observe that his *Moreh Nevukhim* (*Guide of the Perplexed*), a philosophical text, was, at times, both illuminated and illustrated.[1]

Originally written by Maimonides in Judeo-Arabic ca. 1190, and translated into Hebrew by Samuel ben Judah Ibn Tibbon, the *Guide of the Perplexed* is divided into three parts, with the third being the climax of the treatise. It deals with mystical issues, beginning with Creation as recounted at the beginning of the Book of Genesis, and terminating with the Heavenly Chariot, the *merkavah*, described in the Book of Ezekiel (1:4–28).

Depictions of the creatures (*ḥayot*) of the chariot in Ezekiel's vision exist from all three European centers of medieval manuscript production: Spain, Ashkenaz, and Italy. In each, rather than following the biblical account of the Chariot (*Maʿaseh Merkavah*) in which each creature has four faces – that of a human, a lion, an ox, and an eagle – they are depicted as four separate entities. Their appearance, therefore, is consistent with the artistic tradition that developed in medieval Christian art. Although based on the text in Ezekiel, each creature was depicted individually and ultimately associated with a specific Evangelist, with Matthew as a man, Mark a lion, Luke an ox, and John an eagle.

An early Jewish representation of Ezekiel's vision in which the *ḥayot* are envisioned as four separate figures appears in a commentary on the Bible from thirteenth-century Italy.[2] Depicted in the decoration above the opening of the Book of Ezekiel, the nimbed heads of the four creatures, presented in pairs, face each other. At the top, a lion at the left and an

* I am grateful to Benjamin R. Gampel, Ari G. M. Kinsberg, and especially Havva Charm Zellner for their assistance during the preparation of this essay.

1 See cat. no. 7, n. 3.

2 Florence, Biblioteca Medicea Laurenziana, MS Plut. 3.8. The creatures of the *merkavah* appear on fol. 287v, at the opening of the text of Ezekiel. The manuscript has been digitized; this particular folio is available at http://mss.bmlonline.it/s.aspx?Id=AWODlcPXI1A4r7GxMBVw&c=XVII.%20Anonymi%20Commentarius%20in%20Esther#/oro/580 (accessed November 9, 2022). Although this may be the earliest known representation in a Hebrew manuscript from Italy, the depiction of the creatures from the *merkavah* appears early in Ashkenaz in the *Ambrosian Bible*, dated 1236–38, Milan, Biblioteca Ambrosiana B32 inf, fol. 135v, and in micrography formed from Masoretic notes in the *Yonah Pentateuch*, thirteenth–fourteenth century, London, British Library Add MS 21160, fol. 285r. The motif is also found in Ashkenazic prayer books, for example, the *Leipzig Mahzor*, ca. 1310, Leipzig, Universitätsbibliothek, MS Voller 1002–3, vol. I, fol. 31v, and the *Moskowitz Rhine Mahzor*, 1340s, Jerusalem NLI, Heb. 4° 5213–4, fols. 88r and 397v.

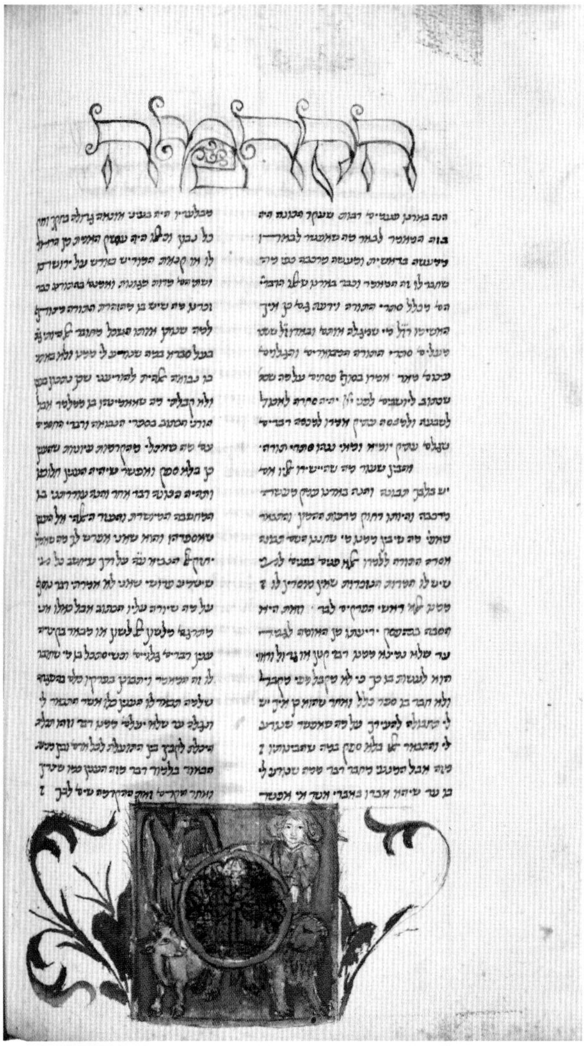

Fig. 74 *Moreh Nevukhim* [Italy, ca. 1465], MS 1, fols. 108v.

ox at the right have wings. At the bottom of the blue panel that embellishes the text, an eagle at the left faces a human head.[3]

The Hartman *Moreh Nevukhim*, also from Italy but dating to the fifteenth century, presents the simplest decoration of the *Guide of the Perplexed* from among the manuscripts under discussion in this essay.[4] It contains only one scene, which appears at the opening of part 3 on folio 108v (Fig. 74). Written at the top of the page, above the two columns of text that begin this section, the letters of the word הקדמה (introduction) are formed by outlines executed in ink that were left hollow. It is possible that the original intention had been to fill in the letters with color or some other form of decoration that was never carried out.

Maimonides begins his introduction to part 3 by stating that he would explain the account of the Creation (Genesis) and the account of the Chariot (*Merkavah*). This text appears on the third line of the first column. Illustrating this concept, a representation of the Heavenly Chariot appears within a square frame at the bottom of the page (Fig. 75). As in the earlier depiction in the biblical commentary in the Laurentian Library, the creatures appear as four separate figures. At the top right corner, the man, depicted as a contemporary

3 It is noteworthy that on fol. 215v the artist included a lion, ox, and eagle as an embellishment for the opening of the Book of Isaiah, which has no overt connection to these animals. Even more striking, all four creatures from the Heavenly Chariot decorate the opening of the Book of Ruth on fol. 451r. Their placement at the four corners of the blue panel decorating the initial words differs from that used for the Book of Ezekiel. The lion at the top left and the human at the top right have gold halos, while the heads of the eagle at the left and the ox at the right are unadorned. Their connection to the biblical text has not been determined.

4 Chicago, Hartman Collection, MS 1. See cat. no. 7.

Fig. 75 *Moreh Nevukhim* [Italy, ca. 1465], MS 1, fols. 108v (detail).

Renaissance figure and sporting a fifteenth-century hairstyle, looks out at the viewer. The eagle opposite him, at the top left corner, turns toward him. Filling the corners at the bottom, a lion at the right and an ox at the left face each other. In the center of the composition a circle filled with ornamentation drawn in ink is displayed for the viewer by the human whose hands hold it in place, while the eagle perches on this form. The lion and ox seem to support much of its weight on their backs. The circle most likely was intended to refer to the wheel that was on the ground next to each of the four-faced creatures described in Ezekiel 1:15. Foliate forms sprout from either side of the panel.

More elaborate illustrations of the creatures of the Heavenly Chariot appear at the beginning of part 3 in two other copies of the *Moreh Nevukhim*. While they were created in two different regions, Spain and Ashkenaz, they were produced only a year apart, in the middle of the fourteenth century when the Black Death was devastating Europe.

The earlier work is the renowned Copenhagen *Moreh Nevukhim*, copied in Barcelona by Levi bar Isaac Figo Karo of Salamanca (לוי בר׳ יצחק פיגו קארו) for the physician R. Menahem Bezalel in 1347 or 1348.[5] The exceedingly fine artwork has been attributed to the Christian workshop of Ferrer Bassa. Each of the openings includes an illustration. Although difficult

5 Copenhagen, The Royal Library, Cod. Heb. 37. In addition to a scene at the beginning of each of the three parts, several text illustrations appear in the margins. See Bezalel Narkiss, *Hebrew Illuminated Manuscripts* (Jerusalem: Encyclopaedia Judaica, 1969), 76, pl. 18; Jørgen H. Barfod, Norman L. Kleeblatt, Vivian B. Mann, and Susan L. Braunstein (eds.), *Kings and Citizens: The History of the Jews in Denmark 1622–1983* (New York: The Jewish Museum, 1983), vol. 2; Ulf Haxen, *Manuscripts and Printed Books from the Collection of The Royal Library Copenhagen* (New York: The Jewish Museum, 1983), cat. no. 6, 18–19; Gabrielle Sed-Rajna, 'Hebrew Illuminated Manuscripts from the Iberian Peninsula,' in *Convivencia: Jews, Muslims, and Christians in Medieval Spain*, ed. Vivian B. Mann, Thomas F. Glick, and Jerrilynn D. Dodds (New York: George Braziller and The Jewish Museum, 1992), 133–55 (esp. 139–40), Fig. 51 and cat. no. 25, 195–96; and Sarit Shalev-Eyni, 'Maimonides's Illuminated Manuscripts,' in *Maimonides: A Legacy in Script* (Jerusalem: The Israel Museum, 2018), 84–78. Digitized images of the entire manuscript are available at http://www5.kb.dk/permalink/2006/manus/293/ (accessed November 9, 2022). Alternative readings have been proposed for the name of the copyist, including פיגוקארו as one word and פיג׳ו קארו as two. The scribe is not known from other manuscripts.

Fig. 76 *Moreh Nevukhim* (Barcelona, 1347 or 1348). Royal Danish Library, Cod. Heb. 37, fol. 202r. Courtesy of the Royal Danish Library.

Fig. 77 *Moreh Nevukhim* (Barcelona, 1347 or 1348). Royal Danish Library, Cod. Heb. 37, fol. 202r (detail). Courtesy of the Royal Danish Library.

to discern because of their damaged condition, facing the introduction by Samuel Ibn Tibbon at the opening of the Guide, within a frame, two scenes appear one above the other on folio 3v. Most likely the scene at the top portrays the presentation of the manuscript to its patron, R. Menaḥem Bezalel. The image beneath it depicts a teacher seated on a cathedra, an open book on his lap, instructing his students who are immersed in their own volumes. Most likely this represents Maimonides as a teacher. Gold borders with painted foliate forms and gold leaf frame the two images. The beginning of the text on the facing page, folio 4r, is embellished with a painted panel bearing the words דברי שמואל בר יהודה. Centered above these words is a golden crest containing a rampant animal. Surrounding the entire page various animals, especially birds, inhabit the foliate borders that embellish the four sides of the page. The opening of the text of the *Moreh Nevukhim* on folio 9r begins with a decorated initial word panel on which the words מורה הנבוכים, placed on a filigree background, are surrounded by an ornamental frame from which leaflike motifs emerge.

Although the most notable illustrations appear in the three openings of the text, some at times unexpected and amusing images are included in the margins of the work, as, for example, the head of a man, a reference to the biblical Adam (אדם) on folio 24r, a leg kicking out illustrating the word foot (רגל) on folio 31r, and a wing (כנף) on folio 44v. There must have been a close collaboration either between the scribe and the artist, or the artist and a Jewish scholar, which fostered the depictions in the scenes at the beginning of each section and the unusual illustrations in the margins.

The opening of part 2 on folio 114r portrays a group of astronomers, an appropriate illustration for a text that deals with the structure of the universe (see Appendix, Fig. 116). The teacher, holding an astrolabe and an open book, lectures to five pupils who stand before him. Some are actively relating to what he is saying, while others look away. The page is framed with an illuminated border containing birds and foliate forms.

As in the other openings, an elaborate border frames the text of the beginning of part 3 on folio 202r, but the scene contained within does not depict a gathering of contemporary people (Fig. 76). The initial word הקדמה is placed within a rectangular filigree panel at the center of a large square space placed above the text. Painted brick red and studded with blue dots, some of which appear within gold, diamond-shaped forms, this panel contains representations of the four creatures of Ezekiel's vision, each of which is winged and placed within a roundel (Fig. 77). The man in the top left corner, the only figure not depicted in its entirety, wears a blue garment and has a blue wing on each shoulder. He points with his right index finger toward the eagle at the top right. This avian figure is the most realistic of the four creatures, as it is naturally winged. The animals at the bottom corners, the lion at the left and the ox at the right, both lie on their stomachs, their heads raised. Although all four figures have wings, each has only two rather than the four described in the biblical text. While clearly intended to represent the Heavenly Chariot described in Ezekiel, in keeping with the tradition followed in medieval Hebrew manuscripts the illustration does not accord with the biblical description.

The appearance of the text of the Copenhagen *Moreh Nevukhim* has a sameness to it. The scribe, Levi ben Isaac, consistently used a semi-cursive Sephardic script; his ink was unvaryingly brown. Although the lines at the beginnings of sections are slightly indented, the writing is justified on the right and the left, forming wide, uniform areas of text. It is the work of the artist – the illuminated panels at the beginning of chapters and section headings, the ornate border designs, and the text illustrations – that enlivens the manuscript and creates a visual delight.

The most elaborate illustration for the opening of part 3 of the *Moreh Nevukhim* is found in a codex from Ashkenaz that until recently was known to relatively few.[6] The manuscript was penned by Jacob ben Samuel Nachlieb, who twice provided the date on which the work was completed.[7] Beneath the end of Maimonides's text on folio 224r the scribe wrote a four-line poem, stating that he finished the manuscript in the year קט (= 109), which is 1349, on Tuesday, the 19th of the month of Adar II. The date appears again, but in a different form, at the end another poem, on folio 225r. Here the scribe's name יעקב בר שמאל נחליף was written in red letters as an acrostic at the beginning of each line of this rhymed colophon. The last four letters of his name were penned, again in red, within the text itself, which otherwise was written in black ink. The name פדה צור, presumably that of the patron, was also written in red letters,[8] as was the year of completion, here presented as עלט (*elet* = 109).

In contrast to the rich pigments used by the illuminator to decorate the text of the Copenhagen *Moreh Nevukhim*, in the Norsa manuscript it is the scribe's skill that frequently achieves striking aesthetic effects.[9] Among his visually interesting practices are the occasional employment of curlicues to adorn letters, the inclusion of Hebrew characters in red and black for words, phrases, and sections of text, the use of vocalization and אותיות משונות (embellished letter forms) for biblical verses, and the shift from a square Ashkenazic script to a sensuous semi-cursive one in parts of the volume. All of these techniques enhance the visual vibrancy of the work.

Unlike the Copenhagen *Moreh Nevukhim*, no illustrations appear in the margins. The scribe included interesting patterns by using the words of the text to create geometric forms, especially at the end of part 2 on folio 140r, where a calligram of the *merkavah* as a two-wheeled chariot was formed utilizing Maimonides's text.

6 The manuscript, which had been in private hands for 500 years, was purchased by the Italian government in 2017; it is now housed in the State Archives of Mantua. It has been studied in several publications. See Thérèse Metzger, 'Le manuscrit Norsa. Une copie ashkenaze achevée en 1349 et enluminée du *Guide des égarés* de Maïmonide,' *Mitteilungen des Kunsthistorischen Institutes in Florenz* 46 (2002), 1–73; *The Austrian Guide for the Perplexed 1349: An Illuminated Manuscript in Hebrew, by the Scribe Jacob ben Samuel Nachlieb [Krems, Austria]* (Alon Shvut: Antiquariat Meir Urbach, 2008); Marcello Moscone, 'The "Norsa Codex" of Maimonides's *Guide for the Perplexed*,' in *Il Codice Maimonides e I Norsa: una famiglia nella Mantova dei Gonzaga: banche, libri, quadri*, ed. Cristina Farnetti (Rome: Ministero per i Bene e le Attività Culturali, 2018), 36–51; and Giulio Busi and Silvana Greco (eds.), *The Renaissance Speaks Hebrew* (Milan: Silvana editoriale, 2019), 248 (cat. no. 14).

7 In addition to the inscriptions, wherever possible within the text the scribe included decorations indicating his name. For a discussion of the scribe, see Menahem Schmelzer, 'Maimonides: The *Guide for the Perplexed*,' in *The Austrian Guide for the Perplexed 1349*, 1–11 (5–7).

8 On the possible identity of the patron, see Schmelzer, 'Maimonides: The *Guide for the Perplexed*,' 8–10.

9 The manuscript's decoration is analyzed in Evelyn M. Cohen, 'The Art of the 1349 *Guide for the Perplexed*: The Scribe, the Artist, the Censors, the Owners,' in *The Austrian Guide for the Perplexed 1349*, 13–50.

Much of the art in this manuscript was created by filigree designs in red and blue, beginning with the introduction by Ibn Tibbon on folio 5r. The display script of the first word דברי, painted red, is placed on a filigree panel of red and blue, framed by filigree borders of the same colors. The result is a page that although devoid of gold leaf and precious colors is lively in its appearance. A similar approach was used on folio 8r, where, in addition to writing in red ink, the scribe added to the vibrancy of the page by alternating the letters of the text with red and black ink. The page comes alive by various means on folio 8v. The initial word, המאמר, written again in display script in red, appears on a panel with an inventive hybrid creature with a camel-like body, beneath which is another level formed of three panels inhabited by animals in pursuit of each other. Penned primarily in black ink, the scribe emphasized various words on the page by writing them in red.

Several pages are embellished with various bright colors and gold leaf. Of special note is the opening of part 1 on folio 14v where both the text and a full-page representation of a Gothic building are adorned with gold leaf. The figure of a lion supports each of the four columns. On a background formed of three registers embellished with red and blue filigree work is written a verse from Isaiah 26:2: פתחו שערים ויבא גוי צדק שומר אמונים (Open the gates and let the righteous nations enter [a nation] that keeps faith). The letters are covered with gold leaf.

The beginning of part 2, on folio 80v, is adorned with decorative penwork in red and blue ink, as well as letters and ornamental forms ornamented with gold leaf (see Appendix, Fig. 117). The framing element above and below the display script that forms the word ההקדמות (the introductions) includes fanciful medieval imagery consisting of dragons and other imaginary creatures.

The decoration for the opening of part 3 is more elaborate than that found in other manuscripts of the *Moreh Nevukhim*. The first words of the text, which appear on folio 142r, are arranged within horizontal panels that display various types of adornment. The word הקדמה (introduction) is placed on a filigree background, its letters embellished with gold leaf. Each panel utilized a different approach toward ornamentation, creating as a consequence a vibrant opening page. However striking the decoration is, it does not prepare the viewer for the extraordinary scene on the verso of the leaf.

The full-page image on folio 142v is an unparalleled visual explication of Maimonides's text, beginning with letters enhanced with gold leaf forming the words ממעשה בראשית ומעשה מרכבה (from the account of Creation and the account of the Chariot) (Fig. 78). Unlike the illustrations in the two other manuscripts under review, which at the opening of part 3 depicted only the four creatures of Ezekiel's vision, here the artist presented a complex composition that reflects Maimonides's fundamental concept. Most of the page is devoted to the account of the Creation, with the words ממעשה בראשית, adorned with gold leaf, appearing on a filigree panel at the top of the page. Immediately beneath it is a horizontal band of blue on which appear twenty stars, under which are five planets and the sun and the moon. All of the celestial bodies are adorned with gold leaf. Below this is another register on which the Hebrew words for the four elements – ארץ (earth), מים (water), אויר (air), and אש (fire) – are written in red ink on a panel decorated with hatching, also in red. The corresponding images of the four elements appear within roundels with gold-leaf frames immediately beneath the words that identify them. They are placed according to the order described in Maimonides's *Guide*. In the middle of the four is a tree, which is part of the scene immediately below.

Depicted in this central area of the composition is an image of the Garden of Eden in which the snake is wrapped around the Tree of Knowledge, shown here with apples growing on it. The depiction is unusual in that rather than enticing Eve, who already appears to be eating the fruit while she proffers another to Adam, the snake seems to be consuming an apple as well. This motif may be based on a *midrash* that recounts that the serpent ate the fruit in order to convince Eve that there was no danger in doing so.[10] In addition, the snake is crowned, which also may be inspired by a legend that God punished the serpent because

10 Louis Ginzberg, *The Legends of the Jews*, trans. Henrietta Szold (Philadelphia, PA: Jewish Publication Society of America, 1968), vol. 1, 73.

Fig. 78 *Moreh Nevukhim* (Ashkenaz, 1349), fol. 142v. Mantua State Archive of the Italian Ministry of Culture.

he was not satisfied with being the king of the animals.[11] Witnessing the Fall of humankind are the animals of the Garden of Eden. This is an unusual image in medieval art, where Adam was often shown naming the animals, but they were not present at the Fall, which took place later. This is another example of the artist following Maimonides's writing, which states that the Fall of humankind took place on the sixth day of Creation.

Adam and Eve stand on a curved, golden surface, which bears an inscription ומעשה מרכבה, written in letters adorned with gold leaf and placed on a filigree background. Beneath it is another curved band on which is written כמראה הקשת (Ezekiel 1:28), a reference to the rainbow.

Only in the horizontal band at the bottom of the page do the four creatures of the Heavenly Chariot appear (Fig. 79). Wingless, each is depicted within its own medallion and identified by an inscription in red ink above it. Reading from right to left they are אדם (man), אריה (lion), שור (ox), and נשר (eagle). As in all other cases found in Hebrew manuscripts, rather than conforming to the biblical description in the Book of Ezekiel, the *merkavah* is alluded to by four separate figures that recall the established iconography of the Four Evangelists.

It is striking that the two most beautiful known examples of the *Moreh Nevukhim* from the Middle Ages were produced while the Black Death was raging throughout Europe. One might wonder why wealthy patrons would have been interested in commissioning lavish copies of Maimonides's *Guide of the Perplexed* at this time. In the case of the Copenhagen manuscript it is clear that the manuscript was produced for a Jewish physician, while the identity of the patron of the Norsa volume remains uncertain. It is tempting to consider that

11 Ginzberg, *Legends of the Jews*, vol. 1, 78.

Fig. 79 *Moreh Nevukhim* (Ashkenaz, 1349), fol. 142v (detail). Mantua State Archive of the Italian Ministry of Culture.

during this calamitous time the *Guide of the Perplexed* provided comfort to the person who commissioned it. As mentioned above, in the *Norsa Moreh Nevukhim*, the scribe first referred to the year of the completion of his text with the customary Hebrew numerical designation of קט, while on the next leaf, he presented the year with the more unusual formulation עלט, meaning darkness, probably intended as an allusion to the Black Death.[12] Perhaps during this dark time people found comfort in Maimonides's closing verses, which cite the Book of Isaiah: אז תפקחנה עיני עורים ואזני חרשים תפתחנה (Then the eyes of the blind shall be opened, and the ears of the deaf shall be unstopped) (Isaiah 35:5) and העם ההלכים בחשך ראו אור גדול ישבי בארץ צלמות אור נגה עליהם (The people that walked in darkness have seen a great light: they that dwelt in the land of the shadow of death, upon them hath the light shined) (Isaiah 9:1). The optimistic and joyful imagery conveyed in the last three words – אור נגה עליהם – written in large display script, would have been impossible to overlook.

12 See Schmelzer, 'Maimonides: The *Guide for the Perplexed*,' 7.

THE RECEPTION OF THE *MISHNEH TORAH* IN THE SIXTEENTH CENTURY

Edward Fram

At the dawn of the sixteenth century, Moses Maimonides's *Mishneh Torah* was the guiding law book for many Jewish communities, but not all. Generally, those living in the Arabic-speaking world saw Maimonides's code as the final word in Jewish law. David Ibn Abi Zimra (d. 1573), who was the leading rabbi in Egypt for much of his life, declared that in Egypt the law followed Maimonides for it was 'the place of the master,' where Maimonides had lived.[1] Joseph Karo (d. 1575), the renowned author of *Shulḥan 'Arukh* and a child of the Spanish Expulsion, reported that Iberian Jews had relied on the *Mishneh Torah* in monetary matters.[2] By 1536, Karo had emigrated to Safed in the Land of Israel. There he said of Maimonides, 'he is the teacher and master of the place in this entire kingdom and all the Arab kingdoms and we live according to his word' (ומפיו אנו חיים).[3] Elsewhere Karo called Maimonides the 'lion of the Land' of Israel and declared that Jews who lived there, as well as those in the 'Arabic-speaking lands and the west' (הארא׳ביסטאן והמערב), followed his *Mishneh Torah*.[4]

The printing history of the *Mishneh Torah* reinforces the regional use of Maimonides's code at the dawn of the early modern age. Despite its length and the necessarily large initial investment required to produce the work, the *Mishneh Torah* was among the first Hebrew books printed. It appeared at the very beginning of Hebrew printing in Rome in the early 1470s and was reprinted in pre-Expulsion Spain (ca. 1480), in Soncino in northern Italy (1490), and in Constantinople (1509), with majestic volumes following in Venice in 1524–1525, twice more in 1550–1551, and again in 1574–1575. Sections of the work, such as the laws of ritual slaughter, also appeared as standalone volumes.

Works printed in the northern Italian regions supplied communities far beyond their borders, but it is noteworthy that Maimonides's legal magnum opus was not published in the German-speaking lands or eastern Europe during the sixteenth or seventeenth centuries.[5] Costs or shortages of materials do not seem to have been the issue. The entire Babylonian Talmud, including the commentaries of Rashi, the twelfth- and thirteenth-century Tosafists, and other legal material, which required reams and reams of paper and had to be set in type by hand, was published a number of times in Cracow and Lublin in the early seventeenth century.[6] Apparently, there was not the same demand for Maimonides's *Mishneh Torah* in these communities as there was elsewhere.

This was not a new development. Historically, the *Mishneh Torah* had not enjoyed the same status in the Ashkenazic world, that is, the cultural sphere of German Jewry, as it

1 See Samuel Morell, *Studies in the Judicial Methodology of Rabbi David Ibn Abi Zimra* (Dallas: University Press of America, 2004), 211–43.

2 Joseph Karo, *She'elot u-Teshuvot Bet Yosef*, with an introduction by Bezalel Landau (Jerusalem: n.p., 1960), no. 10.

3 Joseph Karo, *She'elot u-Teshuvot Avkat Rokhel*, ed. David Avitan (Jerusalem: Siah Yisrael, 2002), no. 201.

4 Karo, *Avkat Rokhel*, nos. 24, 32.

5 A small section of the *Mishneh Torah* dealing only with matters of religious thought did appear in Cracow in 1595.

6 See Raphael Nathan Nata Rabbinovicz, *Ma'amar 'al Hadpasat ha-Talmud*, annotated by Abraham Habermann (repr., 1965; Jerusalem: Mossad Harav Kook, 2006), 80–93.

had in the Arabic-speaking world or on the Iberian peninsula, which had been under Muslim control for centuries before being retaken by Christians. Indeed, when the *Mishneh Torah* arrived in northern Europe in the thirteenth century, it seems to have received a rather lukewarm reception. Maimonides did not engage with the legal thought of the medieval Tosafists, who lived in northern France and the German-speaking lands and developed new ways of understanding texts. Living in Egypt in an age of limited long-distance communication, Maimonides showed no awareness of their efforts. The Tosafists and their students were so involved with their own intellectual efforts to harmonize the Talmudic corpus through reinterpretation that they did not latch onto Maimonides's code of law. Even after Meir ha-Kohen, a student of Meir of Rothenburg (Maharam), added the views of the Tosafists to the margins of the *Mishneh Torah* in the late thirteenth century, the work still did not achieve a pivotal place in the legal thought of Ashkenazic authorities.[7] The *Mishneh Torah* was characterized by apodictic statements that did not offer readers an easy way of grasping the legal foundations for Maimonides's rulings. Asher ben Yeḥiel (d. 1327), who emigrated from the German-speaking lands and settled on the Iberian peninsula in 1304, complained that Maimonides wrote 'like a prophet who heard it from the Almighty without rationales or proofs.'[8] Argumentation was central to the juridic thought of the medieval Tosafists and failure to cite sources was a recurring criticism of the *Mishneh Torah* from its earliest reception to modern times.[9] Maimonides's presentation made it difficult to understand the bases of his conclusions and contributed to his *Mishneh Torah* being left somewhat outside the local legal culture.

In the aftermath of the decimation of Jewish life caused by the Black Death (1348–1349) and the ensuing attacks on Jewish communities, German rabbinic culture tended to focus on its own heritage as it tried to rediscover its own regional customs. While Maimonides was known and cited, his *Mishneh Torah* continued to fail to capture the imagination of local rabbis. Jacob Molin (Rhineland, d. 1427) was perplexed by Maimonides's occasional rulings against the Babylonian Talmud and ultimately said of them, 'our knowledge is insufficient and the depth of his thinking is hidden from us.'[10] Israel Isserlein (Weiner Neustadt, d. 1460) thought that Maimonides had failed to undertake a close reading of the sources. Isserlein did not feel bound by Maimonides's opinions because he believed that Maimonides wrote them based solely on the simple meaning of the Talmud, without the painstaking analysis that characterized the work of the Tosafists and other leading scholars.[11] For most fifteenth-century Ashkenazic rabbis, Maimonides's *Mishneh Torah* remained one source among many.

One exception to this pattern was Jacob Landau, author of *Sefer ha-Agur*, which was printed in Naples sometime between 1490 and 1492. Landau's was the first legal work prepared specifically for the printing press. Landau was from an Ashkenazic family, but he aimed to create a code that was inclusive of the needs of different Jewish communities. He therefore included the opinions of rabbis from various geographical regions and cited the *Mishneh Torah* frequently. The work attained a notable level of popularity and was republished in 1526 (Rimini) and 1546–1547 (Venice), before ultimately being eclipsed by Karo's *Shulḥan 'Arukh*.[12] However, Landau's efforts did not alter the fundamental trend, and Ashkenazic scholars generally maintained a neutral attitude toward the *Mishneh Torah* into the sixteenth century. Copies of Maimonides's work seem to have had a limited place in the libraries of the Jewish communities in Frankfurt and Worms in 1509–1510 when Hebrew

7 Haym Soloveitchik, 'The Halakhic Isolation of the Ashkenazic Community,' *Simon Dubnow Institute Yearbook* 8 (2009): 41–47.

8 See Asher ben Yeḥiel, *She'elot u-Teshuvot le-Rabenu Asher ben Yeḥiel*, ed. Isaac Yudlov (Jerusalem: Makhon Yerushalayim, 1994), 31.9, as well as 94.5.

9 See Isadore Twersky, *Rabad of Posquières: A Twelfth-Century Talmudist* (Philadelphia: Jewish Publication Society of America, 1980), 128–30, 187–88.

10 Jacob Molin, *She'elot u-Teshuvot Maharil*, ed. Y. Satz (Jerusalem: Makhon Yerushalayim, 1979), no. 194.

11 Israel Isserlein, *Pesakim ve-Ketavim* (Venice: Bomberg, 1519), no. 20.

12 See Debra Glasberg Gail, 'The *'Agur*: A Halakhic Code for Print,' *AJS Review* 45, no. 1 (2021): 1–23.

books were confiscated and partially itemized during a campaign against Judaism lead by the Jewish apostate, Johannes Pfefferkorn.[13]

In eastern Europe, Solomon Luria (Lithuania, Lublin, d. 1573) had great respect for Maimonides. He often engaged with Maimonides's opinions, was sensitive to the intricacies of his use of terms, and sometimes went to great lengths to explain his rulings.[14] The margins of Luria's copy of the *Mishneh Torah* are reported to have been filled with his notes on the code, suggesting serious study of the text.[15] Luria thought that one could rely on Maimonides in matters of law, even to be lenient, particularly in those issues connected to science, for Maimonides was 'a great scholar in intellectual and natural [subjects]' (שהיה חכם גדול בסכל ובטבע),[16] the 'father of all the doctors and naturalists' (הוא היה אב לכל הרופאים והטבעיים).[17] This did not mean that Luria did not have his disagreements with Maimonides. Luria found a particular opinion of Maimonides so misguided that he labeled those who followed it 'embarrassing' (חורפי דבר).[18] Moreover, Luria, like some of his predecessors, specifically complained that Maimonides did not cite his sources and that this undermined the reliability of the *Mishneh Torah*.[19] Luria accepted Maimonides's greatness, but he was not in awe of him.

One late medieval code did extensively cite Maimonides's *Mishneh Torah*. In the first half of the fourteenth century, Jacob ben Asher (d. ca. 1343, Toledo) prepared a comprehensive legal work that dealt with all laws applicable in the post-Temple age (i.e., prayer, festivals, rituals, family law, and judicial matters, but not rules related to kingship or Temple worship). Son of the above-mentioned Asher ben Yeḥiel, Jacob's *Arbaʿah Turim* gained broad acceptance in Ashkenazic circles and brought Maimonides's views into Ashkenazic conversations about *halakhah*. Authors such as Moses Isserles (Cracow, d. 1572), Joshua Falk (Lviv, d. 1614), and Joel Sirkes (Cracow, d. 1640) all wrote extensive commentaries on Jacob ben Asher's *Arbaʿah Turim* and had to engage with the opinions of Maimonides cited there. Sirkes was one of the first eastern European authorities truly to embrace Maimonides's *Mishneh Torah*.[20] In his expansive commentary on Jacob ben Asher's *Arbaʿah Turim*, Sirkes constantly considered Maimonides's legal thought. Aware that Maimonides cited the law in the *Mishneh Torah* without explaining how he came to his conclusions, Sirkes sometimes took it upon himself to explain Maimonides's thinking to readers.[21] He deemed Maimonides a *rav muvhak* (literally, 'outstanding rabbi') and felt obliged to follow his views because of his status. In this Sirkes was significantly different than Moses Isserles. Isserles labeled Maimonides a 'pillar of the law' (עמוד התורה) and imbibed much of his philosophical knowledge from the *Guide of the Perplexed* and other writings, but he did not feel duty bound to follow Maimonides's legal decisions based on his reputation. Isserles believed that there were other rabbis over the course of Jewish history who had also attained this level of distinction and there was no reason to favor Maimonides over them.[22] Still, Isserles knew Maimonides's *Mishneh Torah* well. While answering a question without access to his library, the *Mishneh Torah* was one of the very few sources that Isserles cited to make his

13 See Avner Shamir, *Christian Conceptions of Jewish Books: The Pfefferkorn Affair* (Copenhagen: Museum Tusculanum Press, 2011), 110.

14 See, for example, Solomon Luria, *Yam Shel Shelomoh*, ed. Daniel Biton (Jerusalem: Hamaor Institute, 2017), *Gittin* 1:11.

15 Simha Assaf, 'Mashehu le-Toledot Maharshal,' in *Sefer ha-Yovel li-Kevod Levi Ginzberg*, ed. Alexander Marx et al. (New York: American Academy for Jewish Research, 1946), 45–63 (58–59, 62–63).

16 Luria, *Yam Shel Shelomoh*, *Ḥulin* 3:96.

17 Luria, *Yam Shel Shelomoh*, *Ḥulin* 7:15.

18 Luria, *Yam Shel Shelomoh*, *Yevamot* 8:33. Cf. Proverbs 27:11.

19 Solomon Luria, *Yam Shel Shelomoh*, *Ḥulin*, introduction. For an English translation, see Leonard Levin, *Seeing with Both Eyes: Ephraim Luntshitz and the Polish-Jewish Renaissance*, Supplements to *The Journal of Jewish Thought and Philosophy*, vol. 2 (Leiden: Brill, 2008), 234.

20 See Elijah Schochet, *Bach: Rabbi Joel Sirkes: His Life, Work and Times* (Jerusalem: Feldheim, 1971), 55–56.

21 For example, Joel Sirkes, *She'elot u-Teshuvot* (Frankfurt: Johann Vaust, 1697), no. 70.

22 Moses Isserles, *Darke Mosheh*, *Oraḥ Ḥayim* 18:1; Moses Isserles, *She[e'lot] u-T[eshuvot]ha-Rema*, ed. Asher Siev (Jerusalem: Mossad Harav Kook, 2018), no. 17; Sirkes, *Bayit Ḥadash*, *Even ha-ʿEzer* 17:5.

case.[23] As for Sirkes, he sometimes followed Maimonides's views, at least in theory, despite contradictory views among Ashkenazic authorities.[24] No less significantly, Sirkes was among the earliest Ashkenazic users of Maimonides's responsa, some of which appeared in print in Constantinople in 1517 and were republished in Venice in 1544, 1545, and 1574. Sirkes also engaged with Maimonides's responsa found in the work of others, particularly in Karo's writings.[25] Although this material was in print during Isserles's and Luria's lifetimes, they appear to have been generally indifferent to it.

If there was one individual in the sixteenth century who truly saw Maimonides as the most exceptional legal authority of the Middle Ages, it was Joseph Karo. The *Mishneh Torah* was a focal point of Karo's study.[26] Not only did he write a commentary on the *Mishneh Torah* in which he tried to uncover the bases of Maimonides's rulings to dispel misunderstandings, he made Maimonides's legal views one of the pillars of his legal thought in *Shulḥan ʿArukh*. Karo often copied Maimonides's legal formulations in the *Mishneh Torah* directly into his *Bet Yosef*, which was built around Jacob ben Asher's *Arbaʿah Turim* and provided sources for Karo's legal conclusions, and *Shulḥan ʿArukh*. Moreover, to create an efficient rule of thumb to decide between competing legal opinions, Karo said that where there was no clear ruling on a given subject in the Talmud, in subsequent authorities, or a well-accepted custom as to how the law should be observed, he determined the law based on the opinions of three authorities: Isaac Alfasi (North Africa, Spain, d. 1105), Maimonides, and Asher ben Yeḥiel. Karo followed a majority rule system among these three authorities. When two of them agreed on one position, Karo recorded it as the law in his *Shulḥan ʿArukh*. While the importance of this rule in Karo's codification of the law should not be overstated, it further consolidated the central place of the *Mishneh Torah* in his legal decision making and codification project.

Shulḥan ʿArukh was first published in Venice in 1564–1565 and quickly became the legal code of reference for Jewish communities in almost all regions. The margins of the printed text of *Shuḥan ʿArukh* were soon filled with dense commentaries and cross-references, making it the place for the most up-to-date discussions of Jewish law. Karo's proclivity for citing Maimonides's *Mishneh Torah* and his various responsa that were not always known in northern Europe forced legal commentators everywhere to pay close attention to the *Mishneh Torah* and heightened the status of the work in the Ashkenazic cultural world. Even so, Maimonides's *Mishneh Torah* would not take its place as a leading legal source for decision making among Ashkenazic Jews until the uncovering of the sources of Maimonides's rulings became an intellectual genre of its own in Ashkenazic Talmudic culture.

23 Isserles, *Responsa*, no. 34.

24 See, for example, Joel Sirkes, *Bayit Ḥadash*, *Even ha-ʿEzer* 119:7, where he picked up on Maimonides's view through Jacob ben Asher's work.

25 Sirkes, *Bayit Ḥadash*, *Oraḥ Ḥayim* 90, 248, and 269, among others. Also see *Bayit Ḥadash*, *Yoreh Deʿah* 263, where he relied on a citation of one of Maimonides's responsa in Shem Ṭov ben Abraham Ibn Gaon's early fourteenth-century commentary on the *Mishneh Torah* entitled *Migdal ʿOz*. Joshua Falk (d. 1614, Lviv) also accessed one of Maimonides's responsa through Karo's work (see *Derishah*, *Even ha-ʿEzer* 4).

26 Isadore Twersky, 'Ha-Rav Yosef Karo Baʿal ha-Sh[ulḥan] A[rukh],' *Asufot* 3 (1989): 247–50.

MAIMONIDES AND THE KARAITES

Daniel J. Lasker

When Maimonides was born in Córdoba in 1138, there was a significant Karaite Jewish population on the Iberian Peninsula. Although we have no specific demographic information, and this community left no literary remains, its importance can be seen in the lengths to which Rabbanite Jews (followers of rabbinic Judaism) went in combatting it. Most prominent twelfth-century Iberian Rabbanite authors polemicized against this alternative form of Judaism, sometimes in great detail, and they even enlisted the non-Jewish civil authorities in their conflict. Maimonides himself wrote in his *Commentary on the Mishnah* that although Jewish courts in the Diaspora were forbidden from dealing with capital cases, it was nevertheless permitted in his day to execute Karaites as heretics, and, indeed, such sentences were actually carried out in Iberia.[1] Despite this extreme antipathy, Karaism had an impact on Sephardic Rabbanism, as can be seen in the use of imported Karaite literature by Rabbanite authors. Notable examples of such influence are evident in the works of Abraham Ibn Ezra (ca. 1089–ca. 1164), who incorporated many Karaite exegetical insights into his own biblical commentaries. Judah Halevi (ca. 1075–1141) devoted around a tenth of his significant *Book of Kuzari* to a refutation of Karaism, and a number of other contemporary Iberian Rabbanite writings reflect the impact of Karaism in one way or another.[2]

Karaite origins are unclear, but what became Karaism through the centuries seems to have emerged in the Islamic Middle East in the ninth century.[3] It is a form of Judaism that denies the existence of an Oral Torah, given by God to Moses simultaneously with the Written Torah and encapsulated in rabbinic literature, namely the Talmuds and the Midrashim. Most Jews observe a Judaism based on the deliberations of the Rabbis, but, in rejecting the Oral Torah, Karaites developed an alternative, non-rabbinic form of Judaism. Rabbanites considered the denial of the divinity and authority of the Oral Torah as heretical, and, accordingly, Maimonides listed belief in the divine origin of the Oral Torah as an element of one of the thirteen cardinal beliefs that determine who is a Jew.[4]

When Maimonides arrived in Egypt in 1165, he found a vibrant Karaite community living as part and parcel of the larger Jewish community, often intermarrying with the Rabbanite majority. Undoubtedly, he felt it was important to reformulate his policy in dealing with the local dissidents in light of their communal status. On the one hand, he tried to distinguish between the groups by condemning those Egyptian Rabbanite Jews who had adopted certain Karaite practices that were easier to follow than the Rabbanite ones, especially in the realm of post-menstrual purification. On the other hand, Maimonides

1 See Maimonides's comments in *Commentary on the Mishnah*, *Ḥulin* 1:2.

2 For a discussion of Iberian Rabbanite reactions to Karaism, see Daniel J. Lasker, *From Judah Hadassi to Elijah Bashyatchi: Studies in Late Medieval Karaite Philosophy* (Leiden: Brill, 2008), 125–40; for Judah Halevi and Karaism, see Lasker, *From Judah Hadassi to Elijah Bashyatch*, 141–54.

3 For an overview of Karaism from its origins to the present day, see Daniel J. Lasker, *Karaism: An Introduction to the Oldest Surviving Alternative Judaism* (London: Littman Library of Jewish Civilization, 2022).

4 Maimonides's thirteen principles of faith were outlined in his *Commentary on the Mishnah*, Introduction to *Perek Ḥelek*; for a discussion, see Menachem Kellner, *Dogma in Medieval Jewish Thought* (Oxford: Oxford University Press, 1986), 10–65. The obligation to believe in the Oral Torah is part of the eighth principle.

ruled that as long as the Karaites did not curse the Rabbanites, there was an obligation to honor them, to visit their sick, and to circumcise their sons, and he deemed their wine permissible to drink. In other words, Maimonides considered the Karaites as part of the Jewish community in many ways, even if they were schismatic members who followed an illegitimate form of Judaism.

Most importantly, he changed his mind about the permissibility of executing them. In his central law code, the *Mishneh Torah*, he ruled that those heretics who are subject to capital punishment in Jewish law are Jews who actively reject rabbinic Judaism after having been raised in it. A member of a heretical, schismatic group who was born into it was to be considered as a 'baby who was kidnapped by non-Jews' (*tinok she-nishba*) and raised in their religion, giving a Karaite the status of 'a Jew under duress' (*anus*). 'Therefore, efforts should be made to bring them back in repentance, to draw them near, by friendly relations, so that they may return to the strength-giving source, i.e., the Torah. One should not hurry to kill them.'[5] Furthermore, he corrected the text of the *Commentary on the Mishnah* to reflect this new ruling.[6] It would appear that, in contrast to the younger Maimonides, the older, Egyptian one thought that individual Karaites could and should be brought back into the greater Jewish fold in order to distance them from the heresy into which they had been born.

Despite Maimonides's objections to Karaism, his discussions of the nature, origin, and scope of the Oral Torah seem to include concessions to the Karaite view that there was no such Oral Torah. The main Karaite nemesis, Sa'adiah Gaon (882–942), had argued against Karaism by adopting a maximalist position concerning the Oral Torah, namely that all rabbinic interpretations of the Torah and determinations of the law were already revealed to Moses on Mount Sinai. In contrast, Maimonides adopted a minimalist position. He stated that although the Oral Torah revealed at Sinai included the basic principles of understanding the Torah, and a discrete number of specific laws imparted to Moses, the vast majority of Jewish law as developed by the Rabbis was to be considered a product of human effort and not divine intervention. Prophets after Moses may have had a legislative role as sages like other sages, but after Moses there was no divine revelation of laws. Unlike some Rabbanite authorities who explained disagreements between sages as a problem of transmission from Sinai to the Rabbis over the course of more than a thousand years, Maimonides saw contradictory interpretations of the Oral Torah as a consequence of disparate human uses of exegetical reasoning. Like the Karaites, Maimonides was also uncomfortable with many parts of the non-legal rabbinic tradition (the Aggadic Midrash), interpreting seemingly irrational passages as allegorical and not literal, thereby responding to Karaite criticism.[7]

Undoubtedly, Maimonides had a number of different motives for his minimalist view of the Oral Torah and his defense of the Midrash, including his commitment to rationalism and a desire to reject Christian and Muslim views that a post-Mosaic prophet could abrogate the Torah. He was also influenced by trends in Islamic jurisprudence.[8] Nevertheless, a desire to refute the Karaite rejection of the Oral Torah cannot be ruled out as a factor in his theory of the development of Jewish law and lore. Sa'adia's arguments against Karaism were unsophisticated and historically questionable; Maimonides sought to present a reasonable defense of the Oral Torah without making hyperbolic claims as to its contents. As such, he agreed with the Karaites that much of rabbinic law is a result of human initiative and not of divine fiat.

Maimonides's theology shows an awareness of Karaite thought as well. Most Karaites had adopted the Islamic theology known as *Kalam* (literally, word; in this case, words about

5 *Mishneh Torah*, *Mamrim* 3:1–3.

6 This change is documented in Yosef Kafiḥ's edition of Maimonides's *Commentary on the Mishnah*, *Ḥulin* 1:2.

7 See, e.g., Maimonides, *Commentary to the Mishnah*, General Introduction; Introduction to *Perek Helek*.

8 See Marc Herman, 'Situating Maimonides's Approach to the Oral Torah in Its Andalusian Context,' *Jewish History* 31, nos. 1–2 (2017): 31–46.

God, or theology), as had many Rabbanite Geonim.[9] Maimonides considered this school of thought to be apologetic and non-scientific. He polemicized against it at length, having in mind both its Geonic and Karaite followers. In addition, his theory of prophecy, including a division into various levels of revelation, seems to have been a reaction to certain Karaite views of prophecy, including their assumption that post-Mosaic prophets have a legislative role.

Despite what might be seen as ideological concessions to central Karaite beliefs, Maimonides was not himself a Karaite. He was a strong believer in the need for the institutionalization of Jewish law, which only the doctrine of an Oral Torah and its authoritative interpreters could provide. The Karaite ethos summed up in the credo attributed, probably incorrectly, to the proto-Karaite eighth-century Anan ben David – 'Search Scriptures well, and do not rely upon my opinion' – could result in nothing other than legal anarchy. Thus, even if Maimonides felt a certain sympathy toward the Karaite understanding of the Torah and revelation, he rejected it firmly in favor of the traditional rabbinic understanding of the dual Torahs given at Mount Sinai, a Written one and an Oral one.

Karaites, for their part, took much of Maimonides's criticism to heart, especially in the realm of theology. Like Rabbanite Jews who had abandoned *Kalam* for Aristotelianism, they eventually went in the same direction. Starting in the thirteenth century, Karaites in Byzantium began a process of rapprochement with their Rabbanite neighbors, stimulated partially by the accessibility of Rabbanite literature imported from Western Europe, much of which reflected Maimonides's decisive influence. They did not abandon most of the practices which marked the boundaries between the two groups, but they were amenable to Rabbanite theological and exegetical insights that did not threaten their way of life. Thus, although the last great Karaite philosopher, the Byzantine Aaron ben Elijah of Nicomedia (the Younger, d. 1369), tried to defend the intellectual probity of his predecessors among the Karaite theologians, he still accepted many of the Aristotelian positions advocated by Maimonides. By the time of Elijah Bashyatchi (d. 1490), the last major Byzantine Karaite authority and to this day the decisive Karaite legal authority, much of Maimonides's philosophy had already been assimilated into Karaite thinking. The authority of Maimonides was too great for late medieval Karaites to resist.[10]

After adopting major elements of Maimonides's Aristotelian philosophy, some Karaites went one step further and claimed that the Great Eagle was actually a secret Karaite who did not admit his real identity for fear of his Rabbanite colleagues. Maimonides's sanctioning of killing Karaites as heretics was forgotten; his patronizing attitude that they were merely kidnapped babies incapable of seeing the truth of rabbinic Judaism because of their upbringing was ignored. Instead, the Karaites noticed Maimonides's minimalistic approach to the Oral Torah and the fact that he was not always comfortable with rabbinic statements, and they concluded that his devotion to rabbinic Judaism was not wholehearted. They began citing him not only for his theological insights but even for his legal interpretations. In many ways, Maimonides became a Karaite cultural hero.[11]

With the decline of Byzantine (and after 1453, Ottoman) Karaism in the sixteenth century, the center of Karaite life moved to eastern Europe: the Crimea; Poland–Lithuania, especially Troki (Trakai); and Volhynia and Galicia, both now in Ukraine. Although never demographically strong, these communities produced small cadres of intellectuals who wrote a large number of treatises and were responsible for an educational system intended to train Karaite children to grow into believing and knowledgeable adults. Maimonides was often cited in their literary works as an authority, and his *Guide of the Perplexed* was a

9 See Harry A. Wolfson, *The Philosophy of the Kalam* (Cambridge, MA: Harvard University Press, 1976); Wolfson, *Repercussions of the Kalam in Jewish Philosophy* (Cambridge, MA: Harvard University Press, 1979).

10 Maimonides's relation to Karaites and Karaism and the Karaite adoption of Maimonidean philosophy is discussed in Lasker, *Studies*, 60–122, 155–89.

11 See Daniel J. Lasker, 'Maimonides and the Karaites: From Critic to Cultural Hero,' in *Maimónides y su época*, ed. Carlos del Valle Rodriguez et al. (Madrid: Sociedad Estatal de Conmemoraciones Culturales, 2007), 311–25.

mainstay of the curricula of their schools. Even into the modern age, traditional Karaites, like many traditional Rabbanites, were skeptical of new scientific discoveries, such as the heliocentric world with its solar system; thus, Maimonides's medieval theology and science were good fits for their educational needs. His *Guide* was required reading for Karaite students, along with other medieval Rabbanite works, as well as traditional Karaite classics. It is therefore unsurprising that a Crimean Karaite, Isaac ben Moses Mangubi, would have had a copy of the *Guide* and annotated it with explanations of Maimonides's philosophy (see cat. no. 17). There is no Karaite content to these comments, even when Maimonides attacks Karaites for their devotion to *Kalam* (*Guide* 1:71). This volume of the *Guide* in the Hartman Collection is a further indication of how Maimonides was accepted into the Karaite tradition despite his fierce opposition to Karaite doctrines, and the extent to which the boundary lines between the two forms of Judaism were never hermetically sealed.

CHRISTIAN READERS OF MAIMONIDES IN MEDIEVAL AND EARLY MODERN EUROPE

Joanna Weinberg

Maimonides, or rather Rabbi Moyses or Moyses Aegyptius, fared well in the Christian West. His writings were avidly read and translated into Latin over the centuries. Not long after he had completed his magnum opus, the *Guide of the Perplexed*, it was translated in its entirety into Latin under the title *Dux neutrorum* (or *Dux dubiorum*).[1] Based mainly on Judah 'al Ḥarizi's literary Hebrew rendering of the *Guide*, this Latin translation circulated widely – thirteen manuscripts have been discovered to date. The great scholastics such as Albertus Magnus (d. 1280), his student Thomas Aquinas (d. 1274), and Meister Eckhart (1260–1328?) regarded Maimonides as an authoritative spokesman on the major theological questions of the day, citing his *Dux* alongside the Church Fathers and Arabic philosophers including Avicenna and Averroes. Like Maimonides, they had to wrestle with the problems that Aristotelianism and rational philosophy in general posed to their religious faith grounded in Scripture.

Yet Maimonides's opinions were not always accepted; somehow his positions on certain issues appeared too radical. Thus, for example, the 'angelic doctor,' Thomas Aquinas, who cited Maimonides 74 times throughout his writings, challenged him for claiming that the ascription of positive attributes such as merciful or kind to God compromises His perfection and unity. Maimonides concluded that the only way to refer to God is by what He is not (*via negativa*). Aquinas combatted this rigid position by offering a doctrine that facilitated analogy between divine and human attributes.[2] Wishing to allow for a human vision of God, Aquinas argued that human attributes may be predicated of God since these notions are ultimately derived from God in His unitary perfection. Notwithstanding such criticisms, Aquinas and his colleagues respected 'Rabbi Moyses' as a formidable authority whose opinions could not be rejected without serious engagement.

One feature discernible in seven manuscripts of the Latin version of the *Guide* is an additional section at the end of the book in the form of a list of the positive and negative commandments. The addendum is drawn from Maimonides's *Book of Commandments* and their brief listing in the headings of the sections in the *Mishneh Torah*. Clearly, the list is seen as pertinent to part 3 of the *Guide* (chapters 36–50) in which Maimonides accounted for the reasons for the biblical commandments. Christian readers scrutinized these chapters of the *Guide* with the same verve as they did its more philosophical or exegetical sections. When Agostino Giustiniani, bishop of Nebbio (1470–1536?), undertook to produce the first printed translation of the *Guide*, which he renamed *Dux seu Director dubitantium aut perplexorum* (Paris, 1520), he too appended the list of positive and negative commandments

1 On the translation history of the *Guide*, see Josef Stern, James T. Robinson, and Yonatan Shemesh (eds.), *Maimonides' 'Guide of the Perplexed' in Translation: A History from the Thirteenth Century to the Twentieth* (Chicago: University of Chicago Press, 2019).

2 This is a complex topic that alongside other similarly knotty theological problems has been discussed at length by scholars of medieval philosophy. See, for example, the essays in Jacob I. Dienstag, *Studies in Maimonides and St. Thomas Aquinas* (New York: Ktav, 1975).

as the final chapters of the work (56 and 57).[3] Indeed, it would appear that he was basing his transcription on the *Dux neutrorum* and another medieval Latin version. The inclusion of the classification of the commandments is revealing, for it indicates that the enumeration of the commandments was regarded as a basic constituent of at least one main section of the *Guide*.

Though much criticized for its errors in translation, Giustiniani's *Dux* was to be found on many a scholar's bookshelf. Not only did it give readers access to one of the great books of medieval Judaism, Christianity, and Islam, it also provided them with a potted history (in one page) of the life and work of Rambam – Giustiniani noted the conventional Jewish acronym – as well as an index of the most notable concepts. In this brief survey he mentioned Maimonides's medical works, as well as the *Yad* [*Mishneh Torah*] composed of fourteen sections in 'great part based on the Talmud.' The *Guide of the Perplexed* is singled out as a work in which 'not unimportant ideas' are put forward on the basis of numerous rational arguments, and which clarify holy Scripture. Like the majority of Christian readers, Giustiniani's approval of Maimonides is articulated in terms of his truthfulness and disinclination to superstition. Maimonides is therefore implicitly regarded as an exceptional Jew; he did not propagate the fantasies and nonsense that, according to conventional opinion, many a Jewish author articulated.

In passing, Giustiniani referred to the Maimonidean controversy, which he alleged to have been initiated by French Jews who threw Maimonides's writings on the pyre, convinced that they were imbued with Christian heresy. The conflagration was unsuccessful, Giustiniani insisted, for Maimonides's writings survived the fiery onslaught and continued to circulate throughout the world. Giustiniani was clearly privy to one of the many stories connected with the so-called Maimonidean controversy, and to the alleged event of the burning of some of Maimonides's writings in Montpellier in the 1230s.[4] Although the sources for Giustiniani's claim are difficult to establish, he nevertheless exploited them for the sake of propagating the view of a 'kosher' Maimonides whose works were suitable for Christian edification given their rejection by his co-religionists.

Even before the publication of Giustiniani's *Guide*, the writings of 'Rabbi Moyses' had been displayed in print for Latin readers in a variety of ways. Several of Maimonides's medical writings had already come to print in the fifteenth century. For example, Maimonides's ideas permeated the religious philosophy of the physician and kabbalist Paulo Ricci (d. 1541) who had converted to Christianity in about 1500. Not only did Ricci compose his own annotations on a list of the commandments based, though not exclusively, on the enumeration of Moses of Coucy, he also wrote a paraphrase of Maimonides's introduction to the Mishnah with the express purpose of demonstrating the extent to which Jewish law encompassed the goals of Christianity.[5] Of particular significance for Ricci were Maimonides's thirteen principles of faith (*'Ikarim*), dogmas which in his view embodied Christian philosophical truths. It is telling that when Ricci used both the enumeration of the 613 commandments and the listing of *'Ikarim* for the development of his own theology, he singled out two sections of the Maimonidean corpus that became the cornerstone of the

3 Though standard recensions of part 3 of Maimonides's Judeo-Arabic text consist of 54 chapters, Giustiniani based his edition on two medieval Latin versions that did not conform exactly and concluded with 55 chapters.

4 The conventional claim that internal debate over Maimonides's writings led to an inquisitorial investigation that resulted in the burning of the *Guide* and *Sefer ha-Mada* in Montpellier by diktat of Mendicant friars is disputed; see the recent publication of Yossef Schwartz, 'Persecution and the Art of Translation: Some New Evidence of the Latin Translation of the *Guide of the Perplexed*,' *Yod. Revue des études hébraiques et juives* 22 (2019): 49–77.

5 On Ricci, see Bernd Roling, 'Conversio and Concordia: The "statera prudentum" of the Jewish convert Paolo Ricci (d. 1541),' in *Cultures of Conversion*, ed. Jan N. Bremmer, Wout J. van Bekkum, and Arie L. Molendijk (Leuven: Peeters, 2006), 53–64. On the various Latin editions of the enumeration of the commandments, see Siegfried Stein, 'Philippus Ferdinandus Polonus. A 16th Century Hebraist in England,' in *Essays in Honour of the Very Rev. Dr J. H. Hertz*, ed. Isidore Epstein, Ephraim Levine, and Cecil Roth (London: Edward Goldston, 1943), 397–412.

Christian representation of Judaism. When Daniel Bomberg and his editor, the convert Felice da Prato, produced the first Rabbinic Bible (Venice 1516–1517), they chose to stray from the purely biblical realm by including a number of paratexts comprising not only a listing of the commandments, but also 'the thirteen principles which the Rambam of blessed memory composed.' This Jewish 'catechesis' was reprinted many times.

In 1529, the noted Hebraist Sebastian Münster translated the thirteen principles into Latin, claiming that the 'author of this little tract was Rabi Moses son of Maimon whom the Jews revere and regard as very learned. He produced many works and examined the Greek philosophers as his mode of composition clearly indicates.'[6] The designation 'little tract' (*libellus*) demonstrates that Münster translated the text directly from the Rabbinic Bible, unaware of the context in which Maimonides had originally formulated the principles of faith. Another distinguished Hebraist, Johann Buxtorf the elder (1564–1629), though possessor of a substantial collection of Hebrew books, was none the wiser on this matter. In his famous *Jüden Schul* (Hanau, 1603), he listed and expounded the *'Ikarim*, most likely from Münster's bilingual edition. Unlike Ricci, Buxtorf did not interpret them to promote concord; rather, he viewed the Maimonidean principles as a deliberate attempt to undermine Christian beliefs. Buxtorf's condemnation of the *'Ikarim* was typical of his negative characterisation of rabbinic Judaism as a whole, but it was also probably inspired by the last section of the *Mishneh Torah* on the messianic age. There, Maimonides had implicitly rejected the messiahship of Jesus when he wrote, 'he, too, imagined that he would be the messiah, but was killed by the High Court… He caused Israel to be destroyed by the sword … and was instrumental in changing the Torah and causing the majority of the world to err and serve a deity that was not God.'[7] This patent allusion to Jesus did not escape the attention of Christian readers who, rather than ignore the passage, either censored or translated it.[8] The Catholic Hebraist Gilbert Génébrard printed the Hebrew text of chapters 11 and 12 from the Venice 1524 edition with accompanying Latin translation in 1572 (see cat. no. 18). A gentle marginal note on the passage 'he is referring to our Christ' was his only reference to the potentially controversial statement.[9]

Naturally, Christian readers brought their own religious sensibilities to their reading of the writings of the Great Eagle. But it should be stressed that above all Maimonides was their guide. Whether they wished to fathom the theological and linguistic problems that confronted medieval scholars or become proficient in the ancient laws of the Jews, Maimonides's writings provided the requisite goods. By the seventeenth century scholars of all denominations were reading and discussing the contents not only of the *Guide of the Perplexed* but also the *Mishneh Torah*. The distinguished humanists Joseph Scaliger (1540–1609) and Isaac Casaubon (1559–1614) exchanged letters about the language of the *Guide*, and Scaliger himself acquired a manuscript of the Arabic text in Hebrew characters, which he then compared with Giustiniani's edition.

Scaliger's efforts to retrieve the original text were part of a more general trend. In 1655, Edward Pococke (1604–1691), Regius Professor of Hebrew and Laudian Professor of Arabic in the University of Oxford, propelled the study of Maimonides to a different level when he published the *Porta Mosis*, an edition and Latin translation of Maimonides's six introductions to sections of his *Commentary on the Mishnah*. Maimonides's original Judaeo-Arabic text was now available in Hebrew characters for the ever-increasing scholarly elite who were intent on studying and acquiring proficiency in Oriental languages and literature. There was even a proposal by the Bodleian librarian, Thomas Hyde, in 1690 to produce an edition of the Arabic text of the *Guide of the Perplexed* with a facing Latin translation. The work was supposed to supersede the most recent Latin translation of the *Guide*, that of Johannes Buxtorf the younger (Basel, 1629), which had itself superseded and supposedly corrected the

6 Sebastian Münster, *Tredecim articuli fidei Iudaeorum* (Worms, 1529), sig. a2 r–v.

7 *Hilkhot Melakhim* 11:4.

8 The printed editions (and also many manuscripts) of the text are not reliable and usually omit the name 'Jesus' and sometimes the entire passage or, as in the case here, simply read 'he.'

9 Gilbert Génébrard, 'Capita R. Mose ben maiemon de rebus Christi regis,' in *Hebraeorum breve chronicon* (Paris, 1572), 47–54.

errors in Giustiniani's rendering. Though Hyde's initiative never came to fruition, it was nonetheless significant, for it represented contemporary scholarly goals: the desire and need to read Maimonides's own precious words in the original. Particularly attractive to Hebraists like John Spencer (1630–1693) who were intent on understanding biblical religion in its historical context were Maimonides's ideas about the origins of idolatry. No less pronounced was the desire to enter the portals of Jewish law by means of Maimonides's crystal-clear exposition in the *Mishneh Torah*. Throughout the seventeenth century and later, sections of the *Mishneh Torah* were taught, translated, and annotated. When Guilielmus Surenhusius produced his monumental edition of the Mishnah in Amsterdam between 1698 and 1703, it was Maimonides's entire commentary alongside that of Bertinoro that he chose to translate into Latin.[10]

Maimonides was a household name among many of the most distinguished scholars of medieval and early modern Europe. This appreciation even extended to the material text on which the immortal words of the master were inscribed: 'The frontispiece is magnificent, in the Jewish manner,' Isaac Casaubon exclaimed, on gazing at Bomberg's edition of the *Mishneh Torah* (Venice, 1524) (see cat. no. 12). What caught his eye was the inscription that framed the frieze's medallion at the top of the page: 'From Moses to Moses there arose none like Moses.'[11]

10 See Piet van Boxel, Kirsten Macfarlane, and Joanna Weinberg (eds.), *The Mishnaic Moment: Jewish Law among Jews and Christians in Early Modern Europe* (Oxford: Oxford University Press, 2022).

11 Anthony Grafton and Joanna Weinberg, *'I have always loved the Holy Tongue': Isaac Casaubon, the Jews, and a Forgotten Chapter in Renaissance Scholarship* (Cambridge, MA: Harvard University Press, 2011), 111.

MAIMONIDES, THE KABBALIST?

Roni Weinstein

Already in his lifetime Maimonides was hailed as an exceptional figure: among the select group of 'Carriers of Jewish Tradition' (גדולי ישראל), as the political leader of Egyptian Jewry and oriental communities in general, and as composer of the first comprehensive *halakhah summa*, the *Mishnah Torah*. His philosophical writings, particularly the *Guide of the Perplexed*, inspired generations of disciples and scholars within the Jewish fold, while also transcending and affecting the thought of Christian scholars and theologians including Thomas Aquinas. Jewish Enlightenment thinkers in the eighteenth and nineteenth centuries presented him as a precursor to religious open-mindedness and as a model for integrating deep religious commitment with non-Jewish culture. Hagiographic stories have been prevalent since the medieval period, and still play out in the contemporary and distinctively anti-Maimonidean custom of going on pilgrimage to his reputed grave in Tiberias.

A lesser-known aspect of the figure of Maimonides is the myth that he, the leading halakhist, abandoned his philosophical approach at the end of his life in favor of kabbalistic beliefs. With the increasing significance of the *Zohar*, and ideas of the ten *Sefirot* in particular, the Jewish believer could relate to and effect emanations from the infinite God by means of religious commandments and meditative prayers. Gershom Scholem presented the various stages that turned Maimonides the Aristotelian into Maimonides the devoted kabbalist and mystic.[1] The first, during his life and shortly after his death, told of him fleeing persecutors and hiding in a cave for three years. The second, during which Maimonides turned toward Kabbalah, gained momentum in the fourteenth century amid the acrimonious polemics surrounding his philosophical writings. The third took off in the sixteenth century as Kabbalah affected processes of modernization in Jewish culture and tradition by inventing new religious practices or imbuing old ones with new mystical weight, establishing new institutions (such as mystical confraternities), and proposing new sources of religious authority.[2] The use of print technology enabled the story to permeate the entire Jewish ecumene through the writings of Isaac Abarbanel, Meir Ibn Gabbai, Elijah of Genazzano, and Gedaliah Ibn Yayha. 'I do testify in relation to Maimonides, the distinguished Rabbi,' remarked Ibn Gabbai in his *Avodat ha-Kodesh*, 'that at the end of his life he regretted what he composed in *The Book of Commandments* and his *Guide of the Perplexed*. These are his very own words in a letter dispatched to Egypt and Yemen: "After coming to the Holy Land I encountered an old person, who illuminated me in the tradition of Kabbalah. Had I known then what I know right now, I would not have written many things."'[3]

What gave rise to the dissemination of such stories about Maimonides? Did they not contradict the bitter polemics over his philosophical stance in Spain and Provence, leading eventually to the burning of his writings? Was it a baseless narrative lacking any historical

1 Gershom Scholem, 'From Philosopher to Cabbalist (a Legend of the Cabbalists on Maimonides)' [Hebrew], *Tarbiz* 6 (1935): 334–42.

2 Roni Weinstein, *Kabbalah and Jewish Modernity* (London: Littman Library of Jewish Civilization, 2016). See also Elisha Russ-Fishbane, *Judaism, Sufism, and the Pietists of Medieval Egypt: A Study of Abraham Maimonides and his Times* (Oxford: Oxford University Press, 2015).

3 Scholem, 'From Philosopher to Cabbalist,' 341. On the awakened interest of early modern Safed kabbalists in Maimonidean thought, see Moshe Hallamish, 'On Maimonides' Status in the Writings of the Safed Kabbalists' [Hebrew], *Daat: A Journal of Philosophy & Kabbalah* 64–66 (2009): 219–34.

validity, unrelated to Maimonides's religious-philosophical ideas? Despite his philosophical motivations, did his thought impact later Jewish mysticism? These questions implicitly assume that Maimonidean philosophy – and, in general, the Aristotelian positions of medieval thinkers – exclude what we nowadays term mystical thinking and practices. The one is supposedly derived from rational discourse while the other leans on revelation and divine inspiration.

The core positions in Maimonides's *Guide of the Perplexed* and in his letters seem to corroborate this perspective. Human reason is the main channel to approach God, necessitating intense and long-term dedication to various and intricate studies. It entails distancing from the basic joys of life, such as sleep, sex, good food, and social status, and obliges the 'philosopher' to live an ascetic life devoted almost entirely to the cultivation of the mind. Maimonides, as a follower of Aristotelian philosophical tradition – mediated to him by Arabic translations – reiterated the importance of knowledge, even in his grand halakhic opus the *Mishneh Torah*, opening the section *Hilkhot Yesode ha-Torah* (Foundations of the Torah) with the command '*To know* that there is a First Being, that He caused all beings to be…' This is one reading of Maimonides's philosophical heritage, adhered to by some Jewish philosophers who underlined the role of knowledge and even radicalized his positions on the mere necessity of religious practice and rituals, or in regard to differences between the Jewish and Muslim religions, or differences between religions in general (a reading of Maimonides following to a large extent the positions of the Arabic philosopher Ibn-Rushd, or Averroes in the latinized version).

Yet examining the Islamicate cultural space in which Maimonides prospered reveals that the exclusion of mystical traits from his philosophical discourse was not entirely clear or valid. The foundations for the philosophical discussion of fundamental religious issues were laid in Muslim Spain a century and half earlier. Ibn Masarra (883–931), a Sufi scholar with ascetic leanings, suggested a course that led increasingly to God. As described lucidly by Sarah Stroumsa and Sara Sviri in their work on the 'Beginnings of Mystical Philosophy,' later generations relied on the Neoplatonic vision, shared by both Jews and Muslims:

> In his treatise *The epistle on contemplation*, Ibn Masarra lays out contemplation (*i'tibar*) as a mental practice which leads the contemplator in an ascending order through the different levels of existence to the uppermost levels of knowledge and to an encounter with his Creator… The main thesis of this epistle, presented from the outset, is the agreement of intellectual contemplation and revelation. Ibn Masarra states this thesis in an unusually forceful and clear way and ties it with the notion of an inner seeing (*baṣira*), a term which may easily be identified as Sufi, but ultimately owes more to neoplatonic teachings. His emphatic formulation of this thesis introduces a line of thought which was to gain particular popularity among Andalusi philosophers, and which is attested in the writings of Ibn al-Sid 'al Batalyawsi, and Ibn Tufayl, Ibn Rushd, and Maimonides.[4]

Seen in this perspective, the philosophy of Maimonides joins a line of previous discussions in Muslim Spain, where rationalist philosophy intersects with Sufi attitudes and terminology.

The Hellenistic philosophical heritage that reached Maimonides and other intellectuals in the Islamicate world through extensive projects of translation did not make a clear distinction between the writings of Plato and Aristotle, and their followers and disciples in later generations. The concept of the 'chain of being' mediating between the divine and the human domains was to a large extent presented in the philosophical writings as shared by both the Neoplatonic traditions and the Aristotelian (or neo-Aristotelian) traditions. In the latter the focus turned to the noetic (intellectual) ladder, as a passage that man is

4 Sarah Stroumsa and Sara Sviri, 'The Beginnings of Mystical Philosophy in Al-Andalus: Ibn Masarra and his *Epistle on Contemplation*,' *JSAI* 36 (2009): 201–53 (204).

undertaking on his course toward God. As the philosopher advances in his studies and immerses in the understanding of reality, not in its temporary and ephemeral appearances but in its eternal aspects (what we might term today the 'laws of nature'), he attaches himself to the roots of the angelic world and its eternal knowledge. As Adam Afterman has explained, 'Neo-Aristotelian union, which occurs through the clinging of the intellect (not the soul) to a divine or metaphysical intellect or thought, could be characterized as a form of "integrative union". By uniting with the noetic metaphysical entity – that is, pure thought – the human mind undergoes a process of integration into a universal entity.'[5] It is precisely this integration with the universal mind that colors the intellectual activity with mystical dimensions.

In the Muslim Aristotelian tradition, to which Maimonides adhered, this noetic voyage relied on clear religious and even mystical roots. Eminent philosophers and thinkers, such as Ibn Sina (980–1037), Ibn Bajja (1085–1138), and Ibn Tufayl (1105–1185) – all well known in Muslim Spain – refer to Sufi sources when they describe unitive experiences in support of their philosophical experiences. No less significant is the fact that their conceptual framework borrows from the Sufi terminology of *ittisal* and *ittihad*, originally referring to the process of approaching and uniting with God and moments of full mystical union.[6]

This blurred line distinguishing Sufi/mystic life and philosophical reasoning in Islam was very much alive in the thought of Maimonides.[7] There are two important preconditions to this noetic voyage toward God. First and foremost is adherence to and performance of *mitsvot* and the study of Torah and Jewish traditions. The second is the study of nature following a long and arduous philosophical course, as presented in the *Guide of the Perplexed*. Such erudition is not interested in knowledge per se, but as a gate to kindle the love of God and what David Blumenthal describes as 'a series of spiritual emotions – awe, fear, insignificance, shame, and embarrassment.'[8] The goal of study resonates and responds to the soul's and body's yearnings for God. Study is not only an intellectual experience, but no less a religious voyage, an initiatory passage to the spiritual and divine realm. After the meticulous observance of the Torah and the arduous philosophical studies, however, 'there are three further stages of true religious life: intellectual apprehension of God, intellectual contemplation of God, and continuous contemplation of God.'[9] The first stage concerns those committed to the study of Torah and philosophy so as to approach God. The second implies a shift of the very few, following arduous study, into an immersion in the divine, a quasi-prophetic state. The last is reserved for unique persons such as the biblical Moses (and Moses Maimonides?) who are endowed with the gift of contemplating God, a mystical state as a permanent experience.

If we accept this reading of Maimonides's religious and noetic heritage, it comes as no surprise that he left a deep imprint on subsequent generations of kabbalists. His towering status as an important leader and ingenious legalist provided them with an important reference upon which to rely and legitimize their positions regarding several fundamental issues:[10] the metaphysics of divine worlds; mediation between humans and God; the psychology of prophecy and moments of revelation; hermeneutic tools for deciphering divine secrets; the importance of exposing the secretive reading of the Jewish canon and especially the Pentateuch and the prophetic messages; the fundamental role of 'Love of

5 Adam Afterman, *'And They Shall Be One Flesh': On the Language of Mystical Union in Judaism* (Leiden: Brill, 2016), 103.

6 Afterman, *'And They Shall Be One Flesh'*, 106.

7 David R. Blumenthal, 'Maimonides' Philosophic Mysticism,' *Daat: A Journal of Jewish Philosophy & Kabbalah* 64–66 (2009): v–xxv.

8 Blumenthal, 'Maimonides' Philosophic Mysticism,' x.

9 Blumenthal, 'Maimonides' Philosophic Mysticism,' ix.

10 Moshe Idel, 'Maimonides and Kabbalah,' in *Studies in Maimonides*, ed. Isadore Twersky (Cambridge, MA: Harvard University Press, 1990), 31–79; Elliot R. Wolfson, 'Beneath the Wings of the Great Eagle: Maimonides and Thirteenth-Century Kabbalah,' in *Moses Maimonides (1138–1204): His Religious, Scientific, and Philosophical* Wirkungsgeschichte *in Different Cultural Contexts*, ed. Görge K. Hasselhoff and Otfied Fraisse (Würzburg: Ergon, 2004), 209–37.

God'; and the possibility and the means to achieve a state of intimacy with or close proximity to God. These aspects demonstrate the profound effects of the Maimonidean on various components of Jewish religious tradition. It is no mere coincidence that the depiction of Maimonides as kabbalist was disseminated in the sixteenth-century Mediterranean basin, in tandem with the growing popularity of Kabbalah and its increasing impact on Jewish religiosity.

When reckoning the Maimonidean impact of medieval and later kabbalistic currents one should not forget the basic differences between Jewish philosophical and kabbalistic attitudes regarding several important elements: the interaction between God and humanity, reading and understanding the Torah, ritual practices and their meaning, the messianic era, individual destiny after death, and finally the impact of religious devotion on the divine domain. The differences derive from the major point of departure: philosophy considers the human mind as a major tool for understanding religious heritage and the cosmos, while kabbalistic lore relies on the concept of the Secret (*Sod*) and its unveiling.

Maimonides has proven relevant to philosophers, halakhic authorities, yeshiva students in early modern Poland studying him secretly, adherents of the modern European Enlightenment, and contemporary scholars of Jewish thought. Amid the kabbalization of Maimonides from the fourteenth century onward, Jewish thinkers echoed the same recurring theme – that each generation and religious-cultural school within Jewish tradition had its own Maimonides. It provided Jewish mysticism with further legitimacy – even the 'Great Eagle' joined their ranks – and justified their commitment to halakhic heritage. This is a further sign of the elasticity of Jewish tradition, and its willingness to absorb further elements into the Jewish religious melting pot.

MAIMONIDES AND THE MODERN JEWISH MIND

IRENE ZWIEP

'This then, was the man, Rabbi Moses ben Maimon, the Rambam. To recall him means to raise a question, a question that is directed to ourselves.'[1] With these words, 81-year-old Rabbi Leo Baeck concluded his lecture, delivered in Düsseldorf on July 7, 1954, to commemorate the 750th anniversary of the death of Maimonides. The Rambam's writings, he explained to his audience, had unified the Jewish people, pointing them toward a life of science and morality. To Baeck, by pairing true Judaism with altruistic humanism Maimonides's personality had foreshadowed the open mindset of Reform Judaism. Thus, through his life and work, the medieval halakhist-philosopher had provided intellectual, social, and religious guidance for the present-day Jew. Written in 1954, Baeck's portrait was but one in a long line of modern reinterpretations of 'Maimonides: The Man, His Work and His Impact,' as the title of the lecture went. In post-war Germany, however, it became a unique gesture of Jewish–German rapprochement.

It is this rich reception history, with its ever-shifting needs and agendas, that will briefly concern us here. Our starting point is the Berlin *Haskalah*, the German-Jewish Enlightenment that brought a revaluation of Maimonides, after a dip in recognition that roughly coincided with the gap between the Sabbioneta (1553) and Jessnitz (1742) editions of the *Guide of the Perplexed*. At the time, the Jewish commercial elite in Prussia faced what seemed a disruptive dilemma: should they accept the recent invitation to 'civic improvement' and join the Enlightenment project of progress and profit? Or should they stay with the Jewish corporate nation and continue its ancient traditions? Also, in shul and in school, should they choose the universal religion of reason over the faith of their fathers, and introduce secular knowledge, indispensable for participating in gentile society, at the cost of rabbinic learning? *Torat ha-Shem* or *Torat ha-Adam*? – that was the question in 1780s Berlin.

Most *maskilim*, if not all, preferred accommodation over rupture and thus opted for integrating the two conflicting paradigms. When trying to fit their innovations into the Jewish continuum, many turned to Maimonides for help. In 1786, Shimon Berz published a biography that portrayed the Rambam as an advocate of secular studies, freedom of conscience, equal rights, and tolerance – in short, as an early prototype of the Berlin *maskil*. In 1761, Mendelssohn himself issued an annotated version of the master's *Treatise on Logic* in an attempt to spread the latest ideas on the relation between language and thought. Thirty years later Solomon Maimon completed *Giv'at ha-Moreh*, a Hebrew introduction to Kantian philosophy disguised as a commentary on the first book of the *Guide*. New wine poured into time-honed wineskins; needless to say, this was no sign of intellectual weakness, but a conscious, deliberate tactic.

Modern scholars have contemplated the irony that *maskilim* identified with medieval thinkers at a time when the gentile Enlightenment was propagating a clean break with the past. 'Imagine a lapsed Catholic *philosophe*,' Abraham Socher has written, 'utterly rejecting the worldly and doctrinal authority of the Church while taking the pen name "Aquinas."'[2] Socher's is a crucial observation: the Enlightenment was all about moving forward.

1 Leo Baeck, *Maimonides: der Mann, sein Werk und seine Wirkung* (Düsseldorf: Verlag Allgemeine Wochenzeitung der Juden in Deutschland, 1954), 30. English translation: Michael Meyer, 'Maimonides and Some Moderns: European Images of the Rambam from the Eighteenth to the Twentieth Centuries,' *CCAR Journal* 44, no. 4 (1997): 4–15 (14).

2 Abraham Socher, taking his lead from Amos Funkenstein, in 'The Spectre of Maimonidean Radicalism in

Accordingly, if we take seriously the maskilic wish to participate in the movement, we should interpret their recourse to a medieval giant not in terms of conservatism, of looking backwards, but of conservation, of trying to preserve a vital essence. In other words, their reaching back to Maimonides was not a matter of temporality (i.e. of anxiously balancing the effects of progress), but of identity, of articulating their Judaism in the face of modern egalitarian humanism. Rational, erudite, cosmopolitan, yet unquestionably Jewish, the Rambam seemed to embody that essence. And so, after two centuries of relative neglect, his work was rediscovered, reinterpreted, and reprinted for the masses, to help transform the European Enlightenment into an authentic Jewish project. In some respects, this was a short-lived scheme; in others, it proved a lasting strategy.

In many ways the initiative that we have come to know as the *Wissenschaft des Judentums* (science of Judaism) was an heir and successor to the maskilic movement. Berlin-based and bent on civic integration, it continued the *Haskalah*'s agenda of progressive universalism in a Jewish key. Simultaneously, its use of the latest academic methods in the (re)construction of Jewish history and culture brought a radically different perspective on the past. Introducing new ideas via old sources, as Mendelssohn and Maimon had done, went out of fashion; in the age of historicism such simple continuities were considered facile and primitive. Henceforth texts should be read as testimonies, as sources of factual (historical) information, not timeless (religious) edification. Wielded by the *Wissenschaft*, the scalpel of critical inquiry made short work of centuries of received authority.

As a result, Maimonides lost his pole position as the paragon of Jewish secular rationalism. In Leopold Zunz's debut *On Rabbinic Literature* (Berlin, 1818) his name appears but twice, each time in a footnote listing medieval Jewish scholars and ending with Moses Mendelssohn.[3] In 1821, Zunz devoted his doctoral thesis not to the Great Eagle but to Shem Tov Ibn Falaquera, a little-known medieval translator of Aristotle into Hebrew. In the context of Zunz's massive oeuvre this may seem a detail, but in fact it shows just how much priorities had shifted. Inspired by the German Classicism of Schiller and Goethe, Zunz and his colleagues no longer wished to absorb gentile knowledge into the Jewish canon but strove to write *themselves* into the cultural fabric of post-Napoleonic Europe. Their model was neither Berlin nor Paris, but medieval Spain, which in their imagination became a haven of tolerance and civilization, where Jews and Arabs had joined forces in the transmission of Greek (read: universal) philosophy and science. Preserving that European legacy for the Christian West had been a matter of craft rather than creativity, a cumulative effort, not the work of single heroes. Picturing the victory of dedication over genius: enter Ibn Falaquera, exit Maimonides.

Literary afterlives are never linear. Some scholars fall into oblivion, others will stand the test of time thanks to the power of canon, a fascinating life, the quality of their work, or a combination of the three. Writing on the brink of modernity, Baruch Spinoza spawned a staggering range of Jewish, Christian, and secular Spinozisms. Operating from medieval Córdoba, Fez, and Cairo, Maimonides inspired an even longer, strictly Jewish, tradition of 'Maimonideanism,' an academic term that covers eight centuries of interpretation, appropriation, and transformation of his thought.[4]

Besides adding new forms of Maimonideanism, modern scholars also explored the mechanics behind that ongoing fascination. Following the dominant conception of history as a serial clash of civilizations, that dynamic was often framed as a choice between Athens and Jerusalem. Being a man for all seasons, Maimonides was fated to spend his afterlife commuting between the two. For some scholars, including the formidable Leo Strauss, Maimonides was a citizen of Athens who only rarely, and always half-heartedly, traveled the

the Late Eighteenth Century,' in *The Cultures of Maimonideanism: New Approaches to the History of Jewish Thought*, ed. James T. Robinson (Leiden: Brill, 2009), 245–58 (248).

3 Reimund Leicht, 'Neu-orientierung an Maimonides?,' in *Orient – Orientalistik – Orientalismus. Geschichte und Aktualität einer Debatte*, ed. Burkhard Schnepel et al. (Bielefeld: transcript, 2011), 93–121 (104).

4 Warren Zev Harvey, 'The Return of Maimonideanism,' *Jewish Social Studies* 42, nos. 3/4 (1980): 249–68; Robinson (ed.), *Cultures of Maimonideanism*; Carlos Fraenkel (ed.), *Traditions of Maimonideanism* (Leiden: Brill, 2009).

road to Jerusalem in search of philosophical truth. The majority of scholars, however, read his oeuvre as a successful, if necessarily imperfect, integration of Greek and Jewish epistemic values.

Over the past two centuries the Hellenism–Judaism opposition has been called upon to express various opposing worldviews: faith or reason, universalism or particularism, mobility or stagnation, detached intellectualization or moral empathy? It is in the study of these binaries that the true 'lessons of history' are found. By placing Maimonides's life and work at a comfortable distance, Jewish scholars created a medieval safe space that allowed them to openly confront the perplexities of modern life and debate their implications for the Jewish future. In doing so, they left intact fundamental incompatibilities while simultaneously affirming their dialectical relationship, much as the master himself had balanced Athens and Jerusalem in his own inimitable *Guide*.

Imagine young Abraham Geiger, *Wissenschaftler* and early Reform rabbi, noting in his diary on April 29, 1831 that he had read the *Guide*, if only 'for linguistic and historical reasons.' Two years later he announced his intent to publish a critical edition, and in August 1834 reported to Zunz that he now considered writing a book on Maimonides's lasting impact on Judaism. By 1836, he framed the Rambam as the harbinger of modern Jewish religious consciousness (*Glaubensbewustsein*) and tried to establish a Maimonides Society to help promote a Jewish theological faculty.[5] The faculty was never realized, but in Geiger's footsteps generations of Reform scholars kept returning to the *Guide* in their efforts at modernizing Jewish doctrine and practice. As historian Heinrich Graetz wrote, it would take a Maimuni, a 'man of extra-ordinary spiritual disposition ... [to] remove the ugly outer forms with a gentle hand' and rejuvenate historical Judaism.[6] Rejuvenation was Graetz's favorite buzzword at the time, and in that context his use of the 'trendy' Arabicized name was far from coincidental.

As a byproduct of anchoring new values in old thinking, some orthodox critics of *Wissenschaft* and Reform ended up rejecting 'the Rambam and his philosophizing' (*Ha-Rambam im kol hitfalsefuto*).[7] In the writings of his most vocal censor, the Italian rabbi Samuel David Luzzatto (Shadal; 1800–1868), Maimonides became the villain of authentic Judaism. Luzzatto had a keen eye for the frosty side of medieval Aristotelianism. He took issue with the master's belief that immortality was no more than a conjunction of the soul with the active intellect, denounced his insistence on dogma when reason failed, and roasted his lack of patience with human ignorance. Maimonides's preference for intellect over ethics, Luzzatto argued, exposed him as a representative of elitist Atticism (aka Athens) as opposed to inclusive, compassionate Abrahamism (Jerusalem). His German colleague Samson Raphael Hirsch (1808–1888) was less categorical in his rejection; instead, he put the blame on the Rambam's Reform readership. Had Maimonides been able to anticipate today's abuse, Hirsch suggested in 1854, he would surely have burned his *Guide* on the spot.[8]

Whether through identification or dissociation, engaging with Maimonides became a matter of Jewish re-sourcing, with Hermann Cohen's *Religion of Reason out of the Sources of Judaism* (1919) as perhaps the most literal example. For many scholars, 'doing Maimonideanism' became a way of professional self-fashioning. For Salomon Munk, making a critical edition of the Arabic *Guide* and adding a French translation and notes was

5 Frank Surall, 'Abraham Geigers Aufruf zur Gründung eines "Maimonidesvereins" für die Errichtung einer jüdisch-theologischen Fakultät,' in *Moses Maimonides (1138–1204): His Religious, Scientific, and Philosophical* Wirkungsgeschichte *in Different Cultural Contexts*, ed. Görge K. Hasselhoff and Ottfried Fraisse (Würzburg: Ergon, 2004), 397–425 (412–15).

6 George Y. Kohler, *Reading Maimonides' Philosophy in 19th-Century Germany: The Guide to Religious Reform* (Dordrecht: Springer, 2012), 79–80.

7 Michah Gottlieb, 'Counter-Enlightenment in a Jewish Key: Anti-Maimonideanism in Nineteenth-Century Orthodoxy,' in Robinson (ed.), *Cultures of Maimonideanism*, 259–87 (267, and n. 33). See also Jay Harris, 'The Image of Maimonides in 19th-Century Jewish Historiography,' *Proceedings of the American Academy for Jewish Research* 54 (1987): 117–39; and Kohler, *Reading Maimonides' Philosophy*, 309–41.

8 Gottlieb, 'Counter-Enlightenment,' 279 n. 112.

an occasion to showcase his philological skills.[9] For the last Lubavitcher Rebbe, Menachem Mendel Schneerson, the Rambam was a paradigm for global leadership.[10] For Abraham Joshua Heschel, tracing Maimonides's journey from metaphysics to medicine was an opportunity to weigh the pros and cons of active versus contemplative life.[11] For Sarah Stroumsa and Joel Kraemer, portraying Maimonides as a 'Mediterranean man' was an exercise in Jewish cosmopolitanism.[12] In the light of this intense reception history, thinkers who ignored the master's work were also making a statement. Franz Rosenzweig's failure to engage in any form of Maimonideanism may thus be read as a sign of his primary self-identification as a *European* thinker.[13]

What do we talk about when we talk about Maimonides? And *who* do we talk about: Moses ben Maimon the Jew, Rambam the halakhist, Maimonides the philosopher, or the man al-Ra'is Abu Imran Musa Ibn Maymun Ibn Abdallah al-Qurtubi al-Andalusi al-Isra'ili?[14] Every community, in order to *be* a community, needs heroes and villains about whom they can agree to disagree. From the day he completed the *Guide*, Maimonides has fulfilled that role in the Jewish world. From Rabad to Shadal and from Crescas to Twersky, scholars have recalled the Rambam in order to raise questions – questions that were directed to themselves and to each other. The human being, Einstein wrote, is a part of the universe that is limited in time and space. Some human beings, however, will accompany us forever, traversing centuries and crossing continents, marking the intersection of the roads to Athens and Jerusalem.

9 Salomon Munk, *Le Guide des égarés* (Paris: A. Franck, 1856–1866). See Alfred L. Ivry, 'Salomon Munk and the Science of Judaism Meet Maimonides,' in Hasselhoff and Fraisse (eds.), *Moses Maimonides*, 479–89.

10 Naftali Loewenthal, 'The Image of Maimonides in Habad Hasidism,' in Fraenkel (ed.), *Traditions of Maimonideanism*, 277–312.

11 Abraham Joshua Heschel, *Maimonides*, Judentum in Geschichte und Gegenwart (Berlin: Erich Reiss, 1935). See also Michael Marmur, 'Heschel's Two Maimonides,' *Jewish Quarterly Review* 98, no. 2 (2008): 230–54.

12 Sarah Stroumsa, *Maimonides in his World: A Portrait of a Mediterranean Thinker* (Princeton, NJ: Princeton University Press, 2009); Joel L. Kraemer, *Maimonides: The Life and World of One of Civilization's Greatest Minds* (New York: Doubleday, 2008).

13 Ottfried Fraisse, 'Die Abwesenheit des Maimonides im Denken Franz Rosenzweigs oder: Zwischen Erfahrung und Interpretation,' in Hasselhoff and Fraisse (eds.), *Moses Maimonides*, 525–47.

14 Kraemer, *Maimonides*, 11. The question was first raised by YU scholar-librarian Jacob Dienstag in 'Rambam or Maimonides; Unity or Duality. A Bibliographical Survey,' in *Hazon Nahum: Studies Presented to Dr. Norman Lamm in Honor of His Seventieth Birthday*, ed. Yaakov Elman and Jeffrey S. Gurock (New York: Yeshiva University Press, 1997), 129–48.

MAIMONIDES AND ORTHODOX JUDAISM

MARC B. SHAPIRO

Maimonides's centrality in Jewish life is obviously a truism. Yet in the last two and a half centuries, his place has become even more prominent than it had been previously. Beginning in the late eighteenth century with the rise of the *Haskalah* in Germany, we find a new encounter with Maimonides. His philosophical teachings, whether in the *Guide of the Perplexed* or in the first book of the *Mishneh Torah*, had been largely ignored for hundreds of years. But with the Jewish Enlightenment, people began to look more closely at the Maimonidean legacy in all its complexity, and the typical response was even greater esteem for the 'Great Eagle,' as people continued to be mesmerized by his incredible achievements.[1]

This does not mean that all were in agreement in seeing the positive significance of Maimonides. Famously, Samuel David Luzzatto (1800–1865) criticized Maimonides from a variety of perspectives, focusing on his philosophy, his approach to dogma, and even his halakhic codification.[2] This criticism of Maimonides led to sharp polemics against Luzzatto, from both Orthodox writers as well as *Haskalah* figures, and illustrates how the dispute over Maimonides was not merely of academic interest but reflected broader disagreements about how Judaism should be structured in the modern world.[3]

In focusing on the 'Orthodox' world, which is the task of this essay, we can note that not only have a number of leading Orthodox figures been prepared to grapple with Maimonides's philosophical ideas, but also that in the area of traditional rabbinic study Maimonides has assumed a new significance. There was even a surprising attack on Maimonides, similar in some ways to that penned by Luzzatto, from a figure who would become a central spokesman for Orthodoxy and is today a household name. I refer to R. Samson Raphael Hirsch (1808–1888). His engagement with Maimonides is significant as he bravely (or brazenly, depending on your perspective) criticized Maimonides's philosophical ideas as leading to a weakening of Judaism.[4]

While Hirsch's words were unusual, they were not unique. Another Orthodox figure, the historian Ze'ev Jawitz (1847–1924), portrayed Maimonides as having compromised authentic Judaism by allowing the entry of certain Greek ideas into his religious philosophy. This led

I thank R. Chaim Rapoport for his helpful comments.

1 See Allan Nadler, 'The "Rambam Revival" in Early Modern Jewish Thought: Maskilim, Mitnagdim, and Hasidim on Maimonides' *Guide of the Perplexed*,' in *Maimonides After 800 Years: Essays on Maimonides and His Influence*, ed. Jay M. Harris (Cambridge, MA: Harvard University Press, 2007), 235–44.

2 See Monford Harris, 'The Theologico-Historical Thinking of Samuel David Luzzatto,' *Jewish Quarterly Review* 52 (1962): 216–44, 309–34.

3 See James H. Lehman, 'Maimonides, Mendelssohn, and the Me'asfim,' *Leo Baeck Institute Yearbook* 20 (1975): 87–108; Jay Harris, 'The Image of Maimonides in Nineteenth-Century Jewish Historiography,' *Proceedings of the American Academy for Jewish Research* 54 (1987): 117–39; George Y. Kohler, *Reading Maimonides' Philosophy in 19th Century Germany: The Guide to Religious Reform* (Heidelberg: Springer, 2012); Michah Gottlieb, 'Counter-Enlightenment in a Jewish Key: Anti-Maimonideanism in Nineteenth-Century Orthodoxy,' in *The Cultures of Maimonideanism*, ed. James T. Robinson (Leiden: Brill, 2009), 259–87.

4 See Marc B. Shapiro, *Changing the Immutable: How Orthodox Judaism Rewrites Its History* (Oxford: Littman Library of Jewish Civilization, 2015), 122.

to an important defense of Maimonides by R. Abraham Isaac Kook (1865–1935), who presented what we can call a traditional portrait of Maimonides, devoid of contradiction between Maimonides the philosopher and Maimonides the halakhist. For R. Kook, Maimonides's relationship with Greek philosophy was more nuanced than Jawitz's portrayal, the latter of which was not much different than certain medieval criticisms of Maimonides.[5]

The critiques just mentioned are noteworthy, but they are really quite insignificant when viewed against the backdrop of Orthodoxy as a whole, for which Maimonides was the most important of rabbinic authorities. His influence was multifaceted, being the primary voice in both rabbinic discussions and theological matters as Orthodoxy confronted new intellectual challenges. Thus, when Orthodoxy had to respond to issues such as the age of the universe or evolution, Maimonides was often cited as support for the notion that Jews are not bound to the literal meaning of the Genesis story. This approach was based on Maimonides's famous statement that if science proved that creation was not *ex nihilo*, as traditionally believed, then he would be able to reinterpret the words of the Torah.[6] This gave license for the later reinterpretation of the creation story due to other scientific challenges. When space exploration was on everyone's mind in the second half of the twentieth century, and the issue of extraterrestrial life raised theological questions, it was Maimonides who provided the basis for an Orthodox theological response based on his rejection of an anthropocentric view of the universe.[7]

In looking at the Orthodox world of the last century or so we can observe Maimonides's influence in some other significant ways.[8] The first point I would note is with regard to the study of Talmud, which is the primary focus in yeshivas. R. Ḥayim Soloveitchik of Brisk (1853–1918) innovated a new method of Talmud study, which has been called the analytic approach. While there were others who also pioneered this general technique, R. Ḥayim's method conquered much of the yeshiva world, and central to his system was the study of Maimonides. We can say that R. Ḥayim transformed the practical halakhic work *par excellence* – Maimonides's *Mishneh Torah* – into both the central feature of his theoretical analyses as well as the most profound commentary on the Talmud. By doing so, he became the first to reveal the profundity of the *Mishneh Torah* in all of its grandeur.

When R. Ḥayim analyzed a dispute between Maimonides and R. Abraham ben David (Rabad; ca. 1125–1198), he did not adopt the traditional approach of commentators who attempted to answer the difficulties raised by Rabad against Maimonides. Rather, he attempted to *clarify* the divergent understandings of these two great figures, those that brought them to their different conclusions. The centrality of Maimonides's *Mishneh Torah* in contemporary Talmudic *shiurim* is a direct result of R. Ḥayim's influence. In modern Lithuanian-style yeshivas, one cannot study a section of Talmud without also looking at how Maimonides codifies the relevant laws.[9]

Another point to be noted is that the great importance of Maimonides in the yeshiva curriculum is really only about the *Mishneh Torah*. It is perhaps a strange phenomenon that for all the stress on Maimonides, other than the *Mishneh Torah* his works have not been a focus in yeshivas. When it comes to the *Guide of the Perplexed*, this is understandable as Maimonides's philosophical ideas – which are also found in the first book of the *Mishneh Torah* – have never achieved acceptance in yeshiva circles. Rather than attempt to make them palatable for traditional audiences, they have simply been ignored, although both

5 See R. Abraham Isaac Kook, *Ma'amre ha-Re'iyah* (Jerusalem, 1984), 105–12.

6 *Guide of the Perplexed* II:25.

7 See Norman Lamm, 'The Religious Implications of Extraterrestrial Life,' *Tradition* 7 (1965): 25–30, 35–36. On Maimonides and anthropocentrism, see Warren Zev Harvey, 'Maimonides' Critique of Anthropocentrism and Teleology,' in *Maimonides' Guide of the Perplexed: A Critical Guide*, ed. Daniel Frank and Aaron Segal (Cambridge: Cambridge University Press, 2021), 209–22.

8 For addition aspects of twentieth-century Orthodox engagement with Maimonides, see David Berger, 'The Uses of Maimonides by Twentieth-Century Jewry,' in David Berger, *Cultures in Collision and Conversation* (Boston, MA: Academic Studies Press, 2011), 190–202.

9 See R. Abraham Isaac Kook, *Igerot ha-Re'iyah* (Jerusalem, 1962), vol. 1, 155, who in 1908 predicted the emerging centrality of the *Mishneh Torah*.

R. Ḥayim Soloveitchik and R. Joseph Rozin (the Rogochover; 1858–1936) were examples of Talmudists who seriously studied the *Guide*.[10]

More surprising, Maimonides's halakhic writings found in both his *Commentary on the Mishnah* and his responsa have been widely ignored as well. It is the *Mishneh Torah* that has been canonized, if we can use that expression, not Maimonides the person. In fact, as R. Joseph B. Soloveitchik (1903–1993) put it, once the *Mishneh Torah* was 'published,' Maimonides was not to be regarded as its 'owner.'[11] The upshot of this is that just because Maimonides himself explains one of his formulations in the *Mishneh Torah*, this does not mean that alternate explanations are not possible. Indeed, in one oft-cited example, R. Ḥayim Soloveitchik offered an explanation of Maimonides's text even though Maimonides himself in a responsum stated that this text was mistaken. There is no question that R. Ḥayim was aware of this responsum as it is quoted in the *Kesef Mishneh*, one of the standard commentaries on the *Mishneh Torah*.[12]

R. Ḥayim's explanations of the *Mishneh Torah* might not have been what Maimonides intended, but he was explaining the *Mishneh Torah* as an independent work in which authorial intent was not the most important consideration. Such an approach would be controversial even if it were only a matter of explaining a text in the *Mishneh Torah* differently than Maimonides explained it. Yet, in the example just mentioned, Maimonides testified that the *Mishneh Torah* text was actually mistaken. For R. Ḥayim, it seems, it really did not matter if the text was historically correct, for it had appeared in print, had been studied for generations, and had been explained by prior commentators. This meant that even the 'incorrect' text had a Torah logic that had to be understood.[13]

While the approach of R. Ḥayim has been of great significance for one segment of Orthodoxy, there is another that has been greatly influenced by Maimonides in a very different way and that is Chabad Hasidim.[14] Hasidic groups have differed in how they related to Maimonides, but it is fair to say that they all revered Maimonides the halakhist.[15] However, there was nothing 'special' when it came to Maimonides until the Chabad movement, led by R. Menachem Mendel Schneerson (the Rebbe; 1902–1994), raised the stature and the everyday presence of Maimonides to a height not seen before.[16] In 1984 he instituted a program of daily *Mishneh Torah* study, much like the Daf Yomi program of Talmud study,[17] and kicked off an initiative for youth, both boys and girls, to complete Maimonides's *Sefer ha-Mitsvot*.

The Rebbe's focus on the centrality of Maimonides went beyond curricular emphasis, as he was also seen as having a qualitative superiority to all other medieval sages. For the Rebbe, if Maimonides described the Menorah in the Temple as having straight arms rather than curved – as depicted in almost all images of the Menorah from the ancient world – then this is how it must have been. (This is the reason why the ubiquitous Hanukkah

10 See Marc B. Shapiro, 'Response to Criticism Part 4; Rabbi Zvi Yehuda and the Hazon Ish,' *The Seforim Blog*, April 12, 2021, https://seforimblog.com/2021/04/response-to-criticism-part-4-rabbi-zvi-yehuda-and-the-hazon-ish/ (accessed November 9, 2022); and Menahem M. Kasher, *Mefa'ane'aḥ Tsefunot* (New York: Mekhon Tsafnat Pane'aḥ, 1959), ch. 7.

11 See R. Michel Zalman Shurkin, *Meged Giv'ot Olam* (Jerusalem, 2005), vol. 2, 7.

12 See *Mishneh Torah, Hilkhot Nizke Mamon* 4:4, and R. Ḥayim's commentary, *ad loc.*

13 See R. Eliyahu Soloveitchik, 'Le-Ḥidushe Rabi Ḥayim ha-Levi 'al ha-Rambam (2),' *Datche* 16 (23 Kislev 5768): 6.

14 See Naftali Loewenthal, 'The Image of Maimonides in Habad Hasidism,' in *Traditions of Maimonideanism*, ed. Carlos Fraenkel (Leiden: Brill, 2009), 277–312.

15 Regarding Hasidism and Maimonides, see Jacob I. Dienstag, 'Maimonides' Guide and Sefer HaMadda in Hasidic Literature' [Hebrew], in *Abraham Weiss Jubilee Volume* (New York: Yeshiva University Press, 1964), 307–30; Louis Jacobs, 'Attitudes of the Kabbalists and Hasidim towards Maimonides,' *The Solomon Goldman Lectures* 5 (1990): 45–55.

16 See Hananel Sari, *Pitron Ḥidat ha-Nevukhim* (Ramat Gan: Bar-Ilan University Press, 2011), 150–55, who discusses how Maimonides became much more central in the Rebbe's outlook as time went on. See also Yaakov Gottlieb, *Sikhletanut bi-Levush Ḥasidi: Demuto shel ha-Rambam be-Ḥasidut Ḥabad* (Ramat Gan: Bar-Ilan University Press, 2009).

17 See the Chabadpedia entry on the *Mishneh Torah* study program at https://tinyurl.com/cpy7uks (accessed November 9, 2022).

menorahs used by Chabad always have straight arms.)[18] It is likely that the Rebbe's well-known geocentrism can also be traced to Maimonides's adoption of this astronomical model. This is so even though, as far as I am aware, the Rebbe never actually cited Maimonides in this regard, and indeed claimed that after the discoveries of Einstein one could just as easily place the earth as the center of the universe as the sun.[19] The great irony is that Maimonides himself stated that science in the Talmud was based on the most advanced knowledge of the time rather than on Jewish tradition.[20] Yet the Rebbe's position was that everything included in the *Mishneh Torah* should be regarded as part of Torah truth, rather than as reflecting transitory scientific knowledge.[21]

Upon the Rebbe's passing, it became crucial in messianist segments of Chabad to show how continued belief in the Rebbe as the messiah did not contradict Maimonides's clear words in the *Mishneh Torah* that the death of a presumed messiah before completing his task proved he was not the messiah.[22] While it would be easier for Chabad messianists to state that their belief is in line with other non-Maimonidean approaches, it is not an option because of Maimonides's supreme status and the fact that the Rebbe himself stated that no halakhic authorities disagreed with Maimonides's description of the stages of the messianic redemption.[23] Fortunately for them, Maimonides had left an opening: he did not actually write 'if the messiah dies,' but 'if the messiah *is killed*.' Although commentators never considered the difference between these two formulations as being of any real consequence, it has taken on great significance for the messianists. In their eyes, since the Rebbe was not killed, it meant that he still could be the messiah.

What about Maimonides's *Guide*? In an early letter the Rebbe claimed that the *Guide* was an apologetic work that did not reflect Maimonides's true views.[24] The Rebbe repeated this position at the end of his life, so it is clear that he did not waver from this view.[25] Nevertheless, the Rebbe saw the *Guide* as an important work and where possible cited it to explain Maimonides's formulations in the *Mishneh Torah*.[26] He also strongly rejected the notion that there were 'two Maimonides,' writing: 'God forbid to regard Maimonides as a split personality, something completely in opposition to Maimonides's own words in *Hilkhot De'ot*, where he described the character of the perfect person.'[27] However, this does not mean that according to the Rebbe Maimonides's philosophical ideas were in any way binding.[28] Indeed, in a few areas, most notably the issue of universal divine providence, the Hasidic approach championed by the Rebbe – following the strong statements of previous Chabad leaders – was in direct opposition to Maimonides, who limited divine providence to humanity.[29]

18 See Steven Fine, *The Menorah: From the Bible to Modern Israel* (Cambridge, MA: Harvard University Press, 2016), 155–62; Maya Balakirsky Katz, 'Trademarks of Faith: "Chabad and Chanukah in America,"' *Modern Judaism* 29, no. 2 (2009): 239–67; Morris M. Faierstein, 'The Maimonidean Menorah and Contemporary Habad Messianism: A Reconsideration,' *Modern Judaism* 32, no. 3 (2012): 323–34.

19 See Jeremy Brown, *New Heavens and a New Earth: The Jewish Reception of Copernican Thought* (Oxford: Oxford University Press, 2013), 256–59.

20 See Menachem Kellner, *Maimonides on the 'Decline of the Generations' and the Nature of Rabbinic Authority* (Albany, NY: State University of New York Press, 1996), ch. 4.

21 See, for example, *Likute Siḥot*, vol. 23, 33–36; *Hitva'aduyot*, 5743, vol. 3, 1571–73. These sources are cited by Yosef Ginzberg and Yirmiyahu Branover, *Mah Rabu Ma'asekha Ha-Shem: Ha-Mada ve-ha-Teknologyah be-Mishnato shel ha-Rebe mi-Lubavitch, R. Menaḥem Mendel Shneerson* (Jerusalem, 2000), 105.

22 *Mishneh Torah, Hilkhot Melakhim* 11:4.

23 See *Likute Siḥot*, vol. 5, 150 n. 51.

24 See *Igerot Kodesh*, vol. 7, 133–34 (no. 1996), *Hitva'aduyot*, 5783, vol. 3, 1601.

25 See *Hitva'aduyot*, 5743, vol. 3, 1571–72. For a contrasting view, see Sari, *Pitron Ḥidat ha-Nevukhim*, 137.

26 See *Hitva'aduyot*, 5749, vol. 2, 369–70.

27 *Hitva'aduyot*, 5748, vol. 2, 253. The Rebbe then suggested ways to explain the contradictions between the *Mishneh Torah* and the *Guide*. For other rejections of the notion of 'two Maimonides,' see *Hitva'aduyot*, 5745, vol. 2, 1028; *Hitva'aduyot*, 5749, vol. 2, 369–70.

28 See, for example, *Hitva'aduyot*, 5747, vol. 3, 585.

29 See the Rebbe's oft-cited letter on divine providence in *Igerot Kodesh*, vol. 1, no. 94. See also Yisrael Netanel Rubin, 'Hashgaḥah Peratit 'al Ba'ale Ḥayim: Hashva'at Mekorot be-Tarbut,' *Moreshet Yisrael* 18 (2020), 235–67.

A completely different approach to that of the Rebbe was reflected in the writings of R. Joseph Kafiḥ (1917–2000). Kafiḥ is significant because of his great importance as a translator and interpreter of Maimonides. Indeed, it was Kafiḥ's translation from the Arabic of Maimonides's *Commentary on the Mishnah* that led to this work being the subject of serious study after having been largely ignored for hundreds of years. Kafiḥ was also the intellectual and spiritual leader of what remained of the Darda'im movement of Yemen, which itself should be regarded as Maimonidean. Founded by Kafiḥ's grandfather, R. Yihye Kafiḥ (1850–1931), this rationalist movement focused on reviving the Yemenite intellectual tradition, which had been based largely on Maimonides before it became immersed in Kabbalah and what the Darda'im regarded as superstition.[30] The Darda'im also strengthened the legal standing of Maimonides by giving him absolute authority in halakhic matters. In this regard, it is noteworthy that Kafiḥ lamented that other authorities did not accept Maimonides's ruling to force a husband to divorce his wife if she demanded it, for in contemporary times such a step would prevent adulterous relationships. For Kafiḥ, the court should use all means at its disposal to bring about the divorce, which according to Maimonides included beating the husband until he proved amenable.[31]

In addition to his translation of Maimonides's *Commentary on the Mishnah*, Kafiḥ published translations and notes on Maimonides's *Guide of the Perplexed* and his major letters, as well as a comprehensive commentary on the entire *Mishneh Torah*. He also wrote many articles clarifying Maimonides's ideas and presenting a spiritual path for those who want to be guided by the 'Great Eagle' in contemporary times. For example, Kafiḥ's article '"Secular Studies" in Maimonides' shows that for Maimonides, a variety of fields of wisdom are necessary for one to be brought to the knowledge, and thus love, of God. Far from being 'secular,' these subjects are to be regarded as 'holy.'[32]

In many other places in Kafiḥ's writings one is presented with a Maimonidean worldview. This is often at odds with 'mainstream' traditional Judaism, which has been greatly influenced by non-rational trends. For example, it would be unimaginable for the typical observant Jew not to mark the anniversary (*yahrzeit*) of a parent's death in some way, even if only to say Kaddish. Yet Kafiḥ pointed out that Maimonides said nothing about commemorating the *yahrzeit* and therefore as far as he was concerned nothing should be done.[33] Similarly, as Kafiḥ explained, Maimonides forbade praying or even reciting Psalms at a cemetery, and for Kafiḥ this was the proper path,[34] once again placing a Maimonidean intellectual Judaism at odds with what we can call popular Judaism. Just as the path of Maimonides during his lifetime was a path for elites, so the Maimonidean Judaism of Kafiḥ was an elitist path.

In a letter to Professor Michael Schwarz, upon receipt of Schwarz's new translation of the *Guide of the Perplexed*, Kafiḥ wrote that Maimonides is like a mirror. 'Anyone who stands in front of it sees his own reflection.'[35] This has been the case throughout Jewish history, with Talmudists, halakhists, philosophers, and mystics all seeing Maimonides in their own image. This trend continued in the modern era, in particular with Orthodox thinkers who had to confront an array of new challenges. Whether the issue was how to relate to Zionism, non-Orthodox forms of Judaism, secular studies, or a host of other issues, Maimonides has usually been front and center, and the conclusions different groups have drawn from his words are often in diametric opposition to each other. This continuing focus on Maimonides is to be expected, for as anyone who has studied in a yeshiva knows, one of the most common questions heard is, 'What does the Rambam say?'

30 See Yehudah Ratzaby, 'On the History of the Controversy over Kabbalah in Sana'a 1913–1914: A Letter by R. Sa'id ben Haim Alnadaf to his brother R. Abraham' [Hebrew], *Pe'amim* 88 (2001): 98–123.

31 See Joseph Kafiḥ (ed.), *Mishneh Torah, Sefer Nashim* (1), 306–07. Maimonides's opinion about beating the husband is found in *Hilkhot Gerushin* 2:20.

32 *Ketavim*, ed. Yosef Tobi (Jerusalem, 1989), vol. 2, 594.

33 Zohar Amar and Hananel Sari (eds.), *Sefer ha-Zikaron le-Rav Yosef ben David Kafiḥ* (Ramat Gan: Bar-Ilan University Press, 2001), 64.

34 *Ketavim*, vol. 2, 625.

35 *Moreh Nevukhim*, trans. Michael Schwarz (Tel Aviv: Tel Aviv University, 2002), vol. 2, 752. See also Kafiḥ (ed.), *Mishneh Torah, Sefer Hafla'ah*, 444.

MAIMONIDES IN POPULAR CULTURE

MAYA BALAKIRSKY KATZ

Maimonides's literary corpus has influenced Jewish visual and material life for centuries, but it was only in the modern era that the author himself secured a place in the popular visual imagination. Maimonides has become the object of ritualistic practices he would have himself eschewed, such as pilgrimages to his grave and amulets evoking his portrait and writings. Despite his own distaste for representations of the human form, his image has appeared in sculpture in the round; in bas-relief on architectural friezes and coins; on paper on stamps, ex libris labels, sukkah decorations, magazines, comic books, and postcards; and, more recently, on film.[1]

This profusion of imagery in the modern era represents a rupture in the reception history of the historical personality of the medieval sage. In contrast to the Christian dissemination of the image of the first-century Jewish historian Flavius Josephus, the Islamic countries in which Maimonides operated eschewed the representation of holy men. The visualization of Maimonides only emerged in the eighteenth century when Jews in Christian Europe self-identified with his persona. In Germany, Moses Mendelssohn (1729–1786), who became a popular subject for art as the father of the *Haskalah*, ascribed his most salient visual feature – his hunched back – to his long hours spent studying Maimonides's *Guide of the Perplexed*. The Polish-Lithuanian writer Salomon Maimon (1753–1800) adopted Maimonides's patronym as his own for his authorial nom-de-plume. The Hungarian Hasidic tsadik Moshe Teitelbaum (1759–1841) was said to have claimed that his soul descended from Maimonides. When the grandson of Jonathan Eybeschütz (1690–1764) published his notes on Maimonides's *Mishneh Torah* in 1819, a full-page engraved portrait of Eybeschütz faced the title page, connecting the two authors in the mind's eye.[2]

Although first published in the eighteenth century, the paradigmatic portrait of Maimonides was popularly embraced only in the mid-nineteenth century, at which point it took on some of the complexities that had earlier been assigned to the Maimonidean literary corpus. In something of a parallel to the printing and reception history of Maimonides's writings, the visual construction of the Maimonidean image embraced the outer limits of Jewish representation, confronting notions of sacralization, standardization, and censorship. At the same time, the 'revival' of Maimonides's physical likeness appealed to both German and British Reform Jews and mystical strains of Orthodox Judaism, partially for its poetic resolution to controversies that surrounded his thirteenth article of faith on the physical resurrection of the dead *in body* and soul after death. As such, depictions of Maimonides are distinctly modern in form, providing a lens into Jewish representational and devotional practices in recent centuries.

1 See Vivian B. Mann, *Jewish Texts on the Visual Arts* (Cambridge: Cambridge University Press, 2000), 19–24.

2 Jonathan Eybeschutz, *Bene Ahuvah* (Prague, Scholl, 1819).

Fig. 80 Blasio Ugolino, *Thesaurus Antiquitatum Sacrarum* (Venice, 1744), vol. 1, xx. Beinecke Rare Book and Manuscript Library, Yale University.

Maimonides and Modern Jewish Liberation Politics

When the portrait with which we associate Maimonides first appeared in an entry on Jewish antiquities in the *Thesaurus Antiquitatum Sacrarum* in 1744, it attracted little attention (Fig. 80).[3] It was only after Austro-Italian scholar Rabbi Isacco Samuele Reggio (1784–1855), a prominent activist in the Jewish emancipation movement or *Haskalah*, publicized the image in the mid-nineteenth century that the modest miniature began to take on, as they say, a life of its own. Reggio, an accomplished artist, made a sketch that he immediately sent to a Berlin printer active in the *Haskalah*, explaining that the *Thesaurus* editor had copied the image from an 'original' life portrait engraved onto a medal. While the evidence was flimsy, Reggio advised that 'there is nothing against assuming the probability that … such a tabula' existed.[4] Satisfied, the Berlin printer issued the portrait with a copy of Reggio's letter of authenticity (Fig. 81). The image of Maimonides was disseminated *en masse* in both Germany and England.

Nowhere was the passion for Maimonides more entrenched than in Germany, where reformers recruited Maimonides as an icon of liberation politics, and the Spanish 'golden age' as a historical model for Jewish integration.[5] A portrait of Maimonides dressed according to Islamic standards, wearing a trim beard without sidelocks, and bearing what appears to be a symbol of his honorary rank in the court of the great Saladin in Cairo, a fact mentioned in Gotthold Ephraim Lessing's *Nathan the Wise*, provided the campaign a poster child.[6]

German Jewish literati adopted a Maimonides they claimed represented a Protestant-like 'aniconism' and 'anti-ocularcentricism' at the same time that they turned Maimonides into an icon in his own right.[7] A cavalcade of artists and printers popularized the image of Maimonides from the oval vignette in the *Thesaurus* – a conventional cameo presentation for bibliographical portraits – through independent large-format prints and as frontispieces to volumes dedicated to his life and work.[8] To enhance the aura of authenticity that Reggio's letter had attempted to provide at the outset, the Maimonides portrait often appeared

3 Richard Cohen, *Jewish Icons: Art and Society in Modern Europe* (Berkeley, CA: University of California Press, 1998), 292–93.

4 Yitzchak Schwartz, 'The Maimonides Portrait: An Appraisal of One of the World's Most Famous Pictures,' *Rambam Maimonides Medical Journal* 2 (2011), https://www.ncbi.nlm.nih.gov/pmc/articles/PMC3678793/#b7-rmmj-2-3-e0052 (accessed November 9, 2022).

5 See Carsten Schapkow, *Role Model and Countermodel: The Golden Age of Iberian Jewry and German Jewish Culture during the Era of Emancipation*, trans. Corey Twitchell (New York: Lexington Books, 2015).

6 Schwartz, 'The Maimonides Portrait.'

7 Zachary J. Braiterman, 'Maimonides and the Visual Image after Kant and Cohen,' *Journal of Jewish Thought and Philosophy* 20, no. 2 (2012): 217–30; Kalman Bland, *The Artless Jew: Medieval and Modern Affirmation and Denials of the Visual* (Princeton, NJ: Princeton University Press, 2000).

8 See, for example, the frontispiece to David Yellin and Israel Abrahams, *Maimonides* (Philadelphia, PA: Jewish Publication Society, 1903).

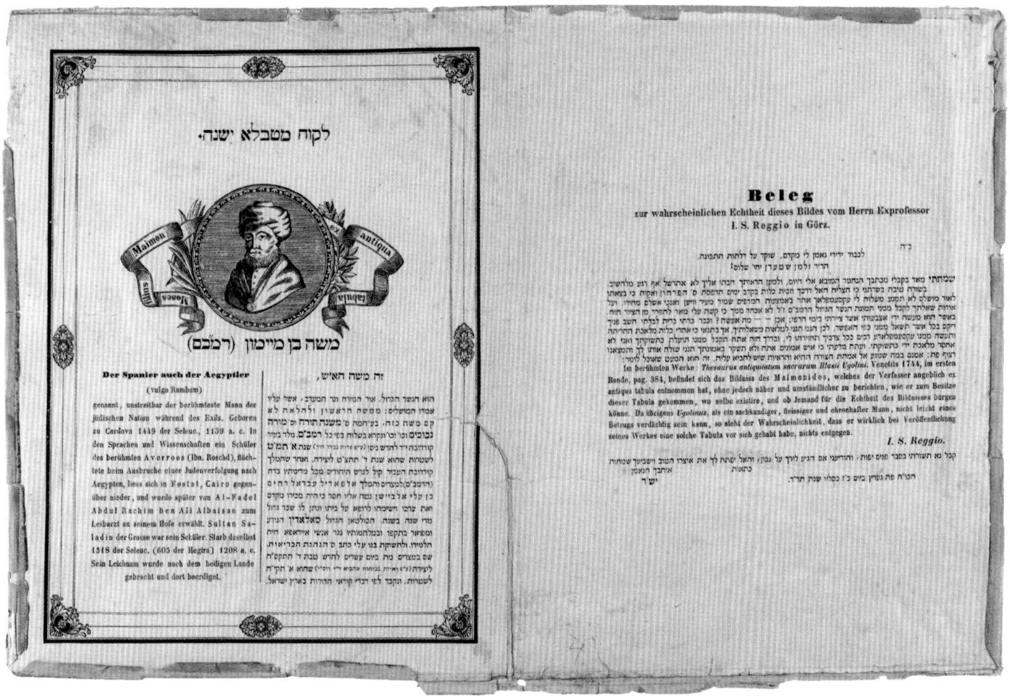

Fig. 81 Typical letters of 'authenticity,' from Isacco Samuele Reggio to Solomon Stern, 1846. Library of the Jewish Theological Seminary, PNT G1020.

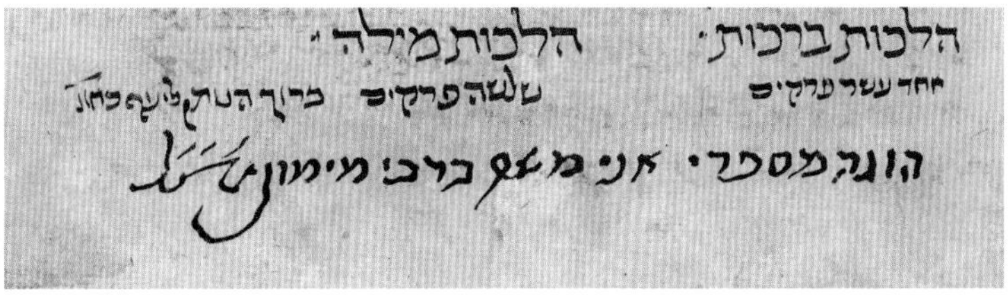

Fig. 82 Maimonides signature. The Bodleian Libraries, University of Oxford, MS. Huntington 80, fol. 165r.

alongside copies of his autograph (Fig. 82).[9] These artistic prints cast Maimonides as a heroic standalone figure, visually apart from conventional images of the persecuted medieval Jew, who challenged the religious conventions of his own people and who was attacked by authorities from all sides.

French semiotician Jacques Derrida captured the anachronism inherent in the modern visual materialization of Maimonides. German Jews drew Maimonides as 'the revealing sign, the mark' of a medieval Jewish Protestantism that presaged the Christian Reformation, rendering him 'the emblem' between these two Reformations. 'Oh, if Maimonides had only known,' waxed Derrida, that one day he would see himself recruited into an alliance with post-Lutheran Germany, 'would his soul rest in peace?'[10]

Reclaiming Maimonides in Jewish Religious Life in Eastern Europe

The popular German claim over the likeness of a reform-friendly Maimonides provoked a backlash from religious quarters in eastern Europe.[11] In 1879, the Warsaw printer Moshe Danziger-Krohn issued a lithograph of the conventional bust portrait in an oval frame but gave Maimonides more familiar physiognomic features, emphasizing the inset oval eyes, outlined with a dark border and crowned with elegant eyebrows, high cheekbones made luminescent with a heavy beard, and a distinctive mustache (Fig. 83). The printer also gave

9 Schwartz, 'The Maimonides Portrait.'

10 Jacques Derrida, *Acts of Religion*, ed. Gil Anidjar (New York: Routledge, 2002), 162–63.

11 Cohen, *Jewish Icons*, 144–45.

Fig. 83 Lithograph (Warsaw: Moshe Danziger-Krohn, ca. 1879). Russian and Hebrew. Moreshet Auction House.

Maimonides a Russian-language pedigree in a bilingual Hebrew–Russian caption and listed the address of his shop in Warsaw.

In 1888, the aspiring Bulgarian artist Boris Schatz, who would found the Bezalel School of Arts and Crafts in Jerusalem in 1906, published a screed in the Hebrew-language newspaper *Ha-Tsefirah* against the misuse of portraits of great Jewish sages for assimilationist efforts. Schatz complained that Jewish artists were squandering their talents and selling their souls for the profitable trade of rabbinical portraits made for the emerging Jewish bourgeoisie.[12] 'The delicate spirit is repulsed to look at these portraits,' wrote Schatz, railing against the painters who depicted Menashe ben Israel and 'the rest of them' like 'an Italian who looks like a bum in the laughing places of the market.' Schatz passionately advocated for 'portraits from life,' which were needed to rehabilitate the living culture of the Jewish people.[13]

The print shop of S. Schottlaender, in its first year of operation that year in Breslau, which had become part of the German Empire in 1871, published a large etching of 'The Great Learned Rabbis of Israel' that likewise challenged the image of Maimonides promoted by German Jewry (Fig. 84). Whereas German Jews preferred a standalone figure in the style of popular images of Martin Luther, the Breslau print showed Maimonides, the largest portrait on the page crowned by the 'Crown of Torah,' among 40 Ashkenazic and Sephardic rabbis from the twelfth to the nineteenth centuries. Even a cursory study of the rabbinic selection demonstrates that Maimonides was situated within a historical pantheon adopted by adherents of Orthodox Judaism, including such luminaries as the Vilna Gaon, Jonathan Eybeschütz, Moses Sofer, and Akiva Eger, alongside medieval Sephardic rabbis like Isaac

12 Boris Schatz, 'Maleket Maḥshevet,' *Ha-Tsefirah* 216 (December 28, 1888): 2–3.

13 *Ha-Tsefirah* 217 (December 30, 1888): 3–4.

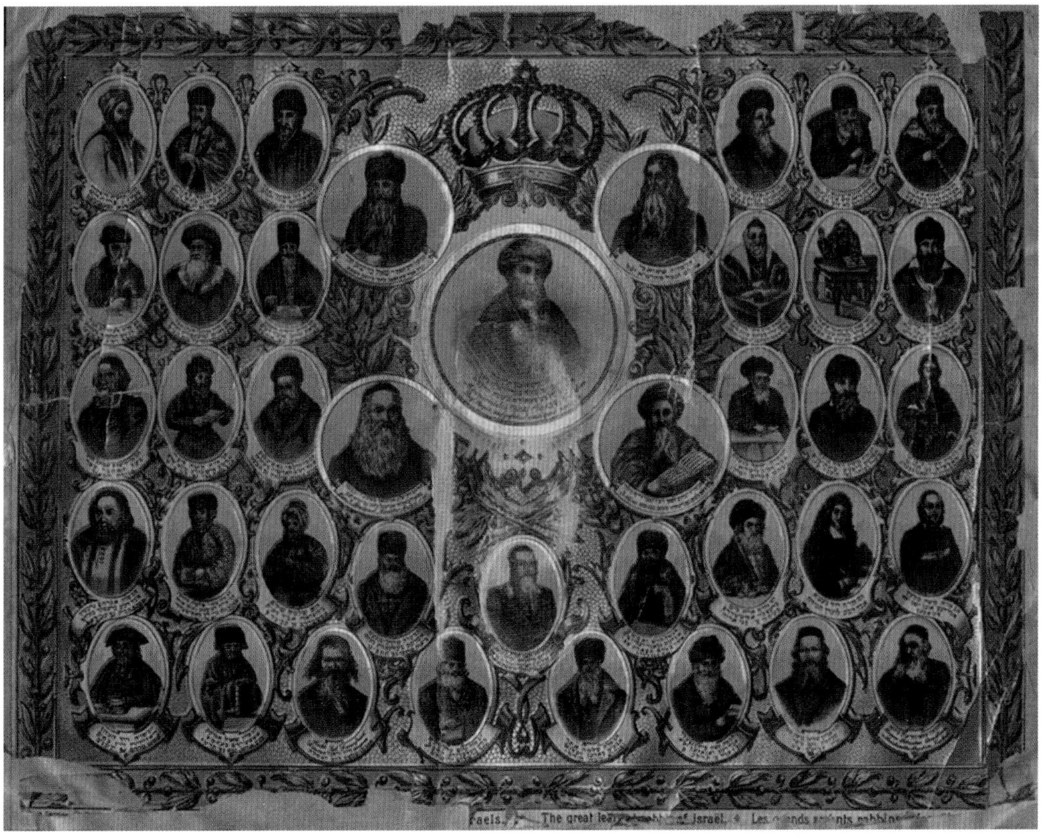

Fig. 84 *The Great Learned Rabbis of Israel* (Breslau: S. Shottlaender, 1888). Courtesy of Special Collections, College of Charleston.

Fig. 85 Eretz Yisrael album (Warsaw, ca. 1910). The Gross Family Collection Trust.

Alfasi (the Rif) and Isaac Abarbanel (depicted, like Maimonides, larger than the other figures). The large frameable print shows Maimonides at the center of a historical pantheon imagined as united, if anachronistically, in anti-reform efforts. He is joined by the sixteenth-century Talmudist Samuel Edels (the Maharsha), who censured the reformers of his day, and the contemporary Meir Loeb ben Jehiel Michael Malbim, who confronted the Reform Judaism promoted by the wealthy Jews in Bucharest, Moghilev, and Konigsberg. The seemingly strange inclusion of less commonly depicted figures such as David Cohen d'Azevedo can be explained by his act of issuing an official statement that Jews were not prepared for unconditional civic commitment in exchange for emancipation. The print, which uses a combination of Hebrew and selective use of German and lists the name, city, magnum opus, and date of death of each rabbinical figure, could be seen as a public petition

Fig. 86 Plaque with a photograph of the Buhuser Rebbe's funeral, 1896. Zusia Efron Archives at the Center for Jewish Art, Hebrew University of Jerusalem.

of protest against the German Reform movement with a reclamation of Maimonides as one of their own.

Many variations on the theme of an imagined historical pantheon of a diverse but uninterrupted line of Orthodoxy circulated in the twentieth century, and it continues to enjoy popularity to this day (Fig. 85). Pre-made frames, such as the one made for the funeral of the Hasidic Zaddik Isaac Friedman, known as the Buhuser Rebbe, in his house in Buhusi (now Romania) in 1896, included portraits of Maimonides, the Vilna Gaon, the Maharsha of Ostroh, Isaac Abarbanel, Saul ben Isaac Halevi of Hague, and Jonathan Eybeschütz (Fig. 86).[14] One could purchase a variety of photographs featuring the crowds at the funeral to insert into the frame for a memorial wall-hanging.

Among Revolution-era Russian Jews, the use of popular culture to represent Maimonides spoke to the sacralizing of mass communication rather than the secularization of religion for consumer culture. Whereas German Jews accorded religious authority to Maimonides's attitudes toward reform, Russian Jews celebrated Maimonides's stature as a physician. In the first decades of the twentieth century, Jewish scholars unearthed Old Russian translations of his medical works to demonstrate the medical contributions of Jewish doctors to Russian culture.[15] In his short story *The Rabbi's Son* (1926), Isaac Babel portrayed Maimonides as a symbol of the Jewish zealotry for communism. Babel's alter-ego surveys the belongings of a dead Jewish soldier who had passionately embraced the Revolution without negating his Jewish roots, wistfully noting that 'The portraits of Lenin and Maimonides lay side by side, the knotted iron of Lenin's skull beside the dull silk of the portraits of Maimonides.'[16]

14 https://cja.huji.ac.il/browser.php?mode=set&id=21495 (accessed November 9, 2022).

15 For example, M. Balaban, 'Evrei-vrati v Krakove I tragedii getto XV–XVII v.,' *Evrejskaja starina* 1 (1912): 38–53. See W. F. Ryan, 'Maimonides in Muscovy: Medical Texts and Terminology,' *Journal of the Warburg and Courtauld Institutes* 51 (1988): 43–65.

16 Isaac Babel, *Red Cavalry*, ed. Nathalie Babel, trans. Peter Constantine (New York: W.W. Norton, 2003), 65.

Fig. 87 Meir Kunstadt, postcard, ca. 1900. Hebrew and English. Courtesy of Special Collections, College of Charleston.

Image Transfer and Immigration

German Jews brought Maimonides along during their migrations to North America, transposing the person of Maimonides onto their new public institutions. In the 1850s, German Reform leaders established the Maimonides cemetery in Brooklyn. Émigré Isaac Leeser (1806–1868) imported the name of Maimonides to Philadelphia, where he opened the first rabbinic school in America in 1867 with the name Maimonides College. The namesake signaled the German Jewish attraction to Maimonides as a codifier who systematized Jewish tradition, a symbol of the *Wissenschaft* approach to modern Jewish studies.[17] In Chicago, the name of Maimonides was invoked as a bridge between the established Reform German community and the recent Orthodox Eastern European immigrants with the opening of the 'Maimonides Kosher Hospital' in 1908.

Eastern European Jews also brought Maimonides along during their immigration, albeit in more intra-Jewish contexts and in more ephemeral media. In Vienna, which had absorbed a large Jewish migration, the partnership between Hungarian émigré artist Meir Kunstadt and his cousins in the Josef Schlesinger Trading and Publishing House in Vienna produced and popularized many of the rabbinical portraits that we have to this day. Under the auspices of Rosa-Reisel, née Strasser (1850–1930), a granddaughter of the Hungarian Ktav Sofer (Abraham Samuel Benjamin Sofer) and widow of a scion of the Sofer and Eiger dynasties, Kunstadt designed several portraits of Maimonides that were printed for Jewish holidays.[18] For an ex-libris sticker of Maimonides repurposed as a postcard, Kunstadt aged

17 Albert M. Friedenberg, 'American Jewish Seminaries,' *The Hebrew Standard*, June 2, 1922, front page.

18 Anna Szalai, 'Korotav shel Bet Mishar la-Sefarim: Viena, Budapesht, Tel Aviv,' http://baderech.hjm.org.il/Mechkarim/He/JosefSchlesingers.pdf (accessed November 9, 2022).

Fig. 88 *Hagadah shel Pesaḥ* (Vienna: Josef Schlesinger, 1929). Meir Kunstadt, illustration for the Rabbis of Bene Berak with Sofer family. Courtesy the Leo Baeck Institute.

Fig. 89 *Hagadah shel Pesaḥ* (Vienna: Josef Schlesinger, 1929). Meir Kunstadt, illustration for the Rabbis of Bene Berak with Maimonides. Private Collection © Archives Charmet / Bridgeman Images.

his subject, added the traditional sidelocks and filled out his beard, and rendered his Iberian Sephardic identity as a Turkish Jew (Fig. 87). Kunstadt gave Maimonides an Ottoman sensibility by placing him before an ornate architectural arch, embellishing his robe with the distinctive chest loops of Ottoman military uniforms and piping in the flavor of insignia, and rendering the medallion with a fringed sash.

In the interwar period, Kunstadt tied Maimonides to the Sofer family by publishing a revised version of his 1922 Haggadah that portrayed the celebrated Sofer family as the

Fig. 90 Hugo Ballin, *Warner Memorial Murals* (Los Angeles, 1929). Photo © Tom Bonner.

'rabbis of Bene Brak,' entitled 'Savants at the Table of Maimonides' (Figs. 88, 89). The scene would be readily recognizable to readers of the wildly popular Berlin Haggadah, but Maimonides replaces Rabbi Simḥah Bunim Sofer, the patriarch of the founder of the printing house. The black *yarmulkas* of the two youths are replaced with Bukharian skullcaps. The extended Sofer family replaced the figures of Joseph Karo, Jacob ben Asher, Solomon Yitsḥaki (Rashi), and Isaac Alfasi. The publisher republished the watercolor as a frameable standalone lithograph throughout the late 1920s in various languages.

In 1929, Maimonides finally made it into the synagogue sanctuary of the Wilshire Boulevard Temple, the most prestigious Reform congregation in Los Angeles, through a partnership between secularized second-generation Russian immigrants known as 'Hollywood Jews' and Rabbi Edgar Magnin, known as the 'rabbi to the stars.' The Hollywood Jews that underwrote Magnin and the Gothic Revival synagogue embraced what Jonathan Sarna called 'a Jewishness rooted in the future,' a secular messianism that shared structural similarities with their brethren in the new Soviet states but that was distinctly American in content.[19] The Russian-Jewish immigrant faith in the transformative power of cinema was such that in the late 1920s the new Wilshire Boulevard Temple designed its sanctuary like a

19 Jonathan Sarna, *The American Jewish Experience* (New York: Holmes and Meier, 1986).

Fig. 91 Advertisement, *The Forward*, October 3, 1938, 5.

Fig. 92 Advertisement, *The Forward*, October 31, 1938, 5 (detail).

movie theater. Funded by the Warner brothers, founding members of the synagogue, Warners' film producer Hugo Ballin painted floor-to-ceiling murals depicting the story of the Jewish people from the Divine creation of light to the invention of cinema. In the narrative cycle Ballin portrayed Rashi and Maimonides as epitomizing the different cultural milieus of Ashkenazic and Sephardic Jewry (Fig. 90). On the left, Rashi sits at a desk, akin to the medieval iconography of St. Matthew the Apostle writing the Gospel. Rashi is surrounded by the messianic imagery of Isaiah, likewise recognizable from Christological imagery (of the tree of Jesse). On the right, Maimonides is removed from the eschatological imagery associated with Jewish history in Christian lands, standing in dramatic repose amid more worldly concerns – a woman with a sick child seeking his help. He is flanked by a symbol of mathematics with an hourglass in the foreground. In the background, five figures, each holding a scroll of the Pentateuch, appear alongside an ecstatic figure representing Aristotle's treatise *On the Soul* (written out in Greek letters).[20] Rashi is cast in dramatic lighting surrounded by an ominous shadow and Maimonides assumes the cinematic through the theatrical pose of heroic film stars of the silent era.

In New York in 1938, the food manufacturer General Foods Corporation recruited Maimonides to advertise its kosher-certified Post Bran Flakes in the Yiddish daily *Forward*.

20 Edgar F. Magnin, *The Warner Murals in the Wilshire Boulevard Temple* (Los Angeles: Wilshire Boulevard Temple, 1974).

Various versions appeared with Maimonides giving medical advice in a speech bubble. In one, Maimonides states that 'constipation is a major obstacle to mental development' (Fig. 91).[21] In another, Maimonides states, 'constipation is the root of all diseases' (Fig. 92).[22] The ads appeared on the same page as the famous 'A Bintel Brief' column, in which Eastern European Jewish immigrants asked for advice on issues related to their acculturation and advised on issues of Americanization. Beneath these heartfelt letters seeking and receiving help, Maimonides appears as a trusted religious medical authority beside graphics of Americans – men in retail or at a business meeting, housewives, siblings, and couples at home over breakfast, or shopkeepers and customers – advising readers to use the fiber-rich Post cereal.

Maimonides in the Holy Land

In the Yishuv, the first Jewish settlers did not initially embrace the visual likeness of Maimonides, perhaps because he had left the depressed economic conditions of Palestine for Egypt, settling in al-Fustat near Cairo. The gravesite of Maimonides in Tiberias inspired pilgrimages as early as the thirteenth century, but it became the subject for art only in the nineteenth century. On the lower left vignette of a watercolor, the tomb of Maimonides concludes the cycle of holy places. Like other Jewish luminaries of the Islamic world, the tomb is imagined with a blue dome and bears an Islamic crescent, which must not have been seen as objectionable in the same way as a Christian cross (Fig. 93).[23] With the growth of the Zionist movement, efforts were made to restore the gravesite, although the nearby graves of Meir Ba'al ha-Nes and Yoḥanan ben Zakkai served as the primary inspiration for visitors. While it is today a popular tourist site in Israel and a number of rituals have developed in connection with mystical symbolism, the grave of Maimonides does not appear centrally in stories of healing or miracles as compared to, for example, those associated with the Rambam Synagogue in the Jewish Quarter (*Ḥarat al-Yahud*) in Old Cairo (Fig. 94).[24]

Despite Maimonides's own eschewal of amulets, printers used his likeness on them, such as one to 'guard the child and the mother' (Fig. 95). The amulet, which originated in the eighteenth century and was attributed to the Baal Shem Tov, contained kabbalistic symbolism and letter combinations. It was reprinted by R. Tzukerman in Jerusalem in the late nineteenth century with the concessionary anti-magic words 'One who trusts in God will turn around [his] fate,' and again later with illustrations of Maimonides and the tomb of the second-century scholar Rabbi Meir Baal HaNeis, utilizing knowledge of their rationalist approaches as visual safeguards against magical thinking.

In Israel, Maimonides appeared most visibly on the 'street' in storefront signage and street names. In the early years of the British administration, the Pro-Jerusalem Society systematically renamed streets, giving Maimonides a place in Palestine with a Rambam Street in Tel Aviv and a 'Ben-Maimon' in the Jerusalem neighborhood of Rehavia. Other streets acquired the Rambam name from private companies, such as in the neighborhood of Raanana, purchased and incorporated by American Jews in 1912. One of the first six street names to be established in the 1920s was Rambam Street, the site of the first medical clinic, apartments for immigrants from Yemen, and allotments of land in lieu of pay to municipal workers. In Tel Aviv, the Schlesinger publishing firm that had produced the bookplates, postcards, and Haggadahs with the image of Maimonides in Vienna opened under its new name Sinai Publishing beside the pharmacy 'Rambam.' Around the corner on Allenby Street was the Rambam Driving School.

21 Advertisement, *Forward*, October 3, 1938, 5.

22 Advertisement, *Forward*, October 31, 1938, 5.

23 Pamela Berger, *Jewish-Muslim Veneration at Pilgrimage Places in the Holy Land* (Boston, MA: Brill, 2011).

24 Notably, when Teddy Kollek and Moshe Pearlman wrote a history of pilgrimage to the Holy Land in 1970, they made no reference to the burial site of Maimonides. Teddy Kollek and Moshe Pearlman, *Pilgrims to the Holy Land: The Story of Pilgrimage through the Ages* (New York: Harper and Row, 1970), 73.

Fig. 93 *View of the Holy Places* (Land of Israel, 19th century). Watercolor and ink on paper. Photo © The Israel Museum by Avshalom Avital.

In 1925, the first sculpture of Maimonides was installed in the Yishuv (Fig. 96). Hebrew University patron Boris Stavski sent a bronze bust of Maimonides by Polish-Jewish artist Abraham Ostrzega (1889–1942) for the laying of the cornerstone of the Mount Scopus campus. A preeminent designer of grave monuments in the Jewish cemetery in Warsaw, Ostrzega was the celebrated sculptor who that same year unveiled his grand Mausoleum for the Yiddish literary trio, I. L. Peretz, S. Ansky, and Yankev Dinezon. Ostrzega's grave sculptures of human subjects frequently violated the religious sensibilities of the locals and were thus often defaced by Jewish visitors, offended by what they saw as idolatry in the consecrated place of the dead. Later, Ostrzega's non-funerary oeuvre was largely lost after

Fig. 94 Photographic postcard of Maimonides's tomb, Tiberias (ca. 1900). Courtesy of Special Collections, College of Charleston.

Fig. 95 Amulet [Jerusalem, ca. 1960]. Collection of Prof. Shalom Sabar, Jerusalem.

Fig. 96 (left) Abraham Ostrzega, *Maimonides* (Poland, 1925). Bronze. Displayed in the Law Faculty building, Hebrew University of Jerusalem.

Fig. 97 (right) Mess Wind-Struski, stamp, issued August 3, 1953 by the Israel Postal Authority. Courtesy of the Leiman Library.

Fig. 98 Benno Elkan, Maimonides from the *Knesset Menorah* (United Kingdom, 1954). Displayed in the Wohl Rose Garden opposite the Knesset. Photographs by Richard McBee.

Fig. 99 Zvi Narkiss and Arie Glazer, 1,000-shekel banknote, Israel, 1983.

the Nazi occupation. As a result, the sculpture of Maimonides has retrospectively taken on the symbolic significance of funerary art and artistic resistance.

Even after the establishment of the State of Israel, the image of Maimonides arrived belatedly. In the early years after independence, official state visual culture preferred the collective concept, although, following the issuing of a stamp to mark the 50th anniversary of the death of Theodor Herzl in 1951 and a centenary stamp commemorating the birth of Chaim Weizmann in 1952, the Israel Postal Authority did issue a single stamp commemorating Maimonides in 1953 as a symbol of 'global and Israeli cogitation' (Fig. 97).[25]

Maimonides made it into the official visual culture of the State of Israel by virtue of a British gift to Israel in 1954 on the occasion of the sixth anniversary of its establishment. German-born British Jewish sculptor Benno Elkan (1877–1960) designed a menorah in bas-relief as a visual historical narrative of the Jewish people, to be installed opposite the Israeli Parliament. Elkan depicted Maimonides in the pose of Rodin's *Thinker* with one hand propping up his head (Fig. 98). The other hand rests on his *Mishneh Torah*, upon which a dove alights as an attribute of faith, and supporting his arm is a volume labeled *Aristotle*, upon which an owl sits as an attribute of wisdom. Elkan paired Maimonides with the figure of Judah Halevi playing the harp to represent the golden age of Jewish culture in Spain. The scene belongs to the arm of the Menorah representing the Hasidic movement, creating a narrative that Jews developed different ways to worship God throughout their history.

Although official civic culture showed a preference for individual personifications in the late 1950s, the Bank of Israel first issued new banknotes dedicated to types, such as a female soldier, a factory worker, and a scientist in his laboratory. Only in 1983 did the bank issue a portrait of Maimonides on the 1,000 shekel bill (Fig. 99), when he thus joined Sir Moses Montefiore and Henrietta Szold as contributors to a proud Jewish national identity. When the Bank of Israel issued the New Israeli shekel to replace the old shekel at a 1,000:1 ratio, they reissued the 1,000 shekel bill design for the most popular single-shekel denomination, signaling the end of hyperinflation. As Alec Mishory has argued convincingly, the Bank of Israel assumed the 'Zionist tendency that puts contributions made by humanists and scholars on a lower rung of hierarchy than that of political figures.'[26] Engravers Zvi Narkiss and Arie Glazer relied on the iconic portrait of Maimonides, which they overlaid on a passage from his handwritten manuscript of the *Mishneh Torah*, slipping in his signature at

25 Alec Mishory, *Secularizing the Sacred: Aspects of Israeli Visual Culture* (Leiden: Brill, 2019), 64.
26 Mishory, *Secularizing the Sacred*, 62.

the bottom. On the reverse, they depicted a stylized view of Tiberias and an ancient candelabrum, using the medieval sage as a bridge in the continuum of classical Judaism and its modern rebirth. When the banknote is held up to the light, a triangle on the front merges with a triangle on the back to form a Star of David.

1935 Commemorations and the Rise of Fascism

In 1935, nations throughout the world celebrated the 800th anniversary of Maimonides's birth, then thought to have been in 1135.[27] More scholarship was published on Maimonides in 1935 than in any other year in history. All over the world, scholarly journals dedicated special issues to his legacy.[28] The import of the celebrations was largely their contemporary political agenda, which drew a poignant parallel between the persecution and suppression of Maimonides and his works and the book-burnings that took place across Germany on May 10, 1933 in a nationwide 'Campaign against the Un-German Spirit.' 'The purest homage' that can be given to Maimonides's philosophical legacy, wrote Emmanuel Levinas, 'consists in blending it with current concerns.'[29]

That was precisely the aim behind the 1935 publications for Maimonides's centennial by the German Jewish Schocken publishing firm, active in Berlin until 1939. Judiciously selecting meaningful texts from the Maimonidean literary corpus and presenting him, as Leo Strauss did in his seminal work 'Persecution and the Art of Writing,' as a writer operating in response to persecution, Schocken transformed Maimonides from an unqualified prototype for the German Enlightenment into a critique of the absolute faith in *Haskalah* values and its naïve liberal utopianism.[30] Beyond the text, the books of the Schocken Verlag in Berlin became material objects in the Jewish home that 'served as visible and touchable reminders of the rich Jewish culture that was being destroyed by Nazism while also bearing witness to the persistence of Jewish life in Germany.'[31]

A national committee was organized in New York – with the participation of Albert Einstein, Louis Finkelstein, Henry Solomon Hendricks, Leo Jung, Henry Pereira Mendes, Abba Hillel Silver, and James Joseph Walsh – for the promotion of the celebration of Maimonides throughout the world, in synagogues, local institutions, and universities. The committee gathered media on the life and works of Maimonides, which included poems, plays, pamphlets, PR releases, and printable images for popular distribution, and published a four-volume set of culturally significant studies on Maimonides.[32] Commemorations paid special attention to Maimonides's *Epistle to Yemen*, offering comfort to embattled Jews by advising that they devote themselves to rational perfection in order to inaugurate the coming of the messiah. The portrait of Maimonides, often paired with an example of his handwriting,

27 For a detailed explanation of the dating of Maimonides's birth, see Herbert A. Davidson, *Moses Maimonides: The Man and His Works* (Oxford: Oxford University Press, 2005), 6–9.

28 There are too many special issues to include here but several examples give a sense of the international scope of these efforts in scholarly circles. *The Jewish Quarterly Review* 25, no. 4 (1935) [Philadelphia]; *Monatsschrift für Geschichte und Wissenschaft des Judentums* 79, no. 2 (1935) [Breslau]; *Bulletin of the Institute of the History of Medicine* 3, no. 7 (July 1935) [Baltimore]; *Tarbiz* 6, no. 3 (1935) [Jerusalem]; *La Rassegna Mensile di Israel* 10, no. 1 (May 1935) [Italy].

29 Originally published as 'L'actualité de Maïmonide,' *Paix et Droit* 15, no. 4 (April 1935), 6–7; reprinted in English translation in Emmanuel Levinas, 'The Contemporary Relevance of Maimonides (1935),' *The Journal of Jewish Thought and Philosophy* 16, no. 1 (2008): 91–94 (91).

30 Marina Urban, 'Persecution and the Art of Representation: Schocken's Maimonides Anthologies of the 1930s,' in *Maimonides and his Heritage*, ed. Idit Dobbs-Weinstein, Lenn E. Goodman, and James Allen Grady (Albany, NY: State University of New York Press, 2009), 153–80.

31 Stefanie Mahrer, 'Texts and Objects: The Books of the Schocken Publishing House in the Context of their Time,' in *The German-Hebrew Dialogue: Studies of Encounter and Exchange*, ed. Rachel Seelig and Amir Eshel (Berlin: De Gruyter, 2017), 121–41 (139).

32 National Organizing Committee for the Maimonides Octocentennial, 1934–1935, Collection of the American Jewish Historical Society, New York, *Maimonides Octocentennial Series*, 4 vols. (New York: Octocentennial Committee, 1935).

Fig. 100 Joseph Hovell working on a bust of Maimonides, New York, January 6, 1936. Federal Art Project, Photographic Division collection, ca. 1920–1965. Archives of American Art, Smithsonian Institution.

played a ubiquitous role in the events surrounding the centennial celebrations, but new works of portraiture were made as well.[33] Artist Joseph Hovell sculpted a bust of Maimonides as part of the Depression-era federal work-relief program (WPA) founded in August of 1935 to implement visual arts programs in local communities across the country (Fig. 100).

In Jerusalem, the Bezalel School of Arts and Crafts reproduced the classic portrait from the *Thesaurus Antiquitatum Sacrarum* (Venice, 1744) with Maimonides's signature beneath it for the occasion. The city of Tiberias prepared for the commemorative events by constructing makeshift buildings 'in the style of the architecture of Rambam's time' and mooring a lightship in the lake.[34] Jewish Agency President Nachum Sokolow led a pilgrimage, complete with a band, to Maimonides's grave, where he read a scroll to the spirit of Maimonides. Addressing him as 'chief of the children of the Diaspora,' Sokolow stated that Maimonides accompanied Israel wherever it was exiled, evoking the 'pillar of fire' that led the children of Israel in their wanderings through the dessert in biblical times. 'Now, when the captivity is returned we shall also walk in thy light and be illuminated thereby,' concluded Sokolow, placing the scroll on the tomb.[35] Two label stamps – unauthorized stamps printed privately primarily for fundraising and the promotion of ideological or political causes – show the very different attitudes that organizations took to the figure of Maimonides in 1935. Keren Tel-Hai, the fund of the Zionist Revisionist Movement (Herut)

33 See layout for David Bernstein, 'From Moses unto Moses: The Life and Death of Moses Maimonides,' *The American Jewish World*, March 29, 1935, 4.

34 *The Palestine Post*, April 15, 1935, 4.

35 *The Palestine Post*, April 23, 1935, 7.

Fig. 101 Label stamp, 1935, for Keren Tel-Hai. Courtesy of the Leiman Library.

Fig. 102 Label stamp, 1935. Courtesy of the Leiman Library.

Fig. 103 Governor of Andalusia speaking at the unveiling of the Maimonides Memorial, Córdoba, March 30, 1935. Courtesy of the Leo Baeck Institute.

established in the wake of the 1929 riots, published a label stamp of Maimonides with his jaw set tight without any embellishment and lacking the requisite medal, dismissing the value of state-awarded 'medals of honor' for an image that projected the need for Jewish self-emancipation and self-defense (Fig. 101). In another label stamp published in 1935, but whose patron is not identified, Maimonides appears haggard amid the entire world that he has traveled, depicting him as paradigmatic of Jews whose history of persecution has created a rich body of knowledge and culture (Fig. 102).

The Republic of Spain, the only liberal democracy to emerge in Europe in the 1930s, and now on the eve of its own Civil War (1936–39), instituted the 'holiday of the Rambam' as an official holiday and announced its intention to issue a commemorative stamp to Maimonides.[36] As Franco's fascist party collected more seats in the government, the leader of the opposition, Niceto Alcalá Zamora, issued a statement of tribute 'to the memory of the sons of Spain who have exalted and carried her fame beyond her own frontiers,' which liberal journalists reported all over the world.[37] On its last legs, the left liberal government renamed the square in which the Córdoba synagogue (built in 1315) was located 'Tiberiadus Square' and erected a plaque declaring 'Plazuela di Maimonides' on one of adjacent buildings (Fig. 103).

The Post-Holocaust Museological Turn to Maimonides

A perceptible 'museological turn' toward Maimonides developed after the Holocaust in the Allied countries, Israel, and sympathetic nations such as Denmark. Those complicit in the extermination of Jews remained silent, while others opposed to the founding of Israel actively allowed the legacy of Maimonides to deteriorate. The Jewish quarter of Old Cairo, the site of the synagogue where Maimonides was believed to have been interred before his burial in Tiberias, decayed and became the site of anti-Zionist protests. Protesting the establishment of the State of Israel, Egyptian authorities put an end to the custom of childless couples spending a night in a special room in the synagogue in the hope of fruitful blessing.[38] It was not until Egyptian president Abdel el-Fattah al-Sisi came to power and decided to reconstruct Jewish historical sites that the synagogue – if not exactly the legacy of Maimonides (whose status as a non-Arab became an issue with the rise of pan-Arab identity following the Arab Spring) – was restored.

In the United States, the first exhibition on Maimonides took place at the Library of the Jewish Theological Seminary of America. Opening May 18, 1948, just days after the declaration of independence of the State of Israel, an exhibition of medical books and manuscripts framed Maimonides as the archetype of modern Jewish life, a quintessential contributor to the progress of Western science.[39] In 1954, the New York Public Library mounted an exhibition in celebration of 300 years of Jewish life in America, displaying the first printed edition of the Hebrew translation of Maimonides's *Guide of the Perplexed* (Rome, pre-1475), alongside Benjamin Franklin's expression of hope that America might become an 'Assylum of all the Oppress'd in Europe' and Emma Lazarus's famous sonnet 'The New Colossus' (inscribed on the base of the Statue of Liberty).[40] In 1983, the Jewish Museum in New York marked efforts to smuggle 7,000 Jews out of Denmark, producing a two-volume catalogues detailing the history of the Jews in Denmark with an impressive collection of Judaica and Hebraica from the Royal Library. It included an illuminated Hebrew translation of Maimonides's *Moreh Nevukhim*, produced in Barcelona in 1348–1349 (see Figs. 76, 116).[41]

In Europe, Maimonides made an important appearance as a point of moving on from the stain of the Holocaust. Throughout the 1950s, the National Museum in Stockholm included copies of Maimonidean manuscripts in multiple exhibitions.[42] In 1973, in honor of

36 Y. Fishman, 'Sakh ha-kol shel Ḥagigot ha-Rambam be-Cordoba,' *Haaretz*, May 20, 1935, 3. Ultimately, the stamp was not produced.

37 A. A. Freedlander, 'Maimonides' 800th Birthday,' *The Sentinel*, March 28, 1935, 4.

38 Tamar Alexander-Frizer, *The Heart is a Mirror: The Sephardic Folktale* (Detroit, MI: Wayne State University Press, 2008), 202–03. I would like to thank Haim Koren, former Israeli ambassador to Egypt, for his insight into Egyptian attitudes towards the memory of Maimonides.

39 William Gross, Orly Tzion, and Falk Wiesemann (eds.), *Catalog of Catalogs: A Bibliography of Temporary Exhibition Catalogs since 1876 that Contain Items of Judaica* (Leiden: Brill, 2019).

40 Joshua Bloch, *The People of the Book: The Background of Three Hundred Years of Jewish Life in America* (New York: New York Public Library, 1954).

41 Jørgen H. Barfod, Norman L. Kleeblatt, Vivian B. Mann, and Susan L. Braunstein (eds.), *Kings and Citizens: The History of the Jews in Denmark 1622–1983* (New York: The Jewish Museum, 1983).

42 Kare Olsen and Carl Nordenfalk (eds.), *Gyllene Böcker. Illuminerade medeltida handskrifter i dansk och svensk ägo* (Golden Books. Illuminated Medieval Manuscripts in Danish and Swedish Hands) (Stockholm: Nationalmuseum Stockholm, 1952). In addition, the National Museum of Stockholm included a Maimonides manuscript (ca. 1300) in its 1957 exhibition 'Oriental Miniatures and Manuscripts in

the 25th anniversary of the founding of the State of Israel, the Ets Haim/Livraria in Amsterdam mounted an exhibition on the 'history of Zionist thinking amongst the Sepharadim in general, and in the Netherlands in particular.'[43] Separate vitrines were dedicated to great Sephardic thinkers, including Benjamin of Tudela, Abraham Ibn Ezra, and Maimonides.

Maimonides in Public American Art

In the aftermath of the Second World War, Maimonides became a subject in American public art. Recognized artists broke out of what had become the conventional image repertoire surrounding Maimonides and created a new figure using a modern aesthetic.

Artist Brenda Putnam, scion of the legendary American Putnam family, sculpted a highly original relief of Maimonides for a series of twenty-three marble plaques dedicated to historical figures 'noted for their work in establishing the principles that underlie American law' (Fig. 104).[44] Installed over the gallery doors of the House Chamber when the United States Capitol was remodeled in 1949–1950, Maimonides appears in classical profile with a heroically taut forehead, jutting collar bone, and prominent neck muscles. A discernable sidelock curled in a Romanesque swirl falls over a stylized classical beard that adorns a cutting jawline. Maimonides's lips are slightly parted as if in measured and dispassionate oration.

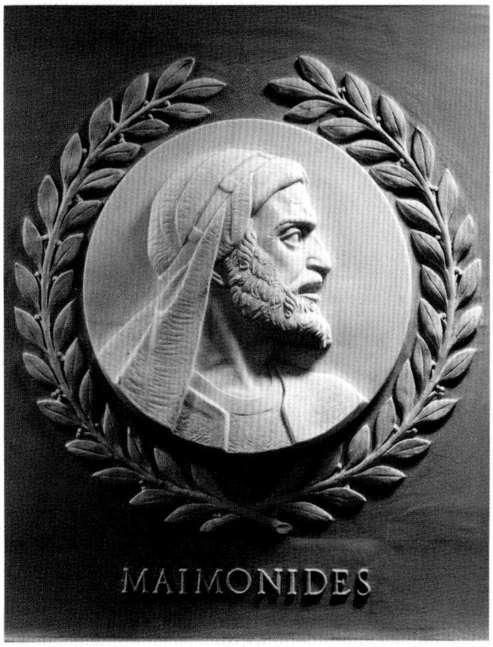

Fig. 104 Brenda Putnam, *Maimonides*, House Chamber, US Capitol, Washington, DC, 1950. Marble. Architect of the Capitol.

In 1950, Arthur Szyk, a Polish émigré artist celebrated for his patriotic wartime anti-Axis images, depicted Maimonides in parallel to George Washington for his illuminated Declaration of Independence. Szyk portrayed Maimonides in orientalist garb, giving him a flowing red velvet robe with golden Persian slippers popularized by seventeenth-century French courtiers and, thus, associated with aristocracy (Fig. 105). Boasting the Star of David on the medal around his neck, the great codifier of Jewish Law holds up a delicate finger while the pages of his manuscript lie strewn at his side, indicating that a sober lesson must be drawn from lived history.

In 1954, Ben Shahn included Maimonides in the plan for his first mosaic mural *Science and the Humanities*, a project for the William E. Grady Career and Technical High School in Brooklyn (Fig. 106). The mosaic depicts a petrified artist holding onto his paintbrushes amid apocalyptic imagery of atomic warfare in an urban landscape. The technological threat to humanity concludes in a moralistic and hopeful image of Maimonides preaching

Scandinavian Collections' and an illuminated *Guide of the Perplexed* from Catalonia (ca. 1347) in the 1960 exhibition 'Great Spanish Masters.'

43 *Catalogus bij de tentoonstelling ter gelegenheid van het 25-jarig jubileum van de staat Israel* [Catalogue of an Exhibition Held in Honor of the 25-Year Jubilee of the State of Israel] (Amsterdam: Livraria D. Montezinos, 1973), in Dutch.

44 https://www.aoc.gov/explore-capitol-campus/art/maimonides-relief-portrait (accessed November 9, 2022).

Fig. 105 (right) Arthur Szyk, *Maimonides*, New Canaan, 1950. Watercolor and gouache on paper. Collection of Yeshiva University Museum, gift of Louis Werner.

Fig. 106 (below and right) Ben Shahn, *Maimonides, Science and the Humanities*, 1957. Mosaic mural. William E. Grady CTE High School, Brooklyn. Photos John Nelle.

humility by way of a book opened to the words 'Teach thy tongue to say I do not know and thou shalt progress.'[45]

In 1955, Boston-based artist and medical historian Doris Appel (1904–1995) made a relief plaque of Maimonides for Marquette University Medical School as part of a group of five famous physicians (Fig. 107). A full-round sculptural bust of Maimonides by the same artist graces the lobby of the 'Hall of Medicine' of the Boston University School of Medicine as one of a dozen figures including Hippocrates, Galen, Vesulius, Pare, Harvey, Morton, Lister,

45 Susan Chevlowe, *Common Man Mythic Vision: The Paintings of Ben Shahn* (New York: Princeton University Press, 1998), plate 23.

Fig. 107 (opposite) Doris Appel, bas-relief bust of Maimonides. From the Doris Appel Papers, Truman G. Blocker, Jr. History of Medicine Collections, Moody Medical Library, University of Texas Medical Branch at Galveston.

Fig. 108 (right) Jack Levine, *Maimonides* (1952). Oil on paper mounted on panel. Library of the Jewish Theological Seminary.

Roentgen, and Marie Curie, to provide future generations of medical students with a 'spiritual hearth.'

Throughout the 1960s and 1970s, artist Jack Levine produced a number of different prints based on his 1952 watercolor of Maimonides for a series called *Teachers and Kings* (Fig. 108). The dramatic perspectival arrangement of the base-line composition renders Maimonides's upper body and especially his hands dominant, giving him the character of the scribe. However, each print creates a different aesthetic presentation of the scribe through an assortment of different etching techniques. In the original, Levine emphasized hyper-realistic contemporary faces that were clearly modeled on life-portraits in his biblical subjects, while the later etchings experiment and play with this juxtaposition, often applying an even-handed expressionistic style to the entire image. The book in which Maimonides inscribes his faraway thoughts is likewise rendered in various styles.

Maimonides and the Multicultural 1980s

Many countries celebrated the 850th anniversary of Maimonides's birth and, unlike the sense of impending terror in 1935, the commemorative products of 1985 were far more globally oriented. Niceto Alcalá Zamora's 1935 efforts to establish a memorial to Maimonides in Spain laid the groundwork for Spanish reclamation of his legacy after the Holocaust with the dedication of a sculpture to Maimonides in Tiberiadus Square in 1985 (Fig. 109).

In honor of the 850th anniversary of Maimonides's birth, the Lubavicher Rebbe, Menachem Mendel Schneerson, sought to increase knowledge and awareness around the world of Maimonides and his values. He asked Barnet Liberman and Sam Malamud to create stamps for the countries they represented for the Inter-Governmental Philatelic Corporation.[46] To commemorate the occasion, nine countries agreed to issue special stamps

46 Personal communication with Sharon Liberman Mintz, January 2023.

Fig. 109 A. R. Oleosa, *Statue of Maimonides* (dedicated in 1985). Bronze. Displayed in Plaza de Tiberiadus, Córdoba. Photo © Ken Welsh. All rights reserved 2022 / Bridgeman Images.

and souvenir sheets, some of which were designed in ways that tied to their own national histories of colonialism and independence. The first stamps of Maimonides were issued by Antigua and Barbuda, former British colonies in the Caribbean, which achieved their independence in 1981 (Fig. 110). Other nations, such as Dominica and Grenada in the Caribbean and Lesotho and Sierra Leone in Africa, each of which declared their own independence from the United Kingdom in the 1960s and 1970s, issued single stamps bearing a portrait of Maimonides in connection with the 40th anniversary of the United Nations. The Dominica stamp stands out for its new representation of Maimonides as a man reading a scroll while seated on the floor in a nondescript space (Fig. 111). Modeled after an ethnographic photograph taken by the studio of Landrock & Lehnert in Tunis at the turn of the twentieth century, this imagined portrait of Maimonides adopts a subject sold as a popular postcard under the generic titles 'old rabbi' and 'old Tunisian.' The redesignation simultaneously recovers an individual character for the anonymized ethnographic subject and gives the imagined portrait of Maimonides a distinctly recognizable oriental character. The depiction directly relates to the accompanying souvenir sheet, which illustrates a rabbi reading from a Torah scroll to a group of young Jewish orphans in the modern State of Israel. For Dominica, this transformation of images most associated with colonialism into images of national independence was a meaningful and self-reflexive narrative journey.

Maimonides continued to resonate in inter-Jewish discourse. In the multicultural 1980s, popular media embraced the image of Maimonides as a global figure. As part of the 850th anniversary commemorations, the Jewish National and University Library mounted an exhibition of its treasures in four sections: Bibles, Literary Works, Maimonides, and Miscellanea.[47] At the same time, Chabad leader Rabbi Menachem Mendel Schneerson, who embraced Maimonides as a source of Chabad Ḥasidut, leaned on Maimonides's drawing of the Temple Menorah for the revitalization of Jewish religious life in the diaspora. In 1982,

47 Mordechai Nadav and Raphael Weiser (eds.), *Selected Manuscripts and Prints: An Exhibition from the Treasures of the Jewish National and University Libraries* (Jerusalem: Jewish National and University Library, 1985).

Fig. 110 Stamps from Antigua and Barbuda, Grenada, and Lesotho (1985). Courtesy of the Leiman Library.

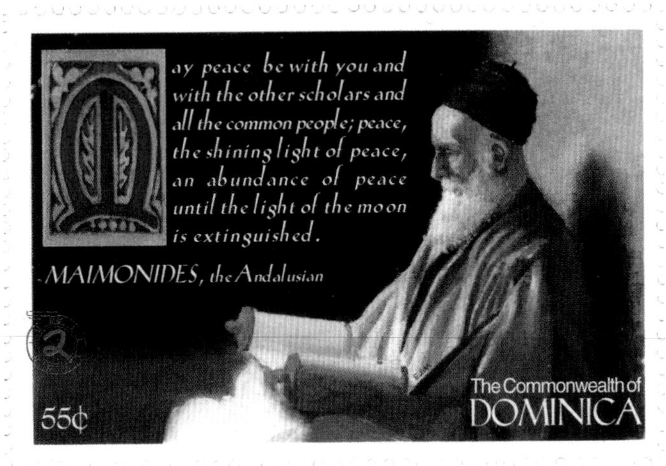

Fig. 111 Stamp from Dominica (1985). Courtesy of the Leiman Library.

Schneerson decried the depiction of the Temple Menorah with semicircular arms and its use for the design of the Hanukkah lamp and called for the use of straight diagonal lines in keeping with a drawing attributed to Maimonides (see Fig. 46).[48] In instructing his Hasidim to utilize straight diagonal lines, Schneerson appropriated the image as a symbol of religious differentiation from secular Zionism.[49] Chabad's Maimonidean Menorah has become the most visible and recognizable symbol of Hanukkah in the world.

In the twenty-first century, the desire to manifest Maimonides in concrete visual and material ways remains unabated, as his image continues to play a role in historical interpretation in a variety of media. After September 11, 2001, peace activist and American director Jacob Bender made the film *Out of Córdoba*, in which he followed in the footsteps of Maimonides and his contemporary Muslim theologian Averroes across Spain, Morocco, France, Egypt, Palestine, and Israel to project the possibility of interfaith dialogue and reconciliation.[50] A marble statue of Maimonides by Spanish sculptor Ángeles Lazaro Guil (b. 1959) is situated among ten other famous figures of Spanish Jewry in the courtyard of the

48 Menachem Mendel Schneerson, *Hilkhot Bet ha-Beḥirah le-ha-Rambam* (Brooklyn, 1986), 46–52. *Perush ha-Mishnayot, Menaḥot* 3:7; *Mishneh Torah, Hilkhot Bet ha-Beḥirah* 3:10.

49 Menachem Mendel Schneerson, 'Parashat Terumah,' *Likute Siḥot*, vol. 21, 169. For further discussion on the shape of the Menorah, see also Menachem Mendel Schneerson, 'Parashat Tetsaveh,' *Likute Siḥot*, vol. 26.

50 *Out of Córdoba*, dir. Jacob Bender. MLK Producciones, Spain and Jacob Bender for Canal Sur, TV de Andalucia, 2009.

Fig. 112 Ángeles Lazaro Guil, Ralli Museum courtyard, Caesarea, 2006. Photograph by Shay Scholnik. Courtesy Caesarea Ralli Museums.

Fig. 113 Solomon Souza, *Maimonides*, Jerusalem, 2015. Photo © Renee Ghert-Zand.

Ralli Museum in Caesarea, designed in a Moorish style evocative of the Alhambra Palace in Grenada. Commissioned by the museum's founder Harry Recanati to capture the breadth of Spanish Jewish culture, Guil designed the figures (unveiled in 2006) on the theme of the 'Convivencia' (coexistence) of three cultures (Fig. 112). Museums have continued to mount exhibitions dedicated to Maimonides and produce lavishly illustrated catalogues in ways that are both internally focused on institution building and on broader Jewish politics.[51] In 2015, the Israel Museum launched the small exhibition 'Together Again,' reuniting two volumes of a lavishly illuminated *Mishneh Torah* produced during the Italian Renaissance.[52]

Maimonides still appears on the street. Today, in the Jerusalem marketplace known as the 'shuk,' a portrait of Maimonides is spray-painted on the garage door of a storefront on the street Derech Ha-Rambam (Fig. 113). As a work of self-creation, Jewish artists and printers brought Maimonides to life, seeing in him their own worldly struggles and aspirations.

51 Avraham David, *The Great Eagle at the JNUL: The Works of Moses Maimonides from the Treasures of the Jewish National and University Library* (Jerusalem: JNUL, 2004); Johannes Wachten, Christine H. Lochow-Dureke, and Johanna Vollmeyer (eds.), *Moses Maimonides. Arzt, Philosophe und Oberhaupt der Juden 1135–1204* (Frankfurt am Main: Museum Judengasse Frankfurt, 2004); Pier Francesco Fumagalli, *Da Mosè a Mosè. Maimonide fra tradizione e modernità* (Milan: Biblioteca Ambrosiana, 2004).

52 The first volume was on temporary loan from the Vatican Library, with the second volume jointly owned by the Israel Museum and the Metropolitan Museum of Art in New York.

APPENDICES

Appendix I:
Additional Exhibition Loans

Appendix II:
Concordance of Catalogue Numbers and Hartman Collection Numbers

Appendix I
Additional Exhibition Loans

1
[Panel from a Torah Ark door]
[Egypt, 11th century, with later carving and paint]. Walnut
The Walters Art Museum (funds provided by the W. Alton Jones Foundation Acquisition Fund, 2000) and Yeshiva University Museum (funds provided by the Jesselson Foundation) (see frontispiece, backmatter image)

2
Commentary on the Mishnah, Nezikin and Kodashim (Autograph)
[Egypt, after 1168]
The Bodleian Libraries, University of Oxford, MS. Pococke 295 (see Fig. 46)

3
Commentary on the Mishnah, Seder Tohorot (Autograph)
[Egypt, 12th century]
Library of the Jewish Theological Seminary, MS 8254.3 (see Fig. 11)

4
Mishneh Torah: Sefer Mada, Sefer Ahavah (Autograph)
[Egypt, 1170–1180]
The Bodleian Libraries, University of Oxford, MS. Huntington 80 (see Fig. 82)

5
Mishneh Torah, Malveh ve-Loveh (Autograph)
[Egypt, 1170–1180]
Library of the Jewish Theological Seminary, MS 8254.4

Fig. 114 *Mishneh Torah, Malveh ve-Loveh* [Egypt, 1170–1180]. Library of the Jewish Theological Seminary, MS 8254.4r.

6
[Circular urging redemption of captives] (Autograph)
[Egypt, 12th century]
Library of the Jewish Theological Seminary, MS 8254.7

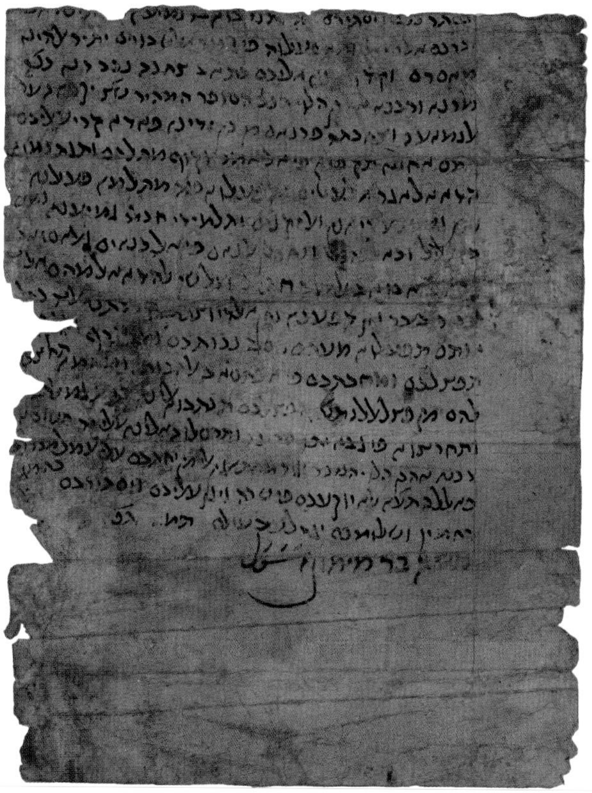

Fig. 115 Circular urging redemption of captives [Egypt, 12th century]. Library of the Jewish Theological Seminary, MS 8254.7r.

7
[Responsa] (Autograph)
[Egypt, 12th century]
Library of the Jewish Theological Seminary, MS 8254.8

8
Mishneh Torah
[Ashkenaz, 13th/14th century]
Library of the Jewish Theological Seminary, MS 8282 / R350 (see Fig. 48)

9
Moreh Nevukhim
Scribe: Levi bar Isaac Figo Karo of Salamanca
Barcelona, 1347 or 1348
Royal Danish Library, Copenhagen, Cod. Heb. 37 (see Figs. 76, 77)

10
Moreh Nevukhim
Scribe: Jacob ben Samuel Nachlieb
[Ashkenaz], 1349
Mantua State Archive of the Italian Ministry of Culture (see Figs. 78, 79)

11
Mishneh Torah
[Spain, 14th/15th century]
Library of the Jewish Theological Seminary, MS 9947 / R1618

Fig. 116 *Moreh Nevukhim* (Barcelona, 1347 or 1348). Royal Danish Library, Cod. Heb. 37, fol. 114r. Courtesy of the Royal Danish Library.

Fig. 117 *Moreh Nevukhim* ([Ashkenaz], 1349), fol. 80v. Mantua State Archive of the Italian Ministry of Culture.

12
Moreh Nevukhim
[Spain, 15th century]
Museum of the Bible, Washington, DC,
GC.MS.000886

Fig. 118 *Moreh Nevukhim* [Spain, 15th century]. Museum of the Bible, GC.MS.000886.

13
Magid Mishneh
Vidal Yom Tov of Tolosa
[Italy, 15th century]
National Library of Israel, Ms. Heb. 8689

Fig. 119 Vidal Yom Tov of Tolosa, *Magid Mishnah* [Italy, 15th century]. National Library of Israel, Ms. Heb. 8689.

14
Mishneh Torah
Lisbon, 1471–1472
British Library Board, Harley MS 5698

15
Mishneh Torah
Venice: Daniel Bomberg, 1524
National Library of Israel, Ms. Heb. 24°9692

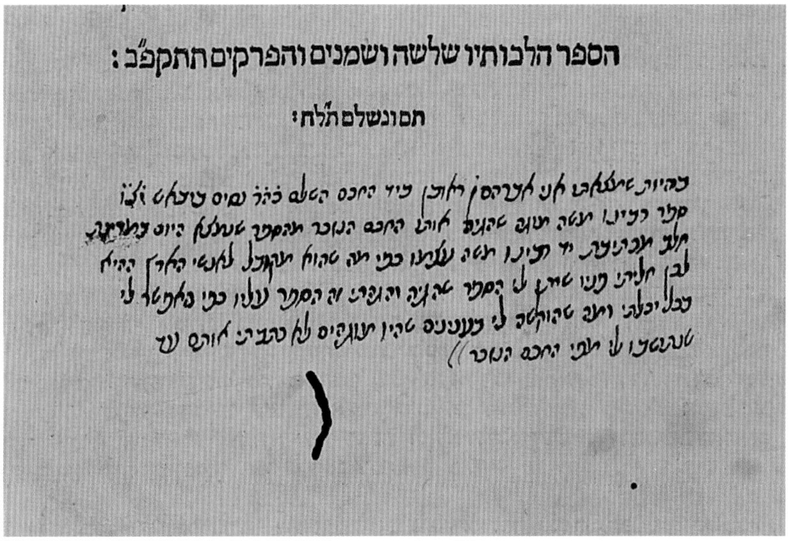

Fig. 120 *Mishneh Torah* (Venice: Daniel Bomberg, 1524–1525). National Library of Israel, Ms. Heb. 24°9692, fol. 763v. Inscription about making corrections to the printed text based on an authoritative manuscript.

16
[Edict ordering confiscation and burning of Talmud]
Venice, 1553
Library of the Jewish Theological Seminary, B (NS)H53

17
Tesoro de Preceptos
Ishac Athias
Venice: Gioanne Caleoni, 1627
Library of the Jewish Theological Seminary, RB417:8

18
Mishnayot
Commentary of Isaac Ibn Gabbai
Constantinople: Solomon Franco, 1643
Hebrew Union College Library, Cincinnati

19
Eyn Sheyn Mayse Bukh
Prague: Sons of Jacob Bak (Wahl), 1665
National Library of Israel, 8°91 A 534

Fig. 121 *Mishneh Torah* (Lisbon, 1471–1472). British Library Board, Harley MS 5698, fol. 11v–12r.

מצותיך

כל המצות שנתנו לו למשה בסיני בפירושן נתנו שנא'
ואתנה לך את לוחות האבן והתורה והמצוה תורה זו
תורה שבכתב ומצוה זו פירושה וצונו לעשות התורה
על פי המצוה ומצוה זו היא הנקראת תורה שבעל פה
כל התורה כתבה משה רבנו קודם שימות בכתב ידו
ונתן ספר לכל שבט ושבט וספר אחד נתנהו בארון
לעד שנא' לקוח את ספר התורה וגו' והמצוה שהיא
פירוש התורה לא כתבה אלא צוה בה לזקנים
וליהושע ולשאר כל ישראל שנא' את כל הדבר
אשר אנכי מצוה אתכם אותו תשמרו לעשות וגו'
ומפני זה נקראת תורה שבעל פה ואע"פ שלא נכתבה
תורה שבעל פה למדה משה רבנו כלה בבית דינו
לשבעים זקנים ואלעזר ופינחס ויהושע שלשתם
קבלו ממשה וליהושע שהוא תלמידו של משה
רבנו מסר לו תורה שבעל פה וצוהו עליה וכן יהושע
למד כל ימי חייו על פה וזקנים רבים קבלו מיהושע
וקבל עלי מן הזקנים ומפינחס ושמואל קבל מעלי

ובית דינו ודוד קבל משמואל ובית דינו ואחיה
השילני מיוצאי מצרים היה ולוי היה ושמע ממשה
רבנו והיה קטן בימי משה והוא קבל מדוד ובית דינו
אליהו קבל מאחיה השילני ובית דינו ואלישע קבל
מאליהו ובית דינו ויהוידע הכהן קבל מאלישע ובית
דינו וזכריה קבל מיהוידע ובית דינו והושע קבל
מזכריה ובית דינו ועמוס קבל מהושע ובית דינו
וישעיה קבל מעמוס ובית דינו ומיכה קבל מישעיה
ובית דינו ויואל קבל ממיכה ובית דינו ונחום קבל
מיואל ובית דינו וחבקוק קבל מנחום ובית דינו
וצפניה קבל מחבקוק ובית דינו וירמיה קבל מצפניה
ובית דינו וברוך בן נריה קבל מירמיה ובית דינו ועזרא
ובית דינו קבלו מברוך ובית דינו בית דינו של עזרא
הם הנקראים אנשי כנסת הגדולה והם חגי זכריה
מלאכי ודניאל וחנניה ומישאל ועזריה ונחמיה בן
חכליה ומרדכי בלשן וזרבבל והרבה חכמים עמהם
תשלום מאה ועשרים זקנים האחרון מהם הוא

הואיל משה
באר את התורה
הזאת
וזאת התורה
אשר שם משה
לפני
בני ישראל

20
Ḥozek Yad
Solomon ben Samuel Ibn Muvḥar
[Italy], 1636
Rare Book & Manuscript Library, Columbia University Libraries, MS X893.15 M88

21
Tsitsat Novel Tsevi
Jacob Sasportas
[Hamburg/Amsterdam, 17th century]
Yeshiva University, Mendel Gottesman Library, MS 1251

22
[Proposals concerning calendar reform (sec. 5)]
Isaac Newton
[England], 1699
National Library of Israel, Ms. Yahuda Var. 1/Newton Papers 24e

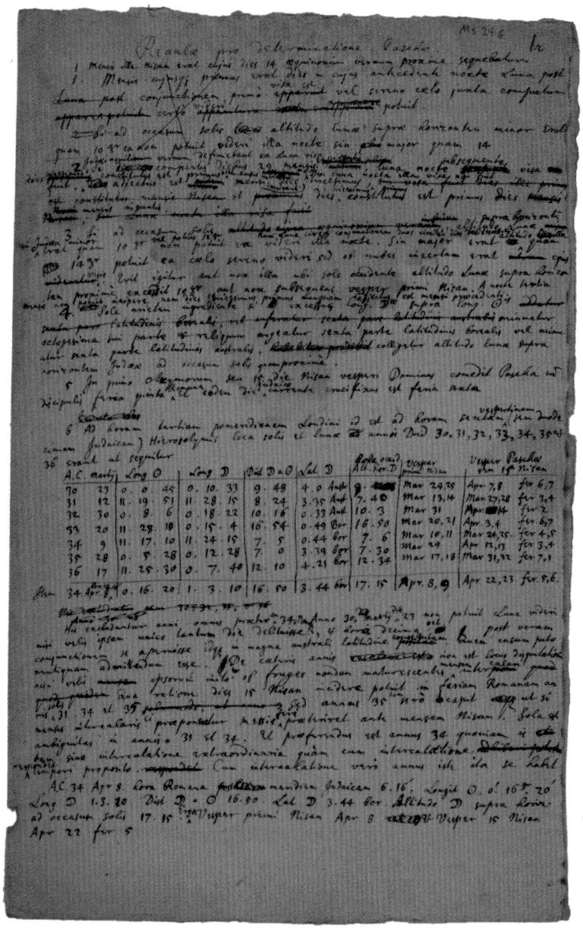

Fig. 122 Isaac Newton, proposals concerning calendar reform (sec. 5) ([England], 1699). National Library of Israel, Ms. Yahuda Var. 1/Newton Papers 24e.

23
Me'am Lo'ez, vol. 1
Jacob Culi
Constantinople: Jonah ben Jacob, 1730
Library of the Jewish Theological Seminary

24
Thesaurus Antiquitatum Sacrarum, vol. 1
Blasio Ugolino
Venice: J. G. Herthz, 1744
Library of the Jewish Theological Seminary (see Fig. 80)

25
[Prayer composed in New York after the Revolution]
Hendla Jochanan van Oettingen
New York, 1784
American Jewish Historical Society, Jacques Judah Lyons papers (P-15), Box 1, Folder 64

26
Sheloshah 'Asar 'Ikarim / De Deritien Geloofs-Artikelen
Amsterdam: J. C. Belinfante, 1850
Library of the Jewish Theological Seminary, B (NS)PP107

27
Moreh Nevukhim
Warsaw: Isaac Goldman, 1872
Library of the Jewish
Theological Seminary

Fig. 123 *Moreh Nevukhim* (Warsaw: Isaac Goldman, 1872). Library of the Jewish Theological Seminary.

28
[Pendant medal of Maimonides wearing an amulet]
[Italy?, before 1935]. Silver
Collection of Ira Rezak

Fig. 124 Pendant medal of Maimonides wearing an amulet [Italy?, before 1935]. Silver. Collection of Ira Rezak.

29
[Maimonides octocentennial medal]
Michael Gur Arie (Bezalel)
Jerusalem, 1935. Bronze
Collection of Ira Rezak

30
Maimonides
Jack Levine
1952. Oil on paper mounted on panel
Library of the Jewish Theological Seminary (see Fig. 108)

31
Maimonides
Ben Shahn
1954. Tempera on paper mounted on panel; study for the mosaic mural *Science and the Humanities* (see Fig. 106)
The Jewish Museum, New York, 2002-29
Bequest of Jacob and Bronka Weintraub

Fig. 125 Ben Shahn, *Maimonides* (1954). Tempera on paper mounted on panel. New York, The Jewish Museum. © 2022 Estate of Ben Shahn / Licensed by VAGA at Artists Rights Society (ARS), NY.

32
[Amulet]
Israel, [ca. 1960]
National Library of Israel, V 183 02 35 (see Fig. 95)

33
[Hotel Maimonides key fob]
Córdoba, [ca. 1970]. Bronze
Collection of Ira Rezak

34
[Commemorative portrait medal of Maimonides]
Victor Douek
[France], 1983. Bronze
Collection of Ira Rezak

35
[Portrait medal of Maimonides]
Alex Shagin
[United States], 1985. Bronze
Collection of Ira Rezak

Fig. 126 Hotel Maimonides key fob (Córdoba, [ca. 1970]). Bronze. Collection of Ira Rezak.

36
[Stamps honoring Maimonides]
Antigua and Barbuda, Grenada, Guinea, Spain, 1985
Barnet Liberman, Inter-Governmental Philatelic Corporation (see Figs. 110, 111)

Appendix II
Catalogue Number and Corresponding Number in the Hartman Collection

Cat. no.	Title (Place/Date)	Manuscript (MS) or Rare Book (RB) no.
1	*Moreh Nevukhim* [Yemen, ca. 1280–1330]	MS 11
1	*Kitab al-Ḥaka'ik* [Yemen, 14th century]	MS 15
2	*Pirke Moshe* [Provence, 14th century]	MS 6
3	*Milot ha-Higayon* [Spain, late 14th–early 15th century]	MS 7
4	*Mishneh Torah* [Yemen, 14th century]	MS 14
4	*Mishneh Torah* [Yemen, 14th century]	MS 2
4	*Mishneh Torah* [Yemen, 15th century]	MS 22
4	*Mishneh Torah* [Yemen, 15th century]	MS 3
5	*Hasagot ha-Rabad* [Italy, 15th century]	MS 4
6	*Seder Nezikin* with Commentary of Maimonides [Yemen, 15th century]	MS 10
6	*Seder Tohorot* with Commentary of Maimonides [Yemen, 15th century]	MS 13
7	*Moreh Nevukhim* [Italy, after 1465]	MS 1
8	*Mishneh Torah* [Rome?, ca. 1475]	RB 1
8	*Mishneh Torah* (Soncino, 1490)	RB 2
9	*Sefer ha-Mitsvot* ([Yemen], 1492)	MS 5
10	*Mishneh Torah* (Constantinople, 1509)	RB 3
11	*Teshuvot, She'elot ve-Igerot* [Constantinople, ca. 1517]	RB 12
12	*Mishneh Torah* (Venice, 1524–1525)	RB 4
12	*Seder Tohorot* with Commentary of Maimonides (Venice, 1528)	RB 30
13	*Igerot le-ha-Ma'or ha-Gadol* (Venice, 1544)	RB 13
13	*Masekhet Avot* with Commentary of Maimonides (Mantua, 1558)	RB 31
14	*Mishneh Torah* (Venice, 1550)	RB 5
14	*Mishneh Torah* (Venice, 1550–1551)	RB 6
15	*Kiryat Sefer* (Venice, 1551)	RB 16
16	*Moreh Nevukhim* (Venice, 1551)	RB 9
17	*Moreh Nevukhim* (Sabbioneta, 1553)	RB 10
18	*De Astrologia Rabbi Mosis filii Meimon epistola elegans* (Cologne, 1555)	RB 32
18	*Chronicon Breve, et Capita R. Mose Ben Maïemon de rebus Regis Messie* (Paris, 1572)	RB 37
19	*Sefer ha-Emunot* (Ferrara, 1556)	RB 18
19	*Hasagot ... Mosheh Al-Ashkar* (Ferrara, 1556)	RB 19
20	*Ru'aḥ Ḥen* (Cremona, 1565)	RB 20
20	*Milot ha-Higayon* (Cremona, 1566)	RB 33
21	*Torat ha-'Olah* (Prague, 1569)	RB 21
22	*Mishneh Torah* (Venice, 1574–1575)	RB 7
23	*Megilat Ester* (Venice, 1592)	RB 34
23	*Sefer ha-Mitsvot* (Berlin, 1733)	RB 35
24	*Mishneh Torah* (Salf Banei al-Qadi, 1559)	MS 16
24	*Mishneh Torah* (Darb al-Ḥanashat, 1594)	MS 18
24	*Mishneh Torah* (Guran, 1596)	MS 17
24	*Masekhet Nidah* with Commentary of Maimonides [Yemen, ca. 1600]	MS 23
24	*Masekhet Ḥulin* with Commentary of Maimonides [Yemen, ca. 1600]	MS 24

Cat. no.	Title (Place/Date)	Manuscript (MS) or Rare Book (RB) no.
25	Commentary of Maimonides on *Masekhet Rosh ha-Shanah* [Middle East, ca. 1600]	MS 12
26	*Leḥem Mishneh* (Venice, 1604–1606)	RB 17
27	*Mishneh Torah* (ʻAmran, 1651)	MS 19
28	*Mada, Ahavah, Zemanim* (Venice, 1665)	RB 27
29	*Mishneh Torah* (Amsterdam, 1702)	RB 8
29	*Pe'er ha-Dor* (Amsterdam, 1765)	RB 14
30	*Yeshuʻah be-Yisrael* (Frankfurt am Main, 1720)	RB 25
30	*Yeshuʻah be-Yisrael* [Central Europe, mid-18th century]	MS 9
31	*Moreh Nevukhim* (Jessnitz, 1742)	RB 11
32	*Seder Sidur ha-Tefilah* (Sanaʻa, 1826)	MS 27
32	*Moreh Nevukhim* [Yemen, 19th century]	MS 25
33	[Responsa] [Oxford, mid-19th century]	MS 8
34	*Pirke Mosheh* (Lviv, [ca. 1830])	RB 15
35	*Ma'amar Teḥiyat ha-Metim* [Rome, ca. 1835]	MS 26
36	*Shene ha-Me'orot* (Berlin, 1847)	RB 23
36	*Shene Ma'amare ha-Mishgal* (Berlin, 1906)	RB 22
37	*Milḥamot Ha-Shem* ([Yemen], 1933)	MS 21
38	*Ḥidushe Rabenu Ḥayim ha-Levi* (Brisk, 1936)	RB 24

Hartman Collection Number and Corresponding Number in the Catalogue

Manuscript (MS) or Rare Book (RB) no.	Title (Place/Date)	Cat. no.
MS 1	*Moreh Nevukhim* [Italy, after 1465]	7
MS 2	*Mishneh Torah* [Yemen, 14th century]	4
MS 3	*Mishneh Torah* [Yemen, 15th century]	4
MS 4	*Hasagot ha-Rabad* [Italy, 15th century]	5
MS 5	*Sefer ha-Mitsvot* ([Yemen], 1492)	9
MS 6	*Pirke Moshe* [Provence, 14th century]	2
MS 7	*Milot ha-Higayon* [Spain, late 14th–early 15th century]	3
MS 8	[Responsa] [Oxford, mid-19th century]	33
MS 9	*Yeshu'ah be-Yisrael* [Central Europe, mid-18th century]	30
MS 10	*Seder Nezikin* with Commentary of Maimonides [Yemen, 15th century]	6
MS 11	*Moreh Nevukhim* [Yemen, ca. 1280–1330]	1
MS 12	Commentary of Maimonides on *Masekhet Rosh ha-Shanah* [Middle East, ca. 1600]	25
MS 13	*Seder Tohorot* with Commentary of Maimonides [Yemen, 15th century]	6
MS 14	*Mishneh Torah* [Yemen, 14th century]	4
MS 15	*Kitab al-Ḥaka'ik* [Yemen, 14th century]	1
MS 16	*Mishneh Torah* (Salf Banei al-Qadi, 1559)	24
MS 17	*Mishneh Torah* (Guran, 1596)	24
MS 18	*Mishneh Torah* (Darb al-Ḥanashat, 1594)	24
MS 19	*Mishneh Torah* ('Amran, 1651)	27
MS 21	*Milḥamot Ha-Shem* ([Yemen], 1933)	37
MS 22	*Mishneh Torah* [Yemen, 15th century]	4
MS 23	*Masekhet Nidah* with Commentary of Maimonides [Yemen, ca. 1600]	24
MS 24	*Masekhet Ḥulin* with Commentary of Maimonides [Yemen, ca. 1600]	24
MS 25	*Moreh Nevukhim* [Yemen, 19th century]	32
MS 26	*Ma'amar Teḥiyat ha-Metim* [Rome, ca. 1835]	35
MS 27	*Seder Sidur ha-Tefilah* (Sana'a, 1826)	32
RB 1	*Mishneh Torah* [Rome?, ca. 1475]	8
RB 2	*Mishneh Torah* (Soncino, 1490)	8
RB 3	*Mishneh Torah* (Constantinople, 1509)	10
RB 4	*Mishneh Torah* (Venice, 1524–1525)	12
RB 5	*Mishneh Torah* (Venice, 1550)	14
RB 6	*Mishneh Torah* (Venice, 1550–1551)	14
RB 7	*Mishneh Torah* (Venice, 1574–1575)	22
RB 8	*Mishneh Torah* (Amsterdam, 1702)	29
RB 9	*Moreh Nevukhim* (Venice, 1551)	16
RB 10	*Moreh Nevukhim* (Sabbioneta, 1553)	17
RB 11	*Moreh Nevukhim* (Jessnitz, 1742)	31
RB 12	*Teshuvot, She'elot ve-Igerot* [Constantinople, ca. 1517]	11
RB 13	*Igerot le-ha-Ma'or ha-Gadol* (Venice, 1544)	13
RB 14	*Pe'er ha-Dor* (Amsterdam, 1765)	29
RB 15	*Pirke Mosheh* (Lviv, [ca. 1830])	34

Manuscript (MS) or Rare Book (RB) no.	Title (Place/Date)	Cat. no.
RB 16	*Kiryat Sefer* (Venice, 1551)	15
RB 17	*Leḥem Mishneh* (Venice, 1604–1606)	26
RB 18	*Sefer ha-Emunot* (Ferrara, 1556)	19
RB 19	*Hasagot … Mosheh Al-Ashkar* (Ferrara, 1556)	19
RB 20	*Ru'aḥ Ḥen* (Cremona, 1565)	20
RB 21	*Torat ha-'Olah* (Prague, 1569)	21
RB 22	*Shene Ma'amare ha-Mishgal* (Berlin, 1906)	36
RB 23	*Shene ha-Me'orot* (Berlin, 1847)	36
RB 24	*Ḥidushe Rabenu Ḥayim ha-Levi* (Brisk, 1936)	38
RB 25	*Yeshu'ah be-Yisrael* (Frankfurt am Main, 1720)	30
RB 27	*Mada, Ahavah, Zemanim* (Venice, 1665)	28
RB 30	*Seder Tohorot* with Commentary of Maimonides (Venice, 1528)	12
RB 31	*Masekhet Avot* with Commentary of Maimonides (Mantua, 1558)	13
RB 32	*De Astrologia Rabbi Mosis filii Meimon epistola elegans* (Cologne, 1555)	18
RB 33	*Milot ha-Higayon* (Cremona, 1566)	20
RB 34	*Megilat Ester* (Venice, 1592)	23
RB 35	*Sefer ha-Mitsvot* (Berlin, 1733)	23
RB 37	*Chronicon Breve, et Capita R. Mose Ben Maïemon de rebus Regis Messie* (Paris, 1572)	18

CONTRIBUTORS

Rabbi Dr. **Ari Berman** is the fifth president of Yeshiva University. He lectures widely throughout the world on topics related to medieval Halakhah, contemporary Jewish thought, and modern philosophy. His recent book, *The Final Exam: Letters to our Students*, expands Torah U-Madda as an educational philosophy into a worldview that also embraces truth, dignity, and compassion.

Dr. **Evelyn M. Cohen** is an art historian who specializes in illuminated Hebrew manuscripts and Italian Renaissance art. A recipient of a National Endowment for the Humanities Fellowship, she also has been a Samuel H. Kress Fellow and a Coleman Fellow at the Metropolitan Museum of Art. She has served on the faculty of Columbia University, Brooklyn College, the University of Pennsylvania, and the Jewish Theological Seminary, where she was also the founding Curator of Jewish Art. A widely published author, she is the recipient of the National Jewish Book Award.

Edward Fram is a professor in the Department of Jewish History at Ben-Gurion University of the Negev, where he holds the Solly Yellin Chair in Eastern European and Lithuanian Jewry. His most recent book is *The Codification of Jewish Law on the Cusp of Modernity*, published by Cambridge University Press (2022).

Gabriel M. Goldstein is the Interim Director and Chief Curator at Yeshiva University Museum. He has served in consultant curatorial roles with the Capital Jewish Museum, Washington DC, the Claims Conference, the National Archives, and the North Carolina Museum of Art. He has worked at Yeshiva University Museum for over twenty years and has also held curatorial positions at the Jewish Museum, New York, and the Royal Ontario Museum, Toronto.

Robert Hartman has amassed an impressive collection of manuscripts and rare printed Maimonidean material over the past twenty-five years. For the last forty years, he has been involved in the start-up and creation of over thirty businesses, primarily related to the healthcare and real-estate fields. He has served as a board member of numerous public and private corporations and entities, and his community leadership and philanthropic activities include: current Chairman of the Board of Trustees of Arie Crown Hebrew Day School; current Director of Simon Wiesenthal Center, Los Angeles; former Director of Northeastern Illinois University, Chicago; former Chairman of the Board of Keshet, which serves children and adults with developmental disabilities; and former board member of Chai Lifeline Midwest, an organization serving children with life-threatening illnesses. Mr. Hartman has been married to Debbie (Lefkovich) for forty-six years and is blessed with four children, twenty-two grandchildren, and five great-grandchildren.

Ephraim Kanarfogel is the E. Billi Ivry University Professor of Jewish History, Literature, and Law at Yeshiva University's Bernard Revel Graduate School of Jewish Studies. His most recent books are *The Intellectual History and Rabbinic Culture of Medieval Ashkenaz* (2012) and *Brothers from Afar: Rabbinic Approaches to Apostasy and Reversion in Medieval Europe* (2020), both published by Wayne State University Press.

Maya Balakirsky Katz is a psychoanalyst and an Associate Professor of Jewish Art at Bar-Ilan University. She is the author of *The Visual Culture of Chabad* (Cambridge: Cambridge University Press, 2010), *Drawing the Iron Curtain: Jews and the Golden Age of Soviet Animation* (New Brunswick: Rutgers University Press, 2016), and *Intersections between Jews and Media* (Leiden: Brill, 2020). She is co-editor, along with Steven Fine and Margaret Olin, of the journal *Images: A Journal of Jewish Art and Visual Culture*. Her most recent book, *Freud, Jung, and Jonah* (Cambridge: Cambridge University Press, 2022), explores the exposition of religion during the founding years of the first psychoanalytic periodicals.

Y. Tzvi Langermann received his PhD in History of Science from Harvard University, where he studied under A. I. Sabra and John Murdoch. For fifteen years, he catalogued Hebrew and Judaeo-Arabic texts in philosophy and science at the Institute of Microfilmed Hebrew Manuscripts in Jerusalem, before joining the Department of Arabic at Bar-Ilan University, from which he recently retired. His most recent books are a translation and study of a treatise by Ibn Kammūna, *Subtle Insights Concerning Knowledge and Practice* (New Haven: Yale University Press, 2019) and *In and Around Maimonides: Original Essays* (Piscataway: Gorgias Press, 2021).

Daniel J. Lasker is the Norbert Blechner Professor of Jewish Values (emeritus) in the Goldstein-Goren Department of Jewish Thought at Ben-Gurion University of the Negev, Beer Sheva, Israel. He is the author of eight books and close to over three hundred other publications in the fields of Jewish philosophy, especially the works of Judah Halevi, the Jewish–Christian debate and its philosophical implications, and the thought and history of Karaism. In addition to his position at Ben-Gurion University, Prof. Lasker has taught at Yale University, Princeton University, Boston College, Yeshiva University, and a number of other institutions. His latest book is *Karaism: An Introduction to the Oldest Surviving Alternative Judaism* (London: Littman Library of Jewish Civilization, 2022) which was a finalist in the category of scholarship in the 2023 National Jewish Book Awards.

David Sclar is Department Guest with the Program in Judaic Studies at Princeton University, and History Instructor and Librarian at The Frisch School. He earned his doctorate in history at the Graduate Center of the City University of New York, and has held fellowships at Harvard University, Princeton University, the University of Oxford, and the University of Toronto. His research explores book history, individual intention and communal identity, and the correlation between intellectual and social history. He worked for many years at the Library of the Jewish Theological Seminary, where he maintained, researched, and catalogued rare material and co-curated exhibitions.

Marc B. Shapiro holds the Weinberg Chair in Judaic Studies at the University of Scranton. His most recent book is *Changing the Immutable: How Orthodox Judaism Rewrites Its History* (London: Littman Library of Jewish Civilization).

Yosef Yuval Tobi is a professor (emeritus) of medieval Hebrew poetry at the University of Haifa, Israel, and Head of the Department of Hebrew Language and Literature in Al-Qasemi Academy, Baqa al-Gharbiyya. His main scholarly fields treat the spiritual, cultural, and historical affinities between Judaism and Islam during the medieval period and modern times. His primary publications include *The Jews of Yemen: Studies in Their History and Culture* (Leiden: Brill, 1999), *Proximity and Distance: Medieval Hebrew and Arabic Poetry* (Leiden: Brill, 2004), *Between Hebrew and Arabic Poetry: Studies in Spanish Hebrew Medieval Poetry* (Leiden: Brill, 2010), and *The Judeo-Arabic Literature in Tunisia 1850–1950* (Detroit: Wayne State University Press, 2014). Prof. Tobi is the editor of three periodicals: *TEMA* – Judeo-Yemenite Studies; *Ben 'Ever La-'Arav* – Contacts between Arabic Literature and Jewish Literature in the Middle Ages and Modern Times; and *Hagut Ba-Hinnukh Ha-Yehudi* – Studies in the Thought of Jewish Education.

Joanna Weinberg is Professor Emerita in Early Modern Jewish History and Rabbinics at the University of Oxford, where she taught rabbinic literature and medieval and Jewish literature and history. Together with Anthony Grafton she is presently engaged in an investigation of the major German Hebraist Johann Buxtorf and his paradoxical approaches to Jews and Jewish literature. With Piet van Boxel and Kirsten Macfarlane, she edited the volume *The Mishnaic Moment: Jewish Law among Jews and Christians in Early Modern Europe*, published in the Oxford–Warburg Studies series in 2022.

Dr. **Roni Weinstein** teaches Jewish History at the Hebrew University. His current research revolves around the religious history of the Jews in the Mediterranean basin in the early modern period. His recently published books include *Kabbalah and Jewish Modernity* (London: Littman Library of Jewish Civilization, 2016) and *Joseph Karo and Shaping Jewish Law: The Early Modern Ottoman and Global Settings* (London: Anthem Press, 2022). His forthcoming book, published by Routledge, focuses on the messianic movement of Sabbetai Zvi in the Ottoman context.

Irene Zwiep is Professor of Hebrew and Jewish Studies at the University of Amsterdam. She specializes in European Jewish intellectual history from the Middle Ages onwards, with a special interest in the history of Jewish linguistic thought and the interface of scholarship and politics. Her recent publications include 'Writing in a World of Strangers: The Invention of Jewish Literature Revisited,' *Journal of Latin Cosmopolitan and European Literatures* 7 (2022): 1–20; 'Judaism as Religious Cosmopolitanism: Apologetics and Appropriation in the *Jüdisches Lexikon* (1927–1930),' in *Protestant Bible Scholarship: Antisemitism, Philosemitism, and Anti-Judaism*, edited by René Bloch et al. (Leiden: Brill, 2022), 24–40; and 'Between Past and Future: European Jewish Scholarship and National Temporalities, 1845–1889,' in *Frontiers of Jewish Scholarship: Expanding Origins, Transcending Borders*, edited by Anne O. Albert et al. (Philadelphia: University of Pennsylvania Press, 2022), 21–41.

IMAGE CREDITS

Unless another source is noted, all images are from the Hartman Family Collection.

All photographs of manuscripts and rare books from the Hartman Family Collection are by Ardon Bar-Hama.

Due to space limitations, full information is at times abbreviated in some image captions. Please see below for more complete descriptions and credit information.

v, vi, 237, 238 – Panel from a Torah Ark door, Egypt, 11th century with later carving and paint. Walnut. Jointly owned by the Walters Art Museum, Baltimore (funds provided by the W. Alton Jones Foundation Acquisition Fund, 2000) and Yeshiva University Museum, New York (funds provided by the Jesselson Foundation). Photograph by Susan Tobin.

Front cover and 201 – Circular urging redemption of captives (Autograph), Egypt, 12th century. Courtesy of the Jewish Theological Seminary Library, MS 8254, fol. 7r.

Front cover, 146–47, Figs. 78–79, and 203, Fig. 117 – *Moreh Nevukhim*, Ashkenaz, 1349, Mantua State Archive of the Italian Ministry of Culture (Ministero della cultura – Archivio di Stato di Mantova), 142v, 80v.

Front cover and 210, Fig. 125 – Ben Shahn, *Maimonides,* 1954, Tempera on paper mounted on panel. Collection of The Jewish Museum, New York. Bequest of Jacob and Bronka Weintraub, 2002–29. Photo by John Parnell, The Jewish Museum, New York / Art Resource, NY, ART130601 © 2022 Estate of Ben Shahn / Licensed by VAGA at Artists Rights Society (ARS), NY.

Left cover flap and 86, Fig. 46 – *Commentary on the Mishnah* (Autograph), The Bodleian Libraries, University of Oxford, MS. Pococke 295, fol. 184v.

177, Fig. 84 – *The Great Learned Rabbis of Israel* (Breslau: S. Shottlaender, 1888), William A. Rosenthall Judaica collection, College of Charleston Libraries, Charleston, SC.

179, Fig. 87 – Meir Kunstadt, postcard, ca. 1900. Hebrew and English. William A. Rosenthall Judaica collection, College of Charleston Libraries, Charleston, SC.

180, Fig. 88 – *Hagadah shel Pesaḥ* (Vienna: Josef Schlesinger, 1929). Meir Kunstadt, illustration for the Rabbis of Bene Berak with Sofer family. Courtesy the Leo Baeck Institute, Call no. r (q) BM 675 P4 V5 1929 Copy 2.

182–83, Figs. 91–92 – Advertisement, *The Forward*, October 3, 1938, 5. Historical Jewish Press website founded by the National Library of Israel and Tel Aviv University, *Forverṭs.*

185, Fig. 93 – *View of the Holy Places,* Land of Israel, 19th century. Watercolor and ink on paper. The Israel Museum, Jerusalem, B03819 177/047. Photo © The Israel Museum by Avshalom Avital.

186, Fig. 94 – Photographic postcard of Maimonides's tomb, Tiberias (ca. 1900). William A. Rosenthall Judaica collection, College of Charleston Libraries, Charleston, SC.

188, Fig. 99 – Zvi Narkiss and Arie Glazer, 1,000-shekel banknote, Israel, 1983. Copyright Bank of Israel.

191, Fig. 103 – Governor of Andalusia speaking at the unveiling of the Maimonides Memorial, Córdoba, March 30, 1935, F 21784. Courtesy of the Leo Baeck Institute.

195, Fig. 108 – Jack Levine, *Maimonides*, 1952. Oil on paper mounted on panel. Courtesy of the Jewish Theological Seminary Library.

204, Fig. 118 – *Moreh Nevukhim* [Spain, 15th century]. Museum of the Bible, Green Collection. All rights reserved. © Museum of the Bible, 2022, GC.MS.000886.

204, Fig. 119 – Vidal Yom Tov of Tolosa, *Magid Mishnah*, Italy, 15th century. Ktiv Project, The National Library of Israel, Ms. Heb. 8689.

Back cover and 196, Fig. 109 – A. R. Oleosa, *Statue of Maimonides,* Córdoba, dedicated 1985. Photo © Ken Welsh. All rights reserved, 2022/Bridgeman Images.

Back cover and 206-207, Fig. 121 – *Mishneh Torah*, Lisbon, 1471–1472. British Library, © The British Library Board, Harley MS 5698, fol. 252v, fol. 11v–12r.

BIBLIOGRAPHY

Abate, Emma, Judith Olszowy-Schlanger, and Delio Vania Proverbio, eds. 'Giovanni Giorgi e Andrea Molza Scriptores: Due Volti dell'Orientalistica Romana.' *Miscellanea Bibliothecae Vaticanae* 25 (2019): 264–90.

Abrahamov, Binyamin. '*Kitab al-Haqa'iq* and Its Sources' [Hebrew]. *Daat: A Journal of Philosophy & Kabbalah* 55 (2005): 31–39.

Abrahams, Israel. *Hebrew Ethical Wills*. Philadelphia, PA: Jewish Publication Society of America, 1926.

Adler, Israel. 'Three Musical Ceremonies for Hoshana Rabba in the Jewish Community of Casale Monferrato (1732–1733, 1735)' [Hebrew]. In *Yuval: Studies of the Jewish Music Research Centre, Volume 5: The Abraham Zvi Idelsohn Memorial Volume*, edited by Israel Adler et al., 51–137 (Hebrew section). Jerusalem: Magnes Press, 1986.

Afterman, Adam. *'And They Shall Be One Flesh': On the Language of Mystical Union in Judaism*. Leiden: Brill, 2016.

Alexander-Frizer, Tamar. *The Heart is a Mirror: The Sephardic Folktale*. Detroit, MI: Wayne State University Press, 2008.

Altmann, Alexander. *Moses Mendelssohn: A Biographical Study*. [N.p.]: University of Alabama Press, 1973.

Amar, Zohar, and Hananel Sari, eds. *Sefer ha-Zikaron le-Rav Yosef ben David Kafiḥ* Ramat Gan: Bar-Ilan University Press, 2001.

Amram, David W. *The Makers of Hebrew Books in Italy: Being Chapters in the History of the Hebrew Printing Press*. Philadelphia, PA: Julius H. Greenstone, 1909.

Assaf, Simha. 'Mashehu le-Toledot Maharshal.' In *Sefer ha-Yovel li-Kevod Levi Ginzberg*, edited by Alexander Marx et al., 45–63. New York: American Academy for Jewish Research, 1946.

— 'Mi-Perusho shel ha-Rambam le-Masekhet Shabbat.' *Sinai* 6 (1940): 103–10.

— 'Teshuvot Geonim.' *Kiryat Sefer* 1, no. 2 (1925): 117–41.

— ed. *Teshuvot ha-Geonim*. Jerusalem: he-Universiṭah ha-'ivrit, 1927.

The Austrian Guide for the Perplexed 1349: An Illuminated Manuscript in Hebrew, by the Scribe Jacob ben Samuel Nachlieb [Krems, Austria] (Alon Shvut: Antiquariat Meir Urbach, 2008).

Babel, Isaac, *Red Cavalry*. Edited by Nathalie Babel. Translated by Peter Constantine. New York: W.W. Norton, 2003.

Baeck, Leo. *Maimonides: der Mann, sein Werk und seine Wirkung*. Düsseldorf: Verlag Allgemeine Wochenzeitung der Juden in Deutschland, 1954.

Baer, Fritz. *Die Juden im Christlichen Spanien: Urkunden und Regesten*, vol. 1. Berlin: Akademie Verlag, 1929.

Bareket, Elinoar. 'The Head of the Jews (ra'is al-yahud) in Fatimid Egypt: A Re-evaluation.' *Bulletin of the School of Oriental and African Studies* 67, no. 2 (2004): 185–97.

Barfod, Jørgen H., Norman L. Kleeblatt, Vivian B. Mann, and Susan L. Braunstein, eds. *Kings and Citizens: The History of the Jews in Denmark 1622–1983*. New York: The Jewish Museum, 1983.

Bar-Ilan, Meir. 'He-'arah Numerologit 'al Meḥaber "Kitab al-Haka'ik," Ḥakham she-lo Noda bi-Shemo.' In *'Ateret Yitsḥak: Kovets Meḥkarim be-Moreshet Yehude Teman: Mugashim le-Yitsḥak Kerner*, edited by Yosef Tobi, 73–80. Netanya: ha-Agudah le-Tipu'aḥ Ḥevrah ṿe-Tarbut, 2003.

Bar-Maoz, Danny. 'Beḥinah Historit shel Tarbut ha-Mahaloket ve-ha-Palganut be-Kehilat Yehude Teman.' PhD diss., Bar-Ilan University, 2001.

Baron, Salo W. 'Historical Outlook of Maimonides.' *Proceedings of the American Academy for Jewish Research* 6 (1934–1935): 5–113.

Barukh ben Isaac. *Sefer ha-Terumah* Part 3, edited by David Abraham. Jerusalem: Mekhon Yerushalayim, 2010.

Beit-Arié, Malachi. *Hebrew Codicology: Tentative Typology of Technical Practices Employed in Hebrew Dated Medieval Manuscripts*. Jerusalem: Israel Academy of Sciences and Humanities, 1981.

Beit-Arié, Malachi, Edna Engel, and Ada Yardeni, eds. *Specimens of Hebrew Medieval Hebrew Scripts*, vol. 1: *Oriental and Yemenite Scripts* [Hebrew]. Jerusalem: Israel Academy of Sciences and Humanities, 1987.

Benayahu, Meir. *Copyright, Authorization, and Imprimatur for Hebrew Books Printed in Venice* [Hebrew] (Jerusalem: Mekhon Ben-Tsevi, Mossad Harav Kook, 1971).
— 'Defuse Zaneti.' *Asufot* 12 (1999): 130–45.
— *Hebrew Printing at Cremona* [Hebrew] (Jerusalem: Mekhon Ben-Tsevi, Mossad Harav Kook, 1971).
— *Rabbi Eliyahu Capsali, of Crete* [Hebrew] (Tel Aviv: Tel Aviv University, 1983).
— 'Reshimat ha-Sefarim she-Hadpis ve-she-Hagayah Rabi Yitsḥak Gershon.' *Asufot* 13 (2000): 65–90.
Ben-Sasson, Jonah. *The Philosophical System of R. Moses Isserles* [Hebrew]. Jerusalem: Israel Academy of Sciences and Humanities, 1984.
Ben-Sasson, Menahem, W. Z. Harvey, Y. Ben-Naeh, and Z. Zohar, eds. *Studies in a Rabbinic Family: The de Botons.* Jerusalem: Misgav Yerushalayim, 1998.
Berger, David. 'The Uses of Maimonides by Twentieth-Century Jewry.' In David Berger, *Cultures in Collision and Conversation*, 190–202. Boston, MA: Academic Studies Press, 2011.
Berger, Pamela. *Jewish-Muslim Veneration at Pilgrimage Places in the Holy Land.* Boston, MA: Brill, 2011.
Berkowitz, David Sandler. *In Remembrance of Creation: Evolution of Art and Scholarship in the Medieval and Renaissance Bible.* Waltham, MA: Brandeis University Press, 1968.
Berliner, Abraham. *Censur und Konfiscation hebraeischer Buecher im Kirchenstaate.* Berlin: H. Itzkowski, 1891.
Berman, Ari. *Ger Toshav in the Halakhic Literature of the High Middle Ages.* PhD diss., Hebrew University of Jerusalem, 2016.
Bernstein, David. 'From Moses unto Moses: The Life and Death of Moses Maimonides.' *The American Jewish World,* March 29, 1935.
Bland, Kalman. *The Artless Jew: Medieval and Modern Affirmation and Denials of the Visual.* Princeton, NJ: Princeton University Press, 2000.
Blau, Joshua, ed. *Teshuvot ha-Rambam*, 4 vols. Jerusalem: Meḳitse Nirdamim, 1957–1986.
Blau, Moshe Y., ed. *Shitat ha-Kadmonim: 'Avodah Zarah.* New York: Deutsch Printing & Publishing Co., 1969.
Bloch, Joshua. *The People of the Book: The Background of Three Hundred Years of Jewish Life in America.* New York: New York Public Library, 1954.
Blumenthal, David R. 'Maimonides' Philosophic Mysticism.' *Daat: A Journal of Jewish Philosophy & Kabbalah* 64–66 (2009): v–xxv.
Bodian, Miriam. *The Hebrews of the Portuguese Nation: Conversos and Community in Early Modern Amsterdam.* Bloomington: Indiana University Press, 1997.
Bos, Gerrit. *Maimonides: Medical Aphorisms: A Parallel Arabic-English Edition. Treatises 6–9.* Provo, UT: Brigham Young, 2007.
— *Maimonides: Medical Aphorisms: A Parallel Arabic-English Edition. Treatises 22–25.* Provo, UT: Brigham Young, 2017.
— *Maimonides: On Asthma. A Parallel Arabic-English Text Edited, Translated, and Annotated.* Provo, UT: Brigham Young, 2002.
Boxel, Piet van. 'Hebrew Books and Censorship in Sixteenth-Century Italy.' In *Jewish Books and their Readers*, edited by Scott Mendelbrote and Joanna Weinberg, 75–99. Leiden: Brill, 2016.
Boxel, Piet van, Kirsten Macfarlane, and Joanna Weinberg, eds. *The Mishnaic Moment: Jewish Law Among Jews and Christians in Early Modern Europe.* Oxford: Oxford University Press, 2022.
Braiterman, Zachary J. 'Maimonides and the Visual Image after Kant and Cohen.' *Journal of Jewish Thought and Philosophy* 20, no. 2 (2012): 217–30.
Breger, Jennifer. 'Printers.' In *The Shalvi/Hyman Encyclopedia of Jewish Women.* December 31, 1999. Jewish Women's Archive. http://jwa.org/encyclopedia/article/printers. Accessed November 8, 2022.
Brill, Yeḥiel, ed. *Perush 'al Masekhet Rosh ha-Shanah.* Paris, 1865.
Briquet, C. M. *Les Filigranes: Dictionnaire Historique des Marques du Papier dès Leur Apparition Vers 1282 Jusqu'en 1600. A Facsimile of the 1907 Edition With Supplementary Material Contributed by a Number of Scholars*, edited by Allan Stevenson. Amsterdam: Paper Publications Society, 1968.
Brown, Jeremy. *New Heavens and a New Earth: The Jewish Reception of Copernican Thought.* Oxford: Oxford University Press, 2013.
Burnett, Stephen G. *From Christian Hebraism to Jewish Studies: Johannes Buxtorf (1564–1629) and Hebrew Learning in the Seventeenth Century.* Leiden: Brill, 1996.
Busi, Giulio and Silvana Greco, eds. *The Renaissance Speaks Hebrew.* Milan: Silvana editoriale, 2019.
Carlebach, Elisheva. *Palaces of Time: Jewish Calendar and Culture in Early Modern Europe.* Cambridge, MA: Belknap Press of Harvard University Press, 2011.

Cattaneo, Marcello. 'Between Law and Antiquarianism: The Christian Study of Maimonides' Mishneh Torah in Late Seventeenth-Century Europe.' In *The Mishnaic Moment: Jewish Law Among Jews and Christians in Early Modern Europe*, edited by Piet van Boxel, Kirsten Macfarlane, and Joanna Weinberg, 237–54. Oxford: Oxford University Press, 2022.

Chabás, José, and Bernard R. Goldstein. *Astronomy in the Iberian Peninsula: Abraham Zacut and the Transition from Manuscript to Print*. Philadelphia, PA: American Philosophical Society, 2000.

Chevlowe, Susan. *Common Man Mythic Vision: The Paintings of Ben Shahn*. New York: Princeton University Press, 1998.

Cohen, Evelyn M. 'The Art of the 1349 *Guide for the Perplexed*: The Scribe, the Artist, the Censors, the Owners.' In *The Austrian Guide for the Perplexed 1349: An Illuminated Manuscript in Hebrew, by the Scribe Jacob ben Samuel Nachlieb [Krems, Austria]*, 13–50. Alon Shvut: Antiquariat Meir Urbach, 2008.

Cohen, Jeremy. *The Friars and the Jews: The Evolution of Medieval Anti-Judaism*. Ithaca, NY: Cornell University Press, 1982.

Cohen, Oded. 'Eager to Belong: A Palestinian Jew in Eighteenth-Century Amsterdam.' *Studia Rosenthaliana* 46 (2020): 211–28.

Cohen, Richard. *Jewish Icons: Art and Society in Modern Europe*. Berkeley, CA: University of California Press, 1998.

Conforte, David. *Koreh ha-Dorot*. Piotrków: Aharon Valden, 1895.

David, Avraham. *The Great Eagle at the JNUL: The Works of Moses Maimonides from the Treasures of the Jewish National and University Library*. Jerusalem: JNUL, 2004.

Davidson, Herbert A. 'Further on a Problematic Passage in "Guide for the Perplexed" 2.24.' *Maimonidean Studies* 4 (2000): 1–13.

— *Moses Maimonides: The Man and His Works*. Oxford: Oxford University Press, 2005.

Davidson, Israel. *Thesaurus of Medieval Hebrew Poetry (= Otsar ha-Shirah ve-ha-Piyut)*. 4 vols. New York: Jewish Theological Seminary of America, 1924.

Davis, Joseph. 'The Reception of the *Shulhan 'Arukh* and the Formation of Ashkenazic Jewish Identity.' *AJS Review* 26, no. 2 (2002): 251–76.

Derrida, Jacques, *Acts of Religion*. Edited by Gil Anidjar. New York: Routledge, 2002.

Dienstag, Jacob I. 'Christian Translators of Maimonides' "Mishneh Torah" into Latin: A Bio-Bibliographical Study.' In *Salo Wittmayer Baron Jubilee Volume*, edited by Saul Lieberman and Arthur Hyman, vol. 1, 287–309. Jerusalem: American Academy for Jewish Research, 1974.

— 'Maimonides' Guide and Sefer HaMadda in Hasidic Literature' [Hebrew]. In *Abraham Weiss Jubilee Volume*, 307–30. New York: Yeshiva University Press, 1964.

— 'Maimonides' Treatise on Resurrection: Bibliography of Editions, Translations and Studies, Revised Edition.' In Jacob I. Dienstag, *Eschatology in Maimonidean Thought: Messianism, Resurrection and The World to Come*, 226–41. New York: Ktav, 1983.

— '*Mishneh Torah le-ha-Rambam: Bibliyografiyah shel Hotsa'ot*.' In *Studies in Jewish Bibliography, History and Literature in Honor of I. Edward Kiev*, edited by Charles Berlin, 21–108 (Hebrew section). New York: Ktav, 1971.

— 'Rambam or Maimonides; Unity or Duality. A Bibliographical Survey.' In *Hazon Nahum: Studies Presented to Dr. Norman Lamm in Honor of His Seventieth Birthday*, edited by Yaakov Elman and Jeffrey S. Gurock, 129–48. New York: Yeshiva University Press, 1997.

— *Studies in Maimonides and St. Thomas Aquinas*. New York: Ktav, 1975.

— 'Yaḥasam shel Ba'ale ha-Tosafot le-ha-Rambam.' In *Sefer ha-Yovel li-Khevod Shemu'el Kalman Mirski*, edited by Simon Bernstein and Gershon Churgin, 350–79. New York: Va'ad ha-Yovel, 1958.

Dunkelgrün, Theodor. 'Like a Blind Man Judging Colors: Jospeph Athias and Johannes Leusden Defend Their 1667 Hebrew Bible.' *Studia Rosenthaliana* 44 (2012): 79–115.

Dweck, Yaacob. *Dissident Rabbi: The Life of Jacob Sasportas*. Princeton, NJ: Princeton University Press, 2019.

Efros, Israel. 'Maimonides' Treatise of Logic (Makalah Fi-Sina'at al-Mantik).' *American Academy for Jewish Research* 8 (1938).

Eijk, Philip J. van der. *Medicine and Philosophy in Classical Antiquity*. Cambridge: Cambridge University Press, 2005.

Elior, Ofer. *A Spirit of Grace Passed Before My Face: Jews, Science and Reading, 1210–1896* [Hebrew]. Jerusalem: Mekhon Ben-Tsevi, 2016.

Enelow, H. G. 'Isaac Belinfante – an Eighteenth Century Bibliophile.' In *Studies in Jewish Bibliography and Related Subjects in Memory of Abraham Solomon Freidus (1867–1923)*, 5–30. New York, 1929.

Eybeschütz, Jonathan. *Bene Ahuvah.* Prague: Gabriel Eibeschitz, 1819.

Faierstein, Morris M. 'The Maimonidean Menorah and Contemporary Habad Messianism: A Reconsideration,' *Modern Judaism* 32, no. 3 (2012): 323–34.

Fenton, Paul B. 'Abraham Maimonides (1186–1237): Founding a Mystical Dynasty.' In *Jewish Mystical Leaders and Leadership in the 13th Century*, edited by Moshe Idel and Mortimer Ostow, 127–54. Northvale, NJ: Jason Aronson, 1998.

— 'Maimonides – Father and Son: Continuity and Change.' In *Traditions of Maimonideanism*, edited by Carlos Fraenkel, 103–37. Leiden: Brill, 2009.

— 'A Muslim Polemic in Yemen Against Maimonides' [Hebrew]. In *Le-Rosh Yosef: Texts and Studies in Judaism*, edited by Yosef Tobi, 409–34. Jerusalem: Afikim, 1995.

Fine, Steven. *The Menorah: From the Bible to Modern Israel.* Cambridge, MA: Harvard University Press, 2016.

Fishman, Y. 'Sakh ha-kol shel Ḥagigot ha-Rambam be-Cordoba.' *Haaretz*, May 20, 1935.

Forte, Doron. 'Back to the Sources: Alternative Versions of Maimonides' Letter to Samuel Ibn Tibbon and Their Neglected Significance.' *Jewish Studies Quarterly* 23 (2016): 47–90.

Fraenkel, Sara. 'Who was the Falsificator of Judith Rozanis in Lemberg?' [Hebrew]. *Proceedings of the Ninth World Congress of Jewish Studies*, Division D, vol. 1, 175–82. Jerusalem, 1985.

Fraisse, Otfried. 'Die Abwesenheit des Maimonides im Denken Franz Rosenzweigs oder: Zwischen Erfahrung und Interpretation.' In *Moses Maimonides (1138–1204): His Religious, Scientific, and Philosophical* Wirkungsgeschichte *in Different Cultural Contexts*, edited by Görge K. Hasselhoff and Otfried Fraisse, 397–425. Würzburg: Ergon, 2004.

Franklin, Arnold E. 'Jewish Religious and Communal Organization.' In *The Cambridge History of Judaism: Volume 5, Jews in the Medieval Islamic World*, edited by Phillip I. Lieberman, 450–83. Cambridge: Cambridge University Press, 2021.

— 'The Mystery of Maimonides' Puzzling Name.' *Mosaic*, May 5, 2020. https://mosaicmagazine.com/observation/religion-holidays/2020/05/the-mystery-of-maimonides-puzzling-name/. Accessed November 8, 2022.

Freedlander, A. A. 'Maimonides' 800th Birthday.' *The Sentinel*, March 28, 1935.

Freidenreich, David M. *Foreigners and their Food: Constructing Otherness in Jewish, Christian and Islamic Law.* Berkeley: University of California Press, 2011.

— 'Fusion Cooking in an Islamic Milieu: Jewish and Christian Jurists on Food associated with Foreigners.' In *Beyond Religious Borders: Interaction and Intellectual Exchange in the Medieval Islamic World*, edited by David M. Freidenreich and Miriam Goldstein, 144–60. Philadelphia: University of Pennsylvania Press, 2012.

Freimann, Abraham H., ed. *Teshuvot ha-Rambam.* Jerusalem, 1934.

Freimann, Aron, ed. *Sefer Ma'agal Tov ha-Shalem ve-hu Sipur Masa'ot ha-Rav Ḥayim Yosef David Azulai z'l Asher Nase ve-Savav be-Artsot Shonot.* Jerusalem: Mekitse Nirdamim, 1934.

Freimann, Aron, and Moses Marx, eds. *Thesaurus Typographiae Hebraicae Saeculi XV – Hebrew Printing in the Fifteenth Century.* A Facsimile Reproduction of the Edition 1924–31. Jerusalem: Universitas-Booksellers, 1968.

Friedenberg, Albert M. 'American Jewish Seminaries.' *The Hebrew Standard*, June 2, 1922.

Friedlaender, Israel. 'Ein Gratulationsbrief an Maimonides.' In *Festschrift zu Hermann Cohens siebzigstem Geburtstage*, 257–64. Berlin: Bruno Cassirer, 1912.

Friedman, Mordechai A. 'In Your Lifetime and in the Lifetime of our Lord Moses Maimonides.' *Zion* 62 (1997): 75–78.

— *Maimonides, the Yemenite Messiah, and Apostasy* [Hebrew]. Jerusalem: Ben-Zvi Institute, 2002.

Fuchs, Uziel. 'Iyunim be-Sefer Or Zaru'a le-R. Yitsḥak ben Mosheh me-Vienna.' M.A. thesis, Hebrew University, Jerusalem, 1993.

Fuks, L. and R. G. Fuks-Mansfeld. *Hebrew Typography in the Northern Netherlands 1585–1815: Historical Evaluation and Descriptive Bibliography.* Leiden: Brill, 1987.

Fumagalli, Pier Francesco. *Da Mosè a Mosè. Maimonide fra tradizione e modernità.* Milan: Biblioteca Ambrosiana, 2004.

Gail, Debra Glasberg. 'The 'Agur: A Halakhic Code for Print.' *AJS Review* 45, no. 1 (2021): 1–23.

Gaimani, Aharon. *Changes in the Heritage of Yemenite Jewry* [Hebrew]. Ramat Gan: Bar-Ilan University, 2005.

Galinsky, Judah. 'The Significance of Form: R. Moses of Coucy's Reading Audience and His Sefer ha-Miẓvot.' *AJS Review* 35 (2011): 293–321.

Gampel, Benjamin. *Anti-Jewish Riots in the Crown of Aragon and the Royal Response, 1391–1392.* Cambridge: Cambridge University Press, 2016.

Gavra, Moshe. *Entsiklopediyah le-Ḥakhme Teman.* 2 vols. Bene Berak: ha-Makhon le-Ḥeker Ḥakhme Teman, 2001–2003.

— *Meḥkarim be-Sidure Teman.* Bene Berak: ha-Makhon le-Ḥeker Ḥakhme Teman, 2010.

— *Shemot ha-Mishpaḥah shel ha-Yehudim be-Teman.* Bene Berak: ha-Makhon le-Ḥeker Ḥakhme Teman, 2014.

Ghirondi, Mordecai Samuel. *Toledot Gedole Yisrael u-Ge'one Italyah.* Trieste: Tipografia Marenigh, 1853.

Giller, Pinchas. *Reading the Zohar: The Sacred Text of the Kabbalah.* Oxford: Oxford University Press, 2001.

Ginzberg, Louis. *The Legends of the Jews.* Translated by Henrietta Szold. Philadelphia, PA: Jewish Publication Society of America, 1942.

Goff, Frederick R. *Incunabula in American Libraries: A Third Census of Fifteenth-Century Books Recorded in North American Collections.* New York: Bibliographical Society of America, 1964.

Goitein, S. D. 'A Jewish Addict to Sufism: In the Time of the Nagid David II Maimonides.' *Jewish Quarterly Review* 44, no. 1 (1953): 37–49.

Goldish, Matt. *Judaism in the Theology of Sir Isaac Newton.* Dordrecht: Kluwer Academic, 1998.

Goshen-Gottstein, Moshe. 'The Authenticity of the Aleppo Codex.' *Textus* 1 (1960): 17–58.

Gottlieb, Michah. 'Counter-Enlightenment in a Jewish Key: Anti-Maimonideanism in Nineteenth-Century Orthodoxy,' In *The Cultures of Maimonideanism*, edited by James T. Robinson, 259–87. Leiden: Brill, 2009.

Gottlieb, Yaakov. *Sikhletanut bi-Levush Ḥasidi: Demuto shel ha-Rambam be-Ḥasidut Ḥabad.* Ramat Gan: Bar-Ilan University Press, 2009.

Grafton, Anthony, and Joanna Weinberg, *'I have always loved the Holy Tongue': Isaac Casaubon, the Jews, and a Forgotten Chapter in Renaissance Scholarship.* Cambridge, MA: Harvard University Press, 2011.

Green, Abigail. *Moses Montefiore: Jewish Liberator, Imperial Hero.* Cambridge, MA: Harvard University Press, 2010.

Gross, William, Orly Tzion, and Falk Wiesemann, eds. *Catalog of Catalogs: A Bibliography of Temporary Exhibition Catalogs since 1876 that Contain Items of Judaica.* Leiden: Brill, 2019.

Grossman, Avraham. 'From Andalusia to Europe: The Attitude of Rabbis in Germany and France in the Twelfth-Thirteenth Centuries towards the Halakhic Writings of Alfasi and Maimonides' [Hebrew]. *Pe'amim* 80 (1999): 14–32.

Guerrini, Maria Teresa. 'New Documents on Samuel Usque, the Author of the *Consolaçam as tribulaçoens de Israel*.' *Sefarad* 61, no. 1 (2001): 83–89.

Habermann, Abraham M. *Giovanni di Gara: Printer, Venice 1564–1610* [Hebrew]. [Israel]: Mekhon Haberman le-Meḥḳere Sifrut, 1982.

— 'Ha-madpisim bene R. Ya'akov Parenzo be-Vinetsiyah.' *Areshet* 1 (1959): 61–90.

— *Nashim 'Ivriyot be-Tor Madpisot Mesadrot Motsi'ot la-Or ve-Tomkhot ba-Meḥaberim.* Berlin: R. Mas, 1933.

— *The Printer Cornelio Adel Kind, His Son Daniel and a List of Books Printed by Them* [Hebrew]. Jerusalem: R. Mas, 1980.

— *The Printer Daniel Bomberg and the List of Books Published by His Press* [Hebrew]. Safed: ha-Muze'on le-omanut ha-defus, 1978.

Halberstam, S. J. *Kohelet Shelomoh.* Vienna: A. Fanto, 1890.

Halbertal, Moshe. *Maimonides: Life and Thought.* Translated by Joel Linsider. Princeton, NJ: Princeton University Press, 2014.

Halbertal, Moshe, and Avishai Margolit. *Idolatry.* Translated by Naomi Goldblum. Cambridge, MA: Harvard University Press, 1992.

Halkin, Abraham. 'Ma'amar Teḥiyat ha-Metim le-Rambam be-Targumo shel R. Yehudah al-Ḥarizi.' *Kobez al Yad* 9 (1980): 129–50.

Hallamish, Moshe. 'On Maimonides' Status in the Writings of the Safed Kabbalists' [Hebrew]. *Daat: A Journal of Philosophy & Kabbalah* 64–66 (2009): 219–34.

Harris, Jay M. 'The Image of Maimonides in Nineteenth-Century Jewish Historiography.' *Proceedings of the American Academy for Jewish Research* 54 (1987): 117–39.

Harris, Monford. 'The Theologico-Historical Thinking of Samuel David Luzzatto.' *Jewish Quarterly Review* 52, nos. 3/4 (1962): 216–44, 309–34.

Harvey, Warren Zev. 'Maimonides' Critique of Anthropocentrism and Teleology.' In *Maimonides' Guide of the Perplexed: A Critical Guide*, edited by Daniel Frank and Aaron Segal, 209–22. Cambridge: Cambridge University Press, 2021.

— 'Michael Friedländer's Pioneering English Translation of the Guide.' In *Maimonides' 'Guide of the Perplexed' in Translation: A History from the Thirteenth Century to the Twentieth*, edited by Josef Stern, James T. Robinson, and Yonatan Shemesh, 209–24. Chicago: University of Chicago Press, 2019.

— 'The Return of Maimonideanism.' *Jewish Social Studies* 42, nos. 3/4 (1980): 249–68.

Havatzelet, Meir, ed. *Midrash ha-Ḥefets 'al Ḥamishah Ḥumshe Torah* [Zechariah ben Solomon ha-Rofeh]. Jerusalem: Mossad Harav Kook, 1981.

Havatzelet, Meir, and Yosef Tobi, eds. *Sho'el u-Meshiv: Perush Midrashi Alegori 'al ha-Torah ve'al ha-Aftarayot: Teman ha-Me'ah ha-15*. Tel Aviv, 2006.

Haxen, Ulf. *Manuscripts and Printed Books from the Collection of The Royal Library Copenhagen*. New York: The Jewish Museum, 1983

Heller, Marvin J. 'Earliest Printings of the Talmud.' In *Printing the Talmud: From Bomberg to Schottenstein*, edited by Sharon Liberman Mintz and Gabriel M. Goldstein, 61–78. New York: Yeshiva University Museum, 2005.

— 'Israel ben Abraham, His Hebrew Printing-Press in Wandsbeck and the Books He Published.' In Marvin J. Heller, *Further Studies in the Making of the Early Hebrew Book*, 169–93. Leiden: Brill, 2013.

— *Printing the Talmud: A History of the Individual Treatises Printed From 1700 to 1750*. Leiden: Brill, 1999.

— 'Sibling Rivalry: Simultaneous Editions of Hebrew Books.' *Quntres* 2, no. 1 (2011): 22–36.

— *The Sixteenth-Century Hebrew Book: An Abridged Thesaurus*. Leiden: Brill, 2004.

— *Studies in the Making of the Early Hebrew Book*. Leiden: Brill, 2008.

Hellerstein, Kathryn. *A Question of Tradition: Women Poets in Yiddish, 1586–1987*. Stanford, CA: Stanford University Press, 2014.

Henshke, David. 'Maimonides as His Own Commentator' [Hebrew]. *Sefunot* 8 (23) (2003): 117–63.

Herman, Marc. 'Situating Maimonides's Approach to the Oral Torah in Its Andalusian Context.' *Jewish History* 31, nos. 1–2 (2017): 31–46.

Heschel, Abraham Joshua. *Maimonides*. Judentum in Geschichte und Gegenwart. Berlin: Erich Reiss, 1935.

Hill, Brad Sabin. 'A Catalogue of Hebrew Printers.' *British Library Journal* 21 (1995): 34–65.

— *Hebraica (saec. X AD saec. XVI): Manuscripts and Early Printed Books from the Library of the Valmadonna Trust: An Exhibition at the Pierpont Morgan Library, New York*. [London]: Valmadonna Trust Library, 1989.

— 'Hebrew Printing on Blue and Other Coloured Papers.' In *Treasures of the Valmadonna Trust Library: A Catalogue of 15th-Century Printing and Five Centuries of Deluxe Hebrew Printing*, edited by David Sclar, 84–111. London and New York: Valmadonna Trust Library, 2011.

Hirschfeld, Hartwig. *Descriptive Catalogue of the Hebrew Manuscripts of the Montefiore Library*. London: Macmillan, 1904.

Huss, Boaz. *The Zohar: Reception and Impact*. Translated by Yudith Nave. London: Littman Library of Jewish Civilization, 2016.

Iakerson, Shimon. *Catalogue of Hebrew Incunabula from the Collection of the Library of the Jewish Theological Seminary of America*. New York and Jerusalem: Jewish Theological Seminary of America, 2004–2005.

Idel, Moshe. 'Maimonides and Kabbalah.' In *Studies in Maimonides*, edited by Isadore Twersky, 31–79. Cambridge, MA: Harvard University Press, 1990.

Isserles, Moses. *She[e'lot] u-T[eshuvot]ha-Rema*. Edited by Asher Siev. Jerusalem: Mossad Harav Kook, 2018.

Ivry, Alfred L. 'Salomon Munk and the Science of Judaism Meet Maimonides.' In *Moses Maimonides (1138–1204): His Religious, Scientific, and Philosophical* Wirkungsgeschichte *in Different Cultural Contexts*, edited by Görge K. Hasselhoff and Otfried Fraisse, 479–89. Würzburg: Ergon, 2004.

Jacobs, Louis. 'Attitudes of the Kabbalists and Hasidim towards Maimonides.' *The Solomon Goldman Lectures* 5 (1990): 45–55.

Jefferson, Rebecca J. W. *The Cairo Genizah and the Age of Discovery in Egypt: The History and Provenance of a Jewish Archive*. London: I. B. Tauris, 2022.

Kafiḥ, Yosef. *Halikhot Teman*. Edited by Yisrael Yeshayahu. Jerusalem: Ben-Zvi Institute, 2002.

— *Kitab al-Ḥaka'ik: Sefer ha-Amitiyot le-Eḥad me-Ḥakhme Tsa'dah, Teman, ha-Me'ah ha-14*. Tel-Aviv: Afikim, 1997.

— (ed.) *Sefer Bustan al-'Uqul*. Jerusalem: ha-Agudah le-Hatsalat Ginzei Teman, 1953/4.

Kalman, Ruthie. 'What is Venus Doing in the 1574–1576 Hebrew Edition of Maimonides' *Mishneh Torah*?' [Hebrew]. *Pe'amim* 120 (2009): 61–91.

Kanarfogel, Ephraim. 'Assessing the (Non-) Reception of Mishneh Torah in Medieval Ashkenaz.' In *'In the Dwelling of a Sage Lie Precious Treasures': Essays in Jewish Studies in Honor of Shnayer Z. Leiman*, edited by Yitzhak Berger and Chaim Milikowsky, 123–45. Brooklyn, NY: Ktav, 2020.

— 'Between Ashkenaz and Sefarad: Tosafist Teachings in the Talmudic Commentaries of Ritva.' In *Between Rashi and Maimonides: Themes in Medieval Jewish Thought, Literature, and Exegesis*, edited by Ephraim Kanarfogel and Moshe Sokolow, 237–73. New York: Ktav, 2010.

— *The Intellectual History and Rabbinic Culture of Medieval Ashkenaz*. Detroit, MI: Wayne State University Press, 2013.

— *'Peering through the Lattices': Mystical, Magical, and Pietistic Dimensions in the Tosafist Period*. Detroit, MI: Wayne State University Press, 2000.

— 'The Popularization of Jewish Legal and Customary Literature in Germanic Lands during the Thirteenth Century.' In *Jüdische Kultur in den SchUM-Städten*, edited by Karl E. Grözinger 233–45. Weisbaden: Harrassowitz, 2014.

— 'Rabbinic Attitudes toward Nonobservance in the Medieval Period.' In *Jewish Tradition and the Non-traditional Jew*, edited by J. J. Schacter, 3–36. Northvale, NJ: Jason Aronson, 1990.

Kanarfogel, Ephraim, and Moshe Sokolow. 'Rashi and Maimonides Meet in a Genizah Fragment: A Reference to "Mishneh Torah" in a Letter from a Tosafist' [Hebrew]. *Tarbiz* 67 (1998): 411–16.

Kaplan, Yosef. *An Alternative Path to Modernity: The Sephardi Diaspora in Western Europe*. Leiden: Brill, 2000.

Karo, Joseph. *She'elot u-Teshuvot Avkat Rokhel*. Edited by David Avitan. Jerusalem: Siah Yisrael, 2002.

— *She'elot u-Teshuvot Bet Yosef*, with introduction by Bezalel Landau. Jerusalem: n.p., 1960.

Karp, Abraham. *From the Ends of the Earth: Judaic Treasures of the Library of Congress*. Washington, DC: Library of Congress, 1991.

Kasher, Menahem M. *Mefa'aneaḥ Tsefunot*. New York: Mekhon Tsafnat Pane'aḥ, 1959.

Kassel, David, ed. *Teshuvot Geonim Kadmonim*. Berlin: Aryeh Leib Zarinzansky, 1848.

Katz, Maya Balakirsky. 'Trademarks of Faith: "Chabad and Chanukah in America."' *Modern Judaism* 29, no. 2 (2009): 239–67.

Kayserling, Meyer. *Biblioteca Española-Portugueza-Judaica: Dictionnaire Bibliographique des Aueurs Juifs, de Leurs Ouvrages Espagnols et Portugais et des Oeuvres sur et Contre les Juifs et le Judaïsme*. Strasbourg: Charles J. Trubner, 1890.

Kellner, Menachem. *Dogma in Medieval Jewish Thought*. Oxford: Oxford University Press, 1986.

— *Maimonides on the 'Decline of the Generations' and the Nature of Rabbinic Authority*. Albany, NY: State University of New York Press, 1996.

Kobler, Franz, ed. *A Treasury of Jewish Letters: Letters from the Famous and the Humble*. 2 vols. Philadelphia, PA: Jewish Publication Society of America, 1953.

Kohler, George Y. *Reading Maimonides' Philosophy in 19th Century Germany: The Guide to Religious Reform*. Heidelberg: Springer, 2012.

Kollek, Teddy, and Moshe Pearlman. *Pilgrims to the Holy Land: The Story of Pilgrimage through the Ages*. New York: Harper and Row, 1970.

Kook, Abraham Isaac. *Igerot ha-Re'iyah*. Jerusalem: Mossad Harav Kook, 1962.

— *Ma'amre ha-Re'iyah*. Jerusalem, 1984.

Kozodoy, Maud. 'Prefatory Verse and the Reception of the *Guide of the Perplexed*.' *Jewish Quarterly Review* 106, no. 3 (2016): 257–82.

Kraemer, Joel L. *Maimonides: The Life and World of One of Civilization's Greatest Minds*. New York: Doubleday, 2008.

Kreisel, Howard. 'Maimonides on Christianity and Islam.' In *Jewish Civilization, Essays and Studies* vol. 3, edited by Ronald A. Brauner, 153–62. Philadelphia: Reconstructionist Rabbinical College, 1985.

Lamm, Norman. 'The Religious Implications of Extraterrestrial Life.' *Tradition* 7 (1965): 5–56.

Langermann, Tzvi. 'Igeret R. Shemu'el ben 'Ali be-'Inyan Teḥiyat ha-Metim.' *Kobez al Yad* 15 (2001): 39–94.

— 'Maimonides' Repudiation of Astrology.' *Maimonidean Studies* 2 (1991): 123–58.

— 'A New Look at *Ma'amar ha-Yihud*, Attributed to Moses Maimonides' [Hebrew]. *Tarbiz* 65 (1996): 109–28.

— 'Sharḥ al-Dalāla: A Commentary to Maimonides' *Guide* from Fourteenth-Century Yemen.' In *Cultures of Maimonideanism*, edited by James T. Robinson, 155–76. Leiden: Brill, 2009.

— 'The "True Perplexity": The *Guide of the Perplexed*, Part II, Chapter 24.' In *Perspectives on Maimonides: Philosophical and Historical Studies*, edited by Joel L. Kraemer, 159–74. Oxford: Littman Library of Jewish Civilization, 1991.
— *Yemenite Midrash: Philosophical Commentaries on the Torah*. New York: Harper Collins, 1996.
— 'Yemenite Philosophical Midrash as a Source for the Intellectual History of the Jews of Yemen.' In *The Jews of Medieval Islam*, edited by Daniel Frank, 335–47. Leiden: Brill, 1992.
Lasker, Daniel J. *From Judah Hadassi to Elijah Bashyatchi: Studies in Late Medieval Karaite Philosophy*. Leiden: Brill, 2008.
— *Karaism: An Introduction to the Oldest Surviving Alternative Judaism*. London: Littman Library of Jewish Civilization, 2022.
— 'Maimonides and the Karaites: From Critic to Cultural Hero.' In *Maimónides y su época*, edited by Carlos del Valle Rodriguez et al., 311–25. Madrid: Sociedad Estatal de Conmemoraciones Culturales, 2007.
— 'Tradition and Innovation in Maimonides' Attitude toward Other Religions.' In *Maimonides after 800 Years: Essays on Maimonides and his Influence*, edited by Jay M. Harris, 167–82. Cambridge, MA: Harvard University Center for Jewish Studies, 2007.
Lehman, James H. 'Maimonides, Mendelssohn, and the Me'asfim.' *Leo Baeck Institute Yearbook* 20 (1975): 87–108.
Leicht, Reimund. 'Neu-orientierung an Maimonides?' In *Orient – Orientalistik – Orientalismus. Geschichte und Aktualität einer Debatte*, edited by Burkhard Schnepel et al., 93–121. Bielefeld: transcript, 2011.
Leicht, Reimund, and Gad Freudenthal, eds. *Studies on Steinschneider: Moritz Steinschneider and the Emergence of the Science of Judaism in Nineteenth-Century Germany*. Leiden: Brill, 2012.
Lerner, Ralph. 'Maimonides' Letter on Astrology.' *History of Religions* 8, no. 2 (1968): 143–58.
Levin, Leonard. *Seeing with Both Eyes: Ephraim Luntshitz and the Polish-Jewish Renaissance*. Supplements to *The Journal of Jewish Thought and Philosophy*, vol. 2. Leiden: Brill, 2008.
Levinas, Emmanuel. 'The Contemporary Relevance of Maimonides (1935).' *The Journal of Jewish Thought and Philosophy* 16, no. 1 (2008): 91–94.
Lewis, Bernard. 'Maimonides, Lionheart, and Saladin.' *Erets-Yisrael* 7 (1964): 70–75.
Loewe, Herbert. *Catalogue of the Manuscripts in the Hebrew Character Collected and Bequeathed to Trinity College Library By the Late William Aldis Wright*. Cambridge: at the University Press, 1926.
Loewe, Louis, ed. *Diaries of Sir Moses and Lady Montefiore: comprising their life and work as recorded in their diaries from 1812 to 1883 ...* Chicago: Belford-Clarke Co., 1890.
Loewenthal, Naftali. 'The Image of Maimonides in Habad Hasidism.' In *Traditions of Maimonideanism*, edited by Carlos Fraenkel, 277–312. Leiden: Brill, 2009.
Luria, Solomon. *Yam Shel Shelomoh*. Edited by Daniel Biton. Jerusalem: Hamaor Institute, 2017.
Magnin, Edgar F. *The Warner Murals in the Wilshire Boulevard Temple*. Los Angeles: Wilshire Boulevard Temple, 1974.
Mahrer, Stefanie. 'Texts and Objects: The Books of the Schocken Publishing House in the Context of their Time.' In *The German-Hebrew Dialogue: Studies of Encounter and Exchange*, edited by Rachel Seelig and Amir Eshel, 121–41. Berlin: De Gruyter, 2017.
Maimon, J. L. 'Akdamot Milin.' *Sinai* 36 (1955): 275–357.
Maimonides, Moses. *Books of Commandments: Arabic Original with New Translation and Commentary*. Edited and translated by Yosef Kafiḥ. Jerusalem: Mossad Harav Kook, 1971.
— *The Guide of the Perplexed*. Translated by Shlomo Pines. Chicago: University of Chicago Press, 1963.
— *Mishnah 'im Perush Rabenu Mosheh ben Maimon: Makor ve-Targum*. Edited and translated by Yosef Kafiḥ. Jerusalem: Mossad Harav Kook, 1963.
— *Mishneh Torah: New Edition with Traditional Commentaries*, 5 vols. New York: Shulsinger Bros., 1947.
— *Moreh Nevukhim*. Translated by Michael Schwarz. Tel Aviv: Tel Aviv University, 2002.
— *Rabbi Moshe ben Maimon (Maimonides) Code of Jewish Law (Mishne-Torah) Ed. Constantinople 1509*, 4 vols. With introduction by S. Z. Havlin. Jerusalem: Makor, 1973.
Mann, Vivian B., ed. *Jewish Texts on the Visual Arts*. Cambridge: Cambridge University Press, 2000.
Mann, Vivian B., Thomas F. Glick, and Jerrilynn D. Dodds, eds. *Convivencia: Jews, Muslims, and Christians in Medieval Spain*. New York: George Braziller and The Jewish Museum, 1992.
Marcus, Ivan. *Sefer Ḥasidim and the Ashkenazic Book in Medieval Europe*. Philadelphia, PA: University of Pennsylvania Press, 2018.
Margoliouth, G. 'Responses of Maimonides in the Original Arabic.' *Jewish Quarterly Review* 11 (1899): 533–550.

Marmur, Michael. 'Heschel's Two Maimonides.' *Jewish Quarterly Review* 98, no. 2 (2008): 230–54.
Marx, Alexander. 'The Correspondence between the Rabbis of Southern France and Maimonides about Astrology.' *Hebrew Union College Annual* III (1926): 311–58.
Mayer, Yakov Z. *Editio Princeps: The 1523 Venice Edition of the Palestinian Talmud and the Beginning of Hebrew Printing* [Hebrew]. Jerusalem: Magnes Press, 2022.
Melamed, Ovadia. *Masoret ha-Tefilah ve-Shoresh ha-Minhag.* Jerusalem: Ovadia Melamed, 2000.
Metzger, David. 'Hagahot ha-Mabit 'al Sifro Kiryat Sefer.' *Moriah* 8 (1979): 14–28.
Metzger, Thérèse. 'Le manuscrit Norsa. Une copie Ashkenaze achevée en 1349 et enluminée du *Guide des égarés* de Maïmonide.' *Mitteilungen des Kunsthistorischen Instituts in Florenz* 46 (2002): 1–73.
Meyer, Michael. 'Maimonides and Some Moderns: European Images of the Rambam from the Eighteenth to the Twentieth Centuries.' *CCAR Journal* 44, no. 4 (1997): 4–15.
Meyerson, Mark D. *A Jewish Renaissance in Fifteenth-Century Spain.* Princeton, NJ: Princeton University Press, 2004.
Mishory, Alec. *Secularizing the Sacred: Aspects of Israeli Visual Culture.* Leiden: Brill, 2019.
Molin, Jacob. *She'elot u-Teshuvot Maharil.* Edited by Y. Satz. Jerusalem: Makhon Yerushalayim, 1979.
Morell, Samuel. *Studies in the Judicial Methodology of Rabbi David Ibn Abi Zimra.* Studies in Judaism. Dallas, TX: University Press of America, 2004.
Mortara, Marco. *Mazkeret Ḥakhme Italiyah.* Padua: F. Sacchetto, 1886.
Moscone, Marcello. 'The "Norsa Codex" of Maimonides's *Guide for the Perplexed.*' In *Il Codice Maimonides e I Norsa: una famiglia nella Mantova dei Gonzaga: banche, libri, quadri*, edited by Cristina Farnetti, 36–51. Rome: Ministero per i Bene e le Attività Culturali, 2018.
Munk, Salomon Munk. *Le Guide des égarés.* Paris: A. Franck, 1856–1866.
Muntner, Süssman, ed. *Pirke Mosheh bi-Refuah be-Targumo shel R. Natan ha-Me'ati, yotsim la-or bi-shelemutam 'al pi kitve yad.* Jerusalem: Mossad Harav Kook, 1959.
— 'Rabenu Mosheh ben Maimon Ma'amar 'al Ḥizuk Ko'aḥ ha-Gavra.' In *Ketavim Refu'iyim*, 4 vols., 4:34–65. Jerusalem: Mossad Harav Kook, 1965.
Nadav, Mordechai, and Raphael Weiser, eds. *Selected Manuscripts and Prints: An Exhibition from the Treasures of the Jewish National and University Libraries.* Jerusalem: Jewish National and University Library, 1985.
Nadler, Allan. 'The "Rambam Revival" in Early Modern Jewish Thought: Maskilim, Mitnagdim, and Hasidim on Maimonides' *Guide of the Perplexed.*' In *Maimonides After 800 Years: Essays on Maimonides and His Influence*, edited by Jay M. Harris, 231–56. Cambridge, MA: Harvard University Press, 2007.
Naor, Bezalel, ed. *Hasagot ha-Ra'avad le-Mishneh Torah: Mugah mi-Tokh 'Asarah Kitve-Yad.* Jerusalem: [n.p.], 1984.
Narkiss, Bezalel. *Hebrew Illuminated Manuscripts.* Jerusalem: Encyclopaedia Judaica, 1969.
Neubauer, Adolf. *Catalogue of the Hebrew Manuscripts in the Bodleian Library and in the College Libraries of Oxford.* Oxford: Clarendon Press, 1886–1906.
Nielsen, Bruce. 'Daniel van Bombergen, a Bookman of Two Worlds.' In *The Hebrew Book in Early Modern Italy*, edited by Joseph R. Hacker and Adam Shear, 56–75, 230–252. Philadelphia, PA: University of Pennsylvania Press, 2011.
Novak, David. 'The Treatment of Islam and Muslims in the Legal Writings of Maimonides.' In *Studies in Islamic and Judaic Traditions*, edited by William M. Brinner and Stephen D. Ricks, 233–50. Atlanta: Scholars Press, 1986.
Oegema, Gerbern S. 'The Uses of the Shield of David on Heraldic Seals and Flags, on Bible Manuscripts, Printer's Marks, and Ex Libris.' *Jewish Studies Quarterly* 5, no. 3 (1998): 241–53.
Offenberg, Adri K. *Catalogue of Books Printed in the XVth Century Now in the British Library: BMC Part XIII Hebraica.* Leiden: Brill, 2004.
— *A Choice of Corals: Facets of Fifteenth-Century Hebrew Printing.* Nieuwkoop: De Graaf, 1992.
— 'The First Printed Book Produced at Constantinople.' *Studia Rosenthaliana* 3 (1969): 96–112.
— *Hebrew Incunabula in Public Collections: A First International Census.* Nieuwkoop: De Graaf, 1990.
— 'The Printing History of the Constantinople Hebrew Incunable of 1493: A Mediterranean Voyage of Discovery.' *The British Library Journal* 22 (1996): 221–35.
Offenberg, Sara. 'The Human Face on the Divine Chariot: Jacob the Knight.' *TheTorah.com.* 2022. https://www.thetorah.com/article/the-human-face-on-the-divine-chariot-jacob-the-knight. Accessed November 9, 2022.

Olsen, Kare, and Carl Nordenfalk, eds. *Gyllene Böcker. Illuminerade medeltida handskrifter i dansk och svensk ägo* (Golden Books. Illuminated Medieval Manuscripts in Danish and Swedish Hands). Stockholm: Nationalmuseum Stockholm, 1952.

Peles, Israel Mordecai. 'Taglit: Ketav Yad Kadum shel Hagahot Maimoniyot - ke-Nusaḥ Defus Kushta.' *Yeshurun* 13 (2003): 744–87.

Penkower, Jordan S. 'The First Edition of the Hebrew Bible That Bomberg Published and the Beginning of His Publishing House' [Hebrew]. *Kiryat Sefer* 58 (1983): 586–604.

— 'Jacob Ben Ḥayyim and the Rise of the *Biblia Hebraica*.' Ph.D. diss., Hebrew University of Jerusalem, 1982.

— 'Rabbinic Bible.' In *Dictionary of Biblical Interpretation*, edited by John H. Hayes, 2 vols, 361a–64b. Nashville, TN: Abingdon, 1999.

Perush Rabenu Efrayim ben R. Shimshon 'al ha-Torah. Jerusalem: J. Klugmann & Sons, 1992.

Perushe R. Yosef Bekhor Shor 'al ha-Torah. Edited by Y. Nevo. Jerusalem: Mossad Harav Kook, 1994.

Peters, Madison C. 'Famous Jews of the 19th Century.' *The Hebrew Standard*, September 24, 1909.

Piccard, Gerhard. *Wasserzeichen Fabeltiere.* Stuttgart: W. Kohlhammer, 1980.

Piske R. Yeshayah di-Trani 'al Masekhet Shevu'ot. Edited by A. Y. Wertheimer. Jerusalem: Mekhon ha-Talmud ha-Yisra'eli ha-Shalem, 1996.

Popper, William. *The Censorship of Hebrew Books*, with introduction by Moshe Carmilly-Weinberger. New York, 1899, repr. New York: Ktav, 1969.

Poznanski, S. A. *Mavo 'al Ḥakhme Tsarefat Mefarshe ha-Mikra.* Warsaw: Mekitse Nirdamin, 1913.

Pribor, Gila. '"*Sefer ha-Zikuk" shel Dominico Yerushalmi.*' *Italia* 18 (2008): 7–302.

Rabbinovicz, Raphael Nathan. *Ma'amar 'al hadpasat ha-Talmud.* Edited by Abraham M. Habermann. Jerusalem: Mossad Harav Kook, 2006.

Ratzaby, Yehudah. 'Inyene dat be-fulmus ben Muslemim li-Yehudim be-Teman.' *Yeda 'Am* 14 (1970): 12–21.

— 'On the History of the Controversy over Kabbalah in Sana'a 1913–1914: A Letter by R. Sa'id ben Haim Alnadaf to his Brother R. Abraham' [Hebrew]. *Pe'amim* 88 (2001): 98–123.

Raz-Krakotzkin, Amnon. *The Censor, the Editor, and the Text: The Catholic Church and the Shaping of the Jewish Canon in the Sixteenth Century.* Translated by Jackie Feldman. Philadelphia, PA: University of Pennsylvania Press, 2007.

Richler, Benjamin, ed. *Hebrew Manuscripts in the Vatican Library: Catalogue* (Studi e testi 438), Palaegraph. and Codicolog. Malachi Beit-Arié and Nurit Pasternak. Vatican City: Biblioteca Apostolica Vaticano, 2008.

Rivkind, Isaac. 'Dikduke Sefarim.' *Kiryat Sefer* 4 (1927): 275–76.

— 'Dikduke Sefarim.' In *Alexander Marx Jubilee Volume on the Occasion of His Seventieth Birthday*, ed. Saul Lieberman, 404. New York: Jewish Theological Seminary of America, 1950.

Rodov, Ilia. *The Torah Ark in Renaissance Poland: A Jewish Revival of Classical Antiquity.* Leiden: Brill, 2013.

Roest, Meijer. *Catalog der Hebraica und Judaica aus der L. Rosenthal'schen Bibliothek.* 2 vols. Amsterdam: B.M. Israël, 1966.

Roling, Bernd. 'Conversio and Concordia: The "statera prudentum" of the Jewish Convert Paolo Ricci (d. 1541).' In *Cultures of Conversion*, edited by Jan N. Bremmer, Wout J. van Bekkum, and Arie L. Molendijk, 53–64. Leuven: Peeters, 2006.

Rosner, Fred, ed. *Maimonides' Commentary on the Aphorisms of Hippocrates.* Haifa: Maimonides Research Institute, 1987.

— *Maimonides' Treatises on Poisons, Hemorrhoids and Cohabitation.* Haifa: Maimonides Research Institute, 1984.

Roth, Cecil. *The History of the Jews of Italy.* Philadelphia, PA: Jewish Publication Society of America, 1946.

— *The Jews in the Renaissance.* Philadelphia, PA: Jewish Publication Society of America, 1964.

— 'The Marrano Press at Ferrara, 1552–1555.' *Modern Language Review* 38, no. 4 (1943): 307–17.

Roth, Pinchas. *In This Land: Jewish Life and Legal Culture in Late Medieval Provence.* Toronto: Pontifical Institute of Medieval Studies, 2021.

Russ-Fishbane, Elisha. *Judaism, Sufism, and the Pietists of Medieval Egypt: A Study of Abraham Maimonides and his Times.* Oxford: Oxford University Press, 2015.

Ryan, W. F. 'Maimonides in Muscovy: Medical Texts and Terminology.' *Journal of the Warburg and Courtauld Institutes* 51 (1988): 43–65.

Rypins, Stanley. 'The Ferrara Bible at Press.' *The Library* s5-X (1955): 244–69.

Sachs, M. J. L. *Ḥidushe ha-Rambam la-Talmud.* Jerusalem: Mekhon ha-Talmud ha-Yisra'eli ha-Shalem, 1963.

Sachs, Senior, ed. 'Hatimat Sefer Pirke Moshe la-Rambam.' *Ha-teḥiyah* 1, 35–38. Berlin: C. L. Fritzsche, 1850.

Sackson, Adrian. 'From Moses to Moses: Anthropomorphism and Divine Incorporeality in Maimonides's *Guide* and Mendelssohn's *Bi'ur.*' *Harvard Theological Review* 112, no. 2 (2019): 209–34.

Saperstein, Marc. 'The Conflict over the Rashba's Herem on Philosophical Study: A Political Perspective.' *Jewish History* 1, no. 2 (1986): 27–38.

Sari, Hananel. *Pitron Ḥidat ha-Nevukhim.* Ramat Gan: Lishkhat Rav ha-Kampus shel Universitat Bar-Ilan, 2011.

Sarna, Jonathan. *The American Jewish Experience.* New York: Holmes and Meier, 1986.

Sassoon, Solomon David. *A Comprehensive Study of the Autograph Manuscript of Maimonides' Commentary to the Mishnah.* Jerusalem, 1990.

— *Ohel Dawid: Descriptive Catalogue of the Hebrew and Samaritan Manuscripts in the Sassoon Library.* [Oxford]: Oxford University Press; London: Humphrey Milford, 1932.

Schapkow, Carsten. *Role Model and Countermodel: The Golden Age of Iberian Jewry and German Jewish Culture during the Era of Emancipation.* Translated by Corey Twitchell. New York: Lexington Books, 2015.

Schirmann, Jefim. *Studies in the History of Hebrew Poetry and Drama* [Hebrew]. Jerusalem: Bialik Institute, 1979.

Schlossberg, Eliezer. 'Yemenite Midrashic Literature: Between Old and New' [Hebrew]. *Jewish Studies* 54 (2019): 215–44.

Schmelzer, Menahem. 'Maimonides: The *Guide for the Perplexed.*' In *The Austrian Guide for the Perplexed 1349: An Illuminated Manuscript in Hebrew, by the Scribe Jacob ben Samuel Nachlieb [Krems, Austria]*, 1–11. Alon Shvut: Antiquariat Meir Urbach, 2008.

Schochet, Elijah. *Bach: Rabbi Joel Sirkes: His Life, Work and Times.* Jerusalem: Feldheim, 1971.

Scholem, Gershom. *Sabbatai Sevi: The Mystical Messiah.* Trans. R. J. Z. Werblowsky. Princeton: Princeton University Press, 1973.

Scholem, Gershom G. 'From Philosopher to Cabbalist (a Legend of the Cabbalists on Maimonides)' [Hebrew]. *Tarbiz* 6 (1935): 334–42.

Schwartz, Yitzchak. 'The Maimonides Portrait: An Appraisal of One of the World's Most Famous Pictures.' *Rambam Maimonides Medical Journal* 2 (2011): https://www.ncbi.nlm.nih.gov/pmc/articles/PMC3678793/#b7-rmmj-2-3-e0052. Accessed November 9, 2022.

Schwartz, Yossef. 'Persecution and the Art of Translation: Some New Evidence of the Latin Translation of the *Guide of the Perplexed.*' *Yod. Revue des études hébraiques et juives* 22 (2019): 49–77.

Sclar, David, ed. *Treasures of the Valmadonna Trust Library: A Catalogue of 15th-Century Books and Five Centuries of Deluxe Hebrew Printing.* New York: Valmadonna Trust Library, 2011.

Sed-Rajna, Gabrielle. 'Hebrew Illuminated Manuscripts from the Iberian Peninsula.' In *Convivencia: Jews, Muslims, and Christians in Medieval Spain*, edited by Vivian B. Mann, Thomas F. Glick, and Jerrilynn D. Dodds, 133–55. New York: George Braziller and The Jewish Museum, 1992.

Segre, Renata. *The Jews in Piedmont.* 3 vols. Jerusalem: Israel Academy of Sciences and Humanities; [Tel Aviv]: Tel Aviv University, 1986–1990.

Septimus, Bernard. *Hispano-Jewish Society in Transition.* Cambridge, MA: Harvard University Press, 1982.

— 'Petrus Alfonsi on the Cult at Mecca.' *Speculum* 56, no. 3 (1981): 517–33.

Shailat, Itzhak, ed. *Letters and Essays of Moses Maimonides* [Hebrew]. Jerusalem: Shailat Publishing, 1995.

Shalev-Eyni, Sarit. 'Maimonides's Illuminated Manuscripts.' In *Maimonides: A Legacy in Script*, 84–78. Jerusalem: The Israel Museum, 2018.

Shamir, Avner. *Christian Conceptions of Jewish Books: The Pfefferkorn Affair.* Copenhagen: Museum Tusculanum Press, 2011.

Shapiro, Marc B. *Changing the Immutable: How Orthodox Judaism Rewrites Its History.* Oxford: Littman Library of Jewish Civilization, 2015.

— 'Islam and the Halakhah.' *Judaism* 42, no. 3 (1993): 332–43.

— *The Limits of Orthodox Theology: Maimonides's Thirteen Principles Reappraised.* Oxford: Littman Library of Jewish Civilization, 2004.

— 'Response to Criticism Part 4; Rabbi Zvi Yehuda and the Hazon Ish.' *The Seforim blog.* April 12, 2021. https://seforimblog.com/2021/04/response-to-criticism-part-4-rabbi-zvi-yehuda-and-the-hazon-ish/. Accessed November 9, 2022.

Shiffman, Yair. 'The Differences Between the Translations of Maimonides' *Guide of the Perplexed* by Falaquera, Ibn Tibbon and al-Harizi, and their Textual and Philosophical Implications.' *Journal of Semitic Studies* 44 (1999): 47–61.

Sirat, Colette. 'La composition et l'édition des texts philosophiques Juifs au Moyen Âge: quelques exemples.' *Bulletin de Philosophie Médiévale* 30 (1988): 224–32.

Sirkes, Joel. *She'elot u-Teshuvot*. Frankfurt: Johann Vaust, 1697.

Socher, Abraham. 'The Spectre of Maimonidean Radicalism in the Late Eighteenth Century.' In *The Cultures of Maimonideanism: New Approaches to the History of Jewish Thought*, edited by James T. Robinson, 245–58. Leiden: Brill, 2009.

Soloveitchik, Eliyahu. 'Le-Ḥidushe Rabi Ḥayim ha-Levi 'al ha-Rambam (2).' *Datche* 16 (23 Kislev 5768): 6.

Soloveitchik, Haym. 'The Halakhic Isolation of the Ashkenazic Community.' *Simon Dubnow Institute Yearbook* 8 (2009): 41–47.

— '*Mishneh Torah*: Polemic and Art.' In *Maimonides 800 Years After: Essays on Maimonides and his Influence*, edited by Jay M. Harris, 327–43. Cambridge, MA: Harvard University Press, 2007.

— *Principles and Pressures: Jewish Trade in Gentile Wine in the Middle Ages* [Hebrew]. Tel Aviv: Am Oved Publishers Ltd., 2003.

— *Wine in Ashkenaz in the Middle Ages: Yeyn Nesekh – A Study in the History of Halakha* [Hebrew]. Jerusalem: The Zalman Shazar Center for Jewish History, 2008.

Spiegel, Jacob. 'Sefer "Magid Mishneh" she-'al "Mishneh Torah" le-ha-Rambam.' *Kiryat Sefer* 46 (1971): 554–79.

Stampfer, Shaul. *Lithuanian Yeshivas of the Nineteenth Century: Creating a Tradition of Learning*. Translated by Lindsay Taylor-Guthartz. Oxford: Littman Library of Jewish Civilization, 2012.

Stein, Siegfried. 'Philippus Ferdinandus Polonus. A 16th Century Hebraist in England.' In *Essays in Honour of the Very Rev. Dr J. H. Hertz*, edited by I. Epstein, E. Levine, and C. Roth, 397–412. London: Edward Goldston, 1943.

Steinschneider, Moritz. *Catalogus Librorum Hebraeorum in Bibliotheca Bodleiana*. Berlin: Ad. Friedlaender, 1852–1860.

— *Die hebräischen Übersetzungen des Mittelalters*. Berlin: Kommissionsverlag des Bibliographischen Bureaus, 1893.

— 'Moreh Mekom ha-Moreh.' *Kovets 'al Yad* 1 (1885): 1–31.

— 'Salomon de Melgueil et Salomon Orgerius.' *Révue des Etudes Juives* 5 (1882): 277–81.

Steinschneider, Moritz, and David Cassel. 'Jüdische Typographie und Jüdischer Buchhandel.' In *Allgemeine Encyclopädie der Wissenschaften und Künste*, edited by Johann Samuel Ersch and Johann Gottfried Gruber, Section 2, part 28, 21–94. Leipzig: F. A. Brodhaus, 1851.

Stern, Eliyahu. *The Genius: Elijah of Vilna and the Making of Modern Judaism*. New Haven, CT: Yale University Press, 2013.

Stern, Gregg. *Philosophy and Rabbinic Culture*. Abingdon: Routledge, 2009.

Stern, Josef, James T. Robinson, and Yonatan Shemesh, eds. *Maimonides' 'Guide of the Perplexed' in Translation: A History from the Thirteenth Century to the Twentieth*. Chicago: University of Chicago Press, 2019.

Stroumsa, Sarah. *Maimonides in his World: A Portrait of a Mediterranean Thinker*. Princeton, NJ: Princeton University Press, 2009.

Stroumsa, Sarah, and Sara Sviri, 'The Beginnings of Mystical Philosophy in Al-Andalus: Ibn Masarra and his *Epistle on Contemplation*.' *JSAI* 36 (2009): 201–53.

Surall, Frank. 'Abraham Geigers Aufruf zur Gründung eines "Maimonidesvereins" für die Errichtung einer jüdisch-theologischen Fakultät.' In *Moses Maimonides (1138–1204): His Religious, Scientific, and Philosophical* Wirkungsgeschichte *in Different Cultural Contexts*, edited by Görge K. Hasselhoff and Otfried Fraisse, 397–425. Würzburg: Ergon, 2004.

Ta-Shma, Israel. *Creativity and Tradition: Studies in Medieval Rabbinic Scholarship, Literature and Thought*. Cambridge, MA: Harvard University Press, 2006.

— *Ha-Sifrut ha-Parshanit la-Talmud*, vol. 1. Jerusalem: Hebrew University Magnes Press, 1999.

— *Studies in Medieval Rabbinic Literature* [Hebrew]. Jerusalem: Bialik Institute, 2004.

Teplitsky, Joshua. *Prince of the Press: How One Collector Built History's Most Enduring and Remarkable Jewish Library*. New Haven, CT: Yale University Press, 2019.

Tobi, Yosef. *'Iyunim be-Megilat Teman*. Jerusalem: Hebrew University Magnes Press, 1986.

— 'Ketav Haganah mi-Teman 'al Shitat ha-Rambam be-'Inyan Teḥiyat ha-Metim.' *Tema* 6 (1998): 29–57.

— 'Nusaḥ ha-Tefillah shel Yehude Teman.' *Tema* 7 (2001): 29–64.

— 'Shir Ma'aneh 'al 'Yigdal Elohim Ḥai' le-R. David ben Shlomo ha-Levi Dhmarmari.' *Afikim* 111–12 (Tishre 5758/October 1997): 40–42.
— 'Shulḥan 'Arukh le-R. Yosef Karo le-umat "Mishneh Torah" le-ha-Rambam be-Teman.' *Tema* 12 (2012): 5–30.
— *The Talmud in Yemen* [Hebrew]. Tel Aviv: Afikim, 1973.
— 'Tenu'at "Dor-De'ah" mi-Teman u-vikorato shel R. Mosheh Tsarum 'al Minhage ha-Kabalah.' *Deḥak* 6 (2016): 604–22.
— 'Who Was the Author of *Emunat ha-Shem*?' [Hebrew]. *Daat: A Journal of Philosophy & Kabbalah* 49 (2002): 87–98.
— *Yemenite Jewish Manuscripts in the Ben-Zvi Institute* [Hebrew]. Jerusalem: Ben-Zvi Institute, 1982.
Turniansky, Chava. 'Meydlekh in der altyidisher literatur.' In *Jiddische Philologie. Festschrift für Erika Timm*, edited by Walter Röll and Simon Neuberg, 7–20. Tübingen: Niemeyer, 1999.
Twersky, Isadore. 'The Beginnings of *Mishneh Torah* Criticism.' In *Biblical and Other Studies*, edited by Alexander A. Altmann, 161–82. Cambridge, MA: Harvard University Press, 1963.
— 'Ha-Rav Yosef Karo Ba'al ha-Sh[ulḥan] A[rukh].' *Asufot* 3 (1989): 247–50.
— *Introduction to the Code of Maimonides.* New Haven, CT: Yale University Press, 1980.
— *A Maimonides Reader.* Springfield, NJ: Behrman House, 1972.
— *Rabad of Posquieres: A Twelfth-Century Talmudist.* Philadelphia: Jewish Publication Society of America, 1980.
Urbach, Efraim E. *Ba'ale ha-Tosafot.* Jerusalem: Bialik Institute, 1955.
Urban, Marina. 'Persecution and the Art of Representation: Schocken's Maimonides Anthologies of the 1930s.' In *Maimonides and his Heritage*, edited by Idit Dobbs-Weinstein, Lenn E. Goodman, and James Allen Grady, 153–80. Albany, NY: State University of New York Press, 2009.
Usaybi'ah, Ibn Abi. *Anecdotes & Antidotes: A Medieval Arabic History of Physicians.* Edited by Henrietta Sharp Cockrell et al. Oxford: Oxford University Press, 2020.
Usque, Samuel. *Consolation for the Tribulations of Israel.* Translated by Martin A. Cohen. Philadelphia, PA: Jewish Publication Society of America, 1965.
Vinograd, Yeshayahu. *Thesaurus of the Hebrew Book: Listing of Books Printed in Hebrew Letters Since the Beginning of Hebrew Printing circa 1469 through 1863* [Hebrew]. Jerusalem: Institute for Computerized Bibliography, 1993.
Wachten, Johannes, Christine H. Lochow-Dureke, and Johanna Vollmeyer, eds. *Moses Maimonides. Arzt, Philosophe und Oberhaupt der Juden 1135–1204.* Frankfurt am Main: Museum Judengasse Frankfurt, 2004.
Walfish, Barry. *"As it is Written": Judaic Treasures from the Thomas Fisher Rare Book Library.* Toronto: University of Toronto Press, 2015.
Weinstein, Roni. *Kabbalah and Jewish Modernity.* London: Littman Library of Jewish Civilization, 2016.
Weiss, Meir Z. '*Seridim me-ha-Genizah.*' In *Festschrift zum 50 jährigen Bestehen der Franz-Josef-Landesrabbinerschule in Budapest*, edited by Ludwig Blau, 77–97 (Hebrew Section). Budapest: Alexander Kohut Memorial Foundation, 1928.
Westwater, Lynn Lara. *Sarra Copia Sulam: A Jewish Salonnière and the Press in Counter-Reformation Venice.* Toronto: University of Toronto Press, 2020.
Wolfensohn, Ze'ev W. and Schneur Z. Schneursohn, eds. *Ḥemdah Genuzah.* Jerusalem: Yisrael Baeck, 1863.
Wolfson, Elliot R. 'Beneath the Wings of the Great Eagle: Maimonides and Thirteenth-Century Kabbalah.' In *Moses Maimonides (1138–1204): His Religious, Scientific, and Philosophical* Wirkungsgeschichte *in Different Cultural Contexts*, edited by Görge K. Hasselhoff and Otfried Fraisse, 209–37. Würzburg: Ergon, 2004.
Wolfson, Harry A. *The Philosophy of the Kalam.* Cambridge, MA: Harvard University Press, 1976.
— *Repercussions of the Kalam in Jewish Philosophy.* Cambridge, MA: Harvard University Press, 1979.
Woolf, Jeffrey. 'Admiration and Apathy: Maimonides' *Mishneh Torah* in High and Late Medieval Ashkenaz.' In *Be'erot Yitzhak: Studies in Memory of Isadore Twersky*, edited by Jay M. Harris, 427–53. Cambridge, MA: Harvard University Press, 2005.
Yaari, Abraham. *Ha-Madpisim Bene-Fo'ah.* Jerusalem: [n.p.], 1941.
— *Hebrew Printers' Marks, from the Beginning of Hebrew Printing to the End of the 19th Century* [Hebrew]. Jerusalem: Hebrew University, 1944.
— *Hebrew Printing at Constantinople: Its History and Bibliography* [Hebrew]. Jerusalem: Magnes Press, 1967.

— 'Judith Rosanes' Hebrew Press at Lwów' [Hebrew]. *Kiryat Sefer* 17 (1940): 95–108.
— *Studies in Hebrew Booklore* [Hebrew]. Jerusalem: Mossad Harav Kook, 1958.
Yellin, David, and Israel Abrahams. *Maimonides*. Philadelphia, PA: Jewish Publication Society of America, 1903.
Yudlov, Isaac. *Ginze Yisra'el / The Israel Mehlman Collection in the Jewish National and University Library: An Annotated Catalogue of the Hebrew Books, Booklets, and Pamphlets*. Jerusalem: Jewish National and University Library Press, 1984.
— *Hebrew Printers' Marks: Fifty-four Emblems and Marks of Hebrew Printers, Publishers and Authors* [Hebrew]. Jerusalem: Y. Yudlov, 2001.
— 'R. Isaac Gershon and R. Isaac Treves' [Hebrew]. *Kiryat Sefer* 59 (1984): 247–51.
— (ed.) *She'elot u-Teshuvot le-Rabenu Asher ben Yeḥiel*. Jerusalem: Makhon Yerushalayim, 1994.
Zedekiah ben Abraham *ha-Rofe*. *Shibole ha-Leket*, Part 2, edited by Menaḥem Z. Ḥasidah. Jerusalem: [n.p.], 1969.
Zedner, Joseph. *Catalogue of the Hebrew Books in the Library of the British Museum*. London: British Museum, 1867.
Zuroff, Abraham N. 'The Responsa of Maimonides.' Ph.D. diss., Yeshiva University, 1966.
Zwiep, Irene E. 'From Moses to Moses…? Manifestations of Maimonides in the Early Jewish Enlightenment.' In *Moses Maimonides (1138–1204): His Religious, Scientific, and Philosophical* Wirkungsgeschichte *in Different Cultural Contexts*, edited by Görge K. Hasselhoff and Otfried Fraisse, 323–36. Würzburg: Ergon, 2004.

INDEX